THE HEROIC LEGEND OF
ARSLAN

STORY BY
YOSHIKI TANAKA

MANGA BY
HIROMU ARAKAWA

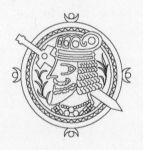

7

The Heroic Legend of
ARSLAN

Table of Contents

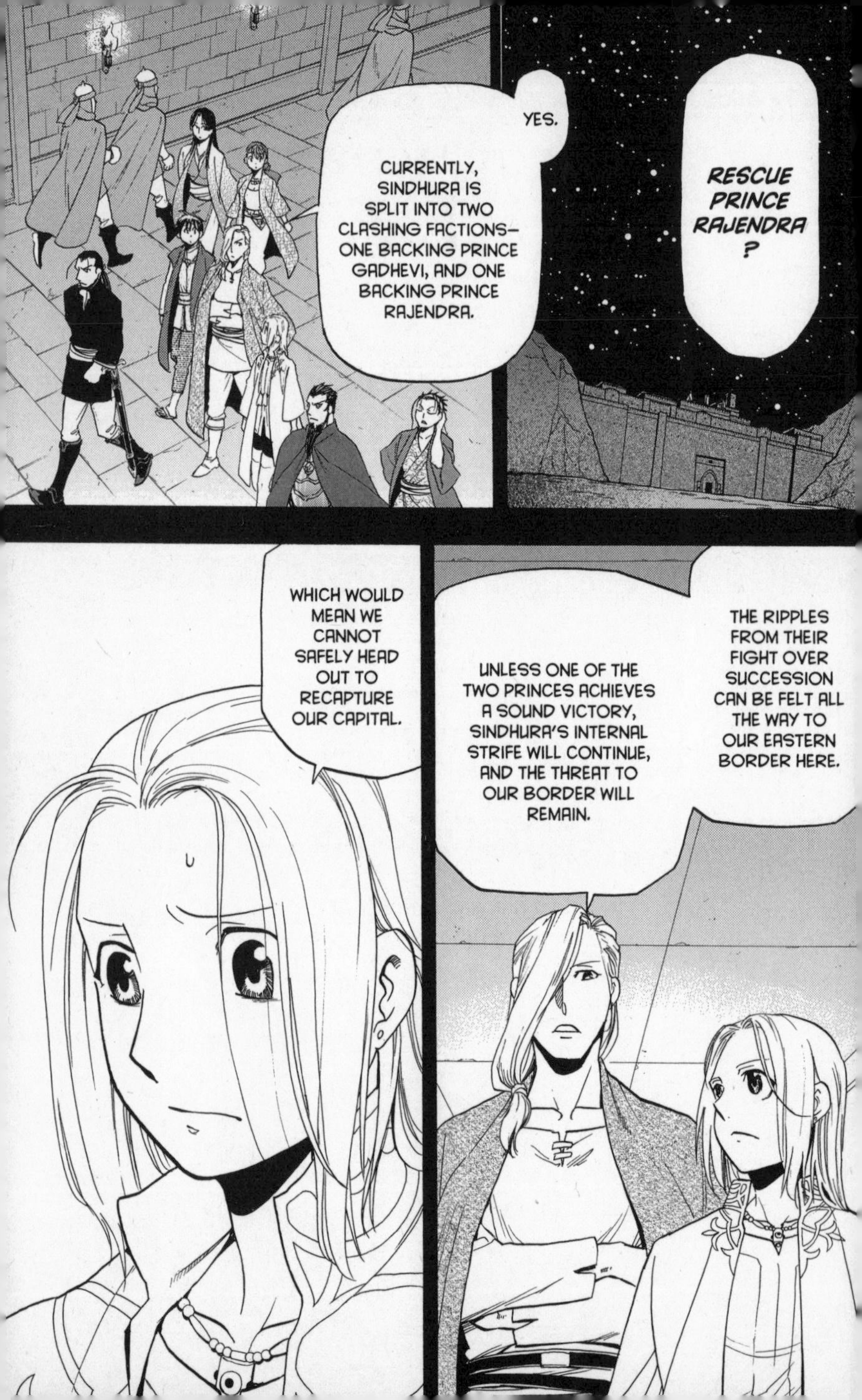
RESCUE PRINCE RAJENDRA?
YES.
CURRENTLY, SINDHURA IS SPLIT INTO TWO CLASHING FACTIONS—ONE BACKING PRINCE GADHEVI, AND ONE BACKING PRINCE RAJENDRA.
THE RIPPLES FROM THEIR FIGHT OVER SUCCESSION CAN BE FELT ALL THE WAY TO OUR EASTERN BORDER HERE.
UNLESS ONE OF THE TWO PRINCES ACHIEVES A SOUND VICTORY, SINDHURA'S INTERNAL STRIFE WILL CONTINUE, AND THE THREAT TO OUR BORDER WILL REMAIN.
WHICH WOULD MEAN WE CANNOT SAFELY HEAD OUT TO RECAPTURE OUR CAPITAL.

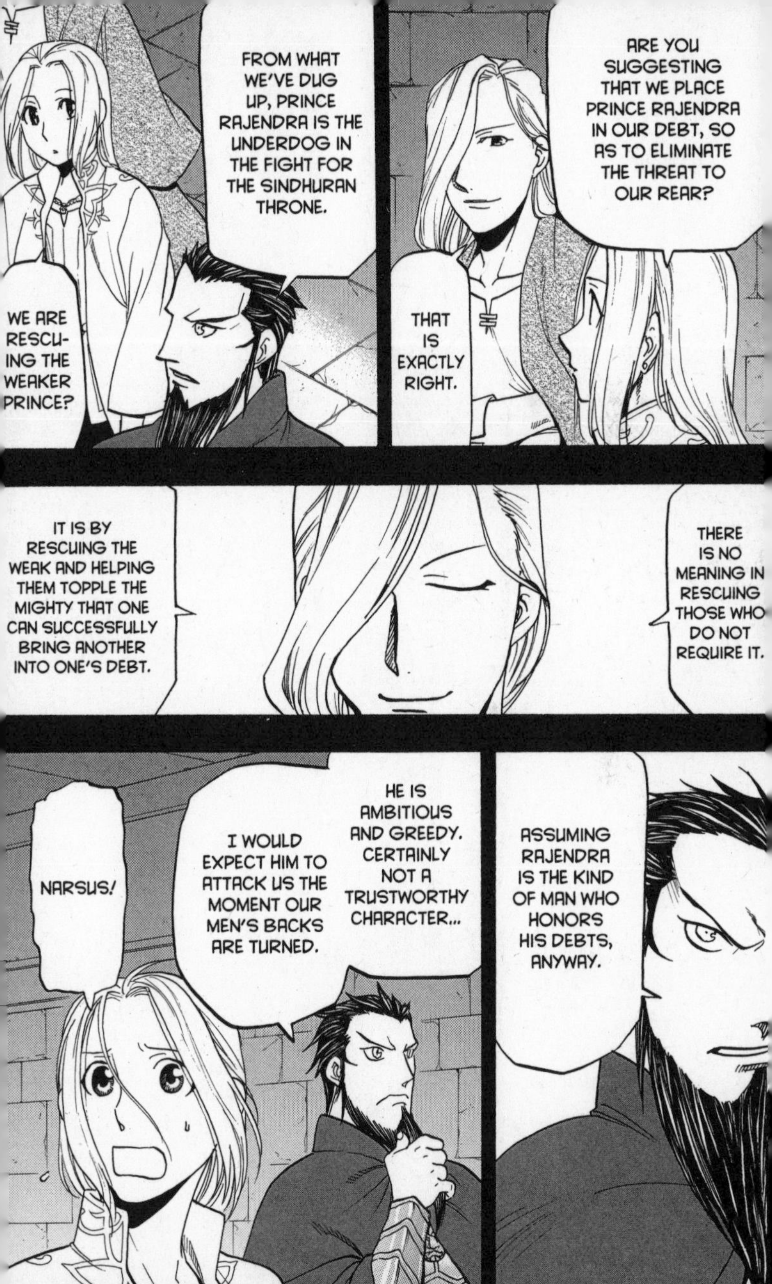
ARE YOU SUGGESTING THAT WE PLACE PRINCE RAJENDRA IN OUR DEBT, SO AS TO ELIMINATE THE THREAT TO OUR REAR?
THAT IS EXACTLY RIGHT.
FROM WHAT WE'VE DUG UP, PRINCE RAJENDRA IS THE UNDERDOG IN THE FIGHT FOR THE SINDHURAN THRONE.
WE ARE RESCU-ING THE WEAKER PRINCE?
THERE IS NO MEANING IN RESCUING THOSE WHO DO NOT REQUIRE IT.
IT IS BY RESCUING THE WEAK AND HELPING THEM TOPPLE THE MIGHTY THAT ONE CAN SUCCESSFULLY BRING ANOTHER INTO ONE'S DEBT.
ASSUMING RAJENDRA IS THE KIND OF MAN WHO HONORS HIS DEBTS, ANYWAY.
HE IS AMBITIOUS AND GREEDY. CERTAINLY NOT A TRUSTWORTHY CHARACTER...
I WOULD EXPECT HIM TO ATTACK US THE MOMENT OUR MEN'S BACKS ARE TURNED.
NARSUS!

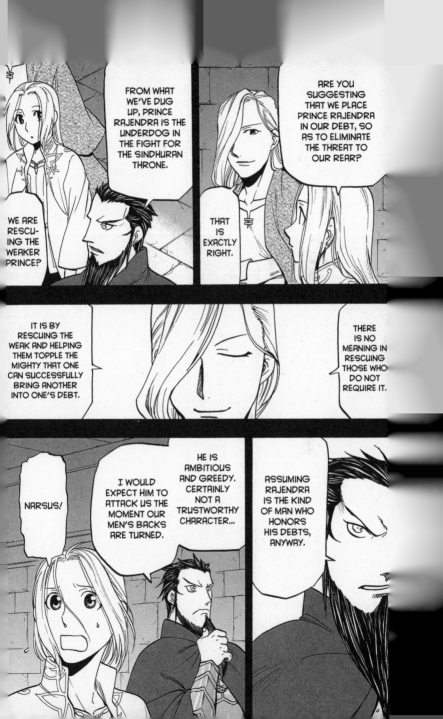

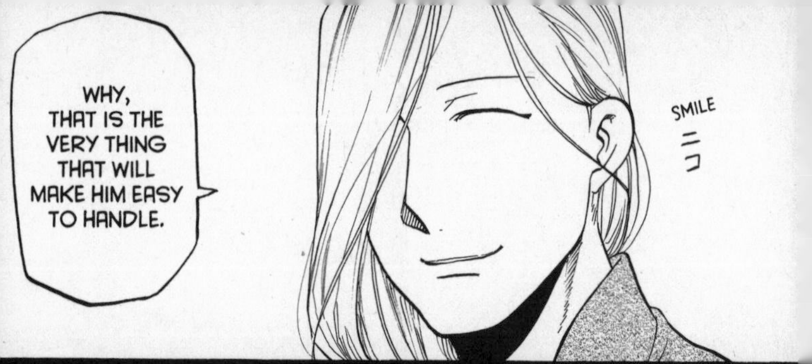
SMILE
ニコ
WHY, THAT IS THE VERY THING THAT WILL MAKE HIM EASY TO HANDLE.

Chapter 41: The Sindhuran Rake

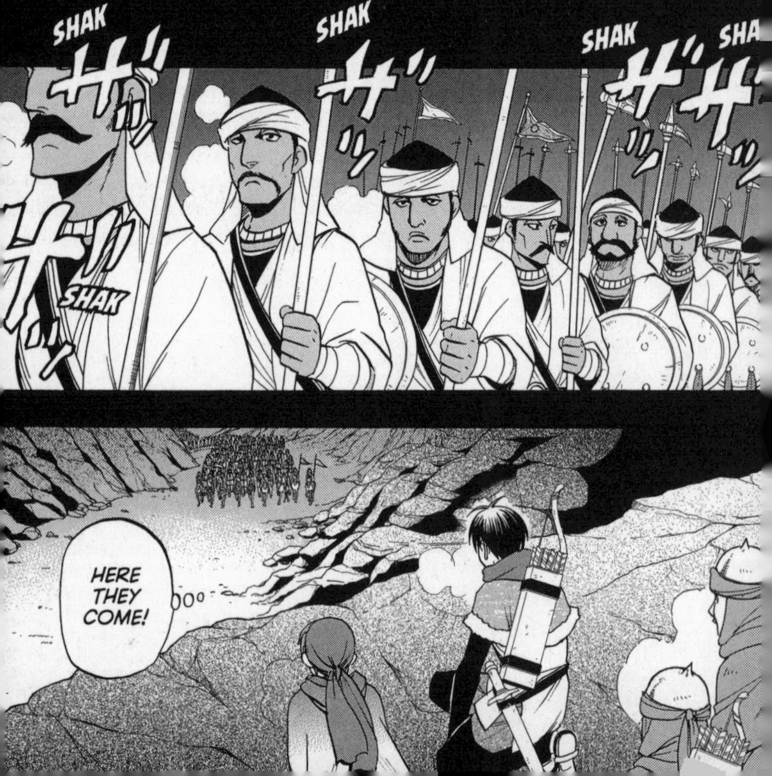
SHAK
SHAK
SHAK
SHAK
HERE THEY COME!

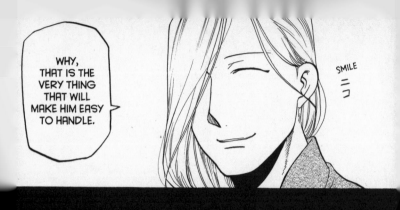

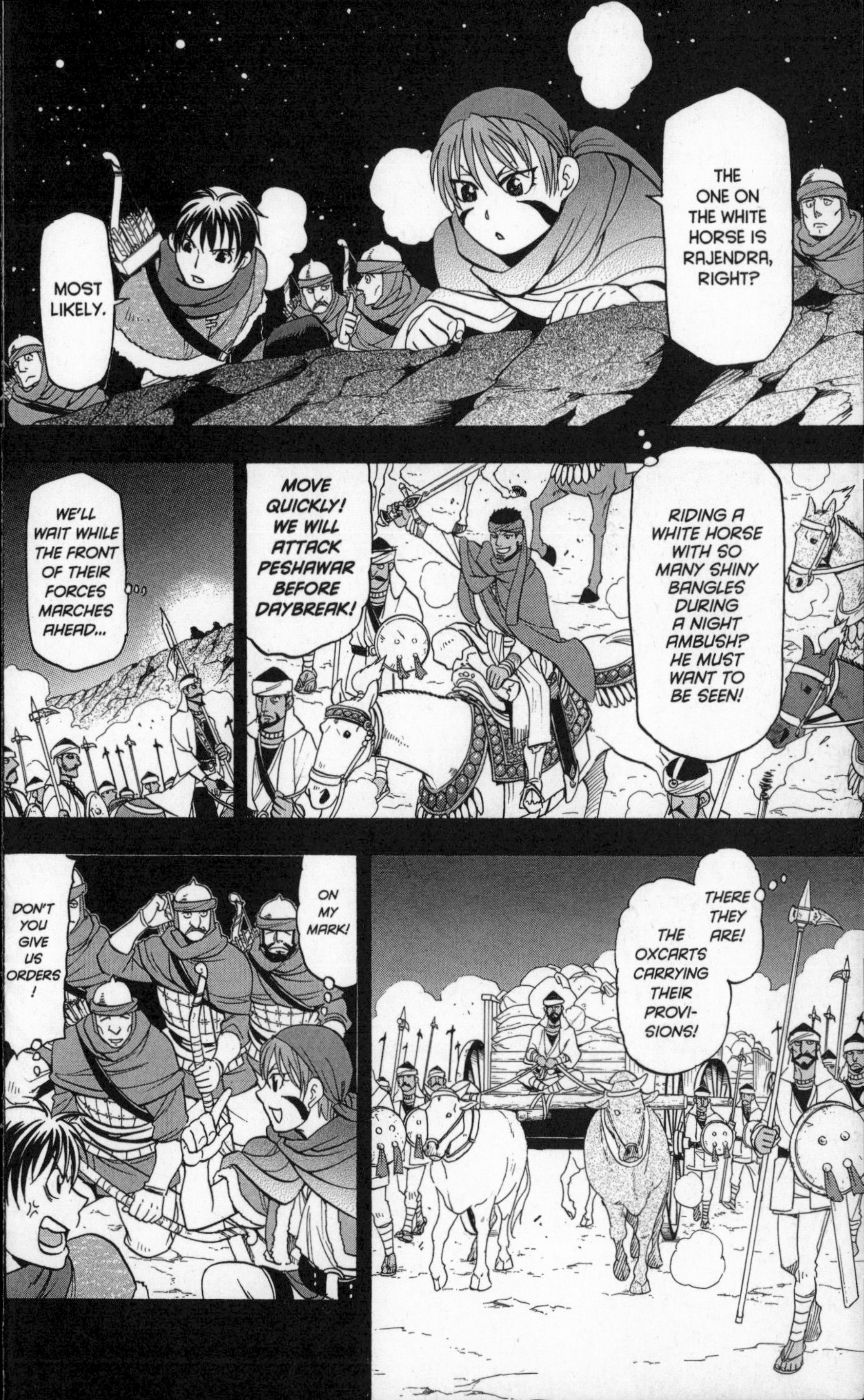
THE ONE ON THE WHITE HORSE IS RAJENDRA, RIGHT?
MOST LIKELY.
RIDING A WHITE HORSE WITH SO MANY SHINY BANGLES DURING A NIGHT AMBUSH? HE MUST WANT TO BE SEEN!
MOVE QUICKLY! WE WILL ATTACK PESHAWAR BEFORE DAYBREAK!
WE'LL WAIT WHILE THE FRONT OF THEIR FORCES MARCHES AHEAD...
THERE THEY ARE! THE OXCARTS CARRYING THEIR PROVISIONS!
ON MY MARK!
DON'T YOU GIVE US ORDERS!

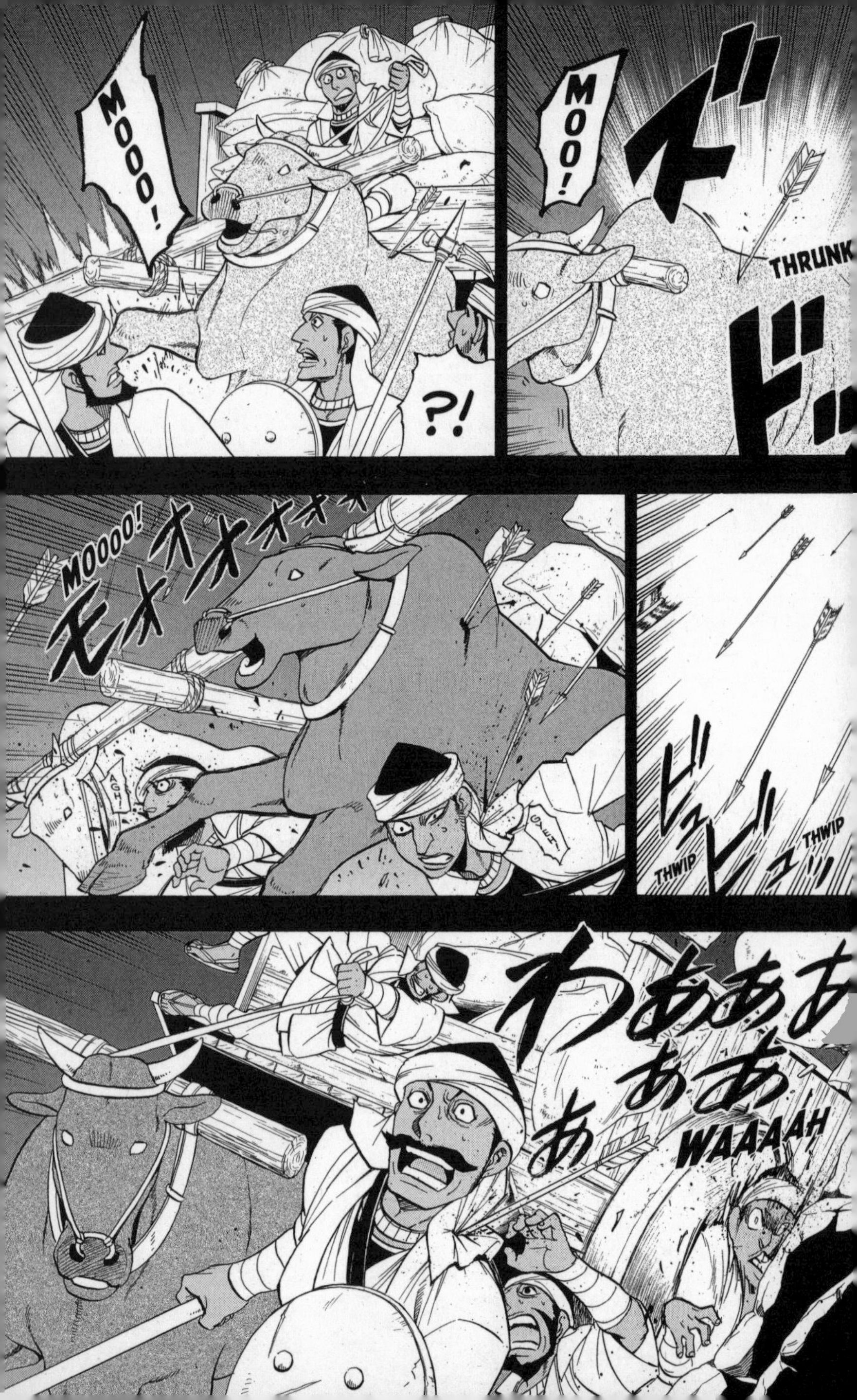

ズ
THRUNK
ド
MOOO!
MOOO!
?!
ビュ
ビュ
THWIP
THWIP
MOOOO!
モオオオオオ
GYEH!
AGH!
わああああああ
WAAAAH

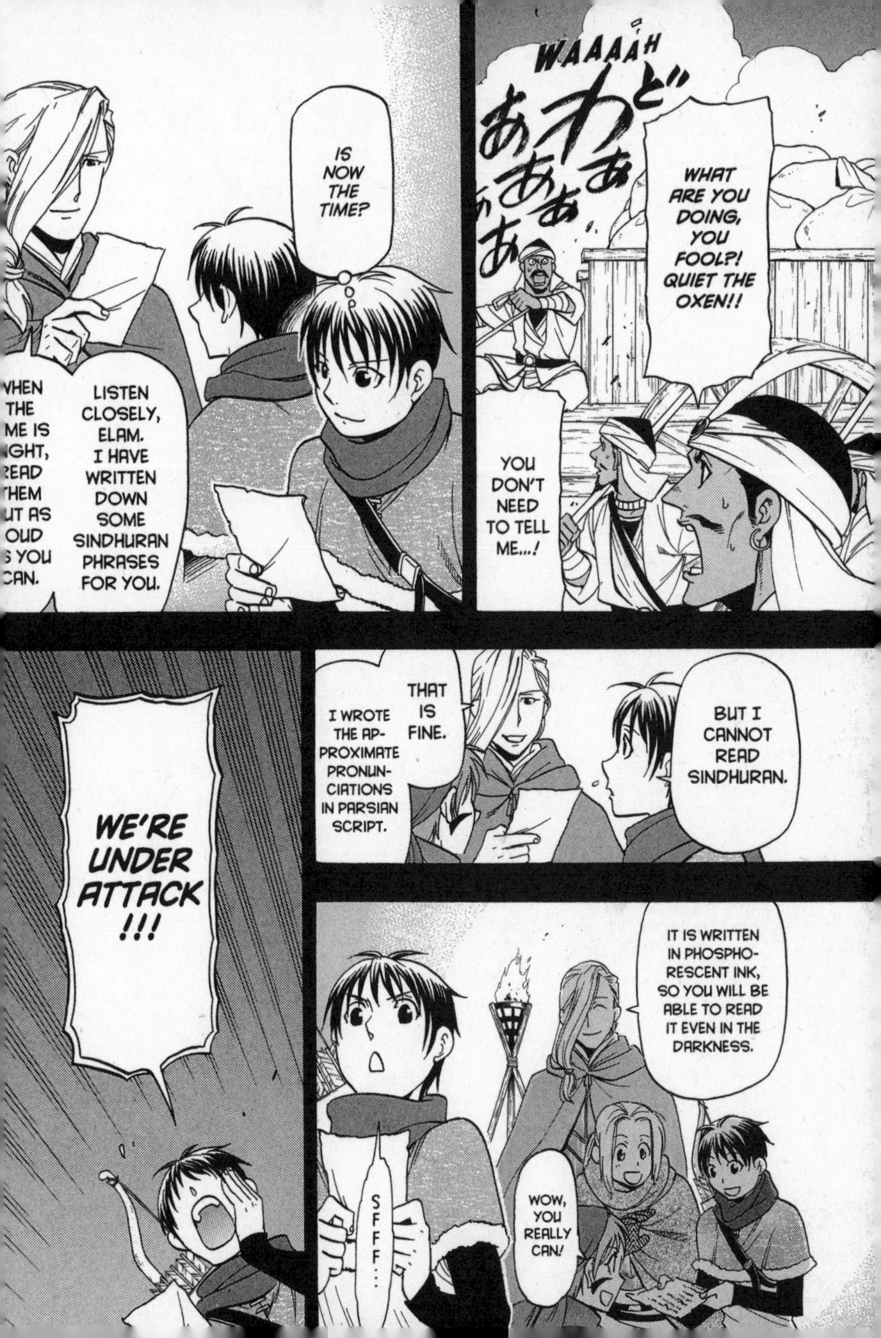
WAAAAH
あわあぁぁぁ
WHAT ARE YOU DOING, YOU FOOL?! QUIET THE OXEN!!
YOU DON'T NEED TO TELL ME...!
IS NOW THE TIME?
LISTEN CLOSELY, ELAM. I HAVE WRITTEN DOWN SOME SINDHURAN PHRASES FOR YOU.
WHEN THE ME IS GHT, READ THEM UT AS OUD S YOU CAN.
BUT I CANNOT READ SINDHURAN.
THAT IS FINE.
I WROTE THE APPROXIMATE PRONUNCIATIONS IN PARSIAN SCRIPT.
IT IS WRITTEN IN PHOSPHORESCENT INK, SO YOU WILL BE ABLE TO READ IT EVEN IN THE DARKNESS.
WOW, YOU REALLY CAN!
SFFF...
WE'RE UNDER ATTACK!!!

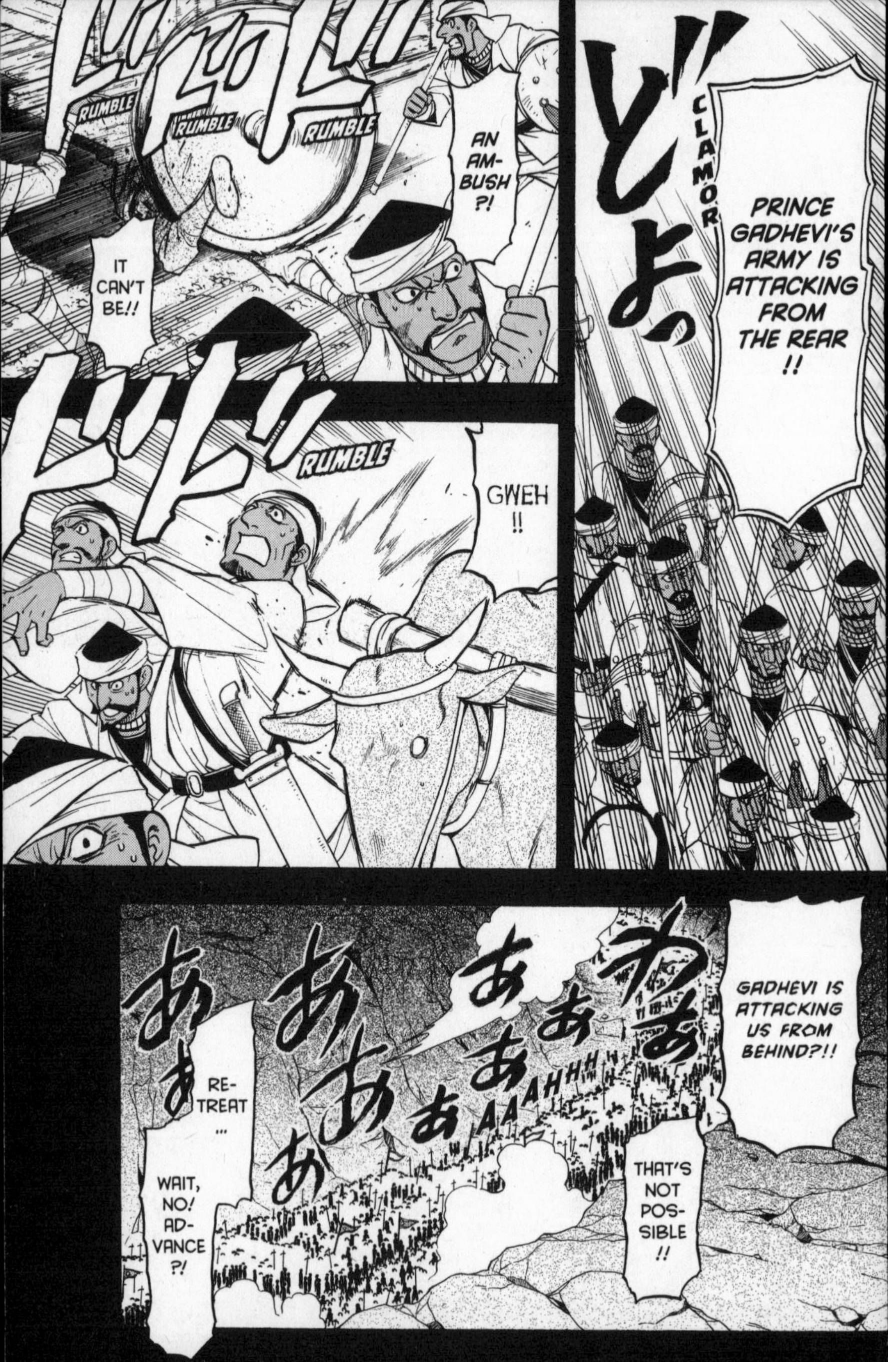
どよっ
CLAMOR
PRINCE GADHEVI'S ARMY IS ATTACKING FROM THE REAR!!
RUMBLE
RUMBLE
RUMBLE
AN AM-BUSH?!
IT CAN'T BE!!
RUMBLE
GWEH!!
GADHEVI IS ATTACKING US FROM BEHIND?!!
THAT'S NOT POS-SIBLE!!
AAAHHH
RE-TREAT...
WAIT, NO! AD-VANCE?!

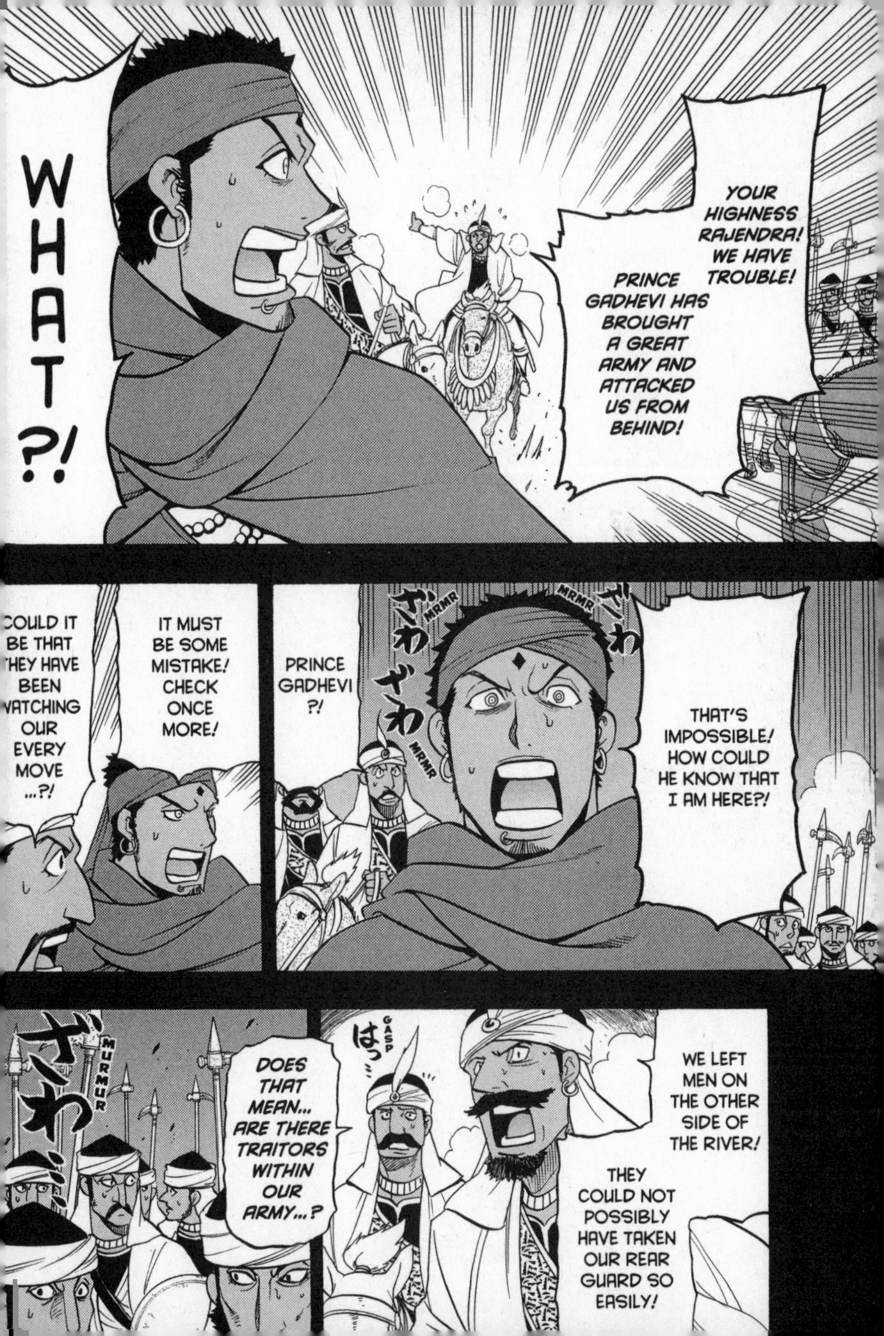
YOUR HIGHNESS RAJENDRA! WE HAVE TROUBLE!
PRINCE GADHEVI HAS BROUGHT A GREAT ARMY AND ATTACKED US FROM BEHIND!
WHAT?!
ざわ MRMR
ざわざわ MRMR
THAT'S IMPOSSIBLE! HOW COULD HE KNOW THAT I AM HERE?!
PRINCE GADHEVI?!
IT MUST BE SOME MISTAKE! CHECK ONCE MORE!
COULD IT BE THAT THEY HAVE BEEN WATCHING OUR EVERY MOVE ...?!
はっ GASP
WE LEFT MEN ON THE OTHER SIDE OF THE RIVER!
THEY COULD NOT POSSIBLY HAVE TAKEN OUR REAR GUARD SO EASILY!
DOES THAT MEAN... ARE THERE TRAITORS WITHIN OUR ARMY...?
ざわっ MURMUR

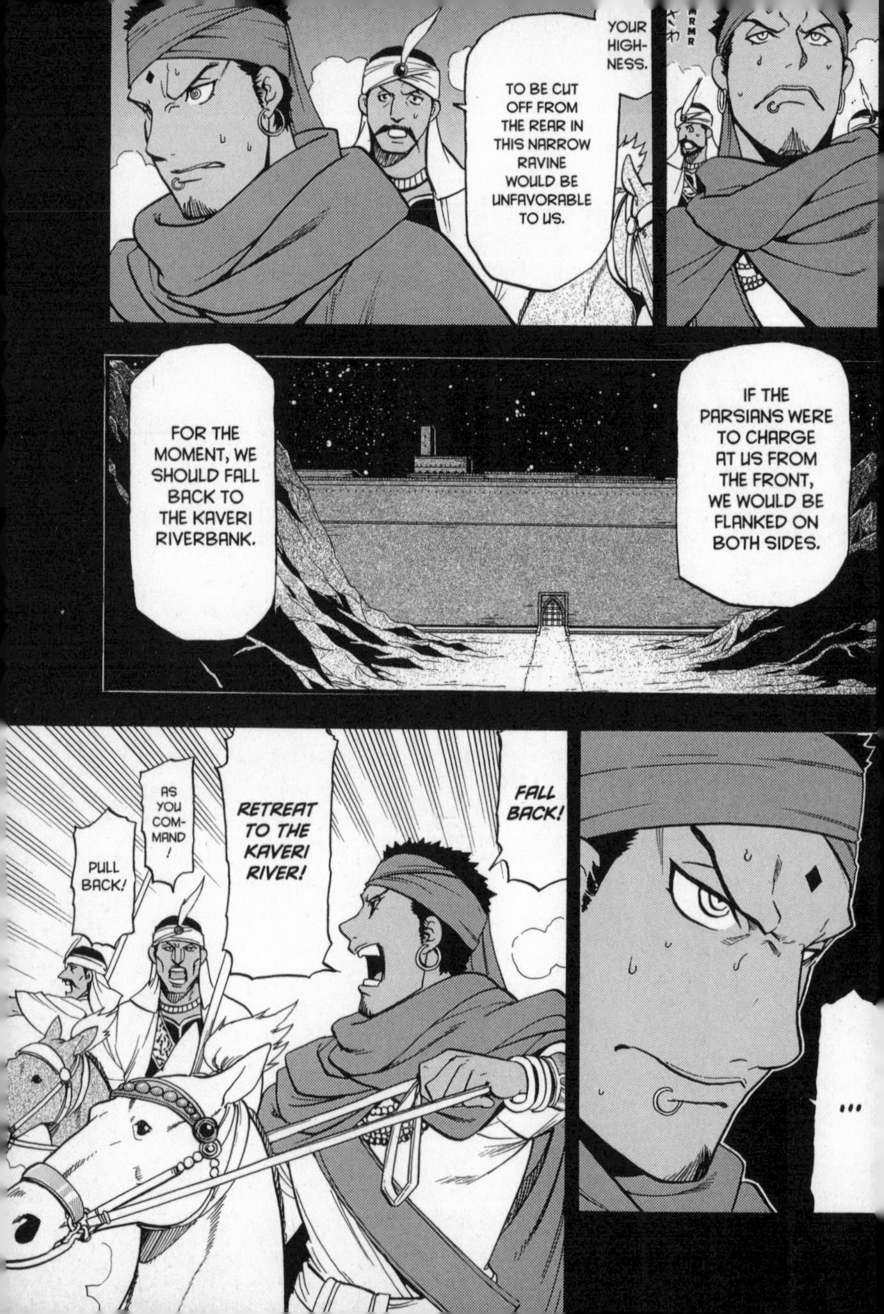
MRMR
YOUR HIGHNESS.
TO BE CUT OFF FROM THE REAR IN THIS NARROW RAVINE WOULD BE UNFAVORABLE TO US.
IF THE PARSIANS WERE TO CHARGE AT US FROM THE FRONT, WE WOULD BE FLANKED ON BOTH SIDES.
FOR THE MOMENT, WE SHOULD FALL BACK TO THE KAVERI RIVERBANK.
...
FALL BACK!
RETREAT TO THE KAVERI RIVER!
AS YOU COMMAND!
PULL BACK!

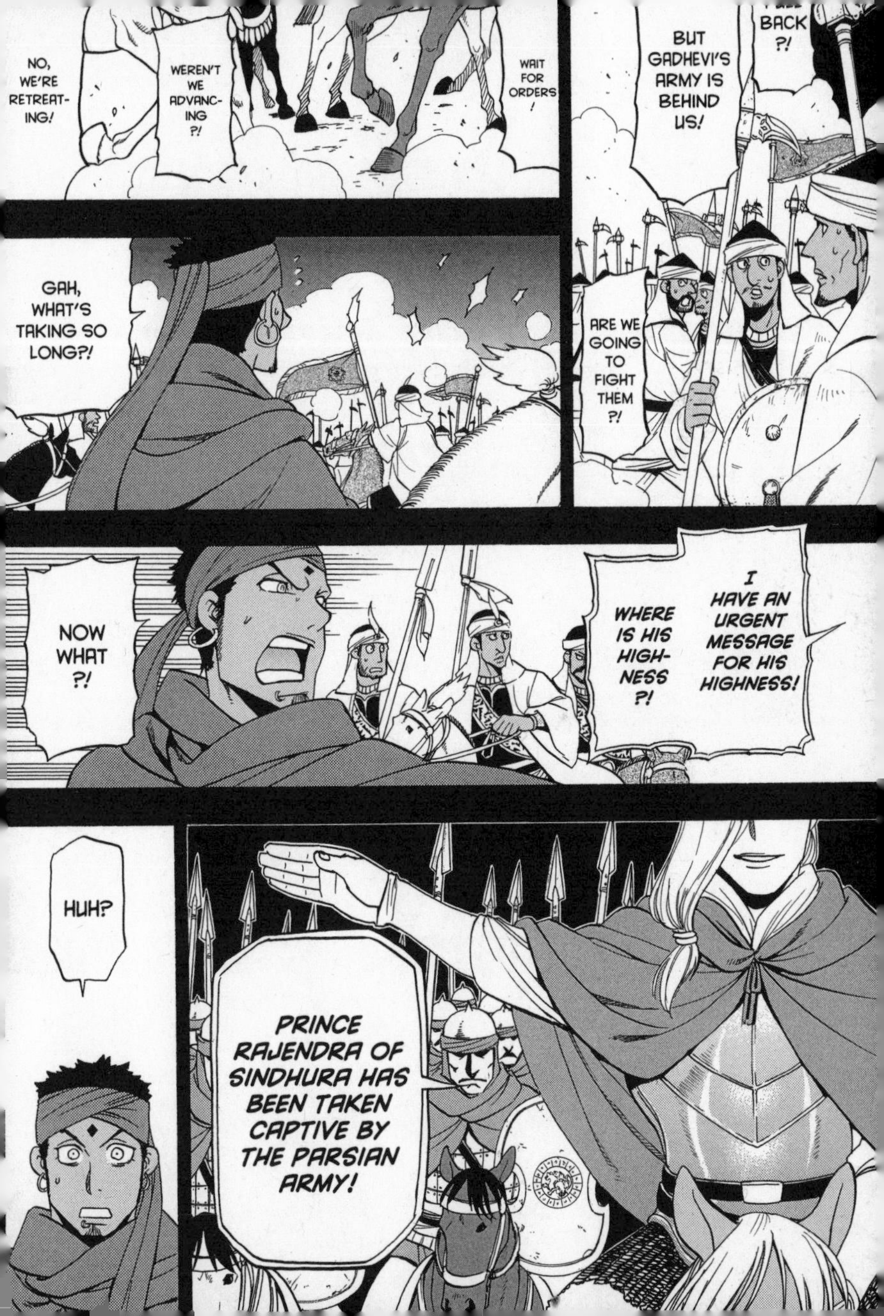
BACK?!
BUT GADHEVI'S ARMY IS BEHIND US!
ARE WE GOING TO FIGHT THEM?!
WAIT FOR ORDERS!
WEREN'T WE ADVANCING?!
NO, WE'RE RETREATING!
GAH, WHAT'S TAKING SO LONG?!
I HAVE AN URGENT MESSAGE FOR HIS HIGHNESS!
WHERE IS HIS HIGHNESS?!
NOW WHAT?!
PRINCE RAJENDRA OF SINDHURA HAS BEEN TAKEN CAPTIVE BY THE PARSIAN ARMY!
HUH?

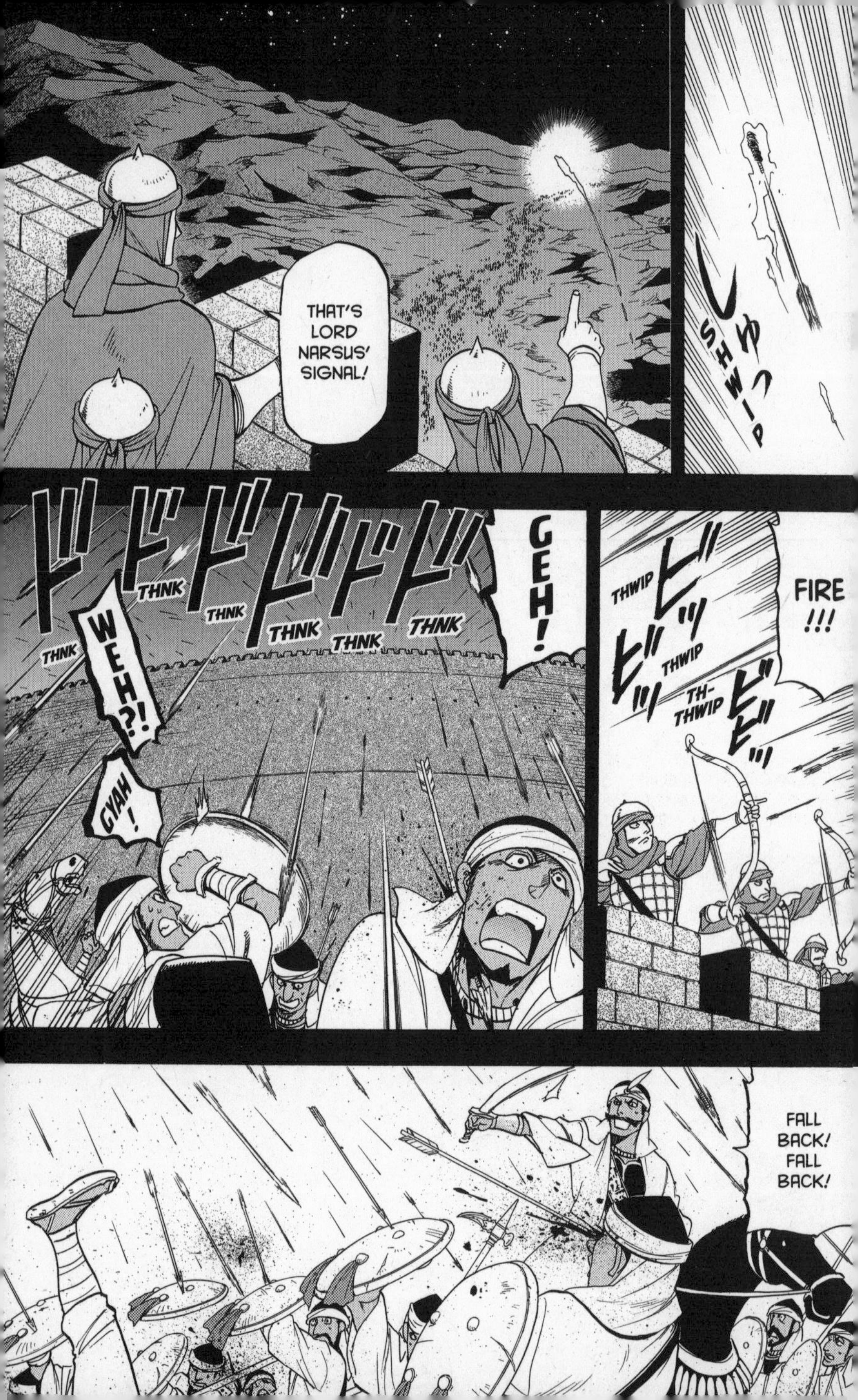
SHWIP
THAT'S LORD NARSUS' SIGNAL!
FIRE!!!
THWIP
THWIP
TH-THWIP
GEH!
THNK
THNK
THNK
THNK
THNK
THNK
WEH?!
GYAH!
FALL BACK! FALL BACK!

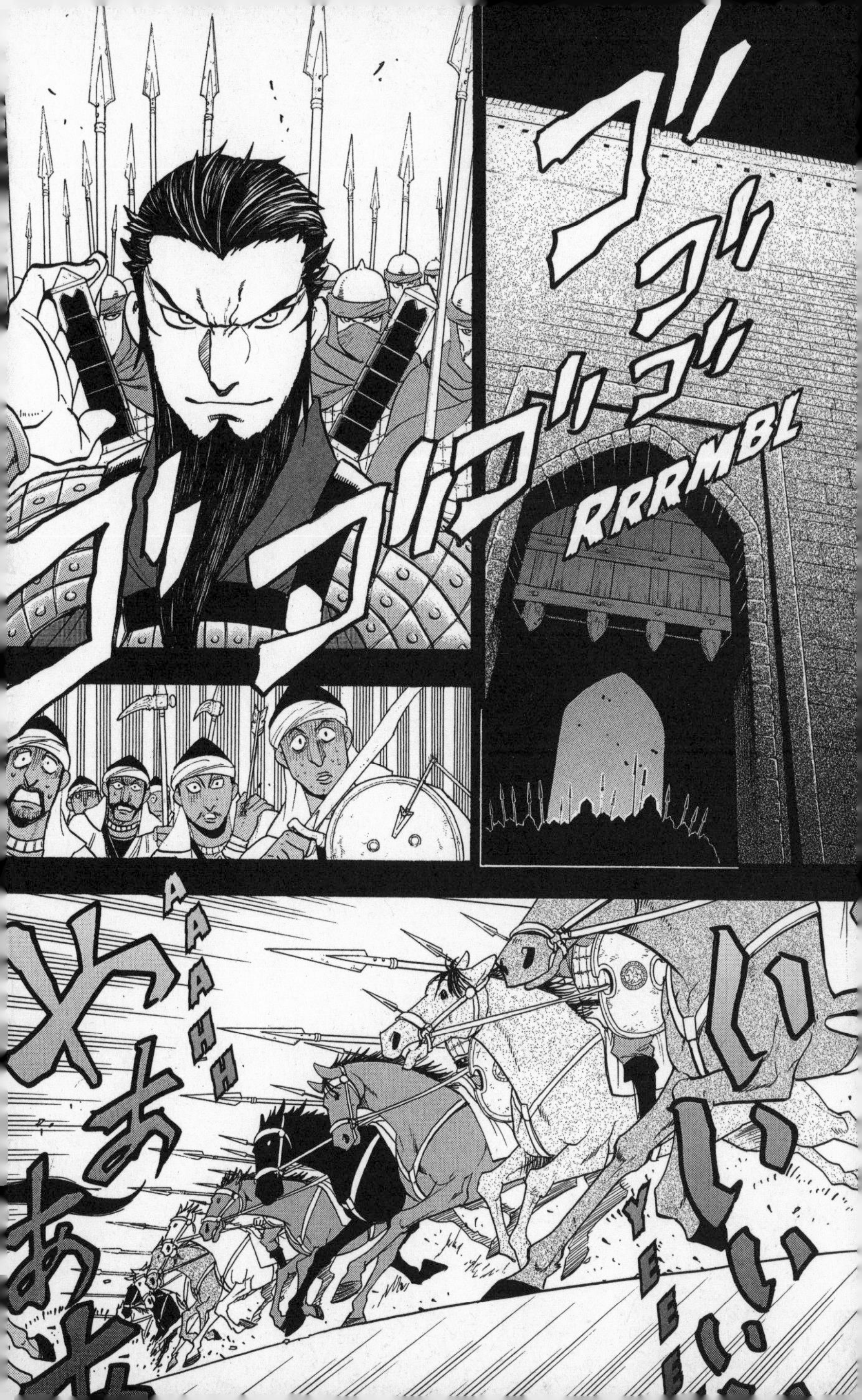
RRRMBL
AAAHH
YEEE

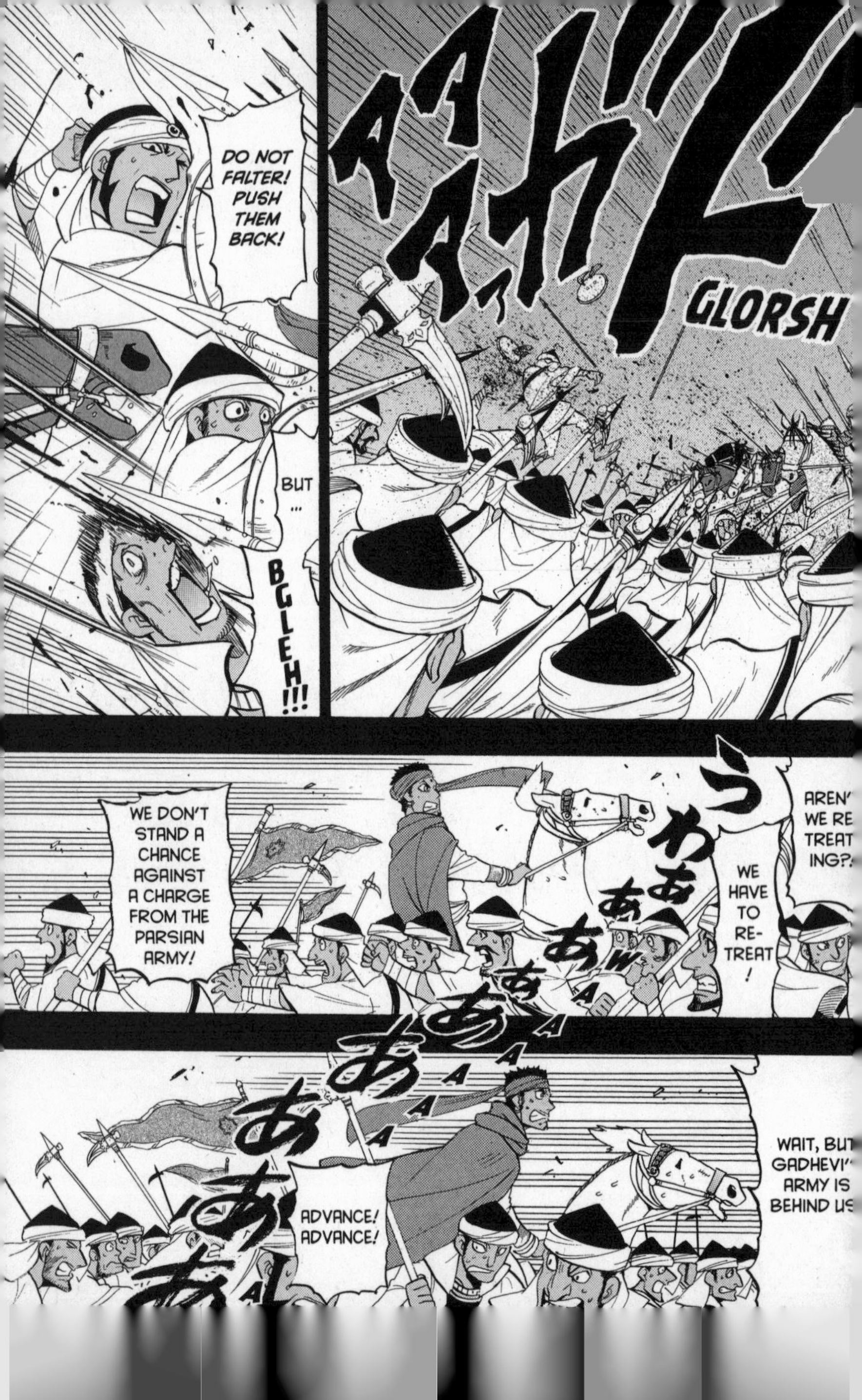
GLORSH
DO NOT FALTER! PUSH THEM BACK!
BUT ...
BGLEH!!!
AREN' WE RE TREAT ING?!
WE HAVE TO RE-TREAT!
うわああああ
WAAAA
WE DON'T STAND A CHANCE AGAINST A CHARGE FROM THE PARSIAN ARMY!
WAIT, BUT GADHEVI' ARMY IS BEHIND US
ああああ
AAAAAA
ADVANCE! ADVANCE!

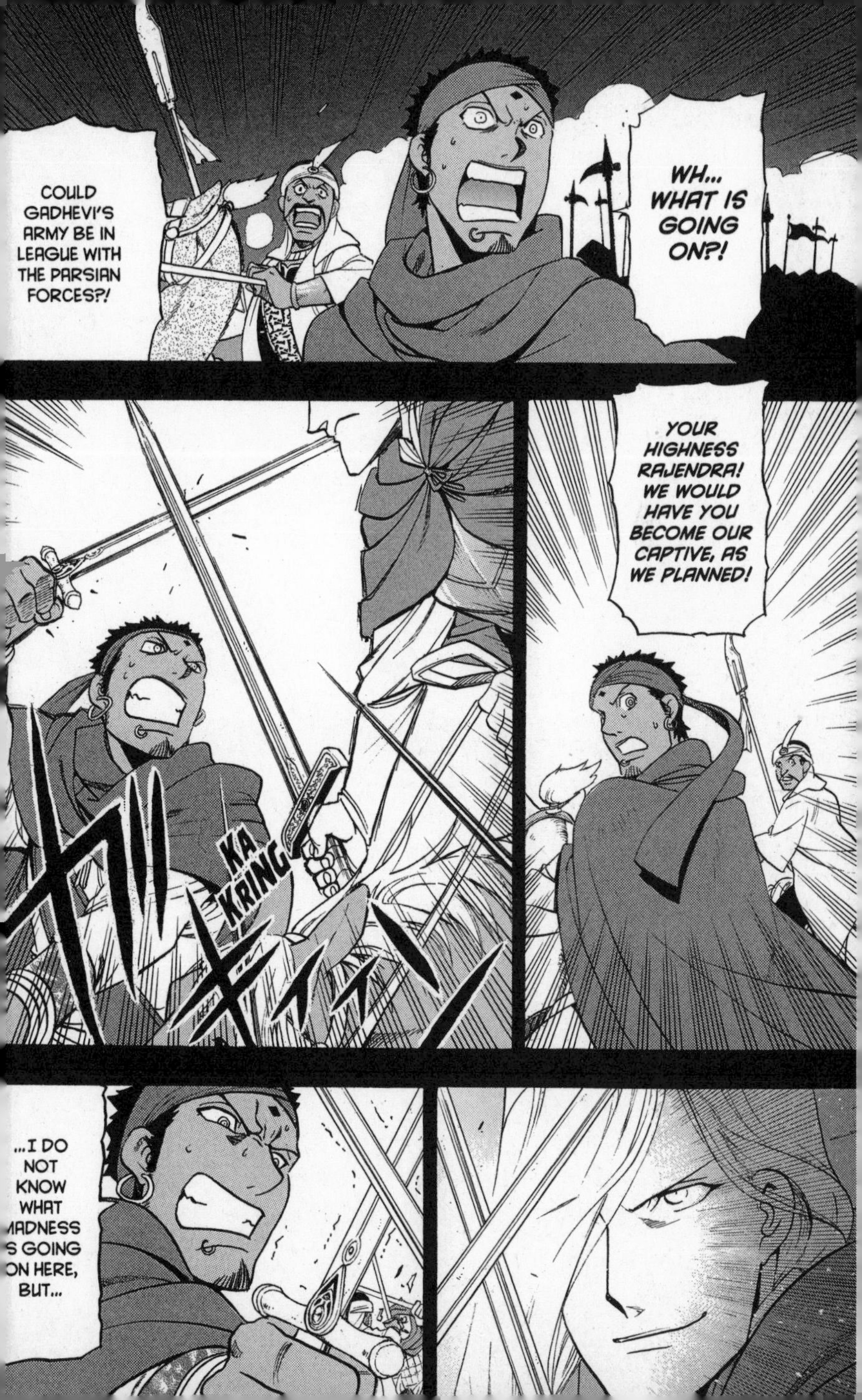
WH... WHAT IS GOING ON?!
COULD GADHEVI'S ARMY BE IN LEAGUE WITH THE PARSIAN FORCES?!
YOUR HIGHNESS RAJENDRA! WE WOULD HAVE YOU BECOME OUR CAPTIVE, AS WE PLANNED!
KA KRING
...I DO NOT KNOW WHAT MADNESS IS GOING ON HERE, BUT...

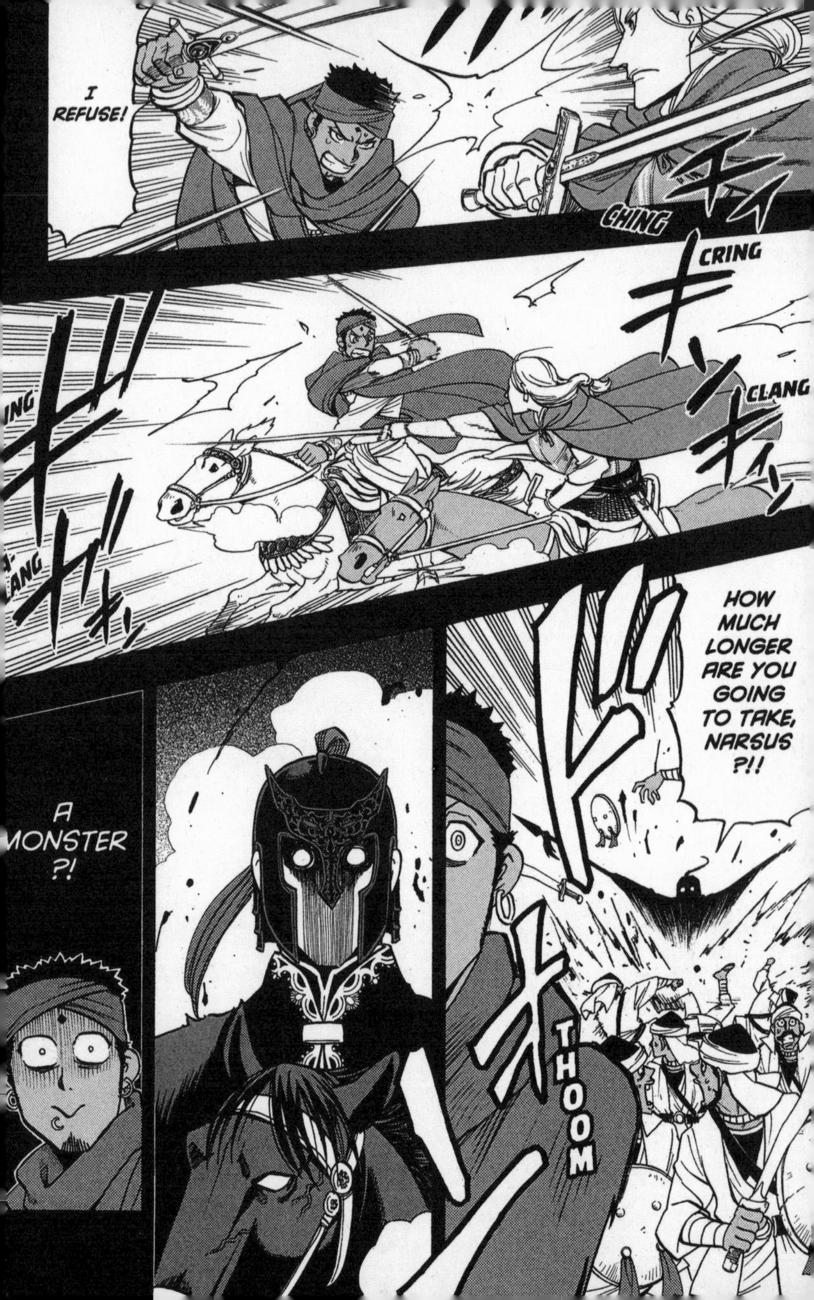
I REFUSE!
CHING
CRING
CLANG
HOW MUCH LONGER ARE YOU GOING TO TAKE, NARSUS?!!
THOOM
A MONSTER?!

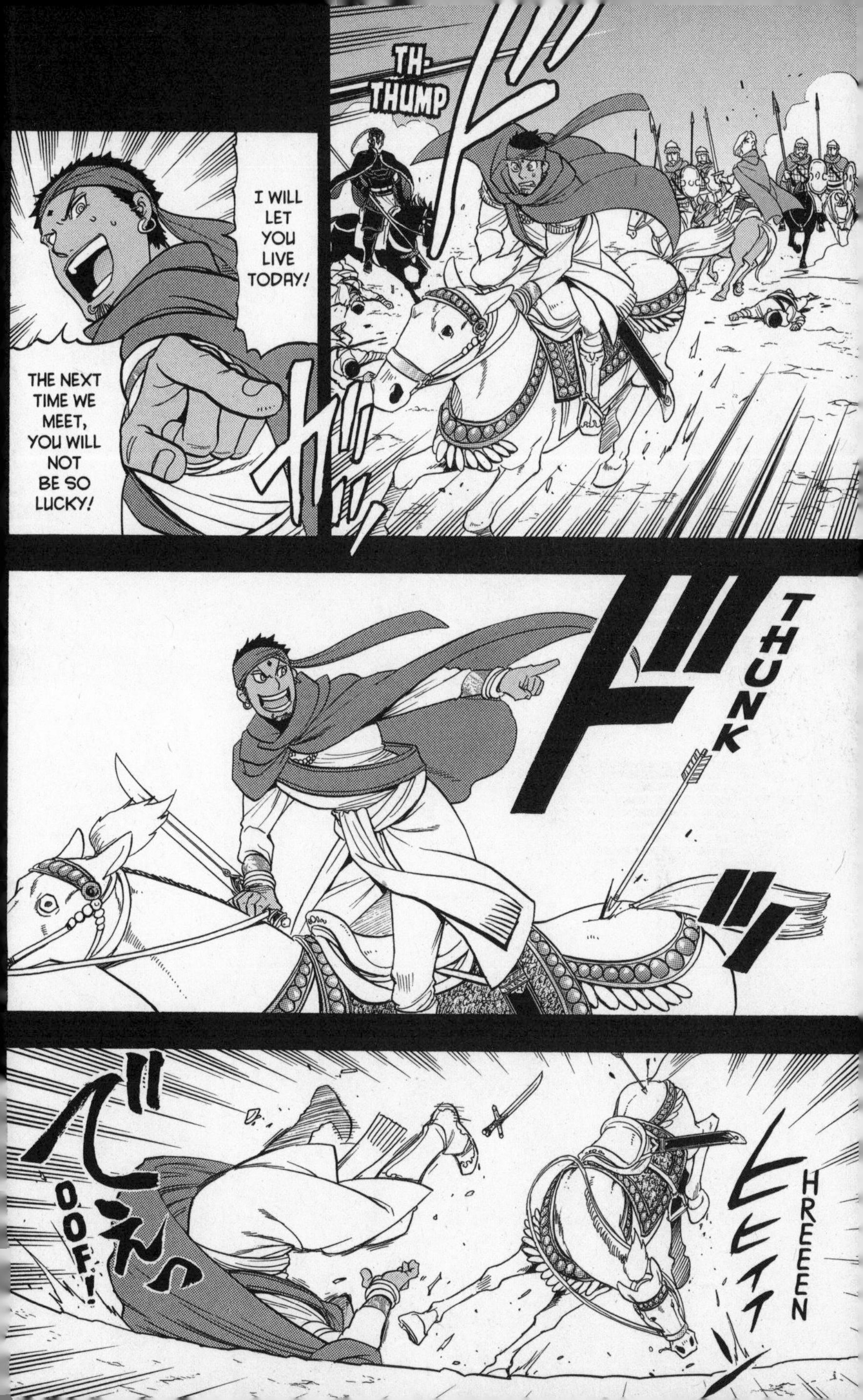
TH-THUMP
I WILL LET YOU LIVE TODAY!
THE NEXT TIME WE MEET, YOU WILL NOT BE SO LUCKY!
THUNK
HREEEN
OOF!

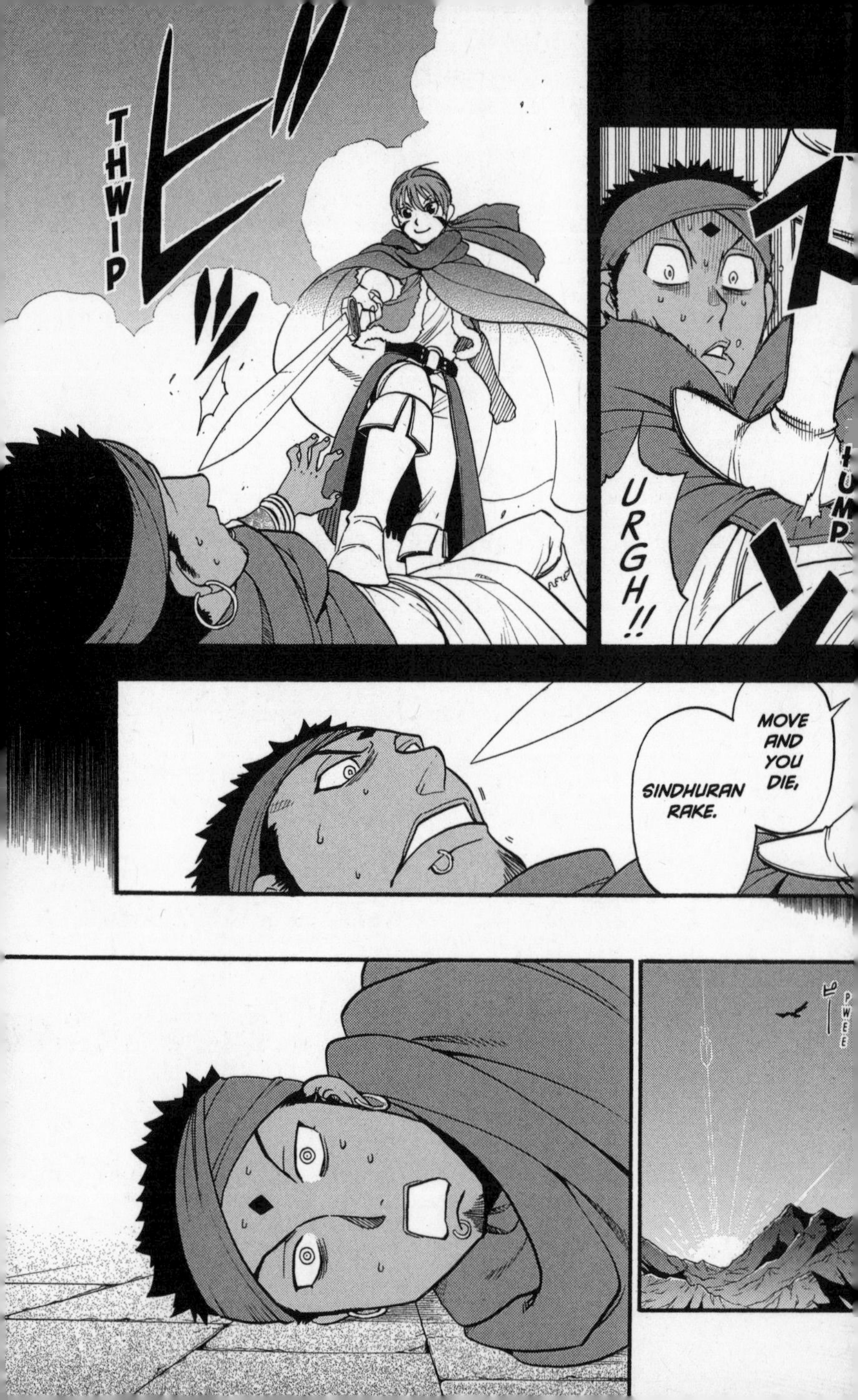
URGH!!
UMP
THWIP
MOVE AND YOU DIE, SINDHURAN RAKE.
PWEE

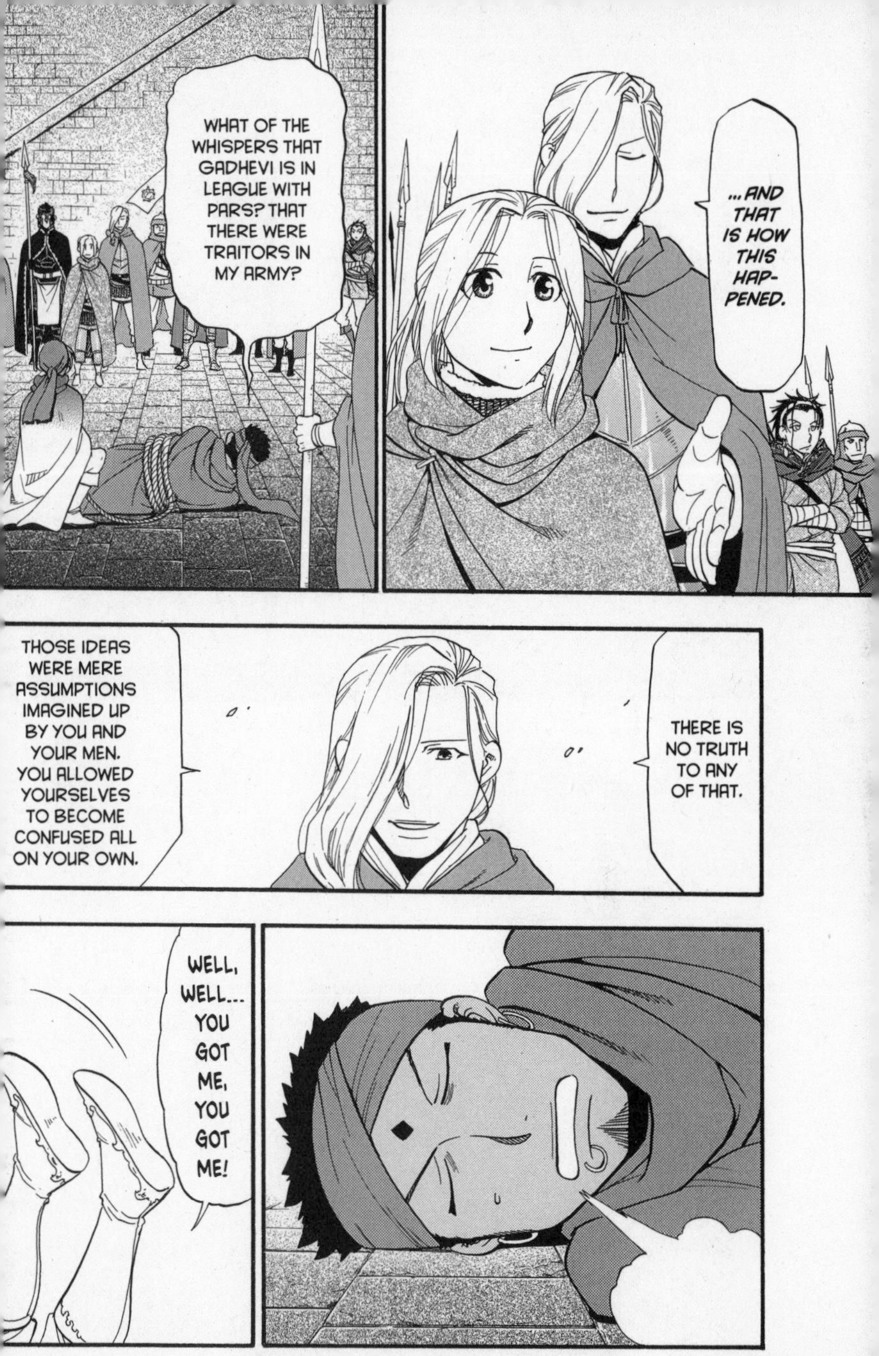
...AND THAT IS HOW THIS HAPPENED.
WHAT OF THE WHISPERS THAT GADHEVI IS IN LEAGUE WITH PARS? THAT THERE WERE TRAITORS IN MY ARMY?
THERE IS NO TRUTH TO ANY OF THAT.
THOSE IDEAS WERE MERE ASSUMPTIONS IMAGINED UP BY YOU AND YOUR MEN. YOU ALLOWED YOURSELVES TO BECOME CONFUSED ALL ON YOUR OWN.
WELL, WELL... YOU GOT ME, YOU GOT ME!

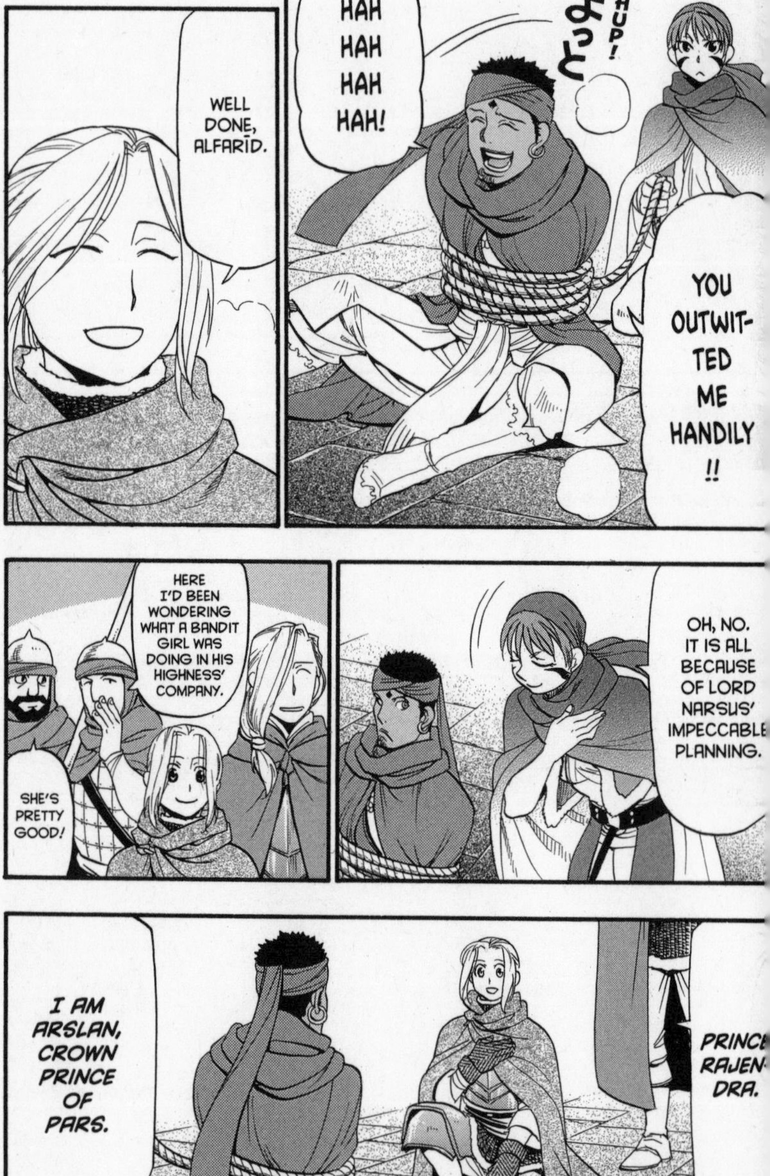

よっと HUP!
HAH HAH HAH HAH!
YOU OUTWITTED ME HANDILY!!
WELL DONE, ALFARĪD.
OH, NO. IT IS ALL BECAUSE OF LORD NARSUS' IMPECCABLE PLANNING.
HERE I'D BEEN WONDERING WHAT A BANDIT GIRL WAS DOING IN HIS HIGHNESS' COMPANY.
SHE'S PRETTY GOOD!
PRINCE RAJENDRA.
I AM ARSLAN, CROWN PRINCE OF PARS.

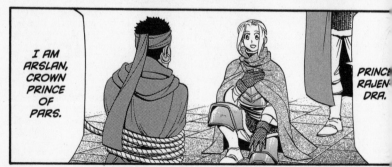

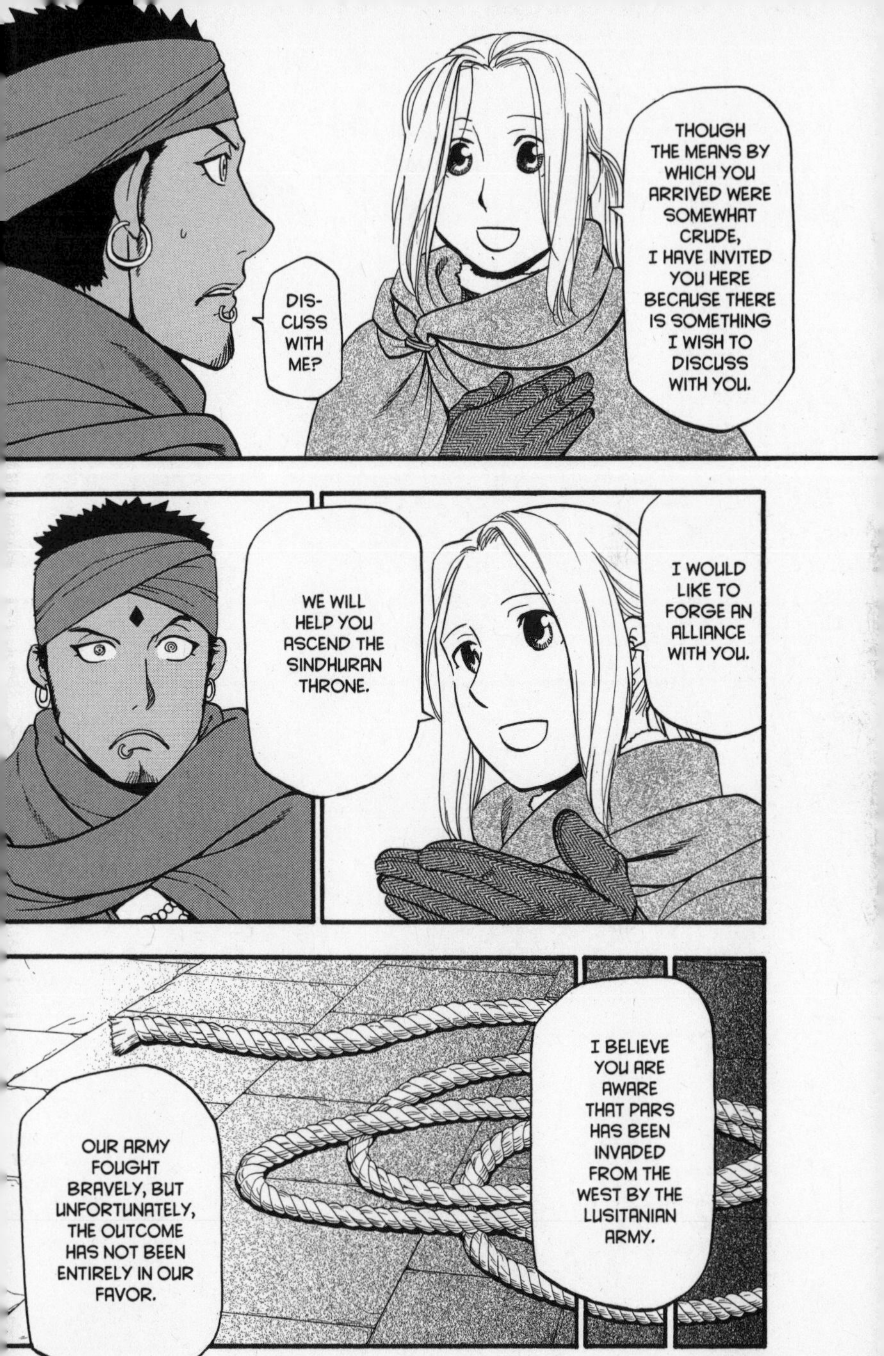
THOUGH THE MEANS BY WHICH YOU ARRIVED WERE SOMEWHAT CRUDE, I HAVE INVITED YOU HERE BECAUSE THERE IS SOMETHING I WISH TO DISCUSS WITH YOU.
DIS-CUSS WITH ME?
I WOULD LIKE TO FORGE AN ALLIANCE WITH YOU.
WE WILL HELP YOU ASCEND THE SINDHURAN THRONE.
I BELIEVE YOU ARE AWARE THAT PARS HAS BEEN INVADED FROM THE WEST BY THE LUSITANIAN ARMY.
OUR ARMY FOUGHT BRAVELY, BUT UNFORTUNATELY, THE OUTCOME HAS NOT BEEN ENTIRELY IN OUR FAVOR.

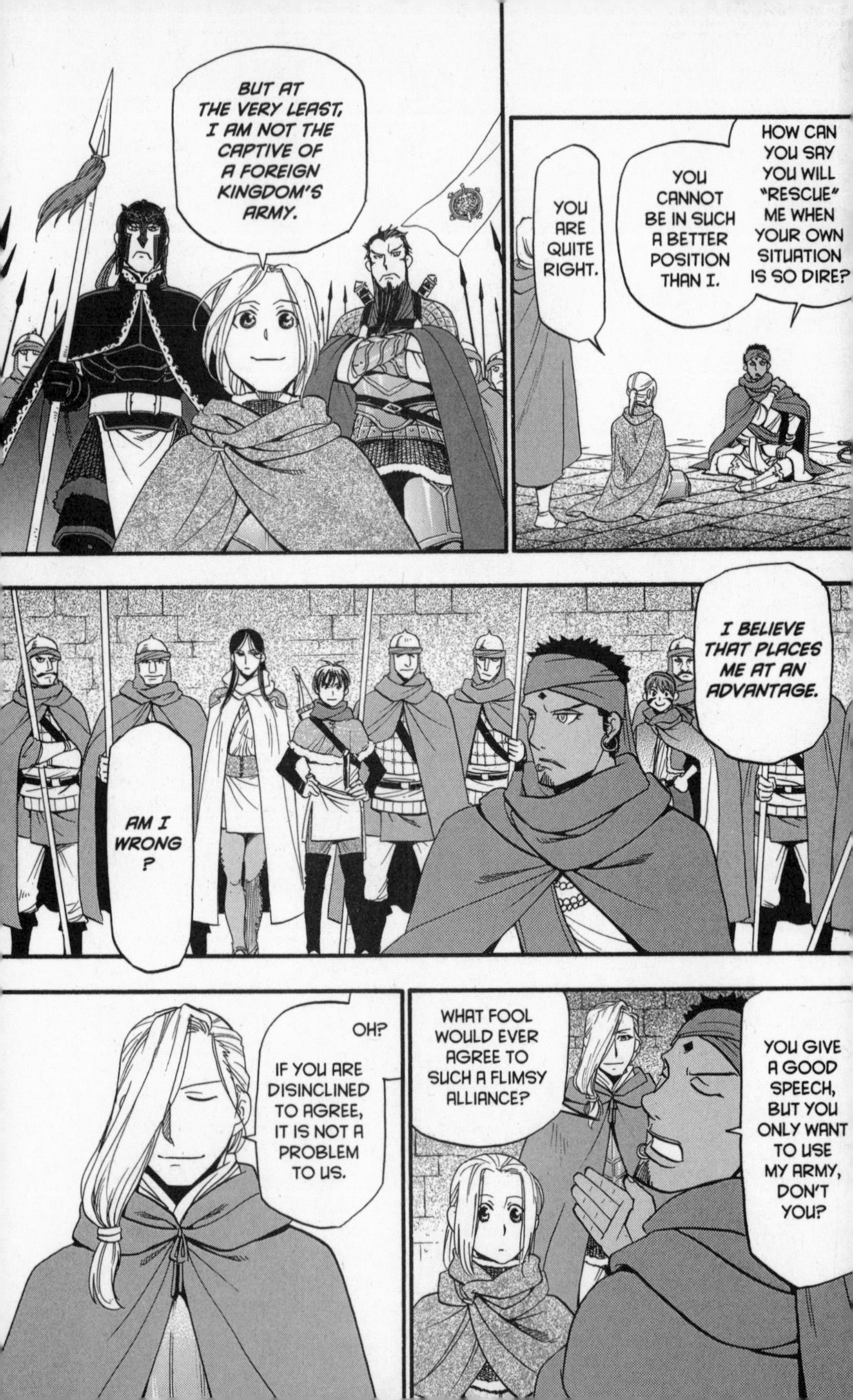

HOW CAN YOU SAY YOU WILL "RESCUE" ME WHEN YOUR OWN SITUATION IS SO DIRE?
YOU CANNOT BE IN SUCH A BETTER POSITION THAN I.
YOU ARE QUITE RIGHT.
BUT AT THE VERY LEAST, I AM NOT THE CAPTIVE OF A FOREIGN KINGDOM'S ARMY.
I BELIEVE THAT PLACES ME AT AN ADVANTAGE.
AM I WRONG?
YOU GIVE A GOOD SPEECH, BUT YOU ONLY WANT TO USE MY ARMY, DON'T YOU?
WHAT FOOL WOULD EVER AGREE TO SUCH A FLIMSY ALLIANCE?
OH?
IF YOU ARE DISINCLINED TO AGREE, IT IS NOT A PROBLEM TO US.

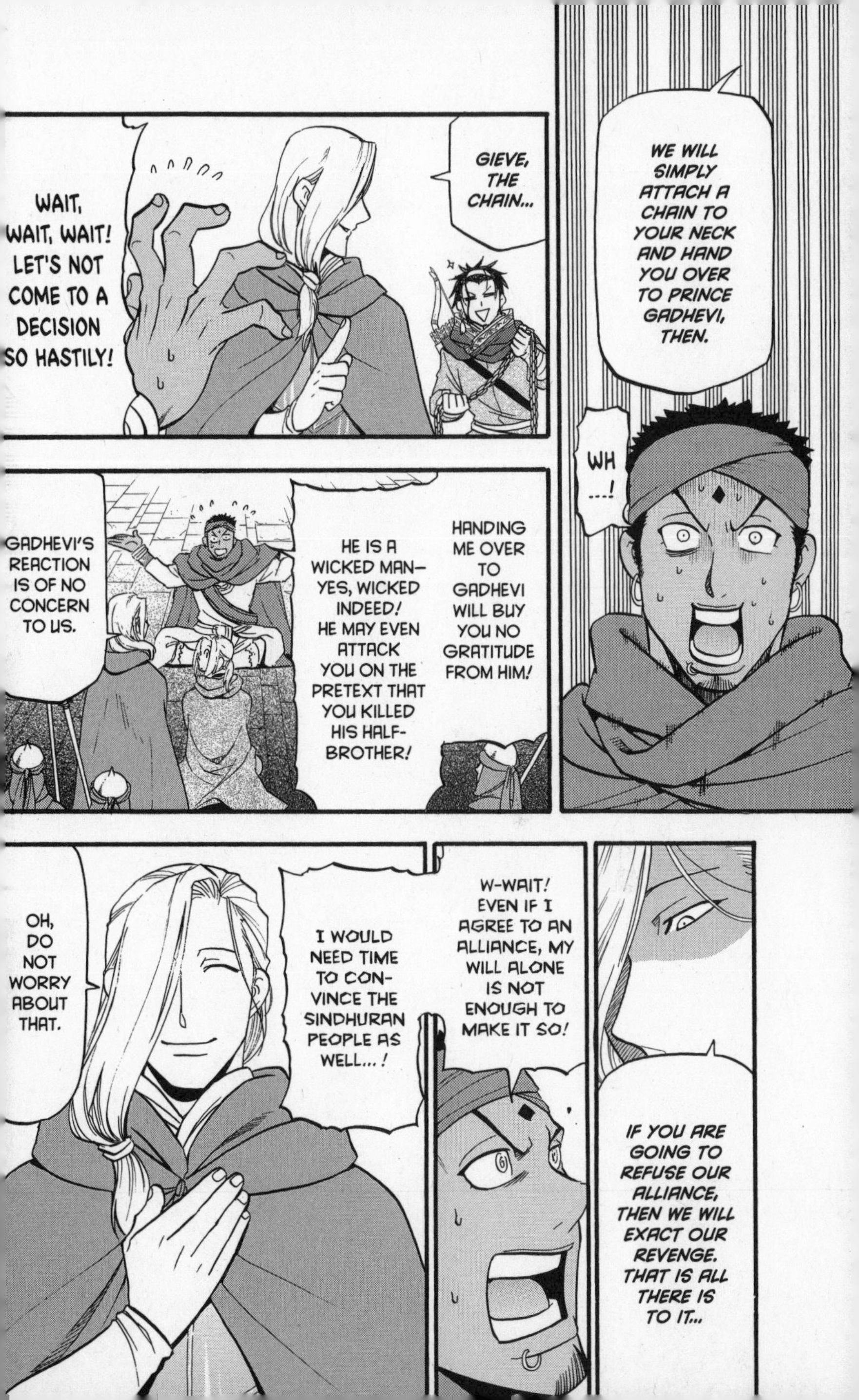
WE WILL SIMPLY ATTACH A CHAIN TO YOUR NECK AND HAND YOU OVER TO PRINCE GADHEVI, THEN.
WH...!
GIEVE, THE CHAIN...
WAIT, WAIT, WAIT! LET'S NOT COME TO A DECISION SO HASTILY!
HANDING ME OVER TO GADHEVI WILL BUY YOU NO GRATITUDE FROM HIM!
HE IS A WICKED MAN— YES, WICKED INDEED! HE MAY EVEN ATTACK YOU ON THE PRETEXT THAT YOU KILLED HIS HALF-BROTHER!
GADHEVI'S REACTION IS OF NO CONCERN TO US.
IF YOU ARE GOING TO REFUSE OUR ALLIANCE, THEN WE WILL EXACT OUR REVENGE. THAT IS ALL THERE IS TO IT...
W-WAIT! EVEN IF I AGREE TO AN ALLIANCE, MY WILL ALONE IS NOT ENOUGH TO MAKE IT SO!
I WOULD NEED TIME TO CON-VINCE THE SINDHURAN PEOPLE AS WELL...!
OH, DO NOT WORRY ABOUT THAT.

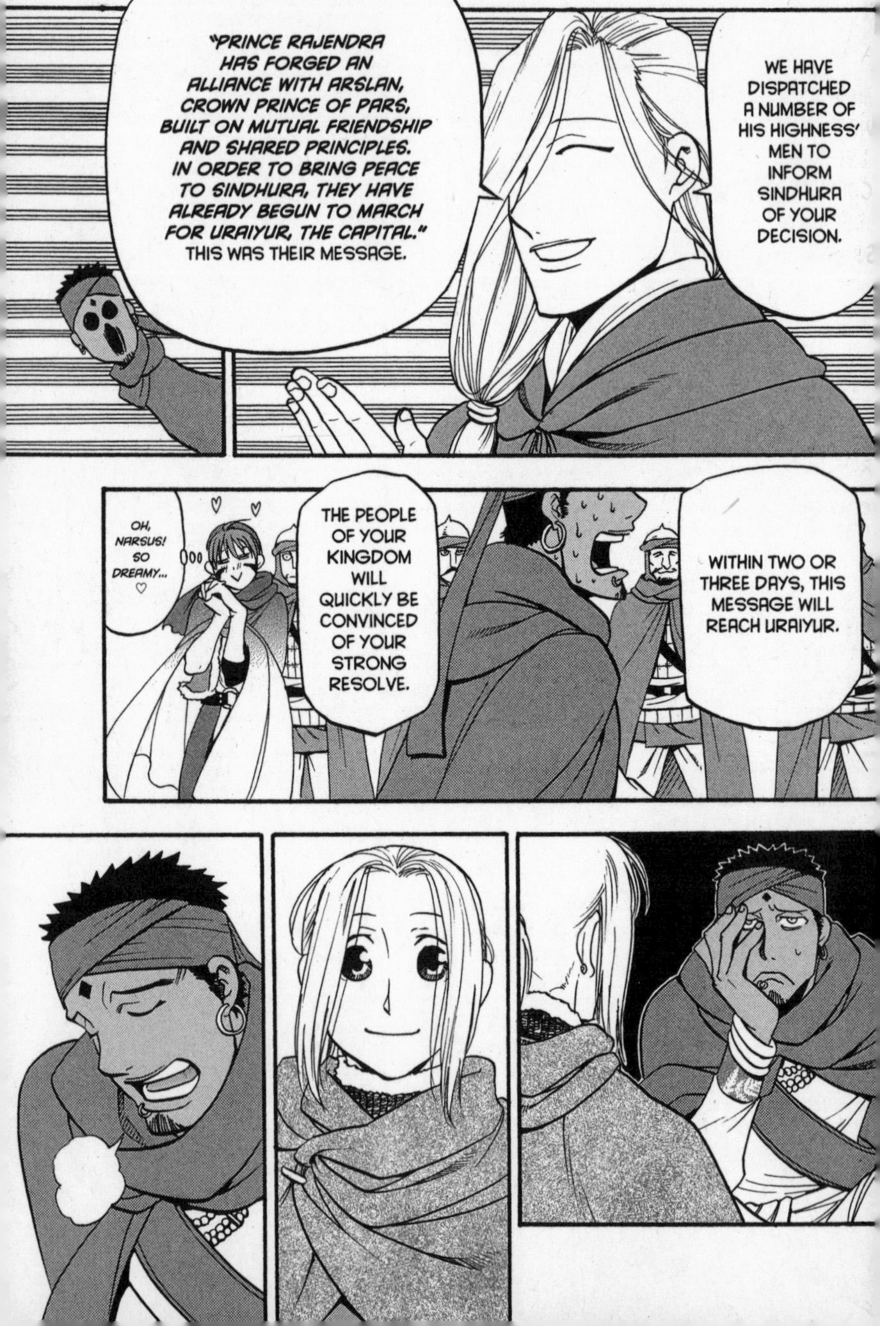

WE HAVE DISPATCHED A NUMBER OF HIS HIGHNESS' MEN TO INFORM SINDHURA OF YOUR DECISION.
"PRINCE RAJENDRA HAS FORGED AN ALLIANCE WITH ARSLAN, CROWN PRINCE OF PARS, BUILT ON MUTUAL FRIENDSHIP AND SHARED PRINCIPLES. IN ORDER TO BRING PEACE TO SINDHURA, THEY HAVE ALREADY BEGUN TO MARCH FOR URAIYUR, THE CAPITAL." THIS WAS THEIR MESSAGE.
WITHIN TWO OR THREE DAYS, THIS MESSAGE WILL REACH URAIYUR.
THE PEOPLE OF YOUR KINGDOM WILL QUICKLY BE CONVINCED OF YOUR STRONG RESOLVE.
OH, NARSUS! SO DREAMY... ♡

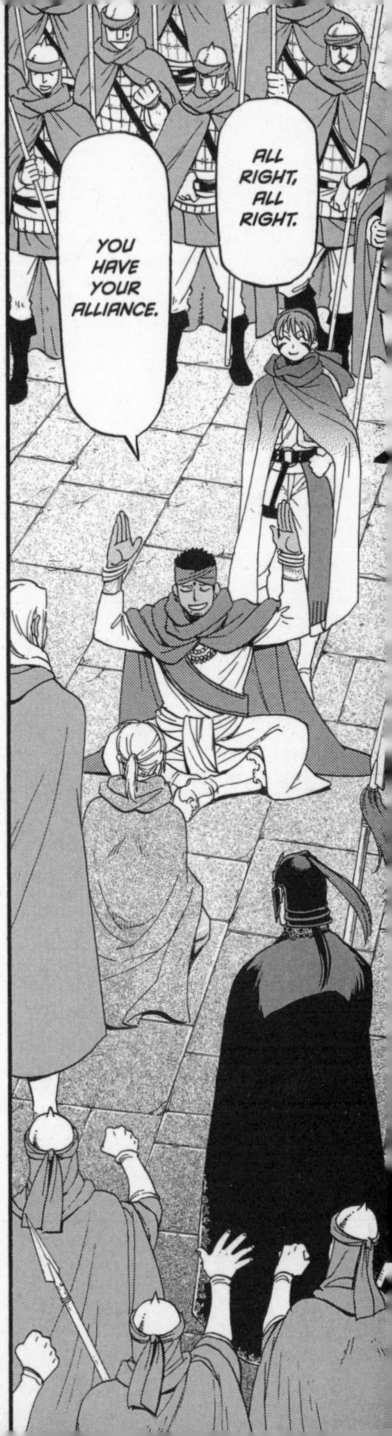
ALL RIGHT, ALL RIGHT.
YOU HAVE YOUR ALLIANCE.

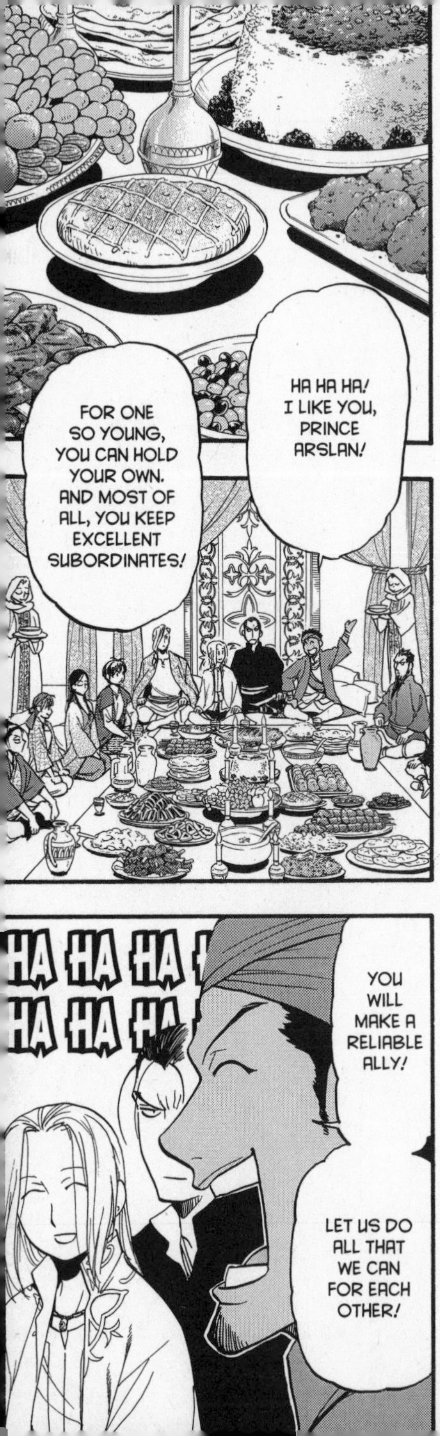
HA HA HA! I LIKE YOU, PRINCE ARSLAN!
FOR ONE SO YOUNG, YOU CAN HOLD YOUR OWN. AND MOST OF ALL, YOU KEEP EXCELLENT SUBORDINATES!
YOU WILL MAKE A RELIABLE ALLY!
LET US DO ALL THAT WE CAN FOR EACH OTHER!
HA HA HA
HA HA

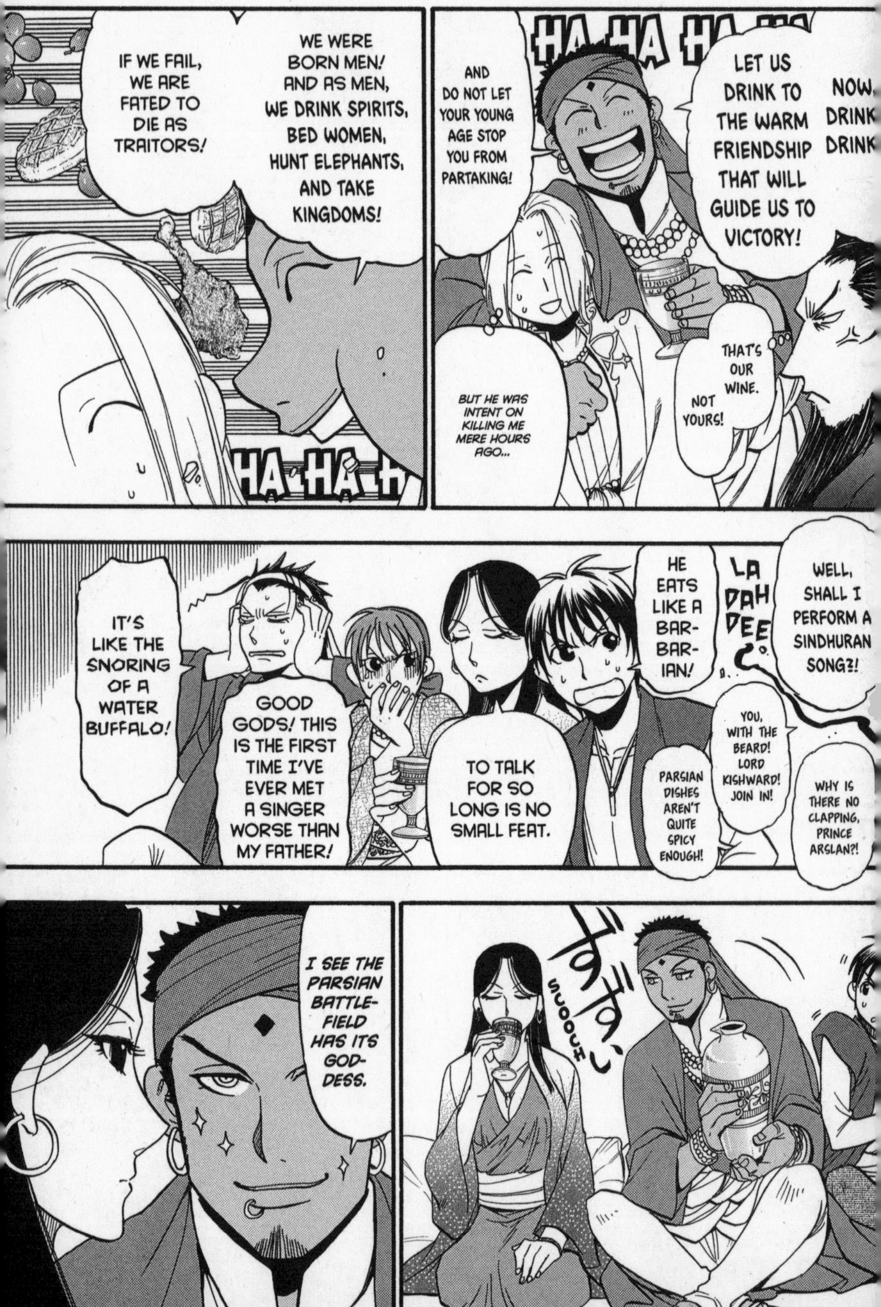
HA HA HA HA
LET US DRINK TO THE WARM FRIENDSHIP THAT WILL GUIDE US TO VICTORY!
NOW, DRINK DRINK
AND DO NOT LET YOUR YOUNG AGE STOP YOU FROM PARTAKING!
THAT'S OUR WINE. NOT YOURS!
BUT HE WAS INTENT ON KILLING ME MERE HOURS AGO...
WE WERE BORN MEN! AND AS MEN, WE DRINK SPIRITS, BED WOMEN, HUNT ELEPHANTS, AND TAKE KINGDOMS!
IF WE FAIL, WE ARE FATED TO DIE AS TRAITORS!
HA HA H
WELL, SHALL I PERFORM A SINDHURAN SONG?!
LA DAH DEE
HE EATS LIKE A BAR-BAR-IAN!
WHY IS THERE NO CLAPPING, PRINCE ARSLAN?!
YOU, WITH THE BEARD! LORD KISHWARD! JOIN IN!
PARSIAN DISHES AREN'T QUITE SPICY ENOUGH!
TO TALK FOR SO LONG IS NO SMALL FEAT.
GOOD GODS! THIS IS THE FIRST TIME I'VE EVER MET A SINGER WORSE THAN MY FATHER!
IT'S LIKE THE SNORING OF A WATER BUFFALO!
ずずい
SCOOCH
I SEE THE PARSIAN BATTLE-FIELD HAS ITS GOD-DESS.

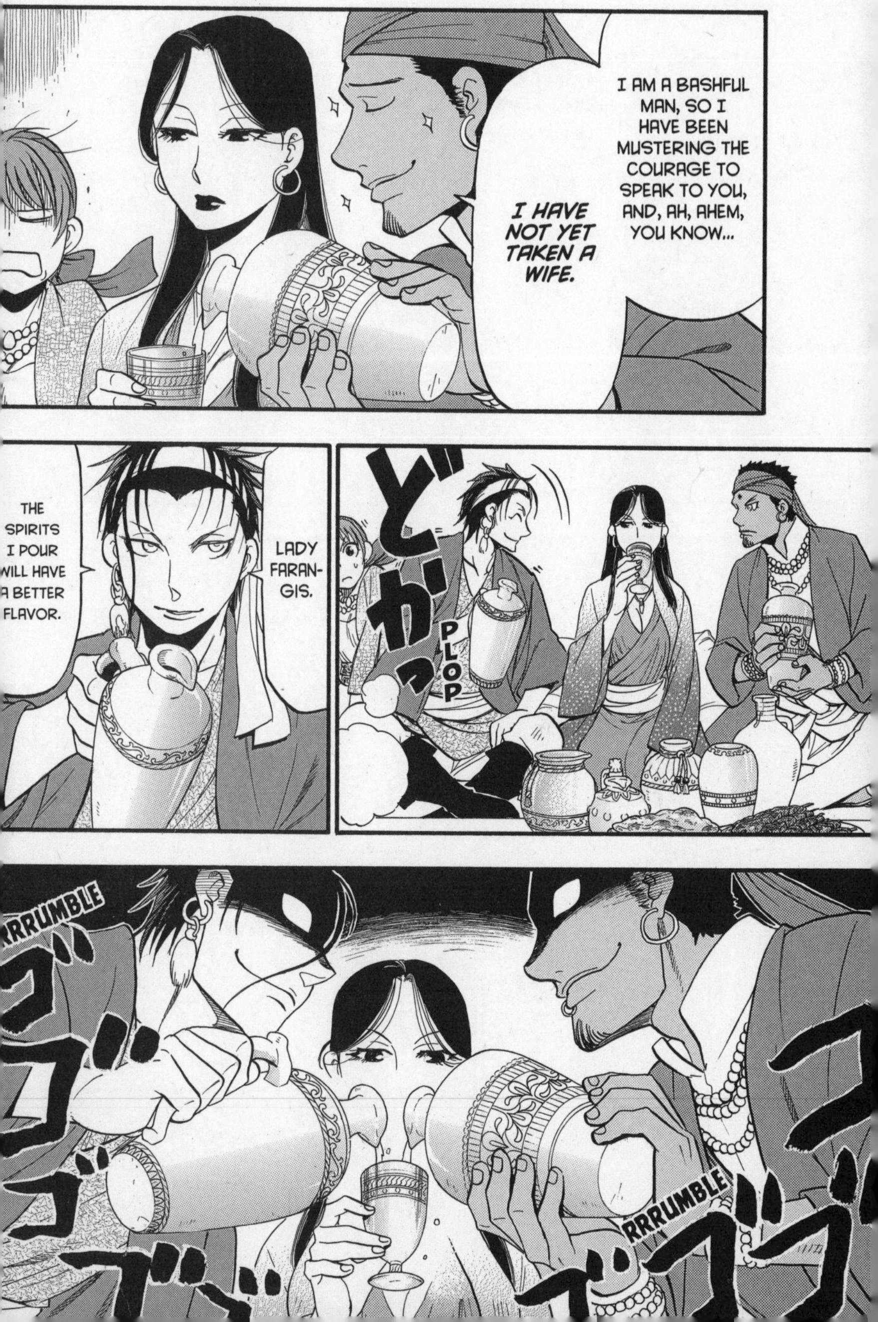
I AM A BASHFUL MAN, SO I HAVE BEEN MUSTERING THE COURAGE TO SPEAK TO YOU, AND, AH, AHEM, YOU KNOW...
I HAVE NOT YET TAKEN A WIFE.
どかっ
PLOP
LADY FARAN-GIS.
THE SPIRITS I POUR WILL HAVE A BETTER FLAVOR.
RRRUMBLE
ゴゴゴ
RRRUMBLE
ゴゴゴ

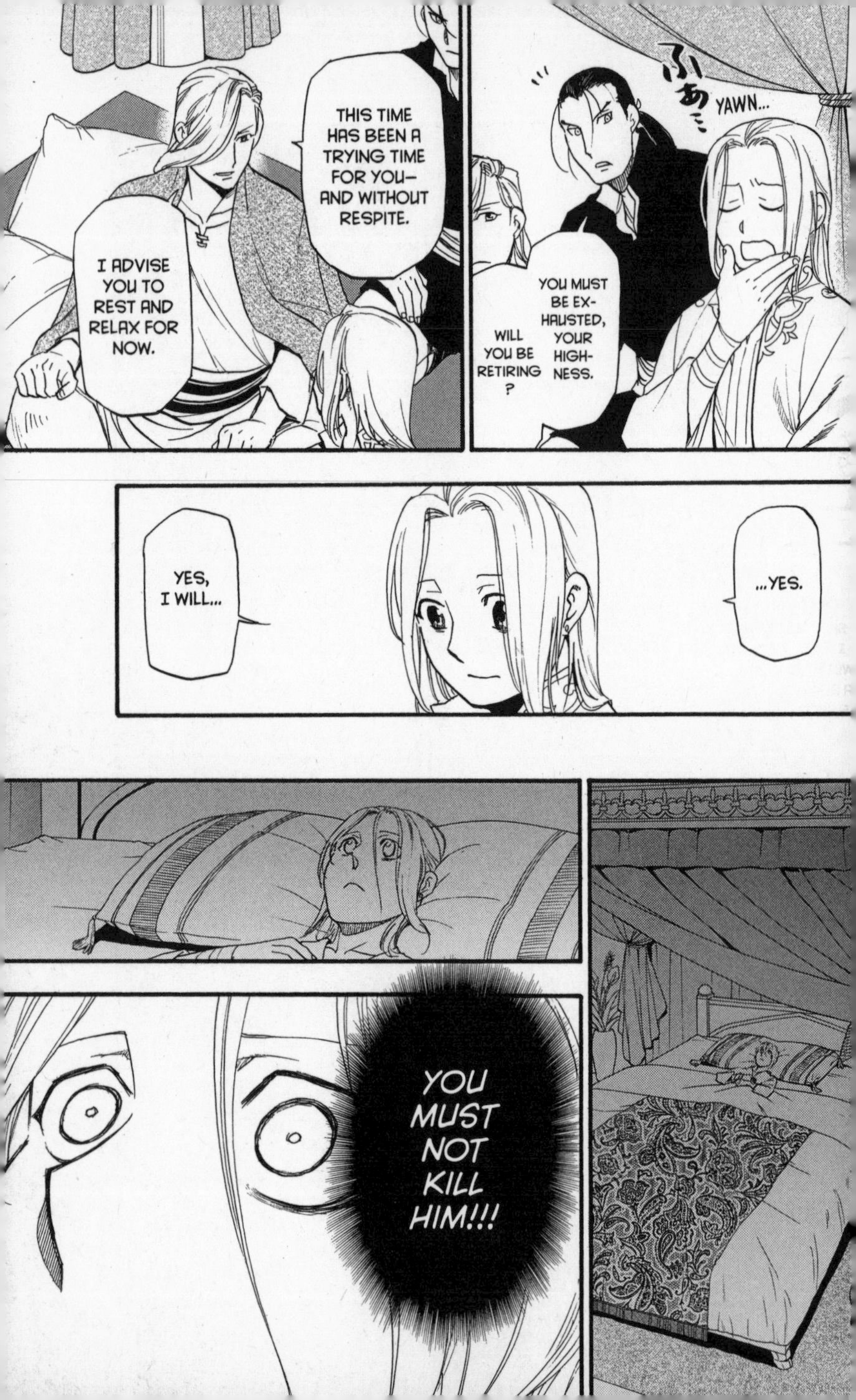
YAWN...
YOU MUST BE EX-HAUSTED, YOUR HIGH-NESS.
WILL YOU BE RETIRING?
THIS TIME HAS BEEN A TRYING TIME FOR YOU—AND WITHOUT RESPITE.
I ADVISE YOU TO REST AND RELAX FOR NOW.
...YES.
YES, I WILL...
YOU MUST NOT KILL HIM!!!

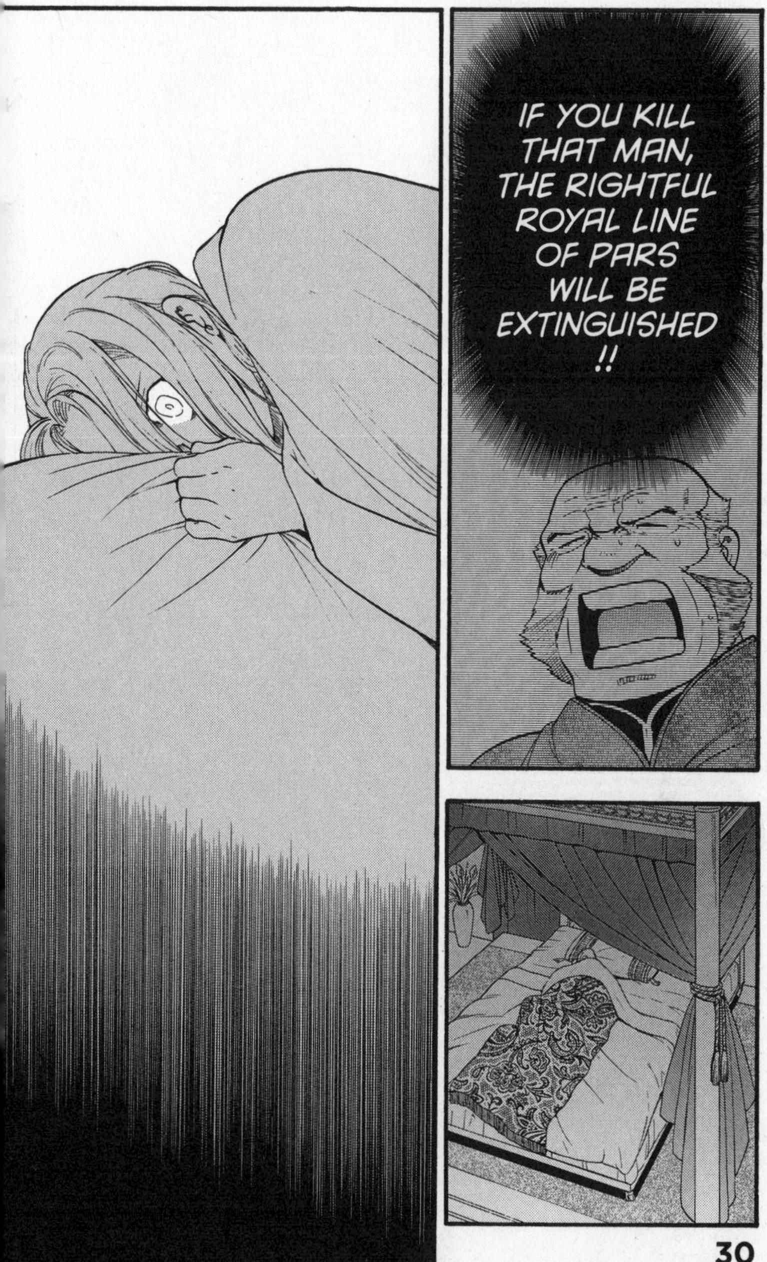
IF YOU KILL THAT MAN, THE RIGHTFUL ROYAL LINE OF PARS WILL BE EXTINGUISHED !!

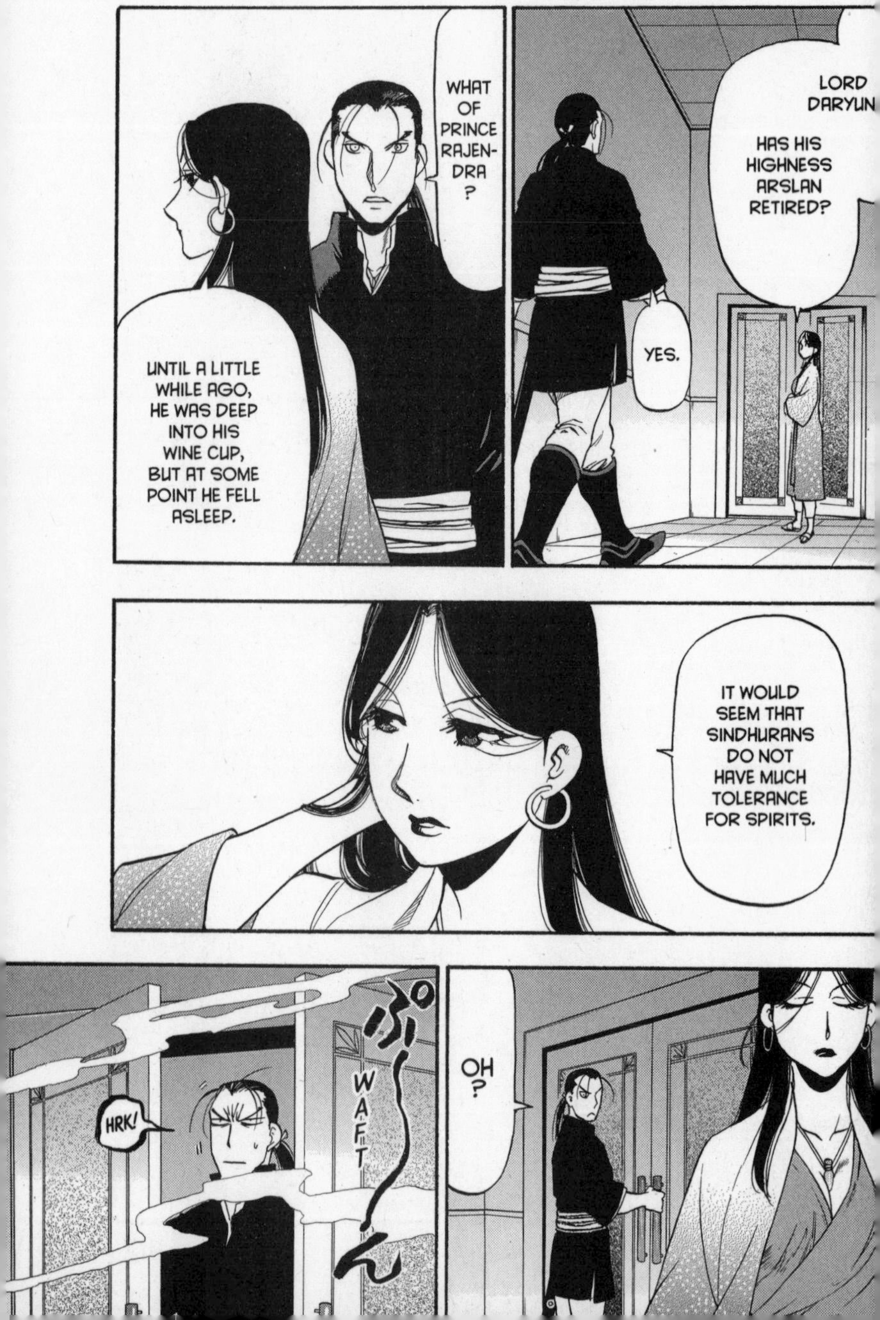
LORD DARYUN
HAS HIS HIGHNESS ARSLAN RETIRED?
YES.
WHAT OF PRINCE RAJEN-DRA ?
UNTIL A LITTLE WHILE AGO, HE WAS DEEP INTO HIS WINE CUP, BUT AT SOME POINT HE FELL ASLEEP.
IT WOULD SEEM THAT SINDHURANS DO NOT HAVE MUCH TOLERANCE FOR SPIRITS.
OH ?
ぷ〜ん
WAFT
HRK!

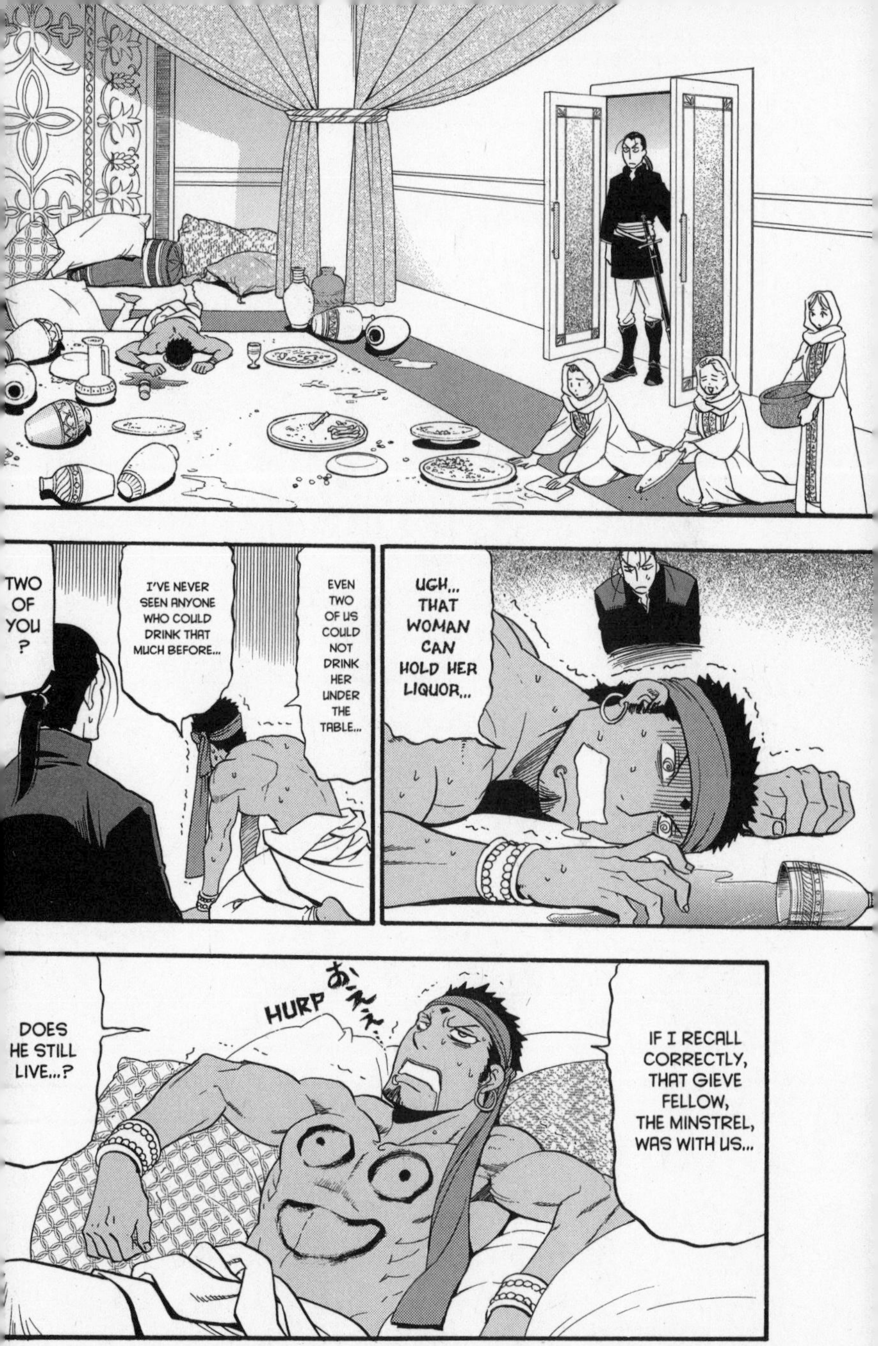
UGH... THAT WOMAN CAN HOLD HER LIQUOR...
EVEN TWO OF US COULD NOT DRINK HER UNDER THE TABLE...
I'VE NEVER SEEN ANYONE WHO COULD DRINK THAT MUCH BEFORE...
TWO OF YOU?
IF I RECALL CORRECTLY, THAT GIEVE FELLOW, THE MINSTREL, WAS WITH US...
HURP
DOES HE STILL LIVE...?

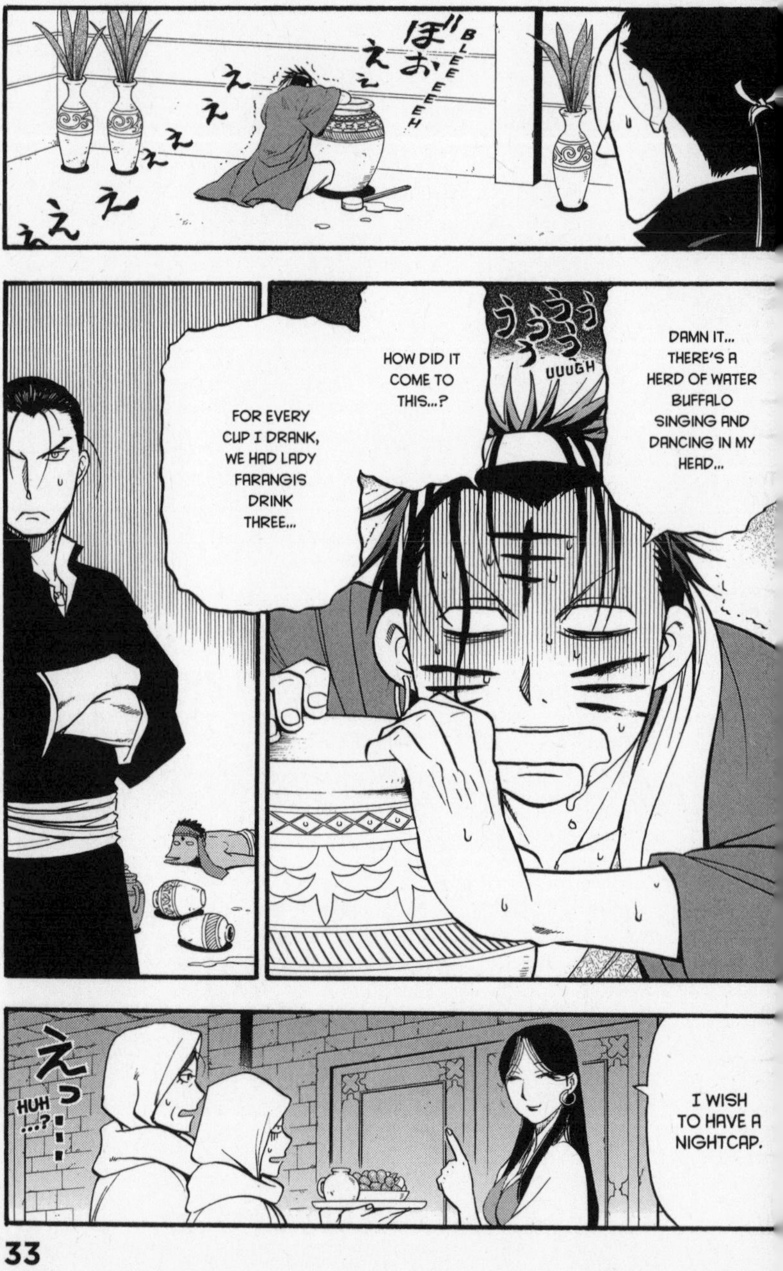

ぼお
BLEEEEEEH
えええええええ
うううううう
UUUGH
DAMN IT... THERE'S A HERD OF WATER BUFFALO SINGING AND DANCING IN MY HEAD...
HOW DID IT COME TO THIS...?
FOR EVERY CUP I DRANK, WE HAD LADY FARANGIS DRINK THREE...
I WISH TO HAVE A NIGHTCAP.
えっ
HUH ...?

THE HEROIC LEGEND OF
ARSLAN

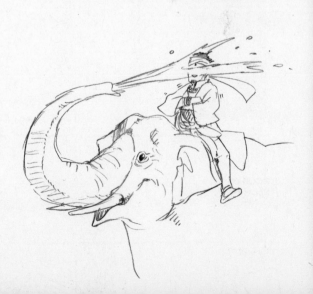

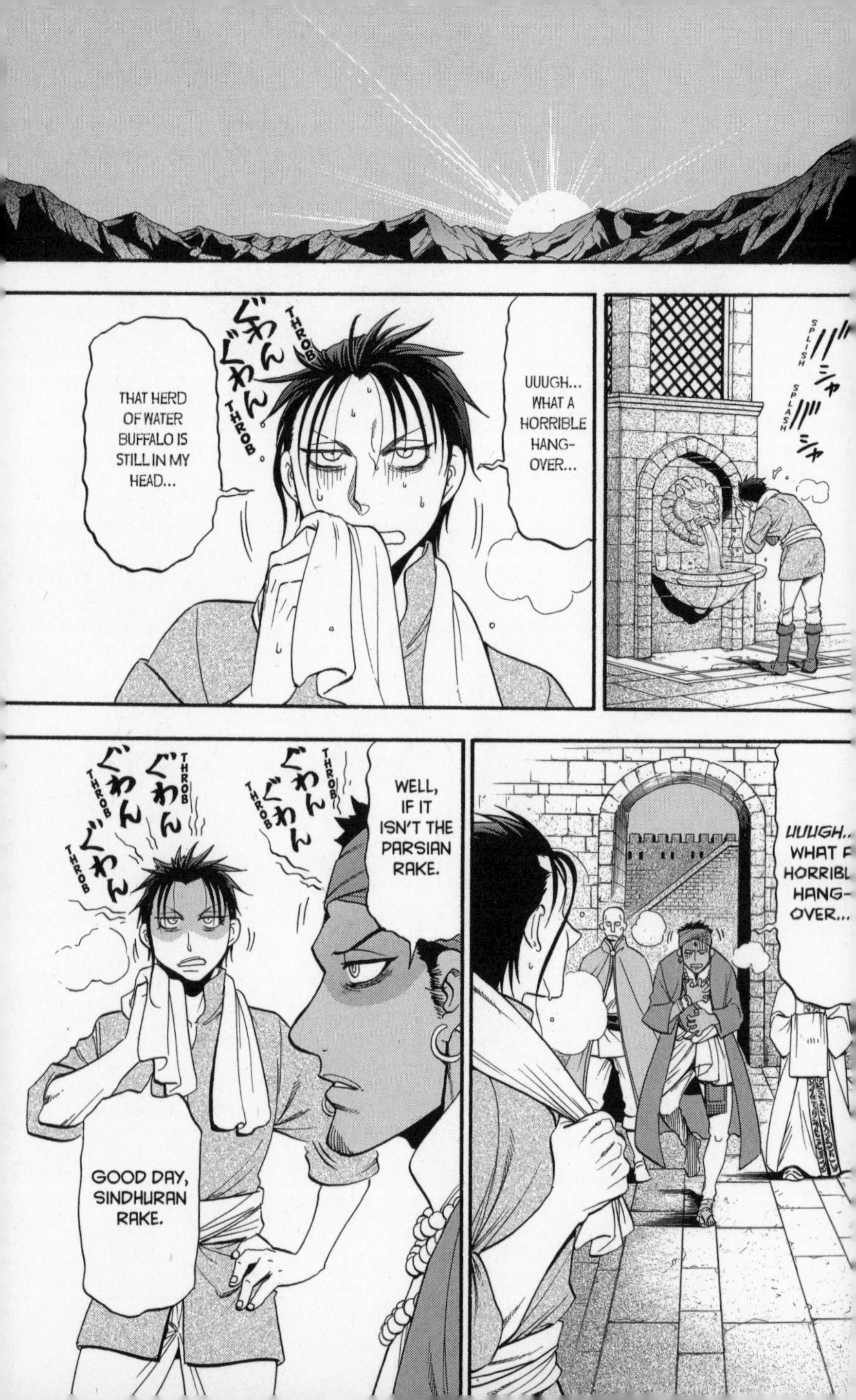
SPLISH
SPLASH
UUUGH... WHAT A HORRIBLE HANG-OVER...
ぐわんぐわん
THROB THROB
THAT HERD OF WATER BUFFALO IS STILL IN MY HEAD...
UUUGH... WHAT A HORRIBL HANG-OVER...
WELL, IF IT ISN'T THE PARSIAN RAKE.
ぐわんぐわん
THROB THROB
ぐわんぐわんぐわん
THROB THROB THROB
GOOD DAY, SINDHURAN RAKE.

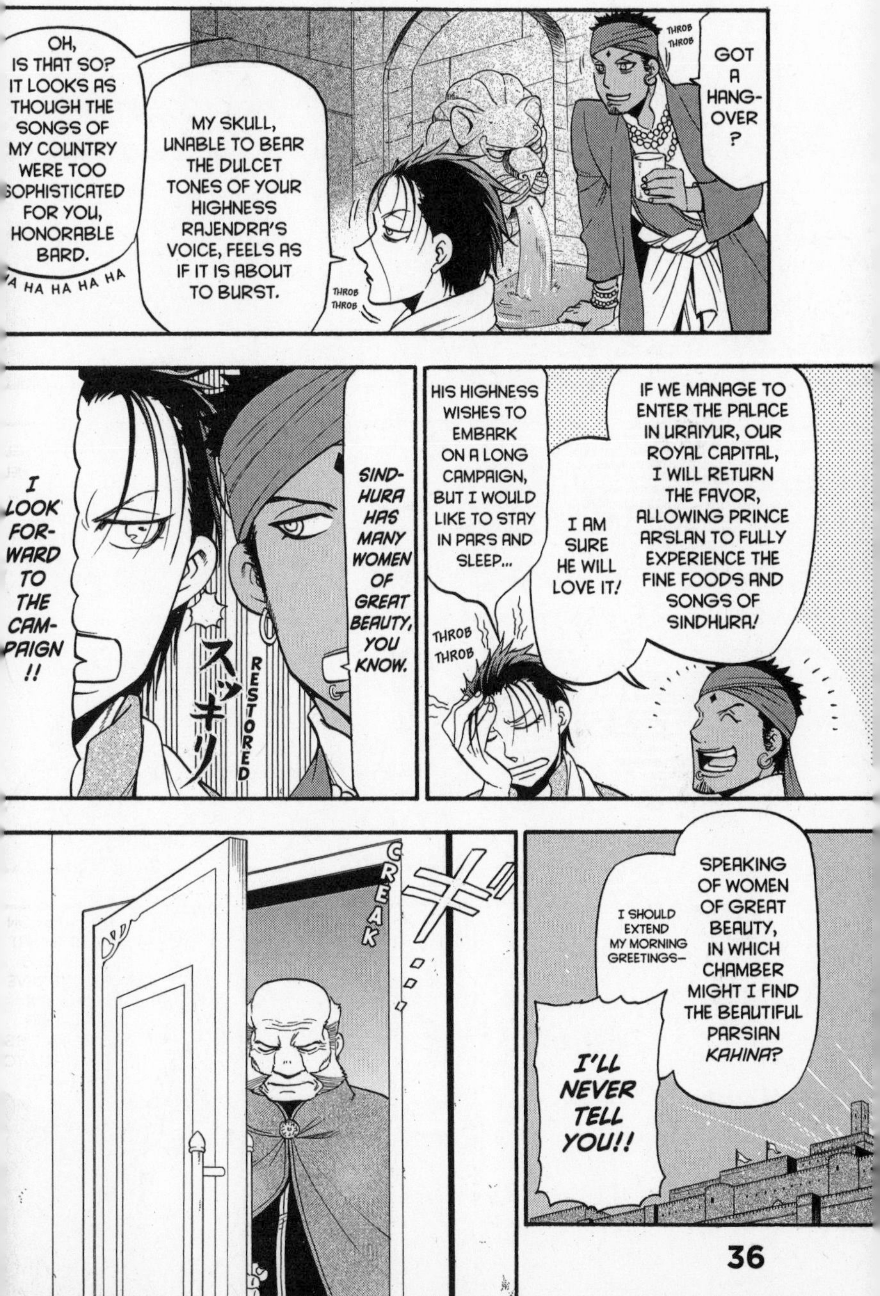
THROB THROB
GOT A HANG-OVER?
MY SKULL, UNABLE TO BEAR THE DULCET TONES OF YOUR HIGHNESS RAJENDRA'S VOICE, FEELS AS IF IT IS ABOUT TO BURST.
OH, IS THAT SO? IT LOOKS AS THOUGH THE SONGS OF MY COUNTRY WERE TOO SOPHISTICATED FOR YOU, HONORABLE BARD.
HA HA HA HA HA
THROB THROB
IF WE MANAGE TO ENTER THE PALACE IN URAIYUR, OUR ROYAL CAPITAL, I WILL RETURN THE FAVOR, ALLOWING PRINCE ARSLAN TO FULLY EXPERIENCE THE FINE FOODS AND SONGS OF SINDHURA!
HIS HIGHNESS WISHES TO EMBARK ON A LONG CAMPAIGN, BUT I WOULD LIKE TO STAY IN PARS AND SLEEP...
I AM SURE HE WILL LOVE IT!
THROB THROB
SINDHURA HAS MANY WOMEN OF GREAT BEAUTY, YOU KNOW.
RESTORED
I LOOK FORWARD TO THE CAMPAIGN!!
SPEAKING OF WOMEN OF GREAT BEAUTY, IN WHICH CHAMBER MIGHT I FIND THE BEAUTIFUL PARSIAN KAHINA?
I SHOULD EXTEND MY MORNING GREETINGS—
I'LL NEVER TELL YOU!!
CREAK

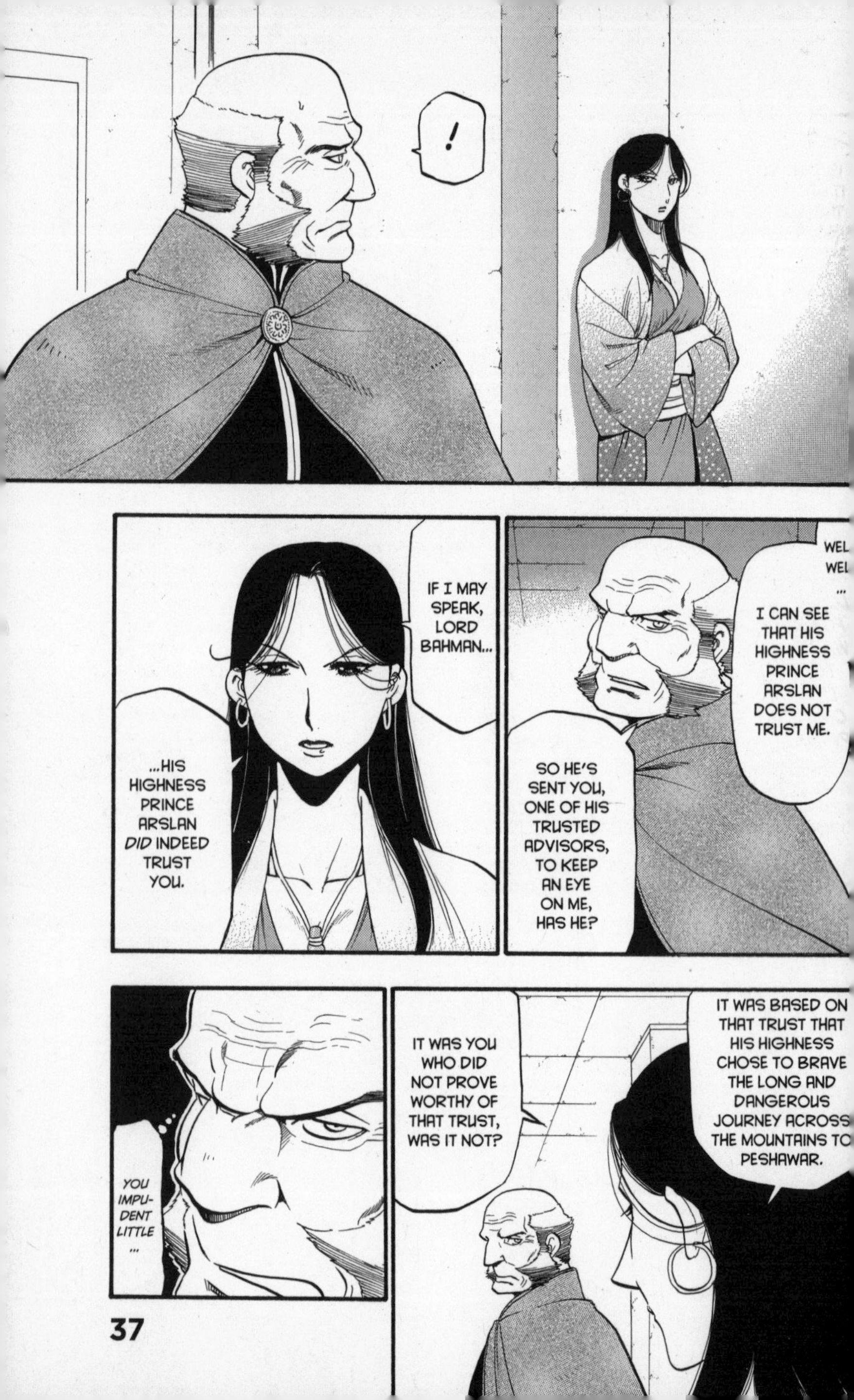
!
WEL WEL ...
I CAN SEE THAT HIS HIGHNESS PRINCE ARSLAN DOES NOT TRUST ME.
SO HE'S SENT YOU, ONE OF HIS TRUSTED ADVISORS, TO KEEP AN EYE ON ME, HAS HE?
IF I MAY SPEAK, LORD BAHMAN...
...HIS HIGHNESS PRINCE ARSLAN *DID* INDEED TRUST YOU.
IT WAS BASED ON THAT TRUST THAT HIS HIGHNESS CHOSE TO BRAVE THE LONG AND DANGEROUS JOURNEY ACROSS THE MOUNTAINS TO PESHAWAR.
IT WAS YOU WHO DID NOT PROVE WORTHY OF THAT TRUST, WAS IT NOT?
YOU IMPUDENT LITTLE ...

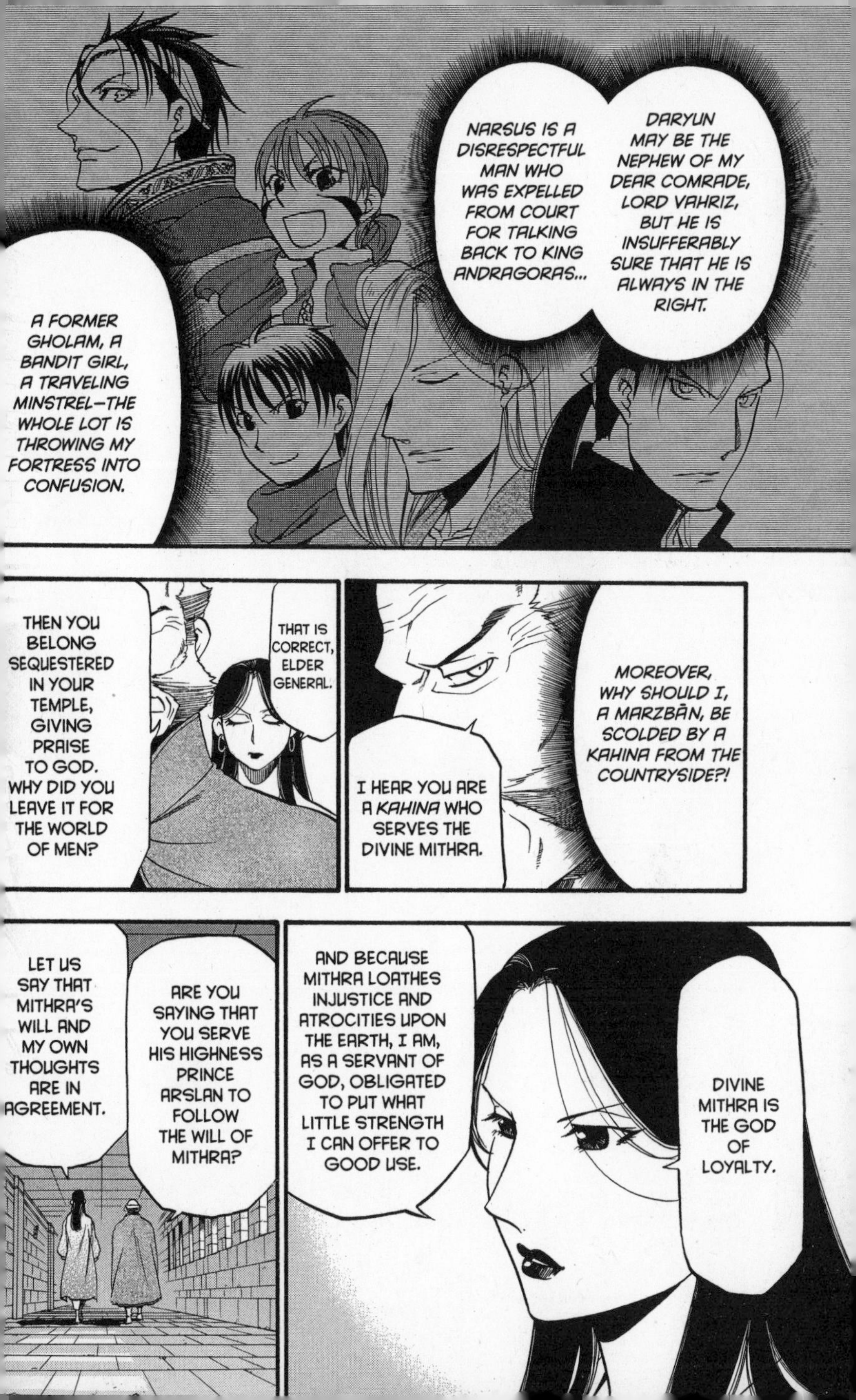
DARYUN MAY BE THE NEPHEW OF MY DEAR COMRADE, LORD VAHRIZ, BUT HE IS INSUFFERABLY SURE THAT HE IS ALWAYS IN THE RIGHT.
NARSUS IS A DISRESPECTFUL MAN WHO WAS EXPELLED FROM COURT FOR TALKING BACK TO KING ANDRAGORAS...
A FORMER GHOLAM, A BANDIT GIRL, A TRAVELING MINSTREL—THE WHOLE LOT IS THROWING MY FORTRESS INTO CONFUSION.
MOREOVER, WHY SHOULD I, A MARZBĀN, BE SCOLDED BY A KAHINA FROM THE COUNTRYSIDE?!
I HEAR YOU ARE A *KAHINA* WHO SERVES THE DIVINE MITHRA.
THAT IS CORRECT, ELDER GENERAL.
THEN YOU BELONG SEQUESTERED IN YOUR TEMPLE, GIVING PRAISE TO GOD. WHY DID YOU LEAVE IT FOR THE WORLD OF MEN?
DIVINE MITHRA IS THE GOD OF LOYALTY.
AND BECAUSE MITHRA LOATHES INJUSTICE AND ATROCITIES UPON THE EARTH, I AM, AS A SERVANT OF GOD, OBLIGATED TO PUT WHAT LITTLE STRENGTH I CAN OFFER TO GOOD USE.
ARE YOU SAYING THAT YOU SERVE HIS HIGHNESS PRINCE ARSLAN TO FOLLOW THE WILL OF MITHRA?
LET US SAY THAT MITHRA'S WILL AND MY OWN THOUGHTS ARE IN AGREEMENT.

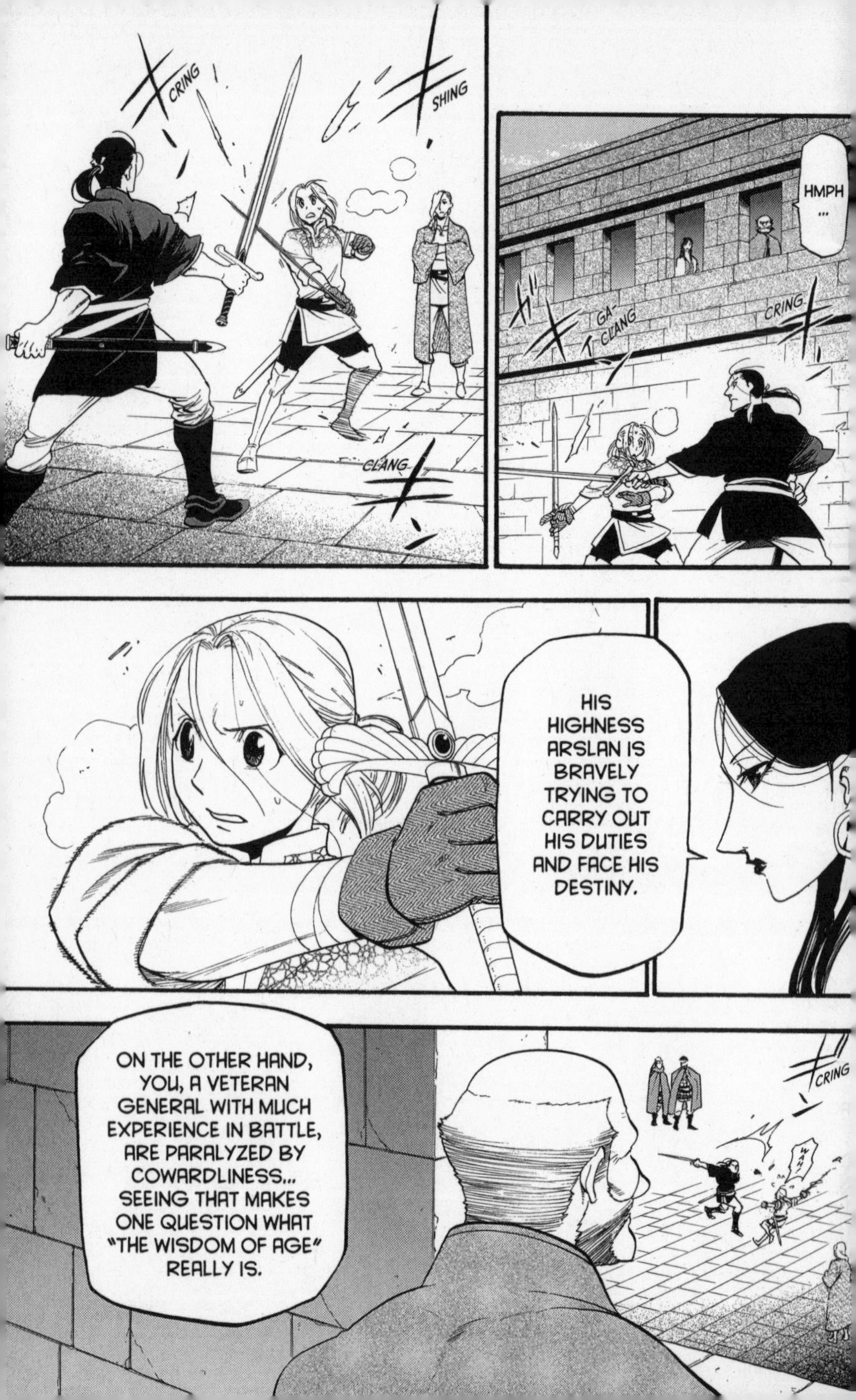
HMPH ...
GA-CLANG
CRING
CRING
SHING
CLANG
HIS HIGHNESS ARSLAN IS BRAVELY TRYING TO CARRY OUT HIS DUTIES AND FACE HIS DESTINY.
CRING
WAH!
ON THE OTHER HAND, YOU, A VETERAN GENERAL WITH MUCH EXPERIENCE IN BATTLE, ARE PARALYZED BY COWARDLINESS... SEEING THAT MAKES ONE QUESTION WHAT "THE WISDOM OF AGE" REALLY IS.

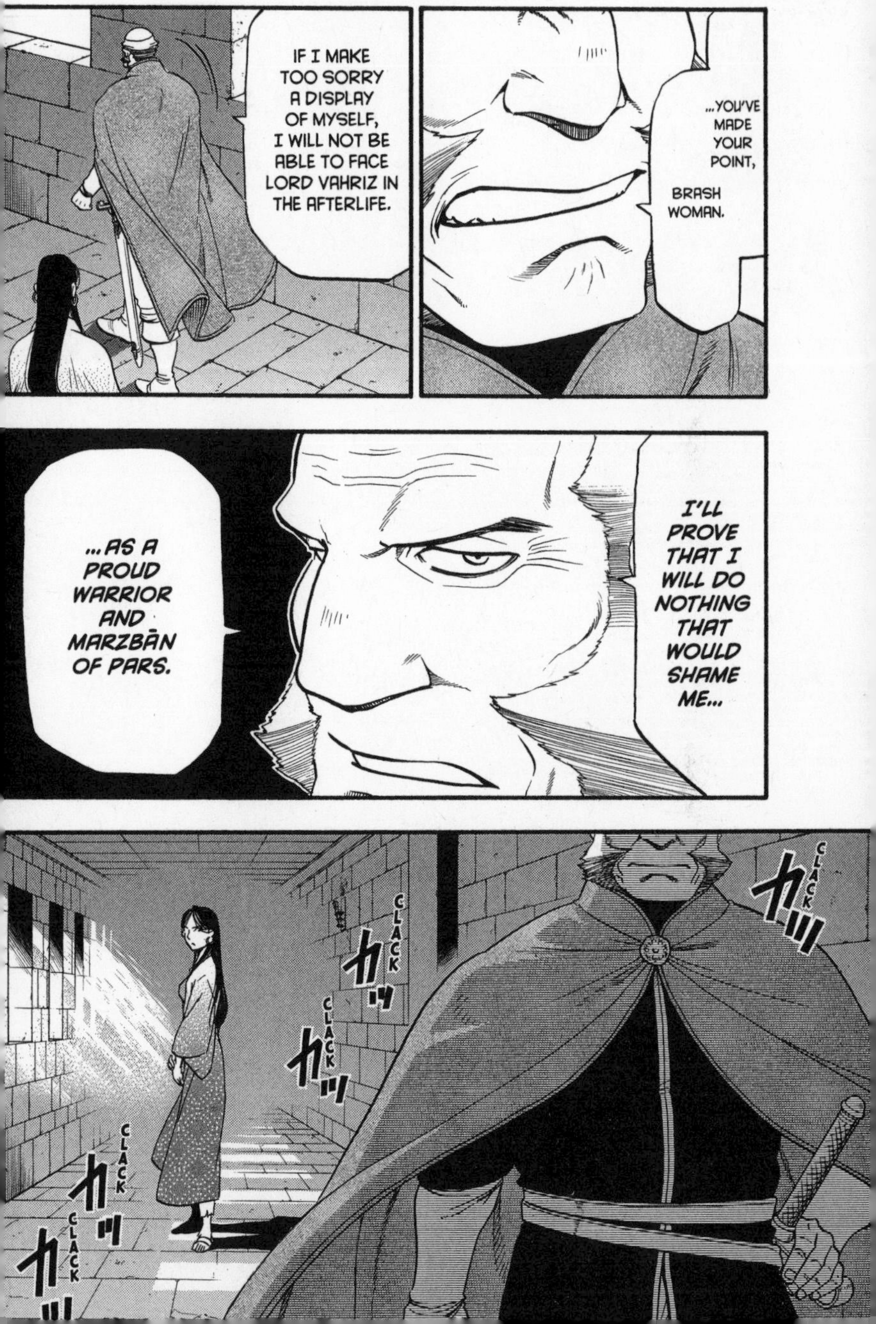
...YOU'VE MADE YOUR POINT,
BRASH WOMAN.
IF I MAKE TOO SORRY A DISPLAY OF MYSELF, I WILL NOT BE ABLE TO FACE LORD VAHRIZ IN THE AFTERLIFE.
I'LL PROVE THAT I WILL DO NOTHING THAT WOULD SHAME ME...
...AS A PROUD WARRIOR AND MARZBĀN OF PARS.
CLACK
CLACK
CLACK
CLACK
CLACK

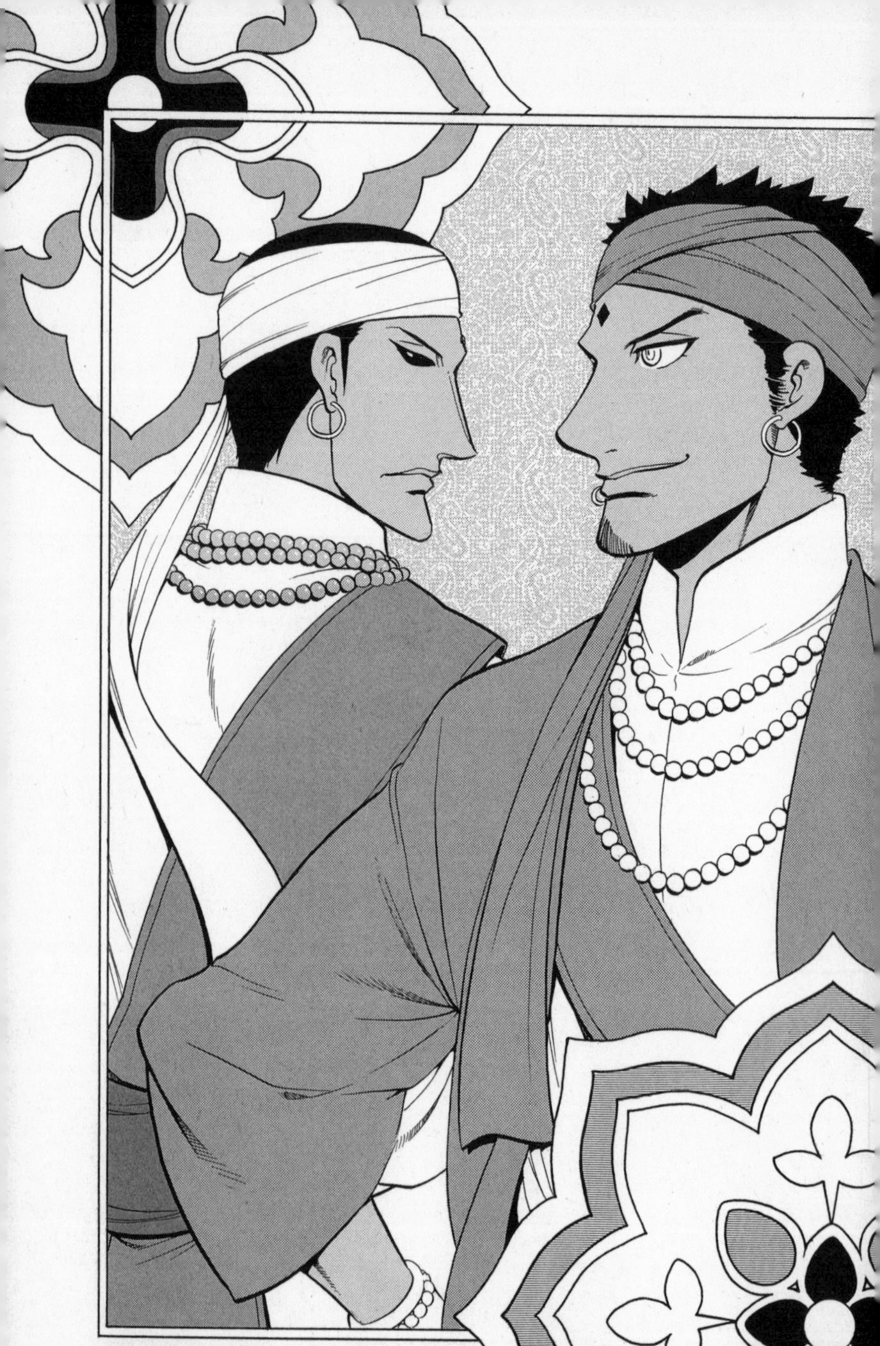

Chapter 42: A Foreign Sky

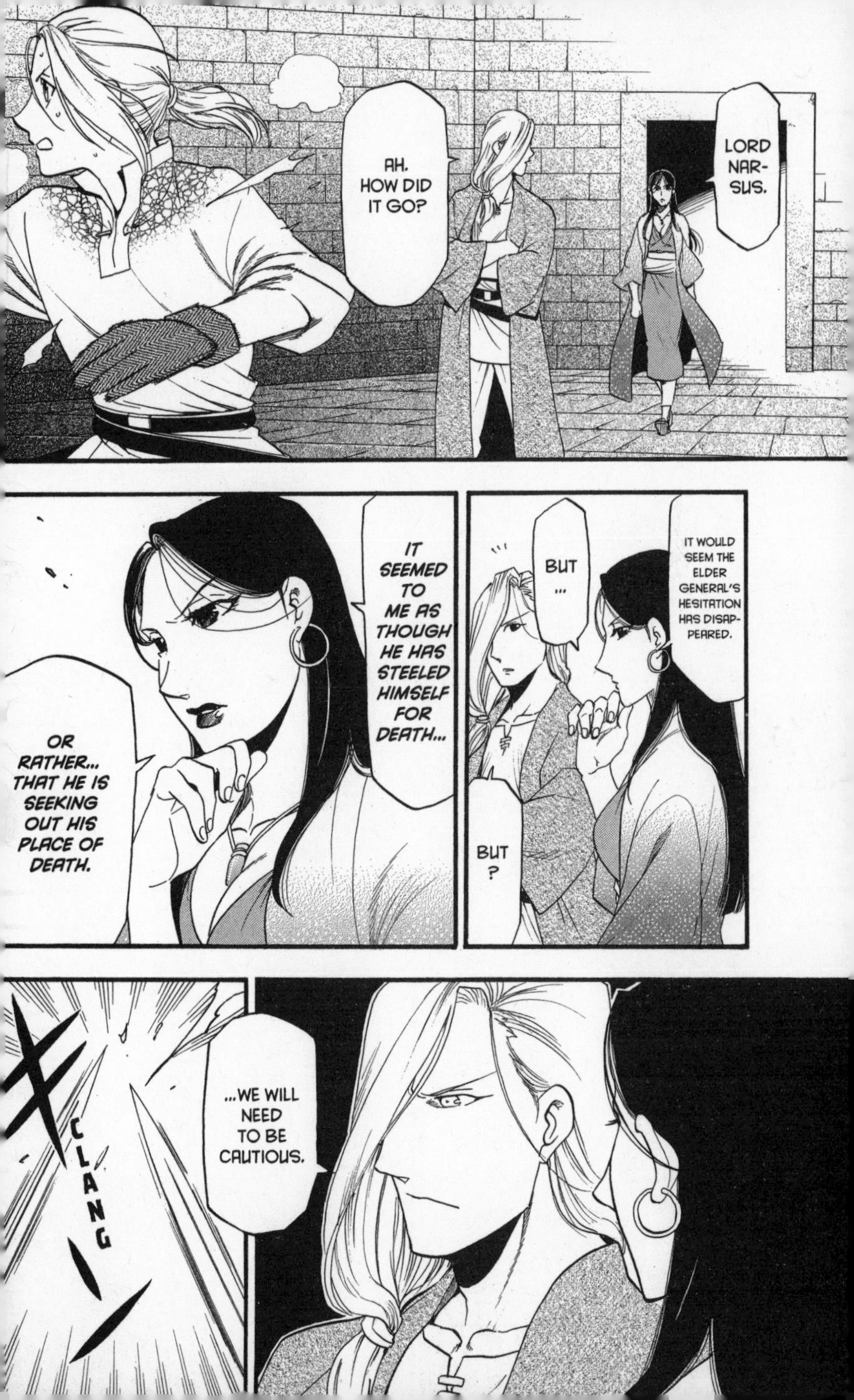
LORD NARSUS.
AH. HOW DID IT GO?
IT WOULD SEEM THE ELDER GENERAL'S HESITATION HAS DISAPPEARED.
BUT ...
BUT ?
IT SEEMED TO ME AS THOUGH HE HAS STEELED HIMSELF FOR DEATH...
OR RATHER... THAT HE IS SEEKING OUT HIS PLACE OF DEATH.
...WE WILL NEED TO BE CAUTIOUS.
CLANG

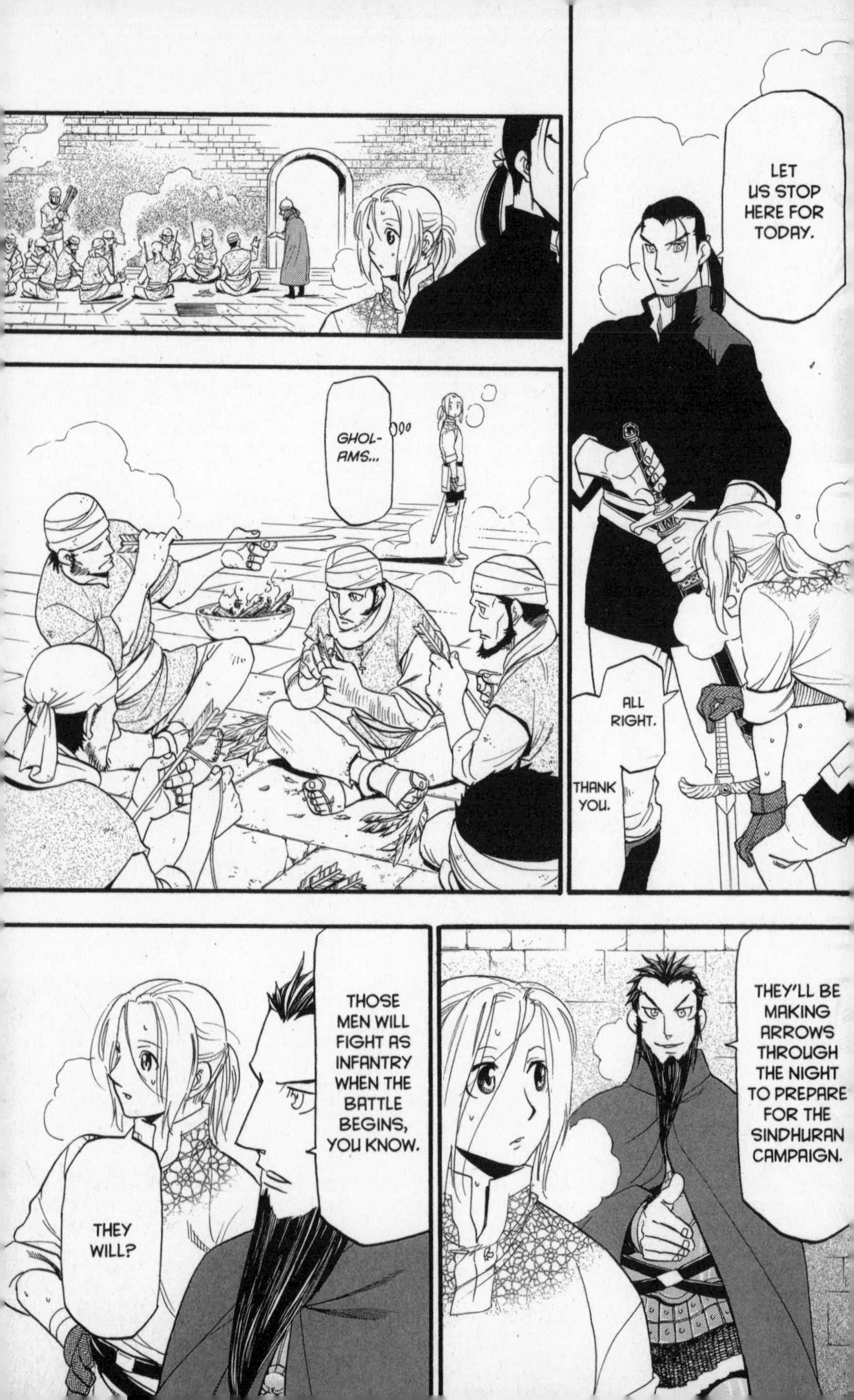
LET US STOP HERE FOR TODAY.
ALL RIGHT.
THANK YOU.
GHOL-AMS...
THEY'LL BE MAKING ARROWS THROUGH THE NIGHT TO PREPARE FOR THE SINDHURAN CAMPAIGN.
THOSE MEN WILL FIGHT AS INFANTRY WHEN THE BATTLE BEGINS, YOU KNOW.
THEY WILL?

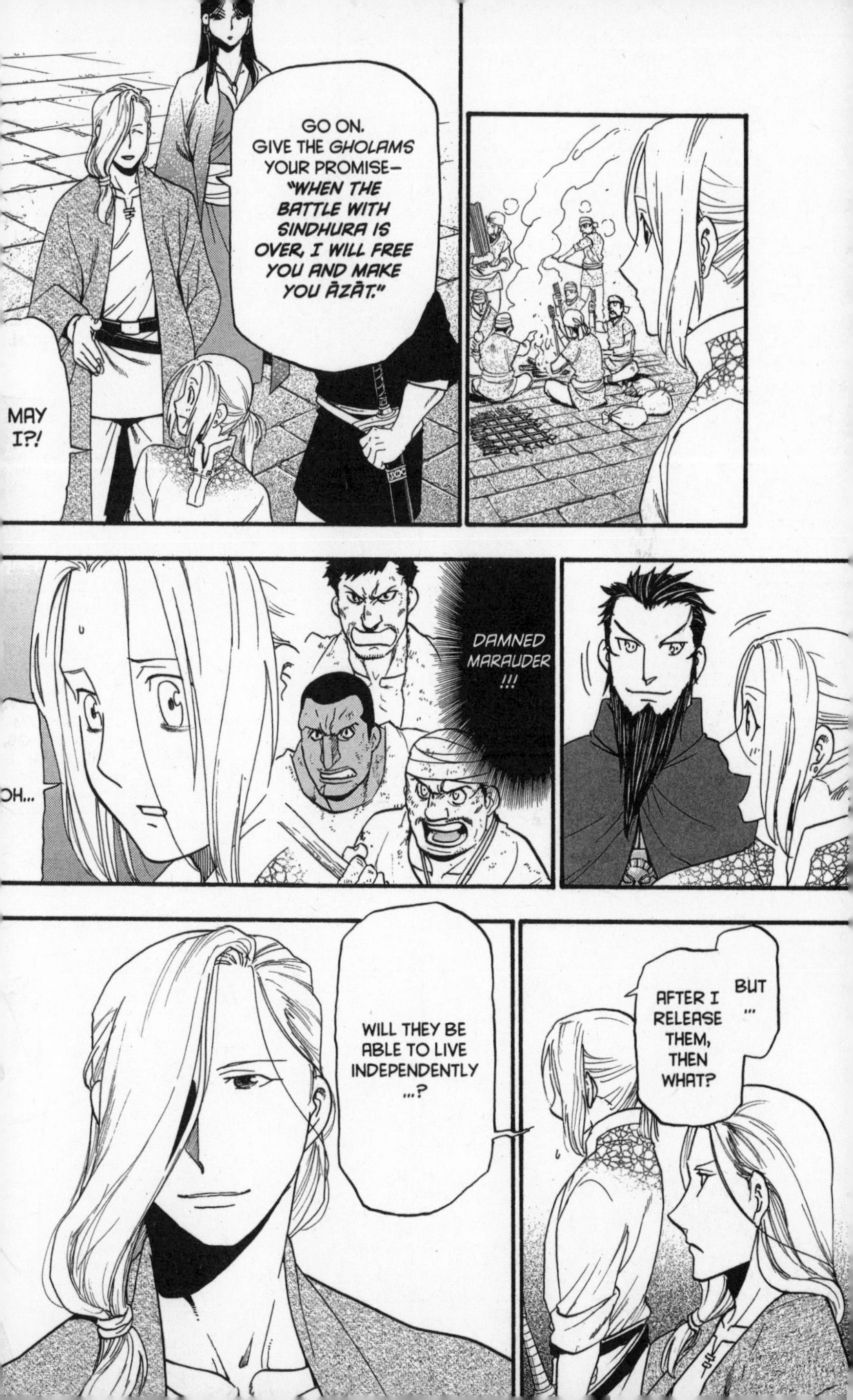
GO ON. GIVE THE GHOLAMS YOUR PROMISE— *"WHEN THE BATTLE WITH SINDHURA IS OVER, I WILL FREE YOU AND MAKE YOU ĀZĀT."*
MAY I?!
DAMNED MARAUDER!!!
OH...
BUT...
AFTER I RELEASE THEM, THEN WHAT?
WILL THEY BE ABLE TO LIVE INDEPENDENTLY...?

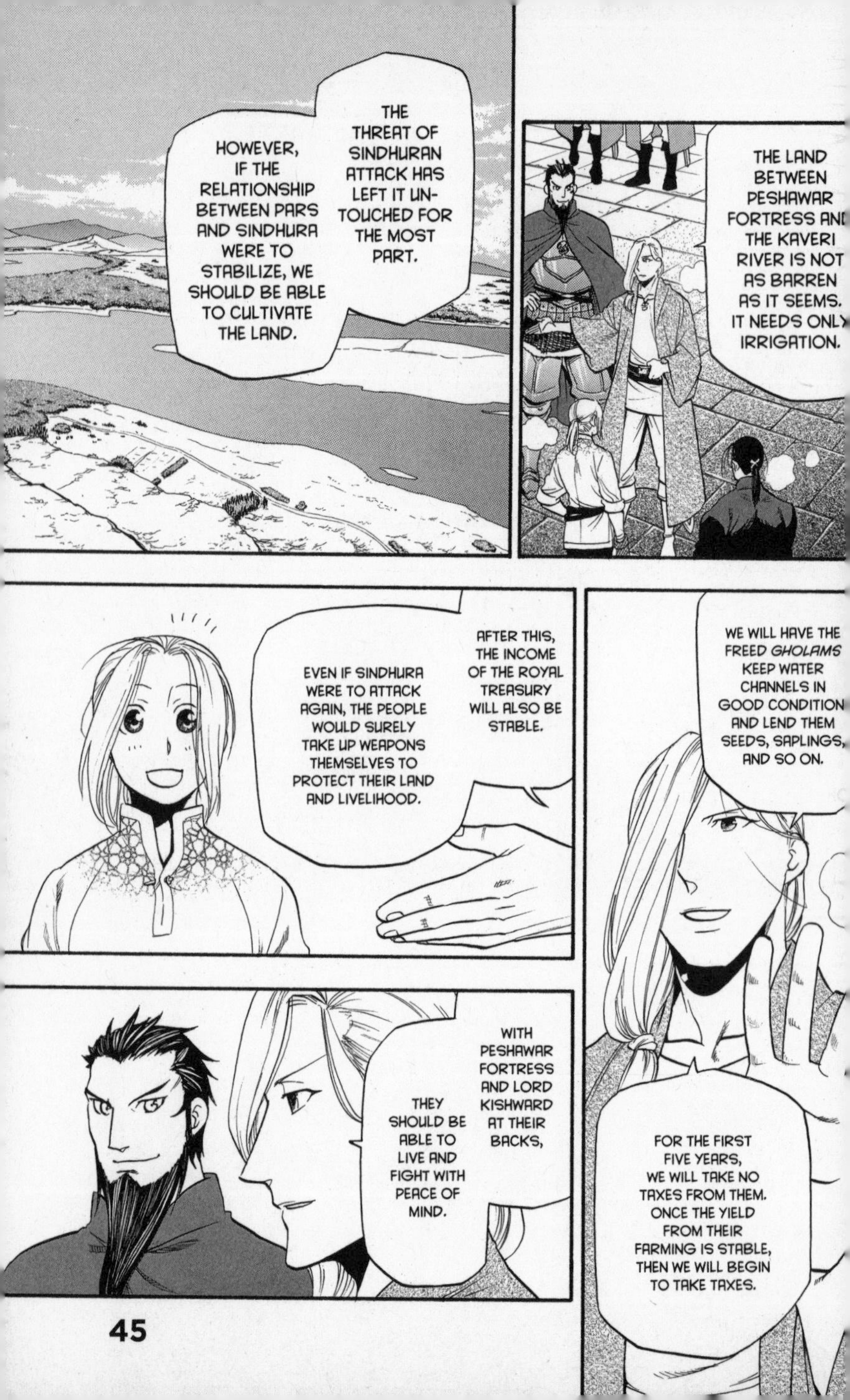
THE LAND BETWEEN PESHAWAR FORTRESS AND THE KAVERI RIVER IS NOT AS BARREN AS IT SEEMS. IT NEEDS ONLY IRRIGATION.
THE THREAT OF SINDHURAN ATTACK HAS LEFT IT UNTOUCHED FOR THE MOST PART.
HOWEVER, IF THE RELATIONSHIP BETWEEN PARS AND SINDHURA WERE TO STABILIZE, WE SHOULD BE ABLE TO CULTIVATE THE LAND.
WE WILL HAVE THE FREED *GHOLAMS* KEEP WATER CHANNELS IN GOOD CONDITION AND LEND THEM SEEDS, SAPLINGS, AND SO ON.
FOR THE FIRST FIVE YEARS, WE WILL TAKE NO TAXES FROM THEM. ONCE THE YIELD FROM THEIR FARMING IS STABLE, THEN WE WILL BEGIN TO TAKE TAXES.
AFTER THIS, THE INCOME OF THE ROYAL TREASURY WILL ALSO BE STABLE.
EVEN IF SINDHURA WERE TO ATTACK AGAIN, THE PEOPLE WOULD SURELY TAKE UP WEAPONS THEMSELVES TO PROTECT THEIR LAND AND LIVELIHOOD.
WITH PESHAWAR FORTRESS AND LORD KISHWARD AT THEIR BACKS,
THEY SHOULD BE ABLE TO LIVE AND FIGHT WITH PEACE OF MIND.

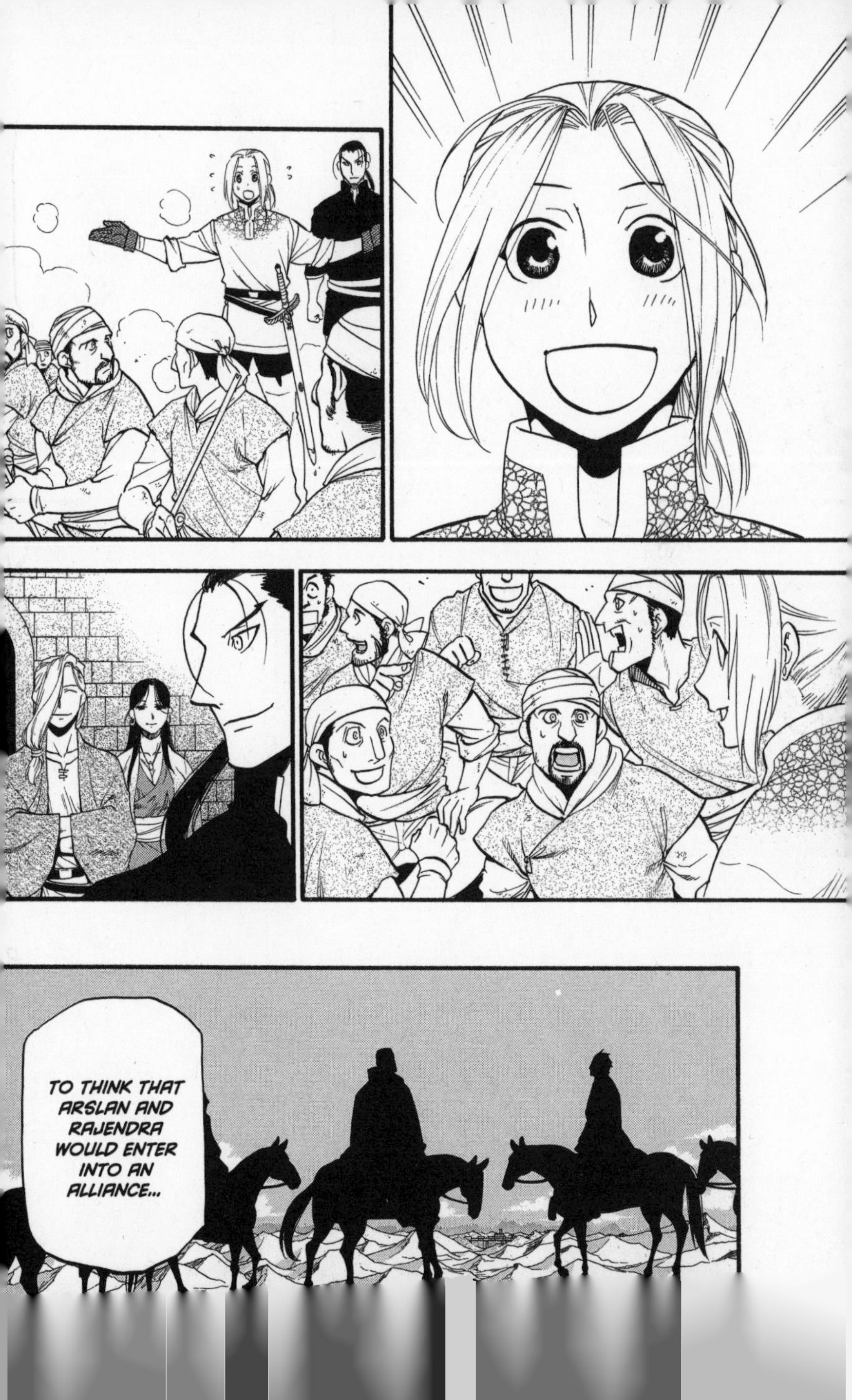
TO THINK THAT ARSLAN AND RAJENDRA WOULD ENTER INTO AN ALLIANCE...

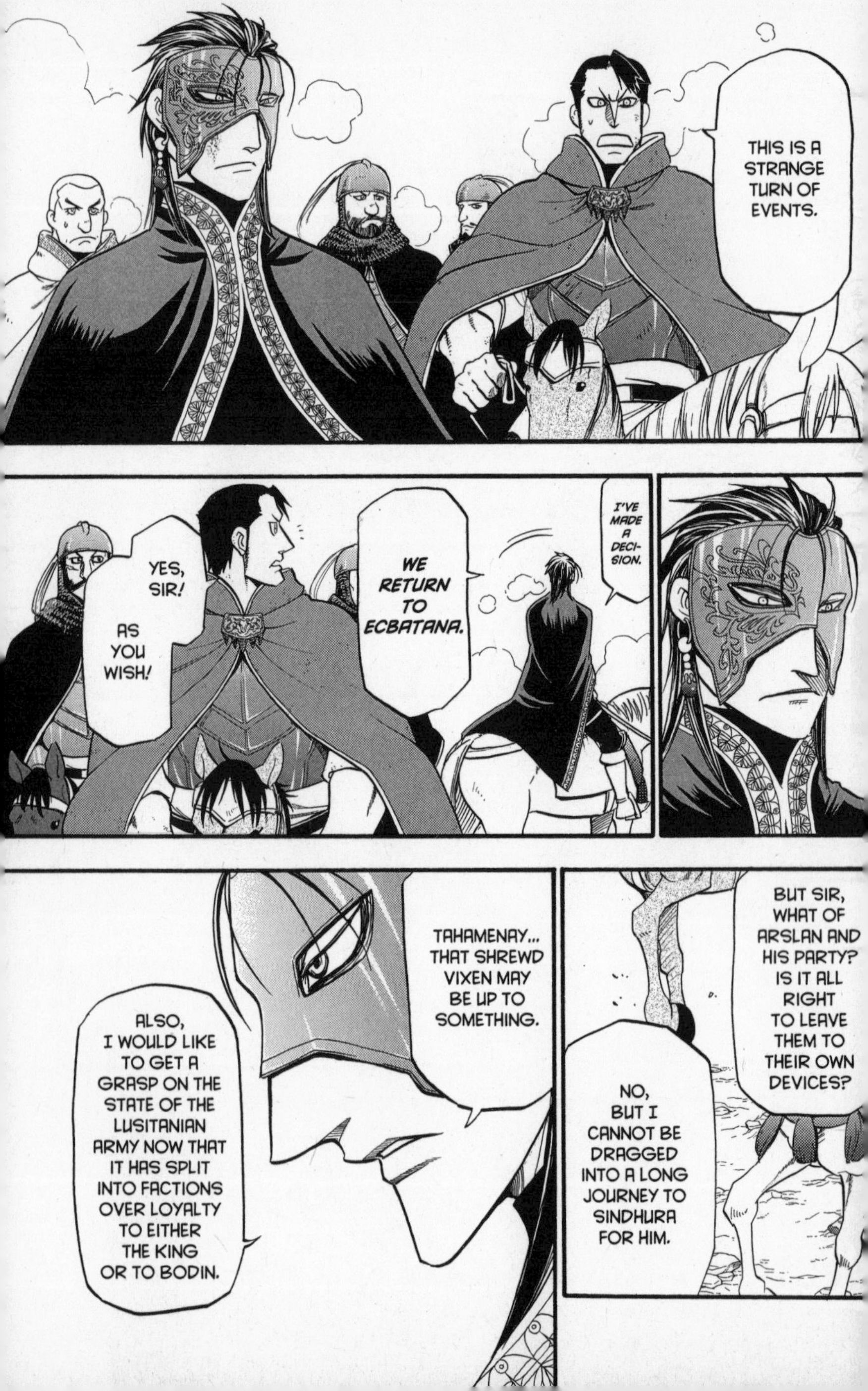
THIS IS A STRANGE TURN OF EVENTS.
I'VE MADE A DECISION.
WE RETURN TO ECBATANA.
YES, SIR!
AS YOU WISH!
BUT SIR, WHAT OF ARSLAN AND HIS PARTY? IS IT ALL RIGHT TO LEAVE THEM TO THEIR OWN DEVICES?
NO, BUT I CANNOT BE DRAGGED INTO A LONG JOURNEY TO SINDHURA FOR HIM.
TAHAMENAY... THAT SHREWD VIXEN MAY BE UP TO SOMETHING.
ALSO, I WOULD LIKE TO GET A GRASP ON THE STATE OF THE LUSITANIAN ARMY NOW THAT IT HAS SPLIT INTO FACTIONS OVER LOYALTY TO EITHER THE KING OR TO BODIN.

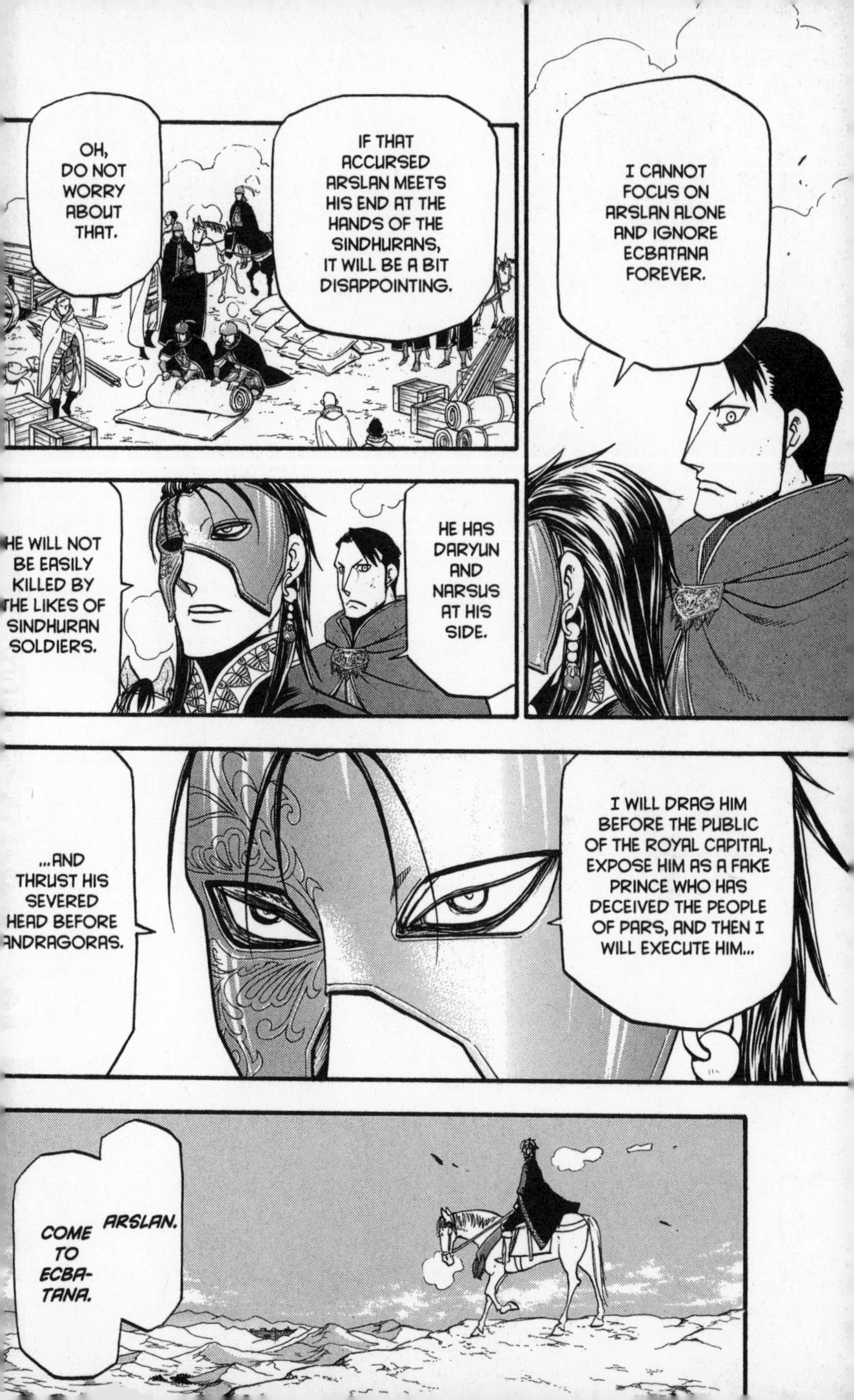
I CANNOT FOCUS ON ARSLAN ALONE AND IGNORE ECBATANA FOREVER.
IF THAT ACCURSED ARSLAN MEETS HIS END AT THE HANDS OF THE SINDHURANS, IT WILL BE A BIT DISAPPOINTING.
OH, DO NOT WORRY ABOUT THAT.
HE HAS DARYUN AND NARSUS AT HIS SIDE.
HE WILL NOT BE EASILY KILLED BY THE LIKES OF SINDHURAN SOLDIERS.
I WILL DRAG HIM BEFORE THE PUBLIC OF THE ROYAL CAPITAL, EXPOSE HIM AS A FAKE PRINCE WHO HAS DECEIVED THE PEOPLE OF PARS, AND THEN I WILL EXECUTE HIM...
...AND THRUST HIS SEVERED HEAD BEFORE ANDRAGORAS.
ARSLAN.
COME TO ECBA-TANA.

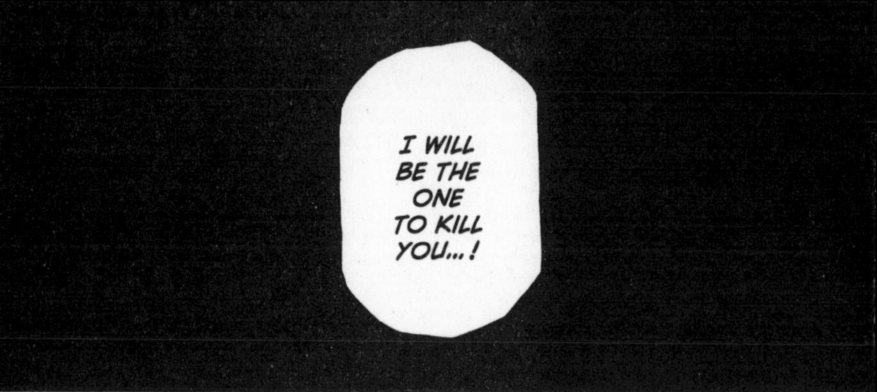
I WILL BE THE ONE TO KILL YOU...!

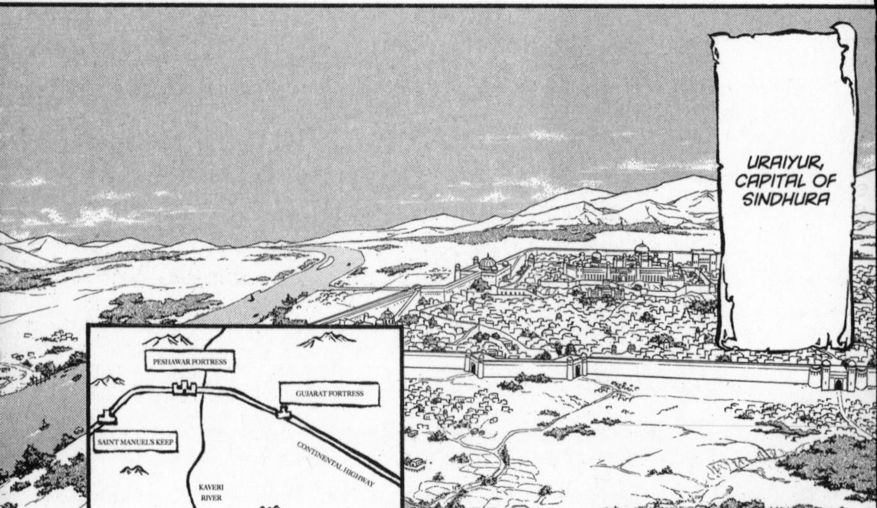
URAIYUR, CAPITAL OF SINDHURA
PESHAWAR FORTRESS
GUJARAT FORTRESS
SAINT MANUEL'S KEEP
CONTINENTAL HIGHWAY
KAVERI RIVER
URAIYUR

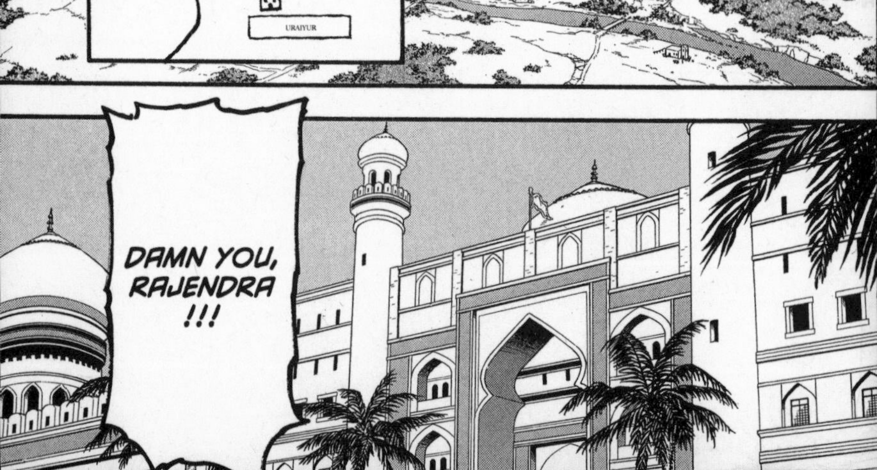
DAMN YOU, RAJENDRA !!!

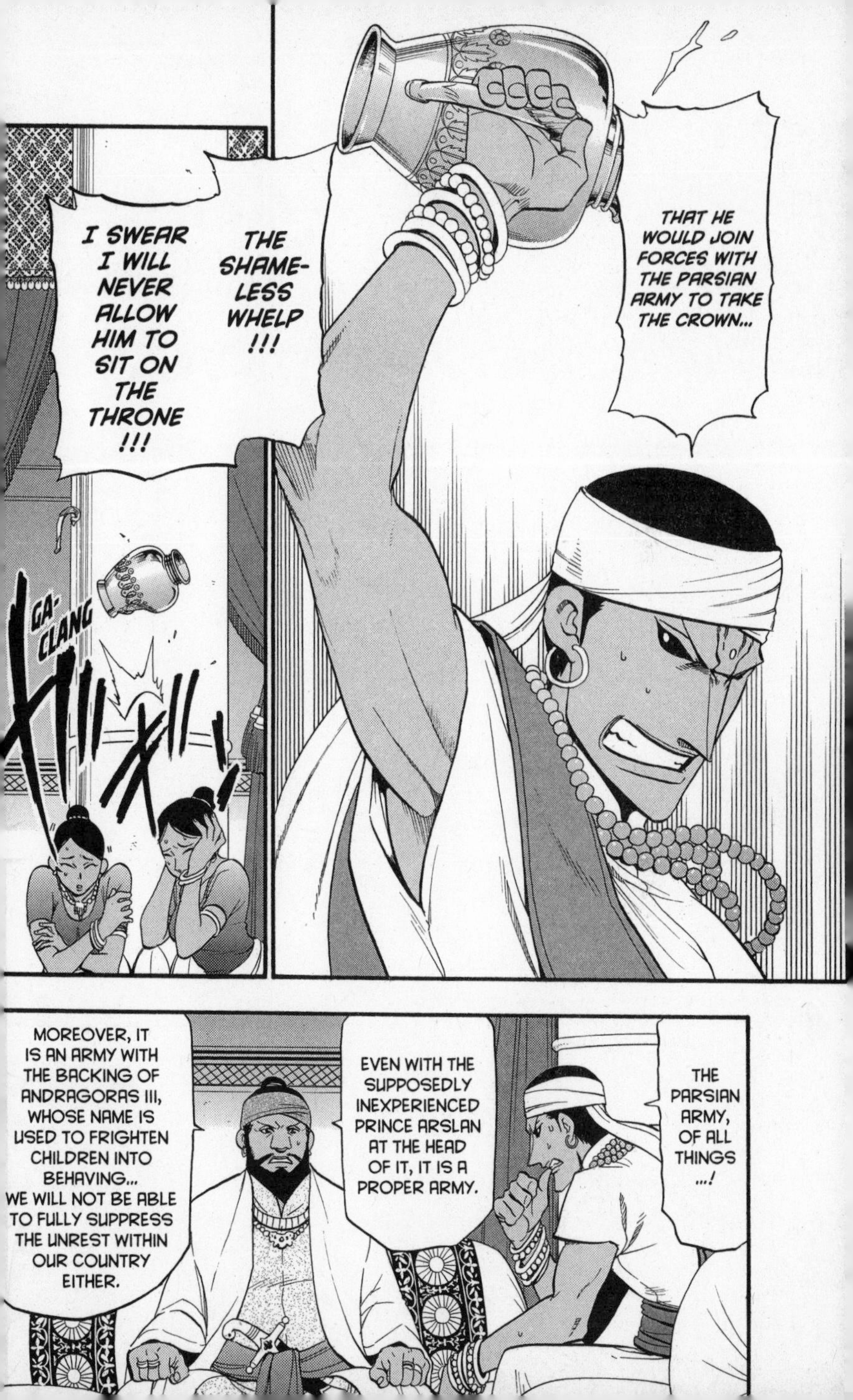
THAT HE WOULD JOIN FORCES WITH THE PARSIAN ARMY TO TAKE THE CROWN...
THE SHAME-LESS WHELP !!!
I SWEAR I WILL NEVER ALLOW HIM TO SIT ON THE THRONE !!!
GA-CLANG
THE PARSIAN ARMY, OF ALL THINGS ...!
EVEN WITH THE SUPPOSEDLY INEXPERIENCED PRINCE ARSLAN AT THE HEAD OF IT, IT IS A PROPER ARMY.
MOREOVER, IT IS AN ARMY WITH THE BACKING OF ANDRAGORAS III, WHOSE NAME IS USED TO FRIGHTEN CHILDREN INTO BEHAVING...
WE WILL NOT BE ABLE TO FULLY SUPPRESS THE UNREST WITHIN OUR COUNTRY EITHER.

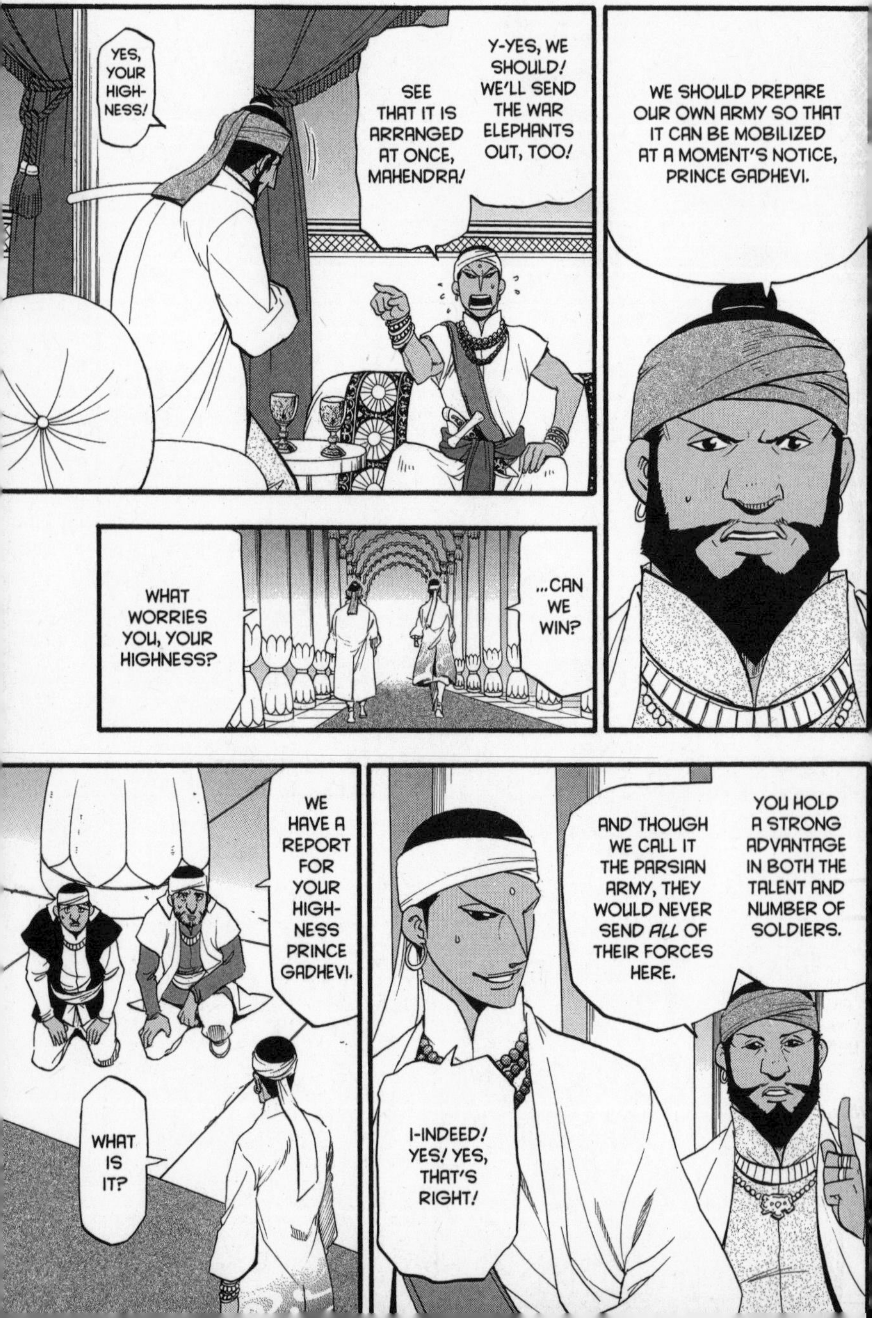
WE SHOULD PREPARE OUR OWN ARMY SO THAT IT CAN BE MOBILIZED AT A MOMENT'S NOTICE, PRINCE GADHEVI.
Y-YES, WE SHOULD! WE'LL SEND THE WAR ELEPHANTS OUT, TOO!
SEE THAT IT IS ARRANGED AT ONCE, MAHENDRA!
YES, YOUR HIGHNESS!
...CAN WE WIN?
WHAT WORRIES YOU, YOUR HIGHNESS?
YOU HOLD A STRONG ADVANTAGE IN BOTH THE TALENT AND NUMBER OF SOLDIERS.
AND THOUGH WE CALL IT THE PARSIAN ARMY, THEY WOULD NEVER SEND ALL OF THEIR FORCES HERE.
I-INDEED! YES! YES, THAT'S RIGHT!
WE HAVE A REPORT FOR YOUR HIGHNESS PRINCE GADHEVI.
WHAT IS IT?

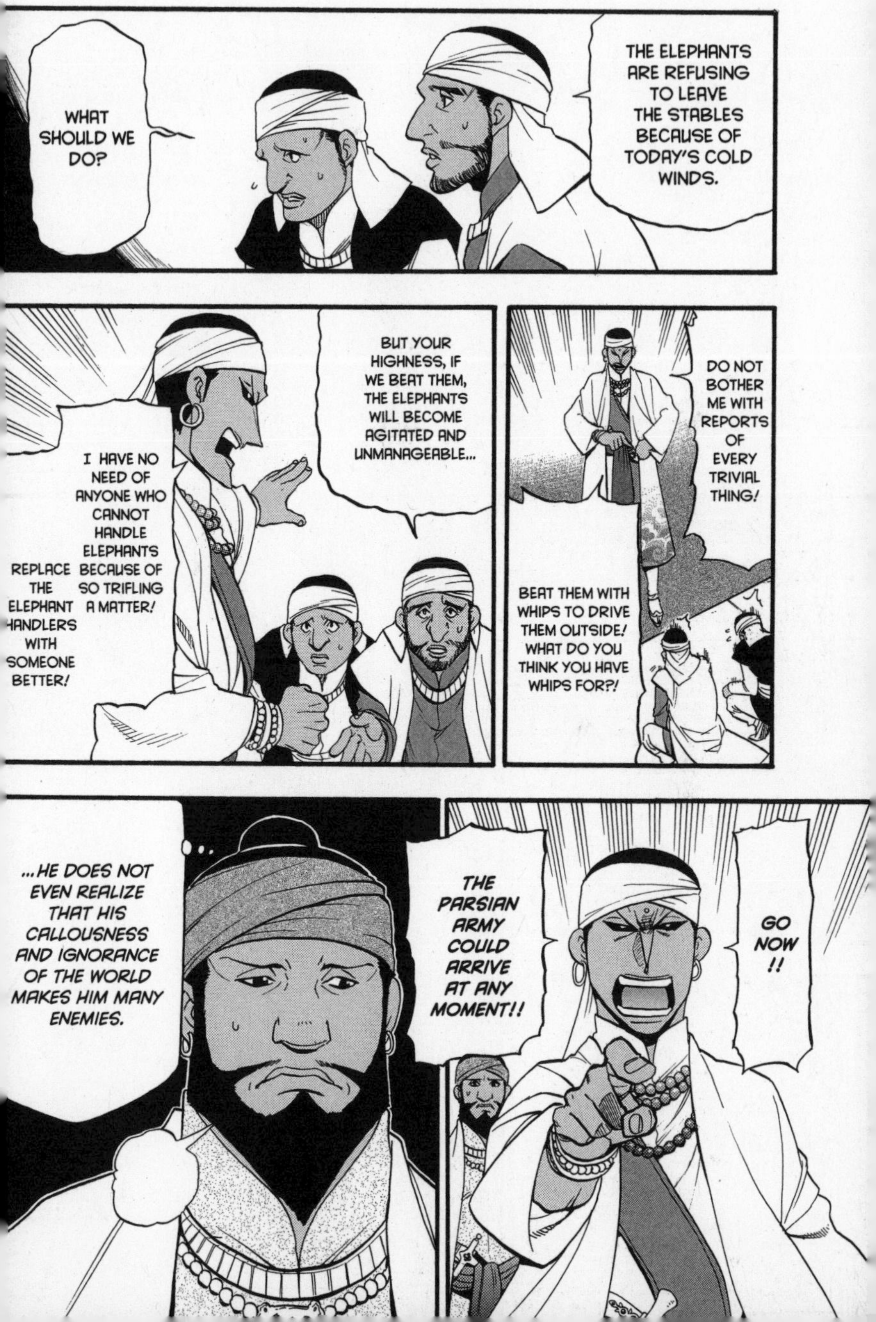
THE ELEPHANTS ARE REFUSING TO LEAVE THE STABLES BECAUSE OF TODAY'S COLD WINDS.
WHAT SHOULD WE DO?
DO NOT BOTHER ME WITH REPORTS OF EVERY TRIVIAL THING!
BEAT THEM WITH WHIPS TO DRIVE THEM OUTSIDE! WHAT DO YOU THINK YOU HAVE WHIPS FOR?!
BUT YOUR HIGHNESS, IF WE BEAT THEM, THE ELEPHANTS WILL BECOME AGITATED AND UNMANAGEABLE...
I HAVE NO NEED OF ANYONE WHO CANNOT HANDLE ELEPHANTS BECAUSE OF SO TRIFLING A MATTER!
REPLACE THE ELEPHANT HANDLERS WITH SOMEONE BETTER!
GO NOW!!
THE PARSIAN ARMY COULD ARRIVE AT ANY MOMENT!!
...HE DOES NOT EVEN REALIZE THAT HIS CALLOUSNESS AND IGNORANCE OF THE WORLD MAKES HIM MANY ENEMIES.

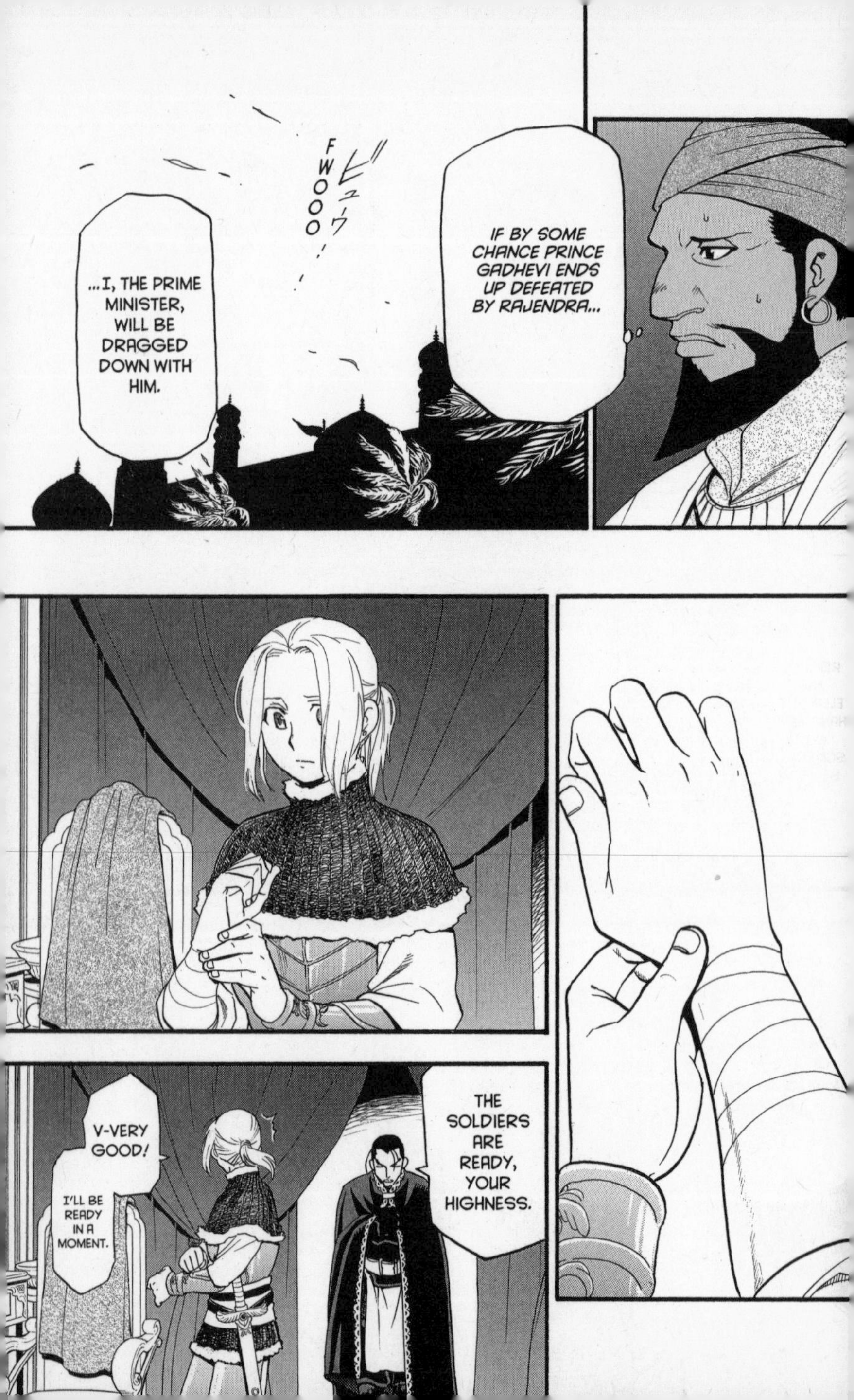

IF BY SOME CHANCE PRINCE GADHEVI ENDS UP DEFEATED BY RAJENDRA...
FWOOO!
...I, THE PRIME MINISTER, WILL BE DRAGGED DOWN WITH HIM.
THE SOLDIERS ARE READY, YOUR HIGHNESS.
V-VERY GOOD!
I'LL BE READY IN A MOMENT.

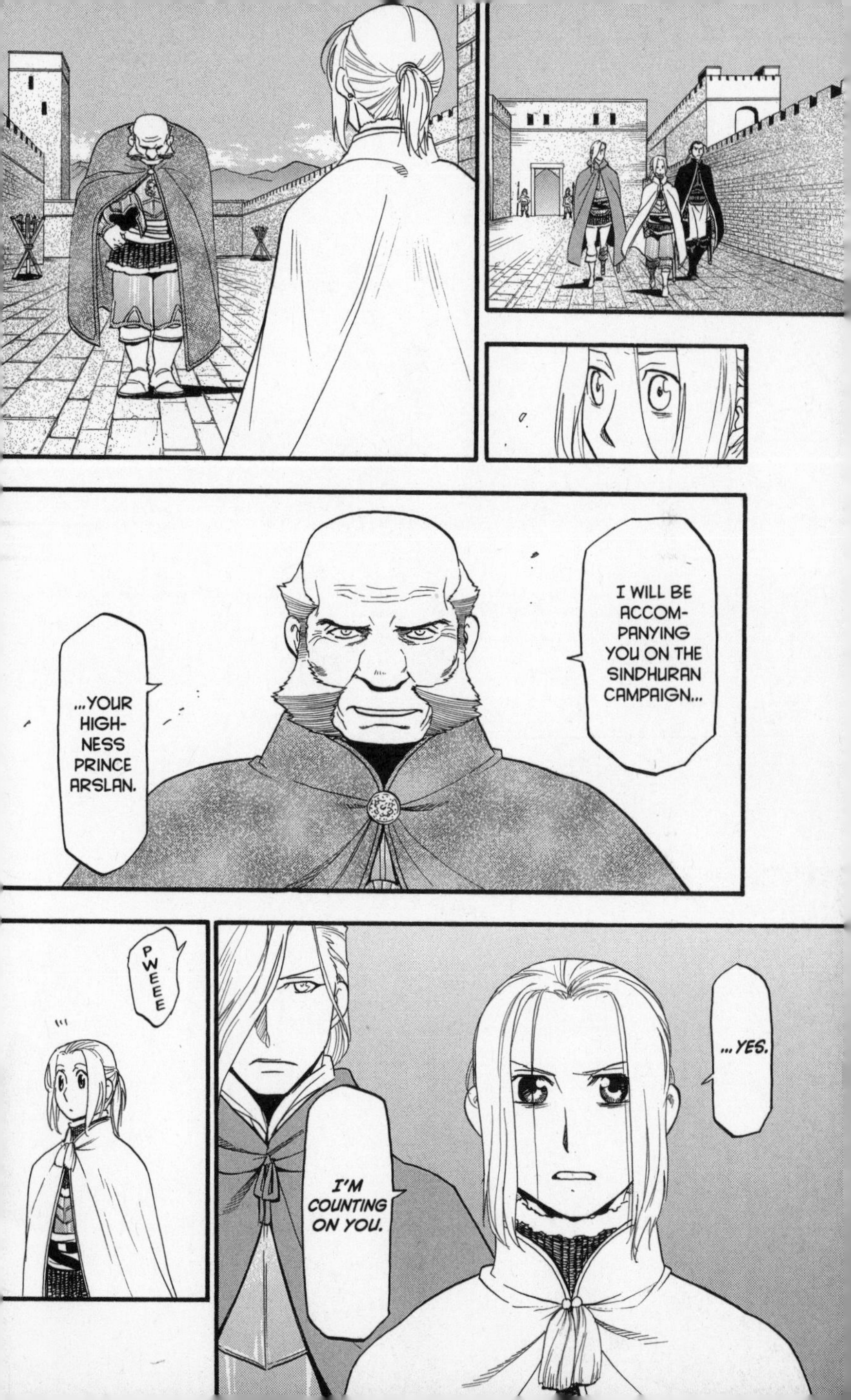
I WILL BE ACCOM-PANYING YOU ON THE SINDHURAN CAMPAIGN...
...YOUR HIGH-NESS PRINCE ARSLAN.
...YES.
I'M COUNTING ON YOU.
PWEEE

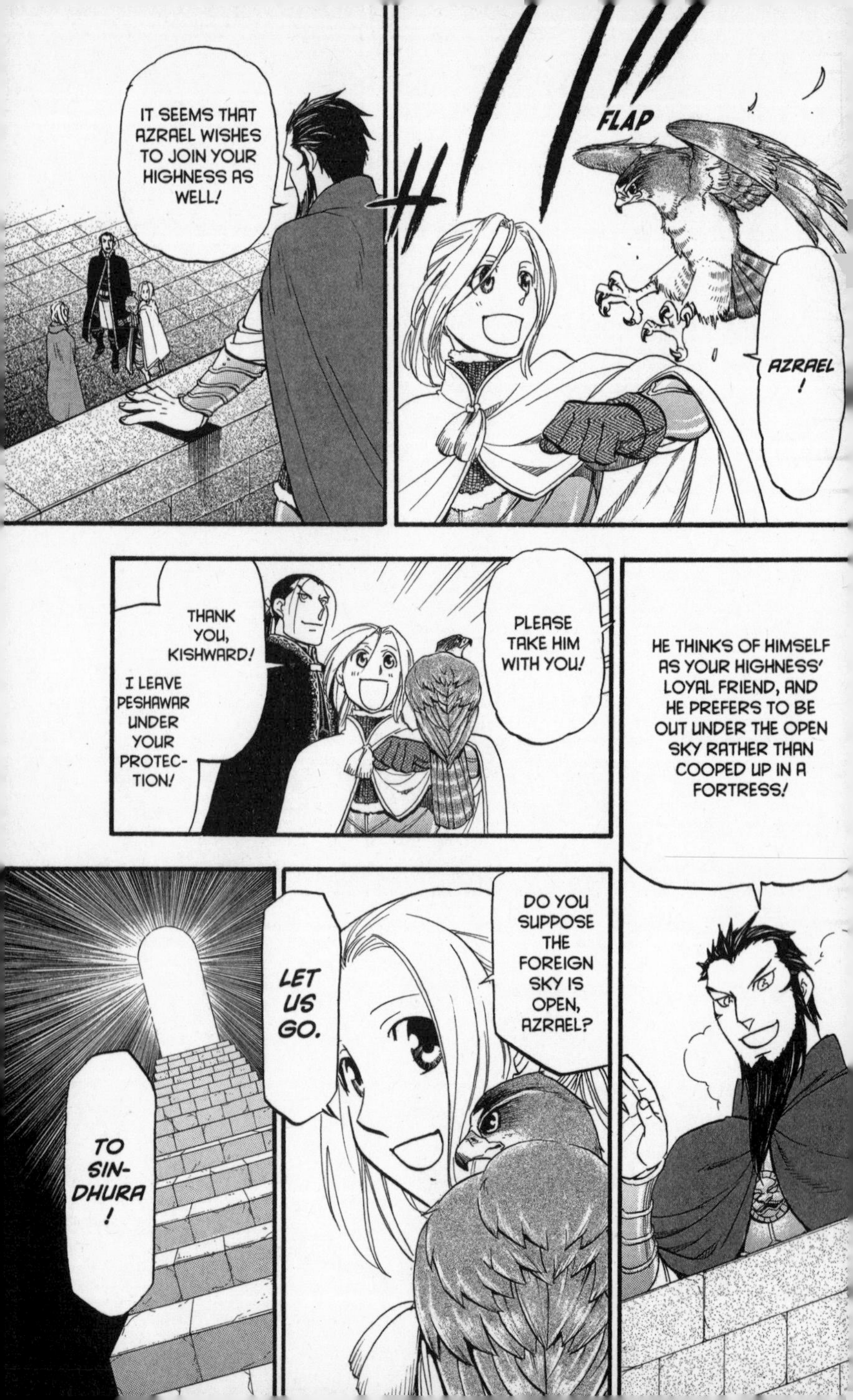
FLAP
AZRAEL!
IT SEEMS THAT AZRAEL WISHES TO JOIN YOUR HIGHNESS AS WELL!
HE THINKS OF HIMSELF AS YOUR HIGHNESS' LOYAL FRIEND, AND HE PREFERS TO BE OUT UNDER THE OPEN SKY RATHER THAN COOPED UP IN A FORTRESS!
PLEASE TAKE HIM WITH YOU!
THANK YOU, KISHWARD!
I LEAVE PESHAWAR UNDER YOUR PROTECTION!
DO YOU SUPPOSE THE FOREIGN SKY IS OPEN, AZRAEL?
LET US GO.
TO SINDHURA!

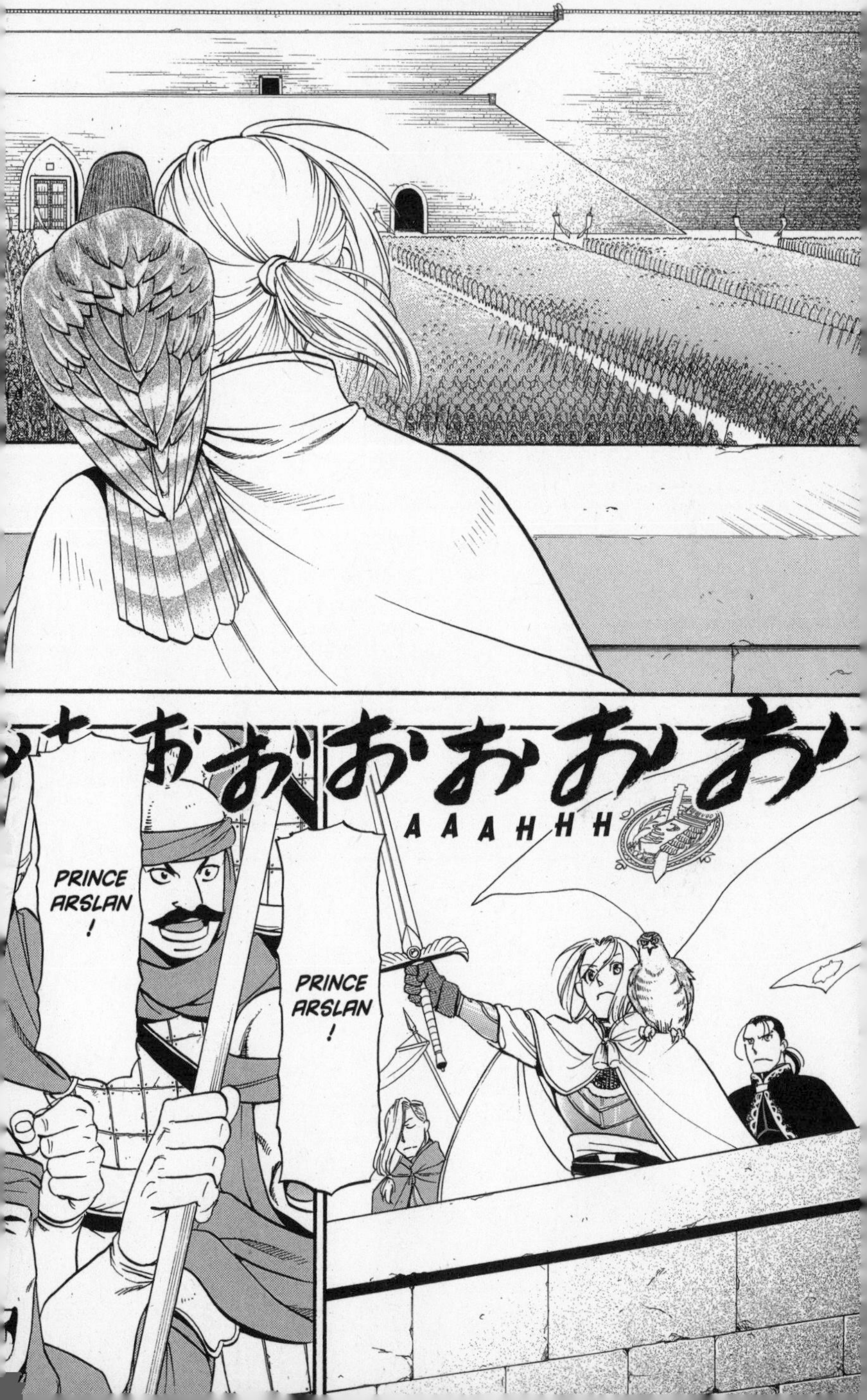
AAAHHH
PRINCE ARSLAN !
PRINCE ARSLAN !

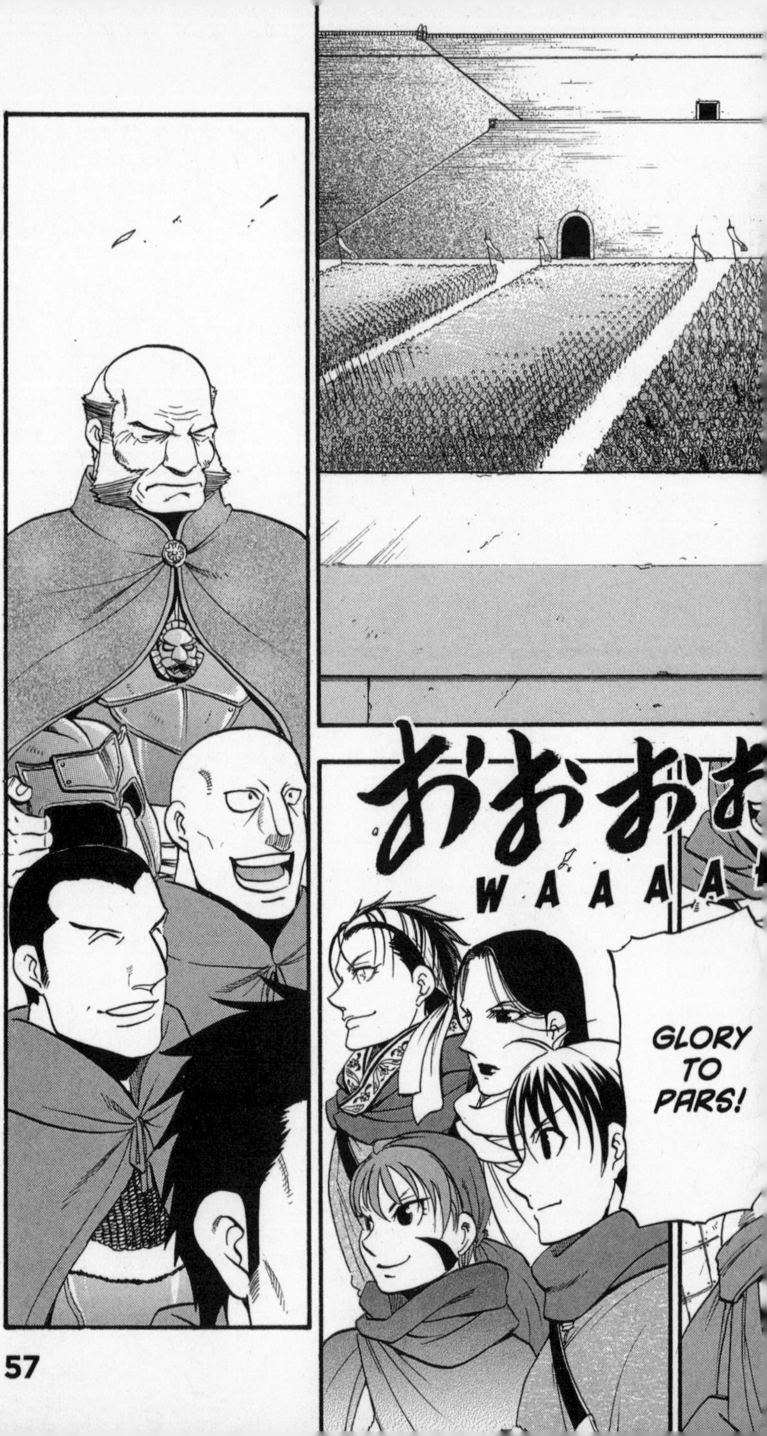
おおお
WAAAA
GLORY TO PARS!

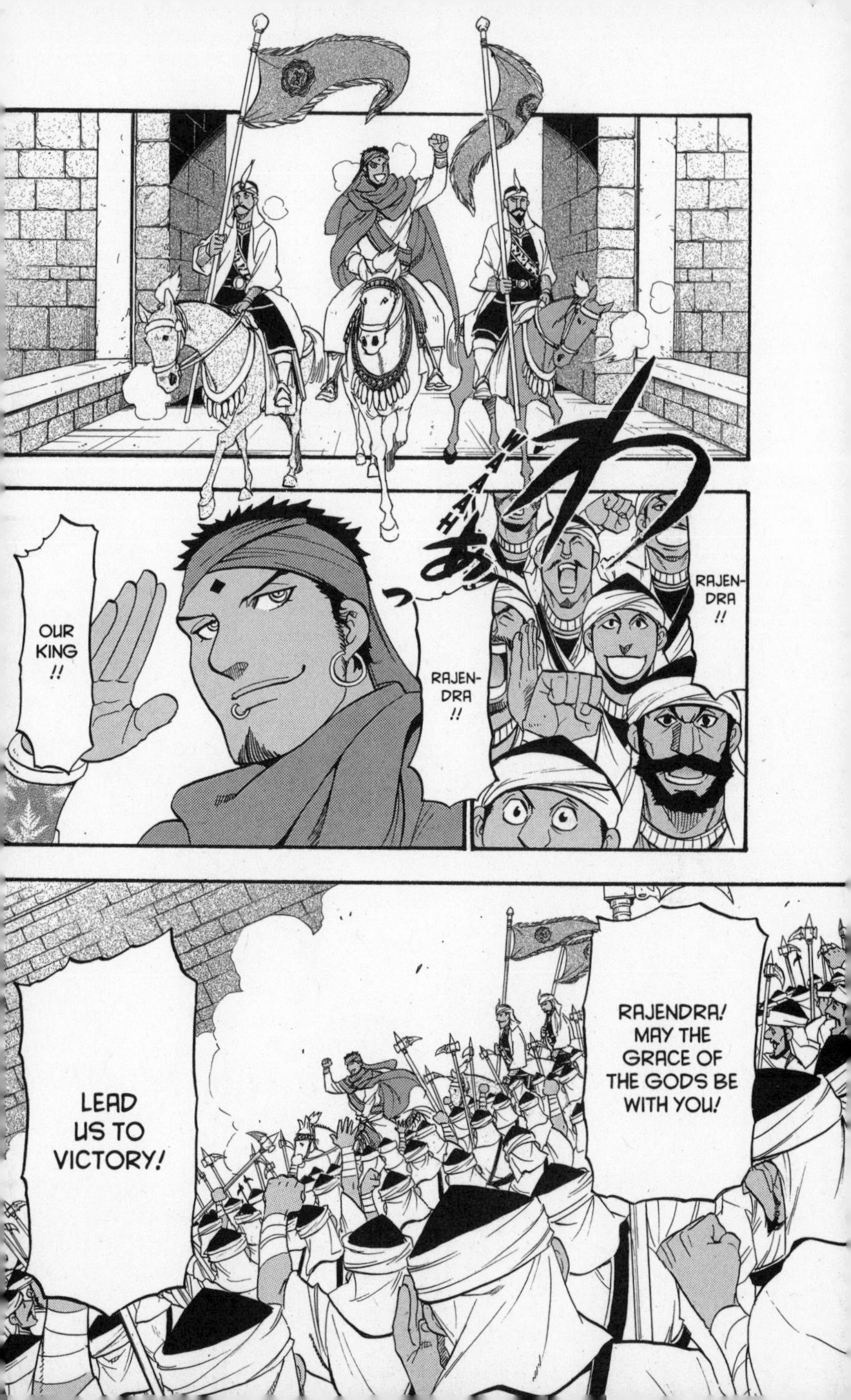
WAAAAH
RAJEN-DRA!!
RAJEN-DRA!!
OUR KING!!
RAJENDRA! MAY THE GRACE OF THE GODS BE WITH YOU!
LEAD US TO VICTORY!

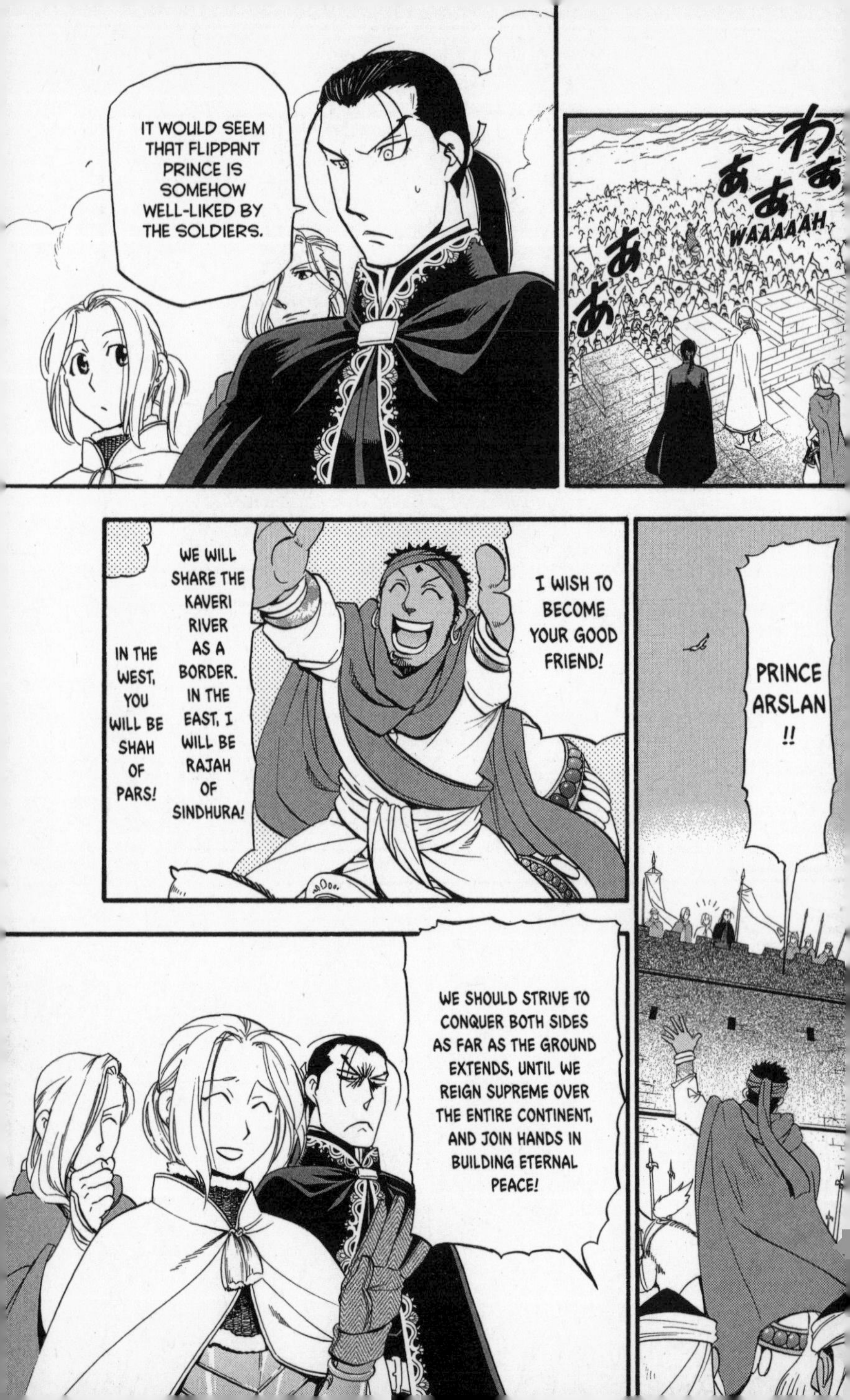
わぁああああ
WAAAAAH
IT WOULD SEEM THAT FLIPPANT PRINCE IS SOMEHOW WELL-LIKED BY THE SOLDIERS.
PRINCE ARSLAN !!
I WISH TO BECOME YOUR GOOD FRIEND!
WE WILL SHARE THE KAVERI RIVER AS A BORDER. IN THE EAST, I WILL BE RAJAH OF SINDHURA!
IN THE WEST, YOU WILL BE SHAH OF PARS!
WE SHOULD STRIVE TO CONQUER BOTH SIDES AS FAR AS THE GROUND EXTENDS, UNTIL WE REIGN SUPREME OVER THE ENTIRE CONTINENT, AND JOIN HANDS IN BUILDING ETERNAL PEACE!

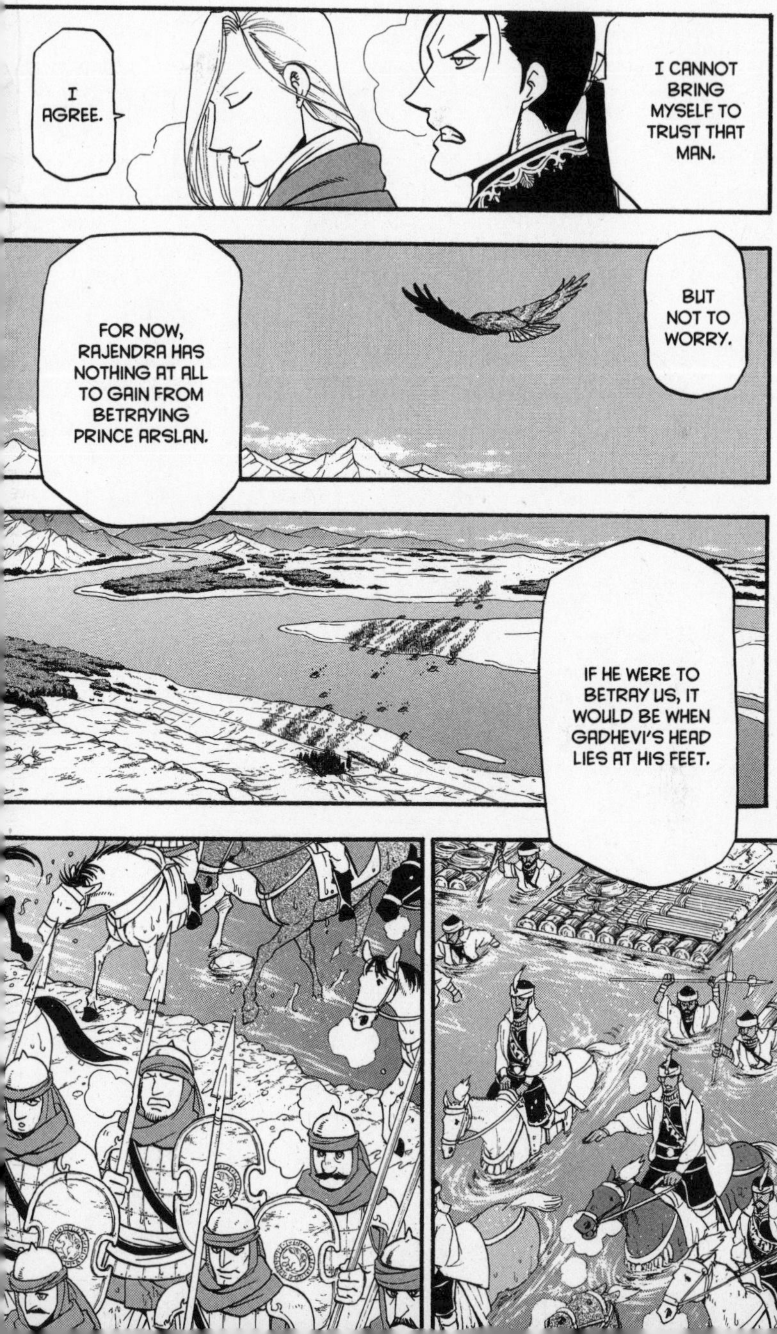
I CANNOT BRING MYSELF TO TRUST THAT MAN.
I AGREE.
BUT NOT TO WORRY.
FOR NOW, RAJENDRA HAS NOTHING AT ALL TO GAIN FROM BETRAYING PRINCE ARSLAN.
IF HE WERE TO BETRAY US, IT WOULD BE WHEN GADHEVI'S HEAD LIES AT HIS FEET.

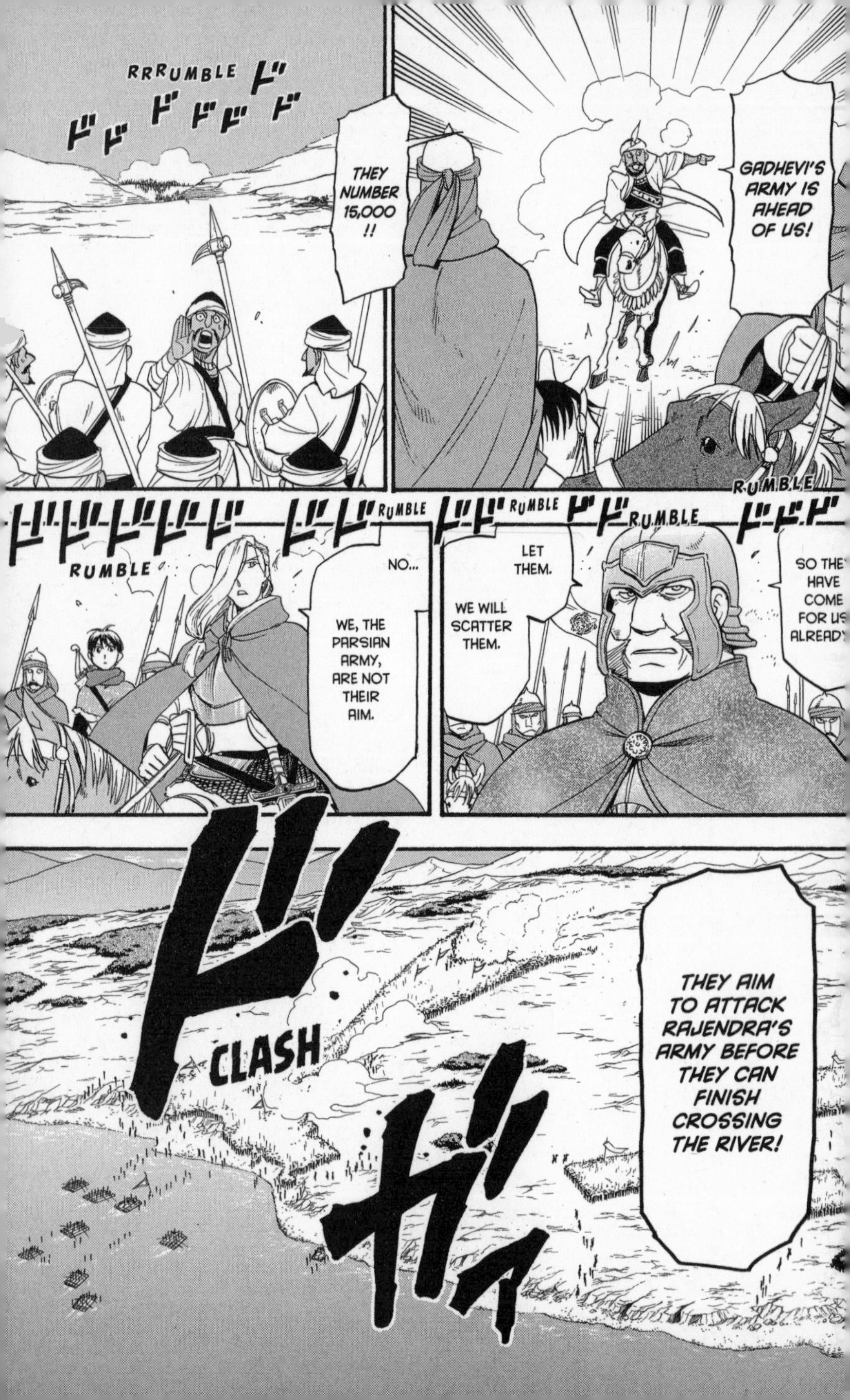

GADHEVI'S ARMY IS AHEAD OF US!
THEY NUMBER 15,000 !!
RUMBLE
RRRUMBLE ドドドドドド
ドドド
RUMBLE
SO THEY HAVE COME FOR US ALREADY
LET THEM.
WE WILL SCATTER THEM.
ドド RUMBLE
ドド RUMBLE
NO...
WE, THE PARSIAN ARMY, ARE NOT THEIR AIM.
ドドドドドド RUMBLE
THEY AIM TO ATTACK RAJENDRA'S ARMY BEFORE THEY CAN FINISH CROSSING THE RIVER!
ド
CLASH

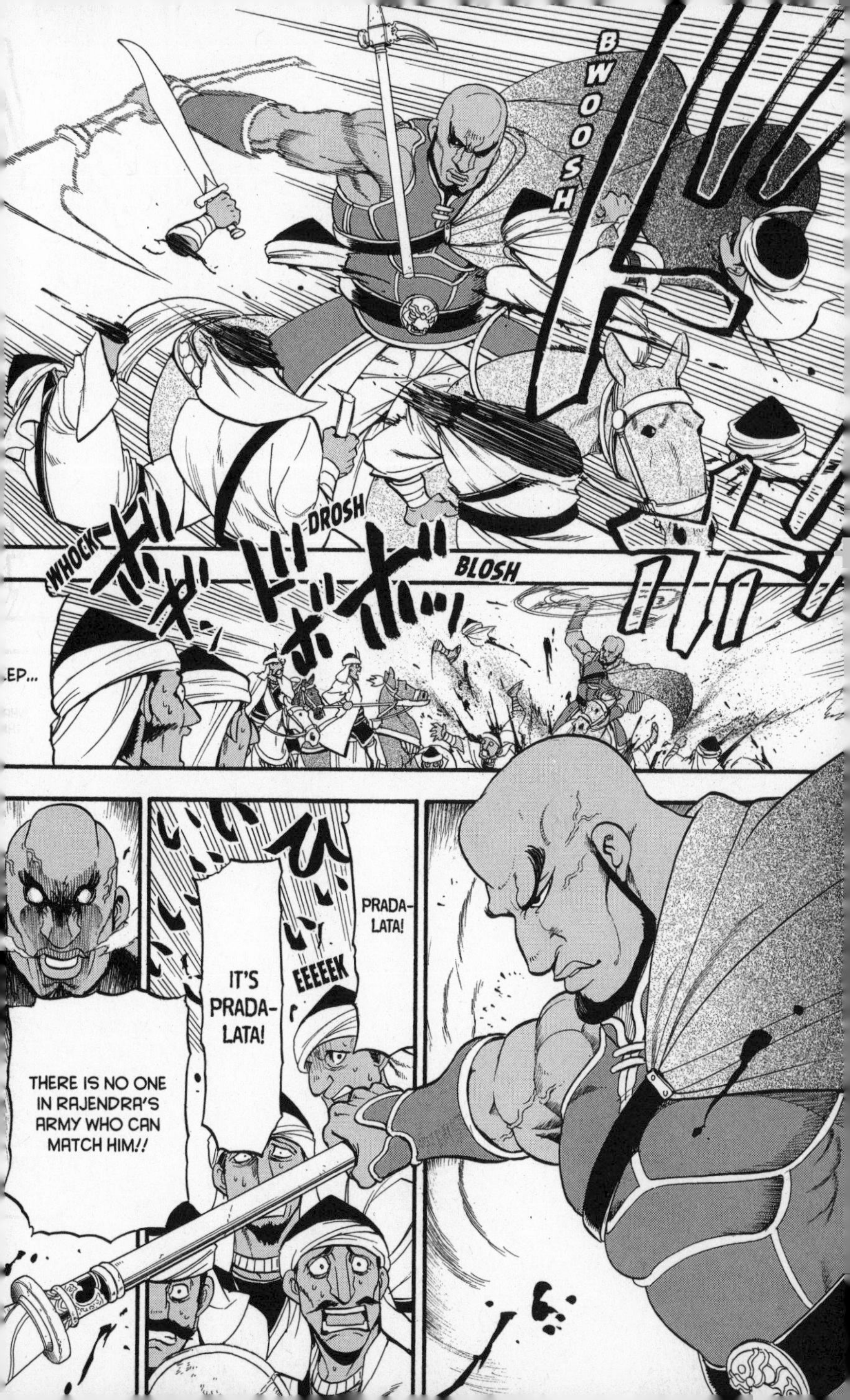
BWOOSH
BLOSH
DROSH
WHOCK
PRADA-LATA!
EEEEEK
IT'S PRADA-LATA!
THERE IS NO ONE IN RAJENDRA'S ARMY WHO CAN MATCH HIM!!

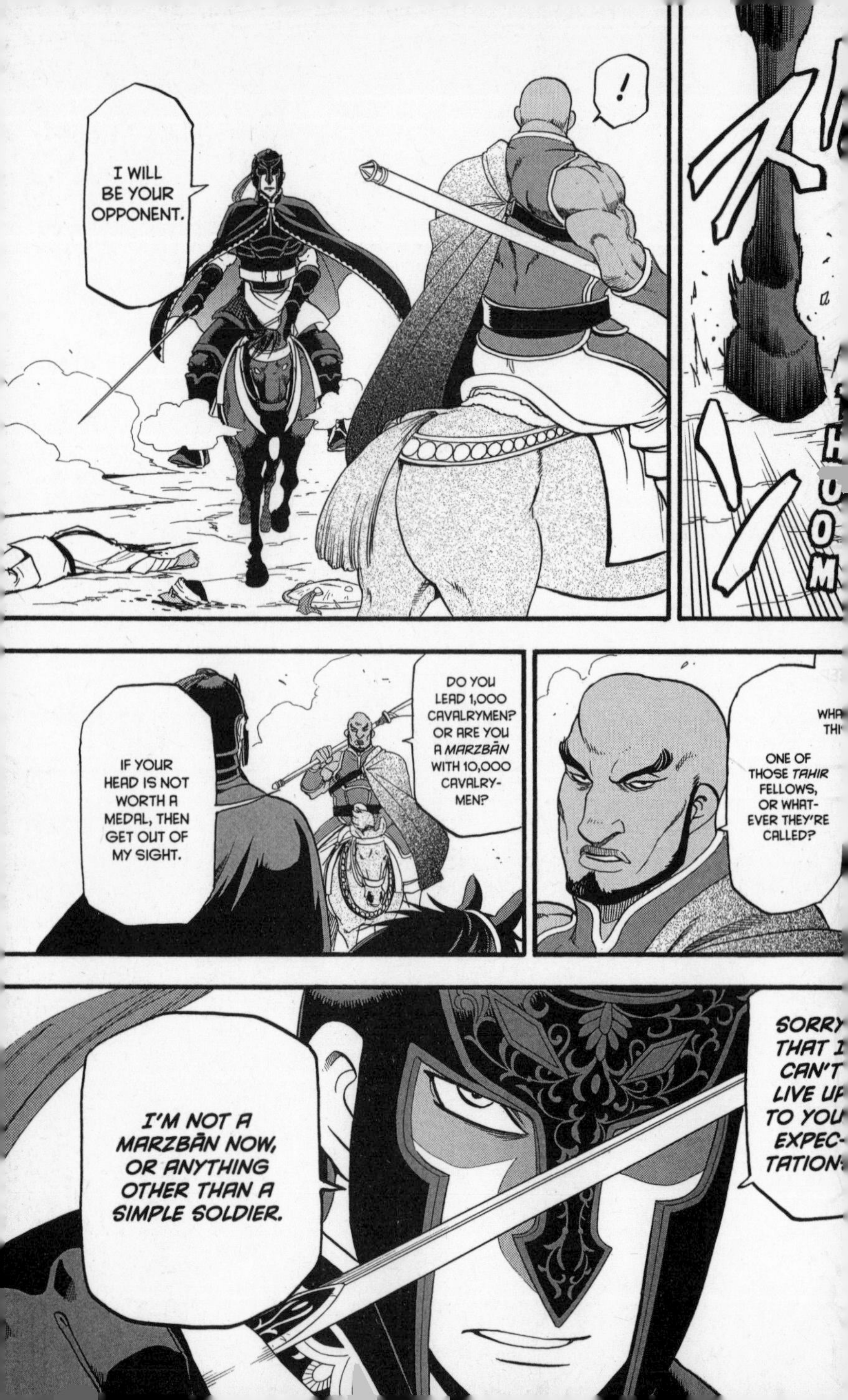
HOOM
!
I WILL BE YOUR OPPONENT.
ONE OF THOSE *TAHIR* FELLOWS, OR WHATEVER THEY'RE CALLED?
DO YOU LEAD 1,000 CAVALRYMEN? OR ARE YOU A *MARZBĀN* WITH 10,000 CAVALRYMEN?
IF YOUR HEAD IS NOT WORTH A MEDAL, THEN GET OUT OF MY SIGHT.
SORRY THAT I CAN'T LIVE UP TO YOU EXPECTATION
I'M NOT A MARZBĀN NOW, OR ANYTHING OTHER THAN A SIMPLE SOLDIER.

THE HEROIC LEGEND OF
A R S L A N

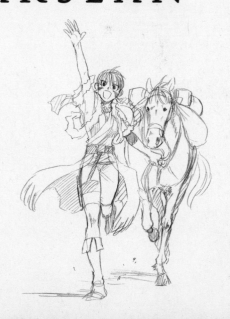

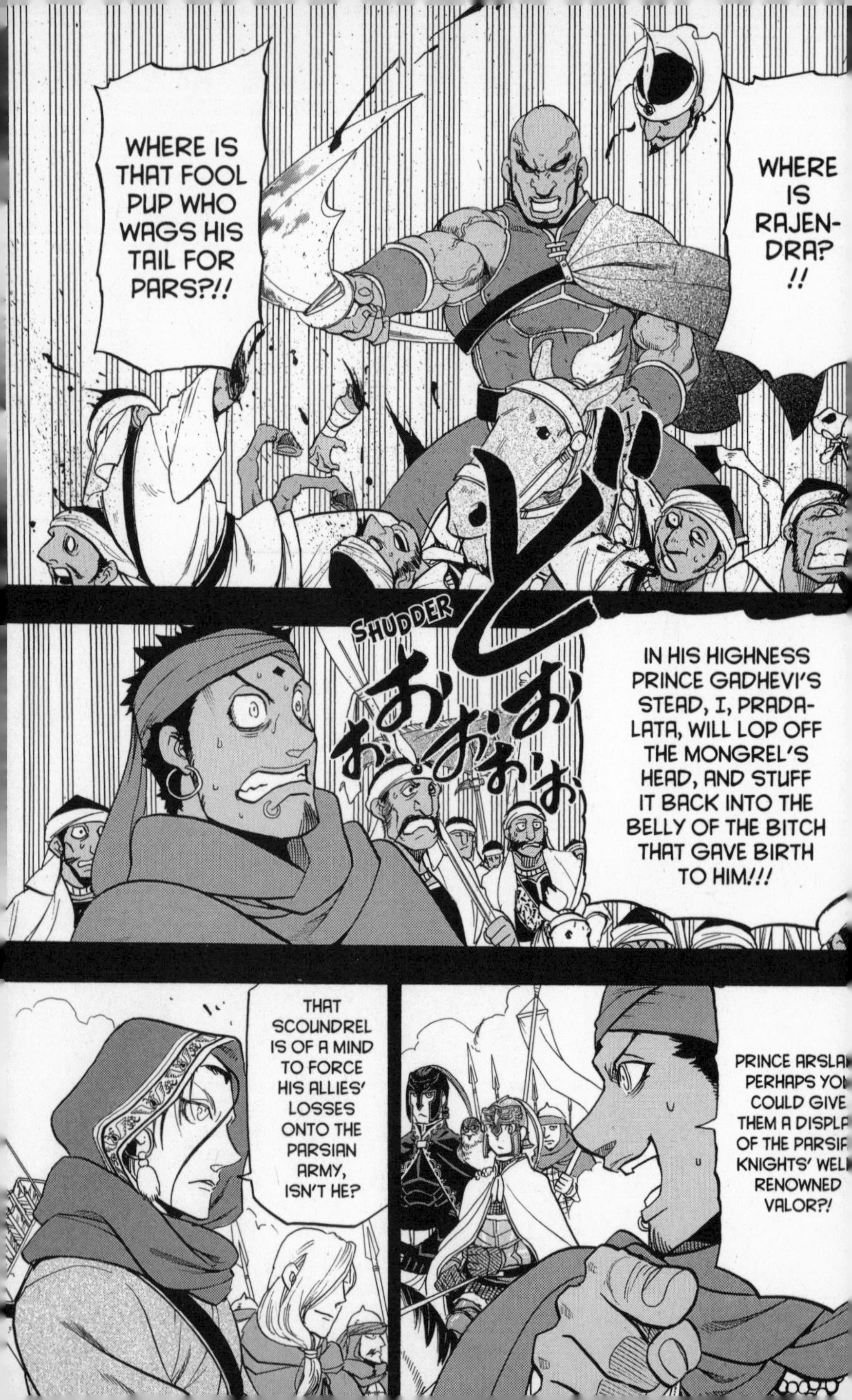
WHERE IS RAJEN-DRA?!!
WHERE IS THAT FOOL PUP WHO WAGS HIS TAIL FOR PARS?!!
どおおおおお
SHUDDER
IN HIS HIGHNESS PRINCE GADHEVI'S STEAD, I, PRADA-LATA, WILL LOP OFF THE MONGREL'S HEAD, AND STUFF IT BACK INTO THE BELLY OF THE BITCH THAT GAVE BIRTH TO HIM!!!
PRINCE ARSLA PERHAPS YO COULD GIVE THEM A DISPLA OF THE PARSIA KNIGHTS' WEL RENOWNED VALOR?!
THAT SCOUNDREL IS OF A MIND TO FORCE HIS ALLIES' LOSSES ONTO THE PARSIAN ARMY, ISN'T HE?

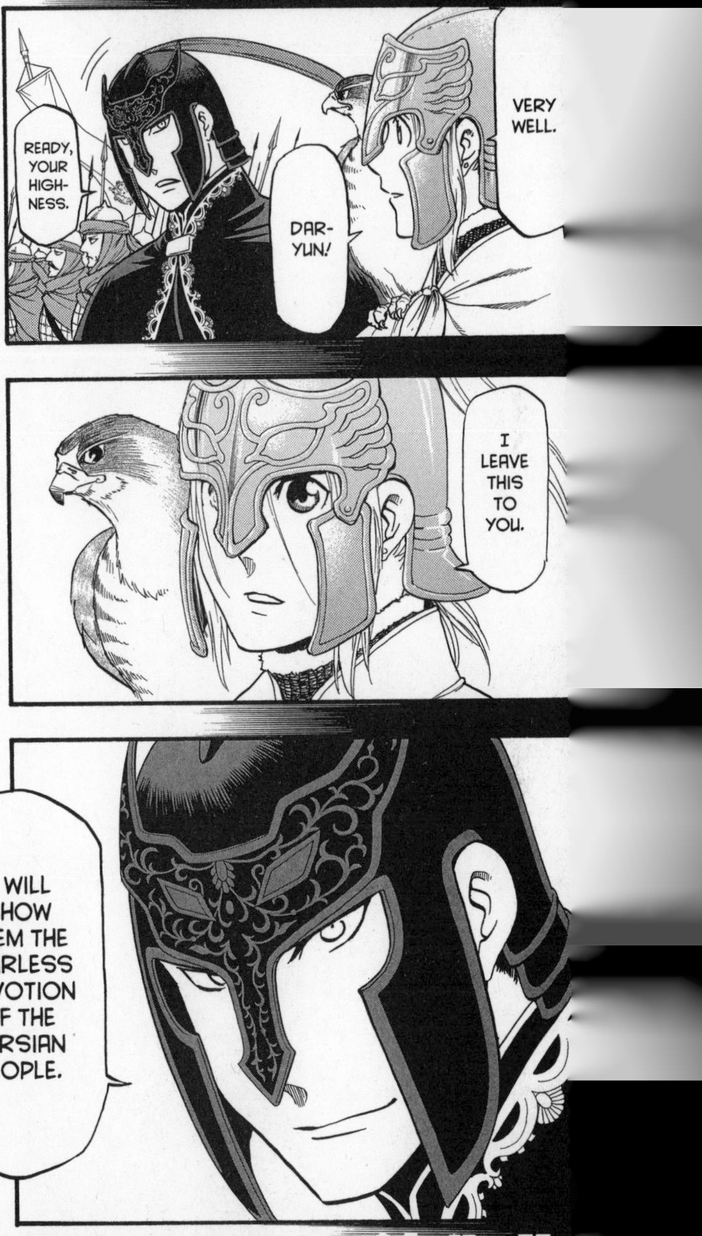
VERY WELL.
DAR-YUN!
READY, YOUR HIGHNESS.
I LEAVE THIS TO YOU.
I WILL SHOW THEM THE FEARLESS DEVOTION OF THE PARSIAN PEOPLE.

Chapter 43: Ceremony of the New Yea

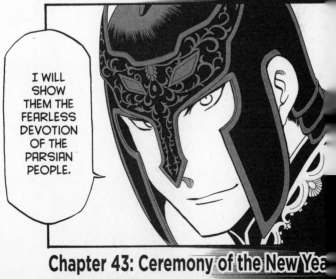

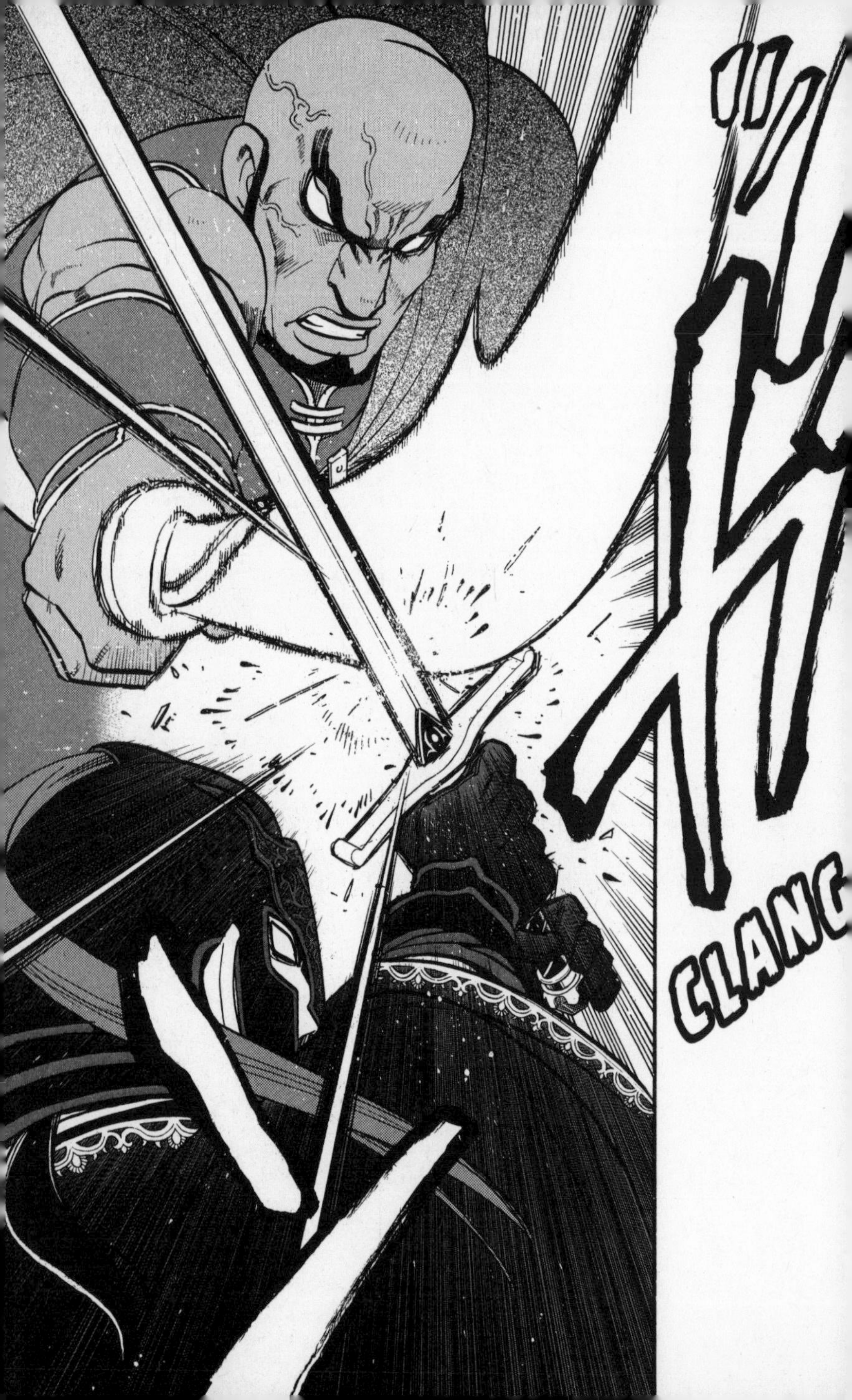
CLANG

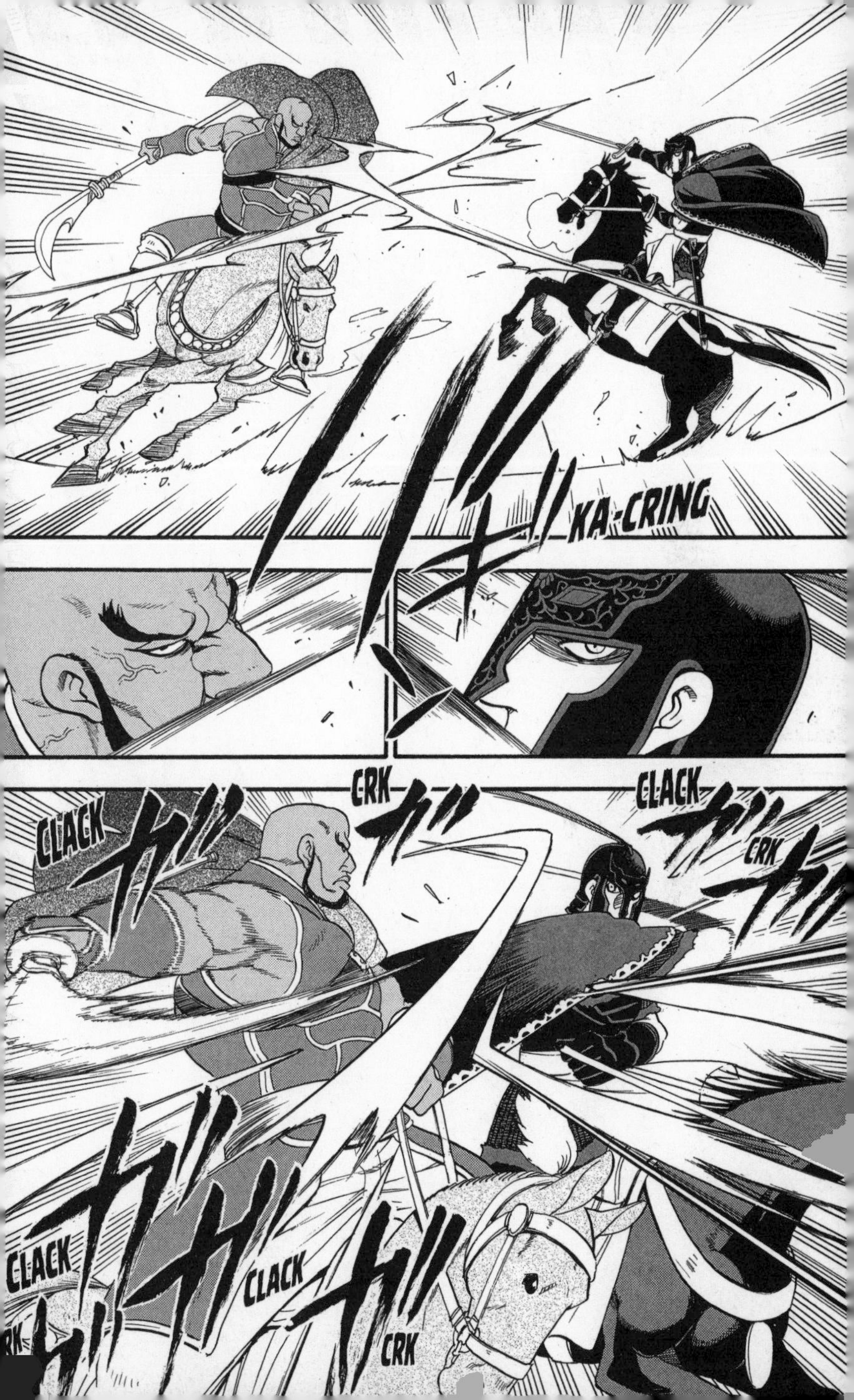
KA-CRING
CLACK
CRK
CRK
CLACK
CLACK
CRK
CLACK

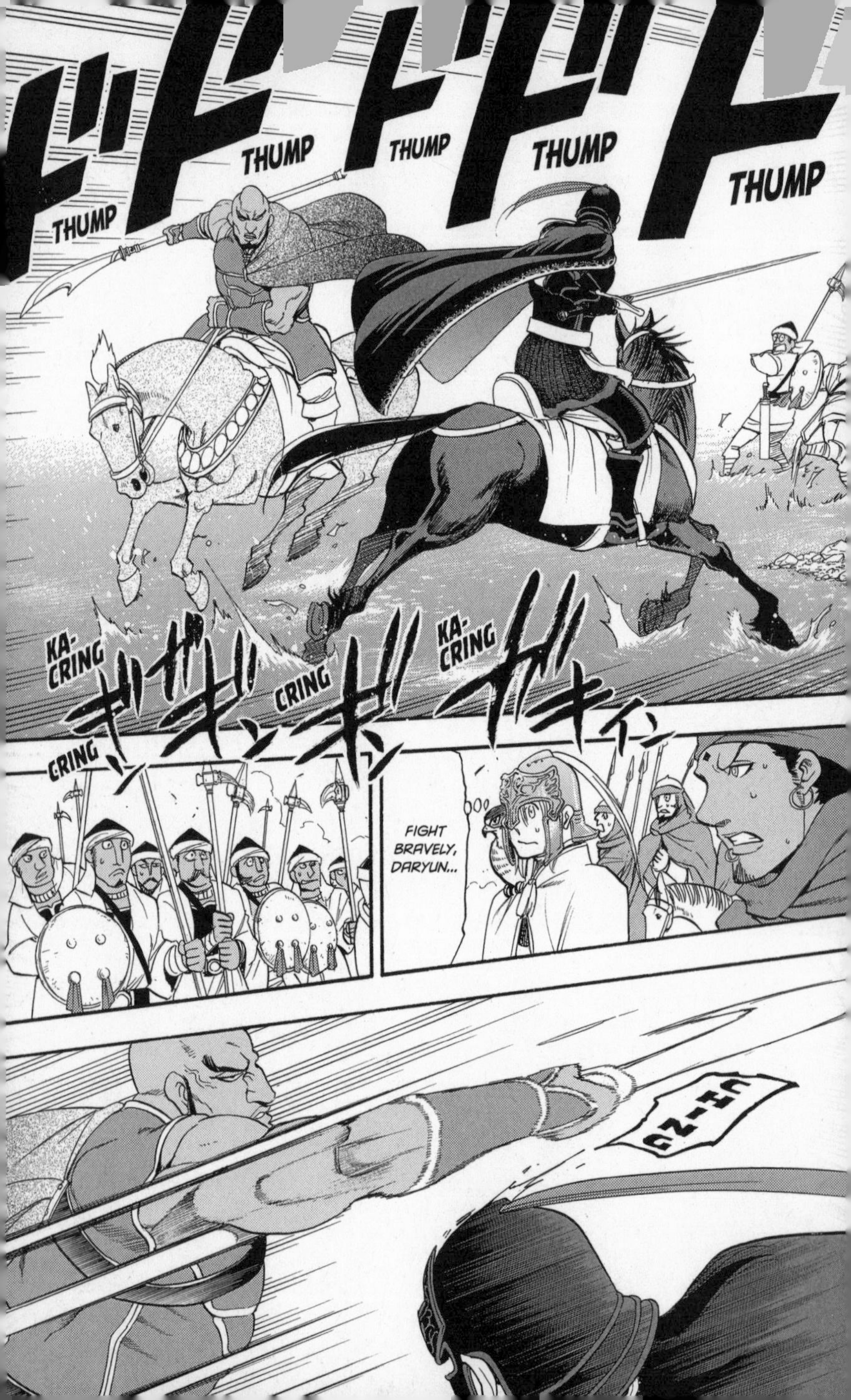
THUMP
THUMP
THUMP
THUMP
THUMP
KA-CRING
CRING
KA-CRING
CRING
FIGHT BRAVELY, DARYUN...

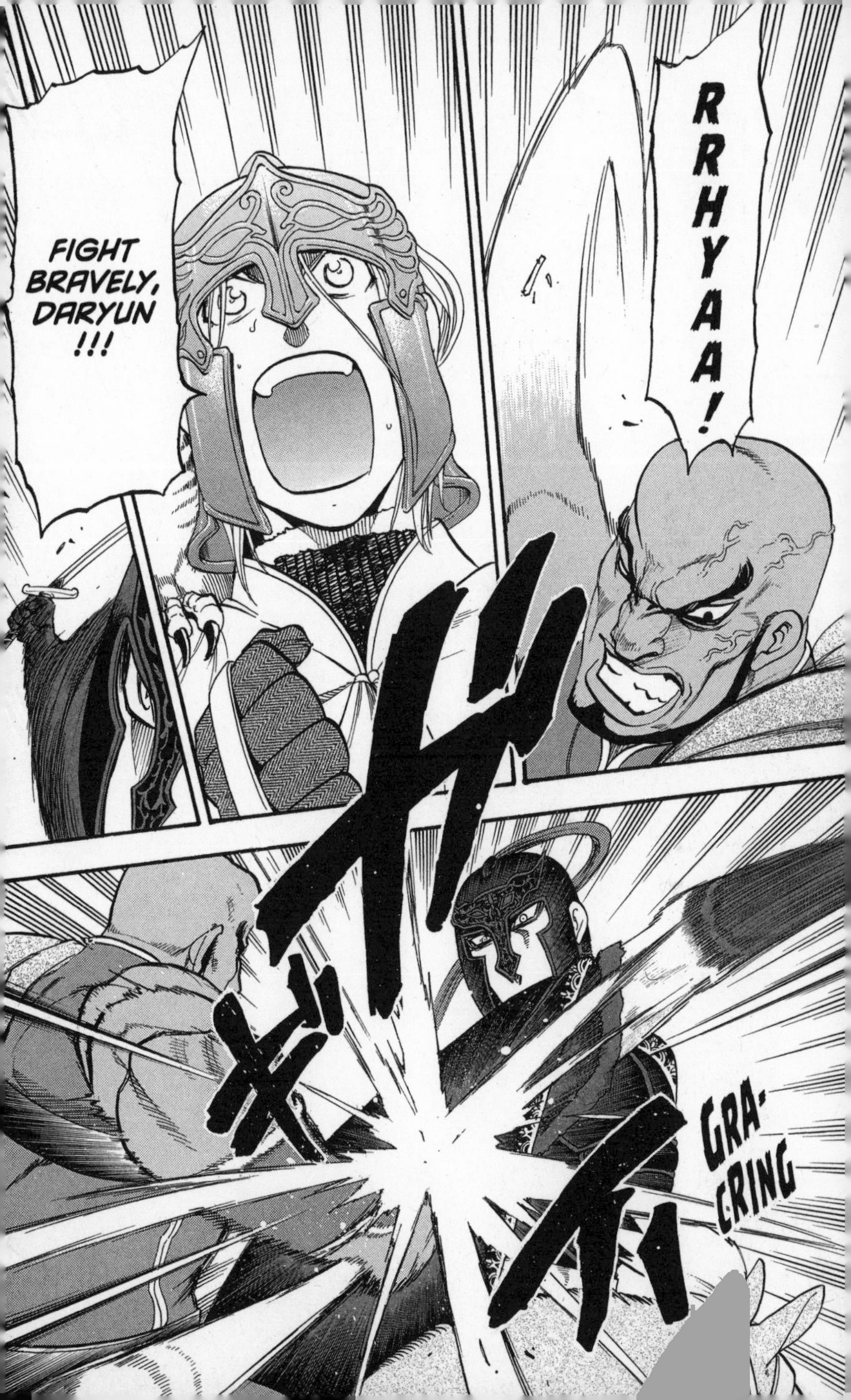
RRHYAAA!
FIGHT BRAVELY, DARYUN!!!
GRA-CRING

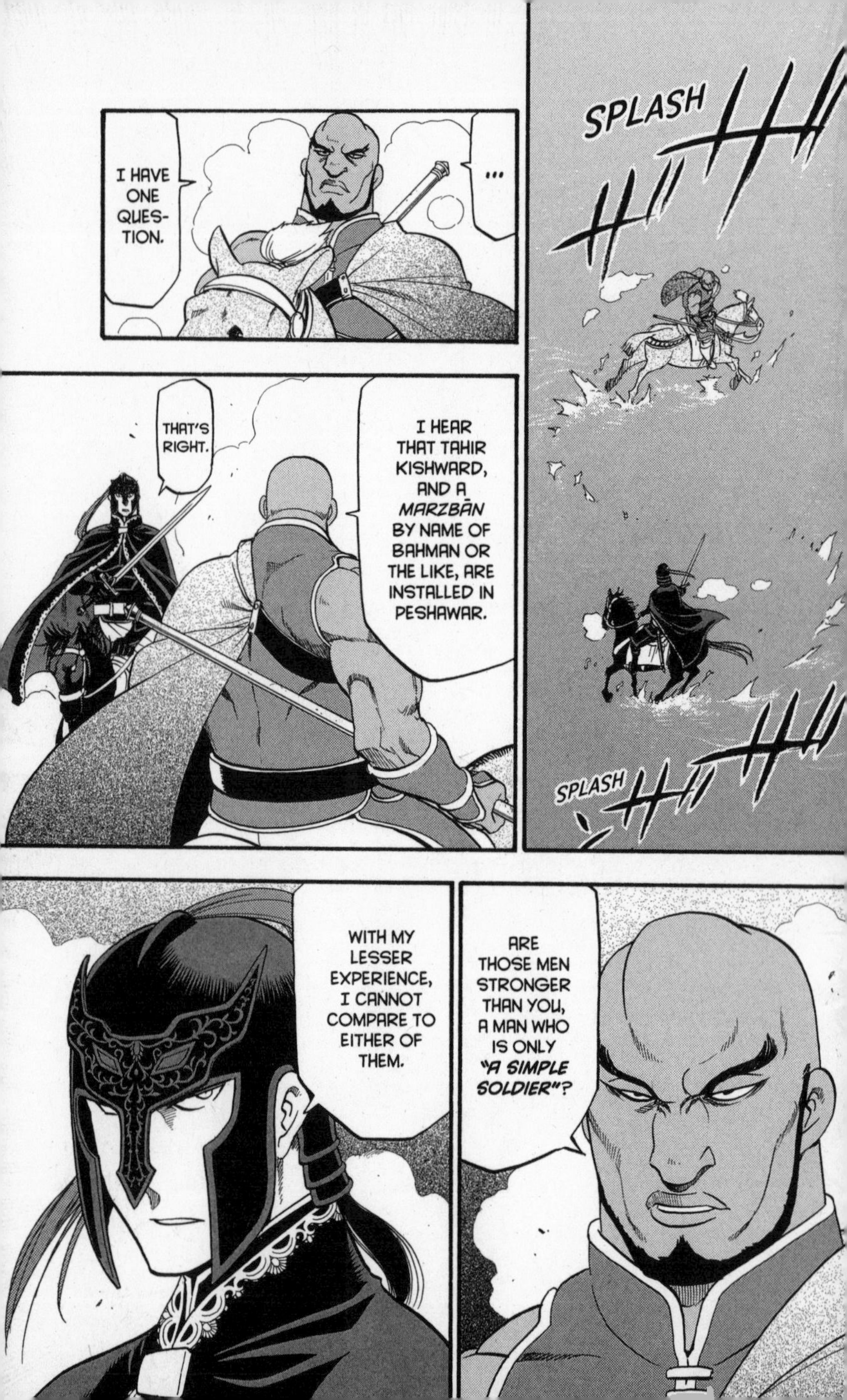

SPLASH
SPLASH
...
I HAVE ONE QUES-TION.
I HEAR THAT TAHIR KISHWARD, AND A *MARZBĀN* BY NAME OF BAHMAN OR THE LIKE, ARE INSTALLED IN PESHAWAR.
THAT'S RIGHT.
ARE THOSE MEN STRONGER THAN YOU, A MAN WHO IS ONLY *"A SIMPLE SOLDIER"*?
WITH MY LESSER EXPERIENCE, I CANNOT COMPARE TO EITHER OF THEM.

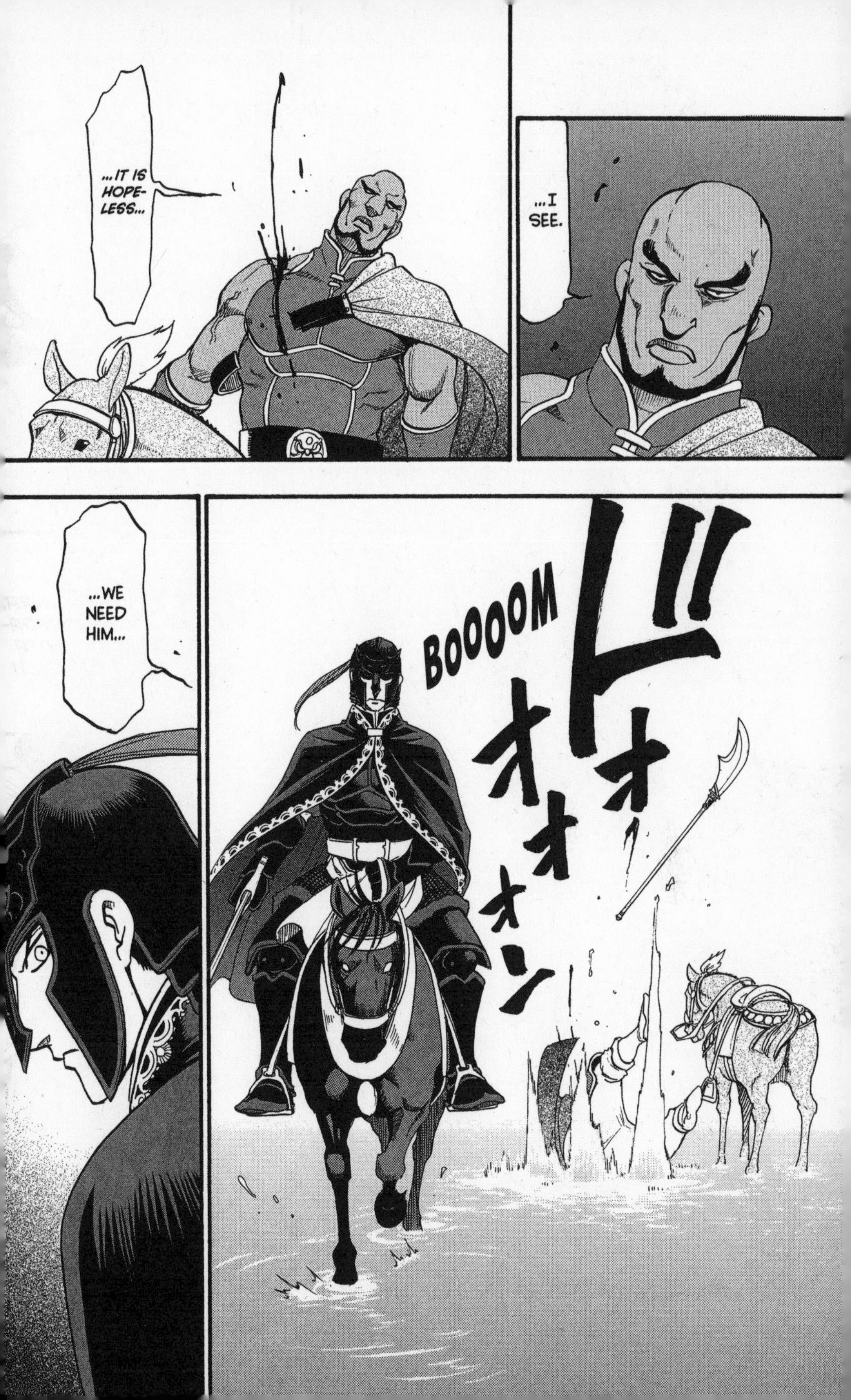
...I SEE.
...IT IS HOPE-LESS...
BOOOOM
ドオオオン
...WE NEED HIM...

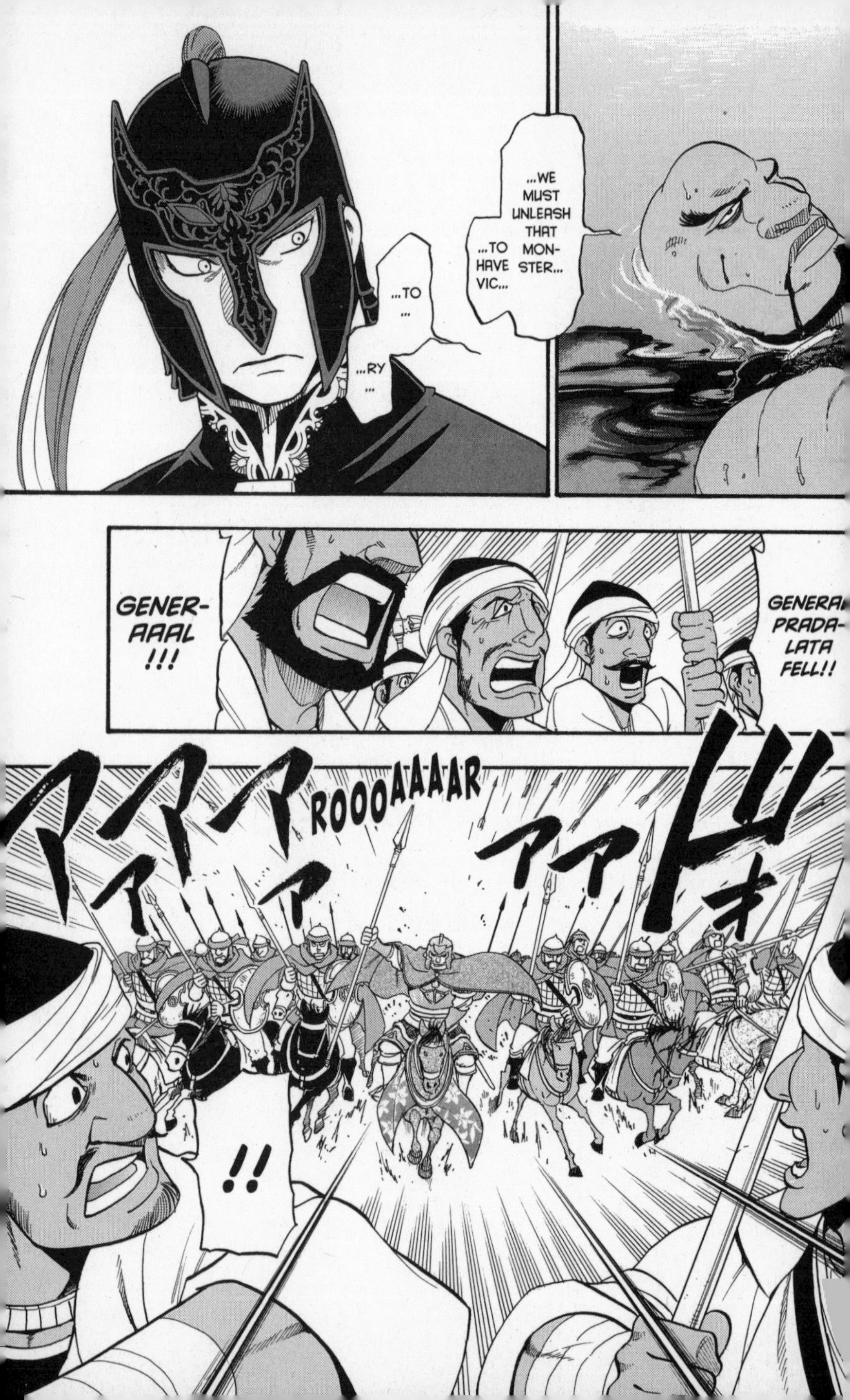
...WE MUST UNLEASH THAT MONSTER...
...TO HAVE VIC...
...TO ...
...RY ...
GENERA PRADA-LATA FELL!!
GENER-AAAL!!!
ROOOAAAAR
!!

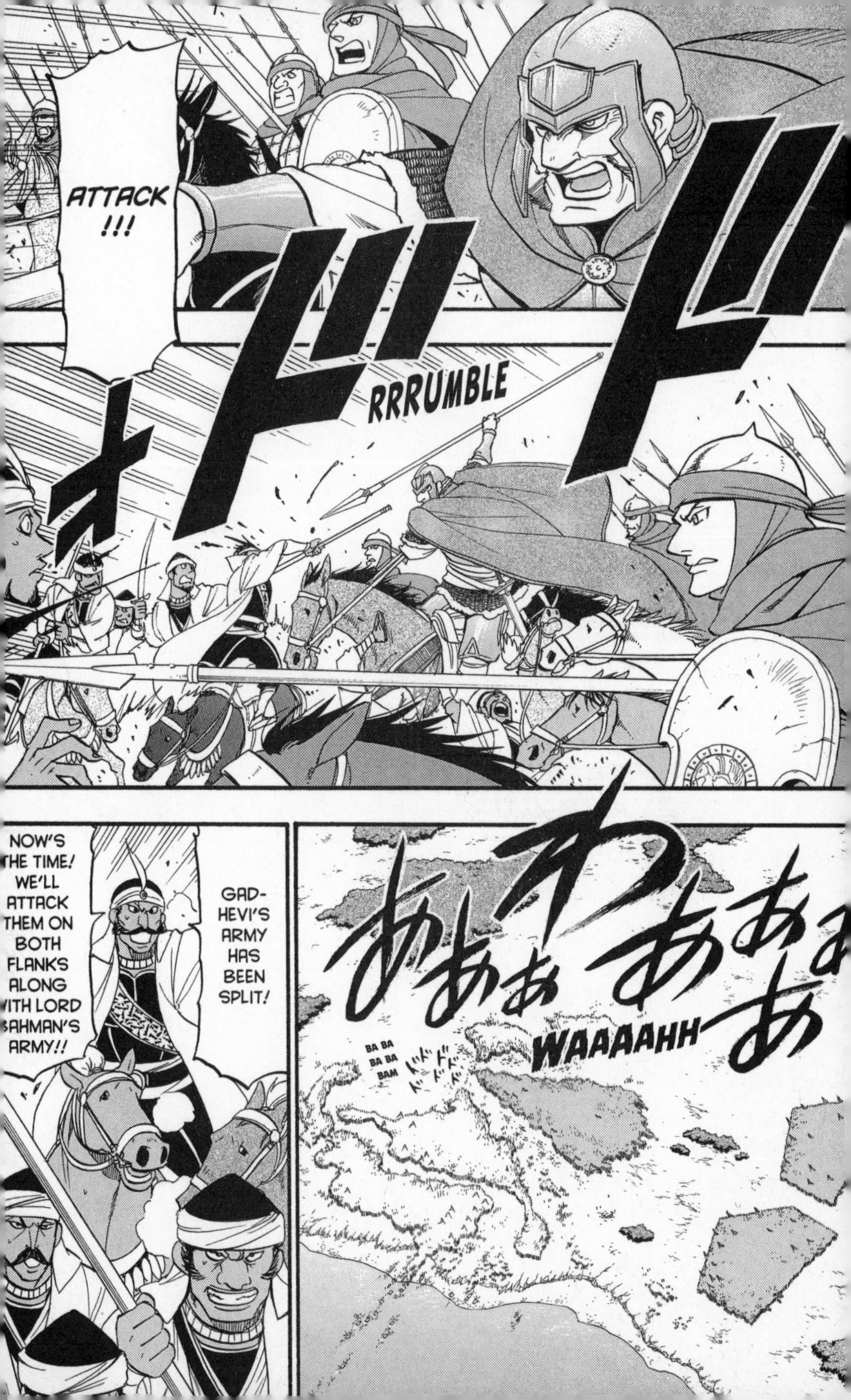
ATTACK !!!
RRRUMBLE
WAAAAHH
BA BA BA BA BAM
GAD-HEVI'S ARMY HAS BEEN SPLIT!
NOW'S THE TIME! WE'LL ATTACK THEM ON BOTH FLANKS ALONG WITH LORD BAHMAN'S ARMY!!

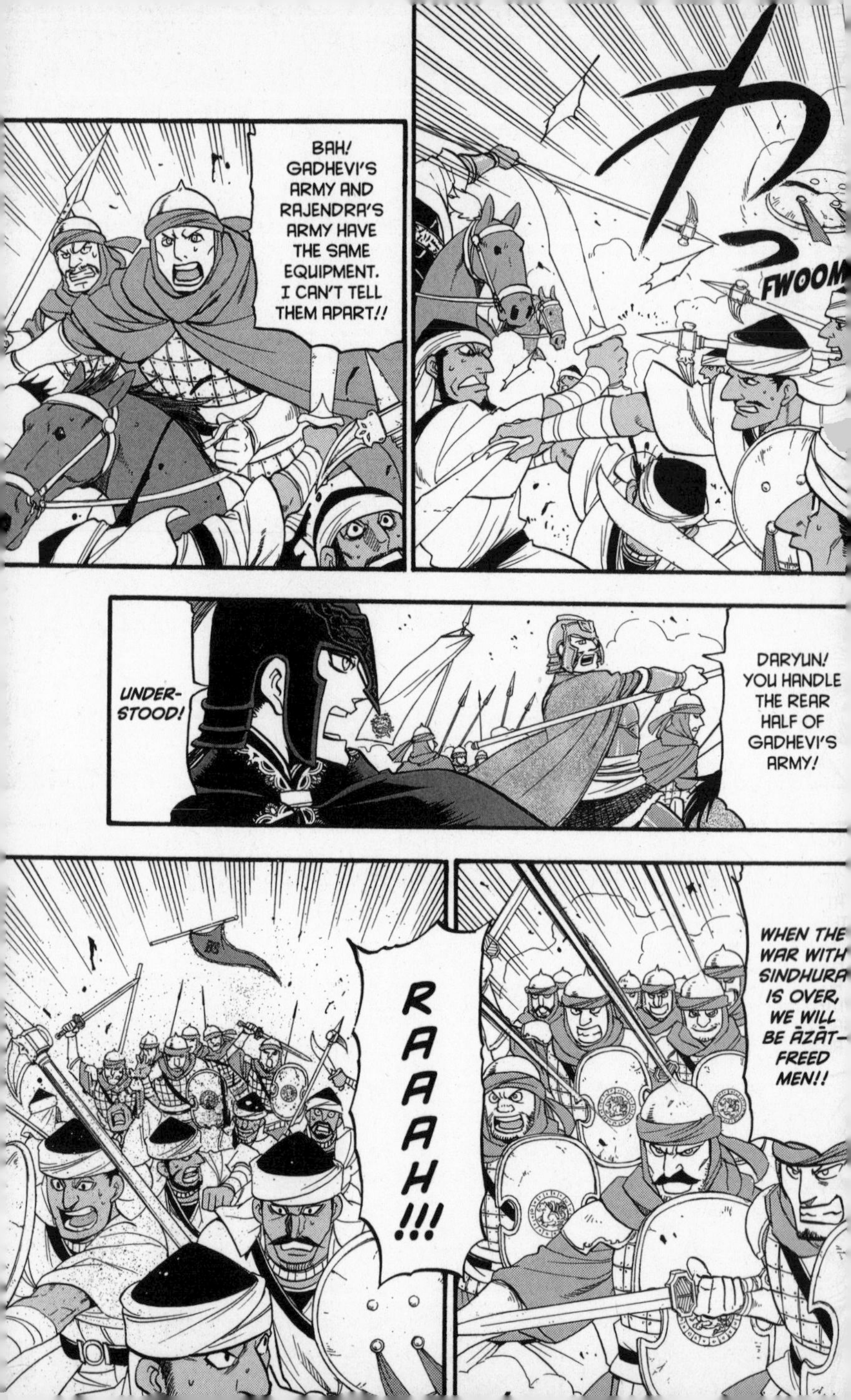
FWOOM
BAH! GADHEVI'S ARMY AND RAJENDRA'S ARMY HAVE THE SAME EQUIPMENT. I CAN'T TELL THEM APART!!
DARYUN! YOU HANDLE THE REAR HALF OF GADHEVI'S ARMY!
UNDER-STOOD!
WHEN THE WAR WITH SINDHURA IS OVER, WE WILL BE ĀZĀT-FREED MEN!!
RAAAAH!!!

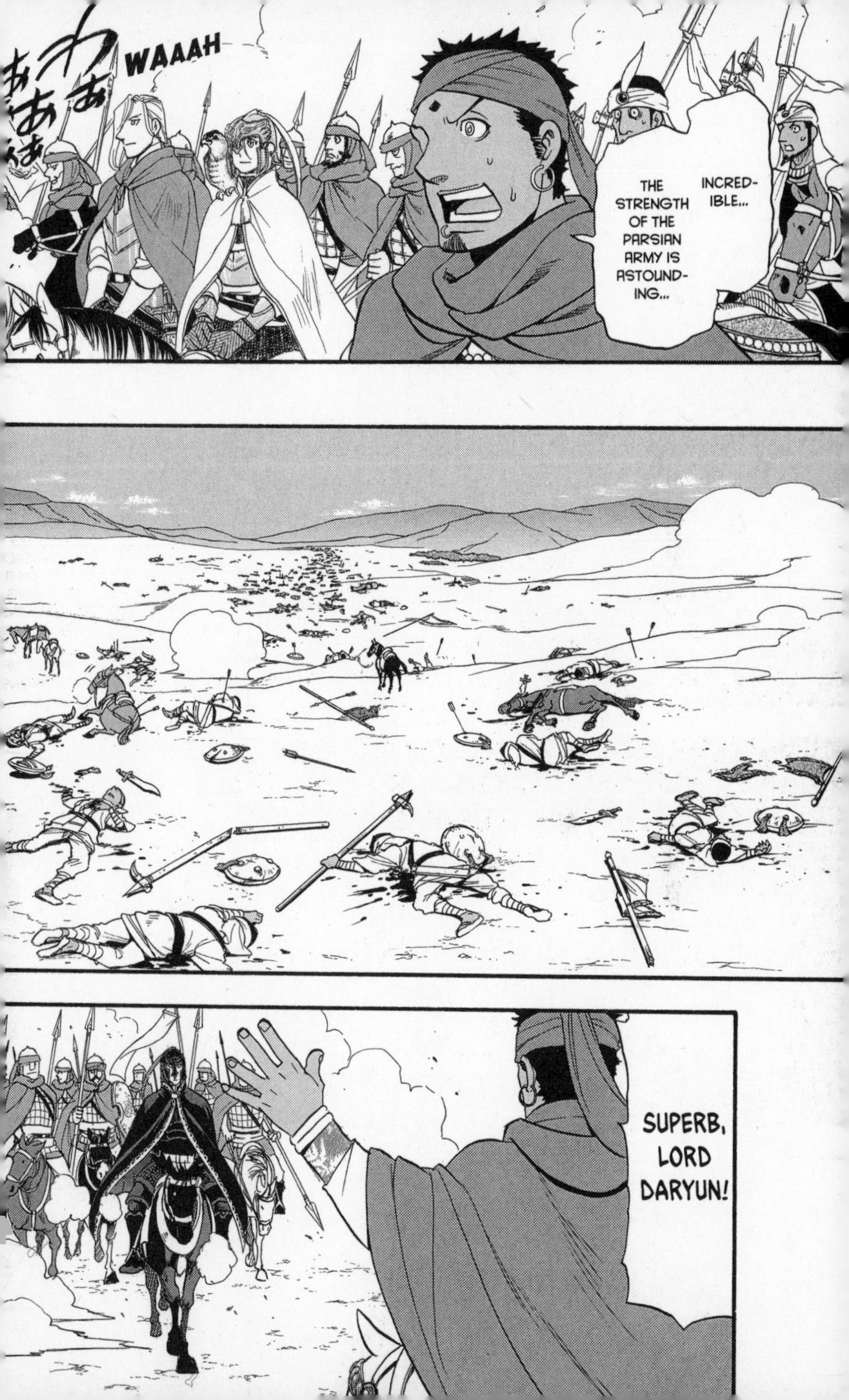
INCREDIBLE...
THE STRENGTH OF THE PARSIAN ARMY IS ASTOUNDING...
わあああ
WAAAH
SUPERB, LORD DARYUN!

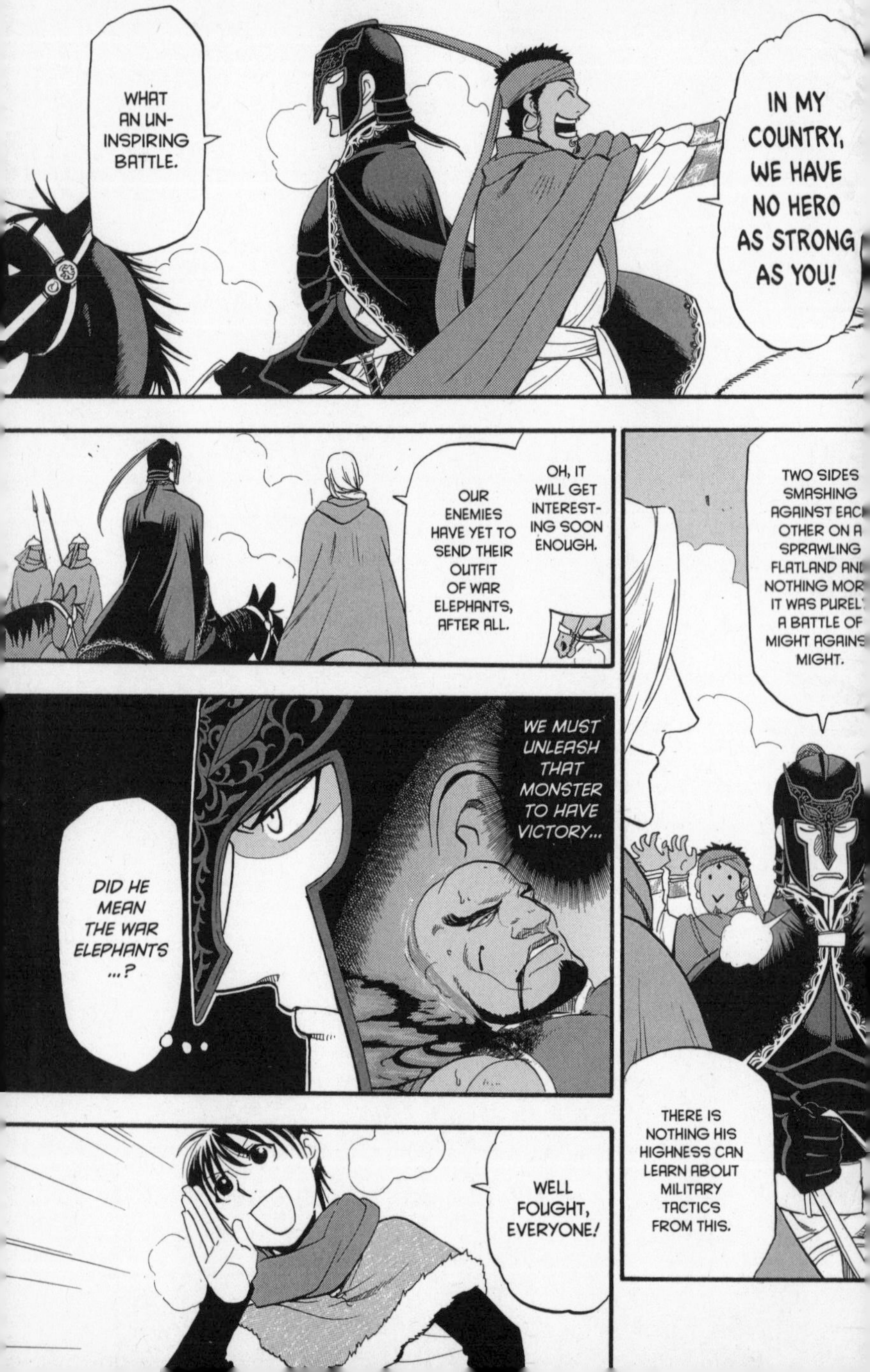

IN MY COUNTRY, WE HAVE NO HERO AS STRONG AS YOU!
WHAT AN UN-INSPIRING BATTLE.
TWO SIDES SMASHING AGAINST EAC OTHER ON A SPRAWLING FLATLAND AN NOTHING MOR IT WAS PUREL A BATTLE OF MIGHT AGAINS MIGHT.
THERE IS NOTHING HIS HIGHNESS CAN LEARN ABOUT MILITARY TACTICS FROM THIS.
OH, IT WILL GET INTEREST-ING SOON ENOUGH.
OUR ENEMIES HAVE YET TO SEND THEIR OUTFIT OF WAR ELEPHANTS, AFTER ALL.
WE MUST UNLEASH THAT MONSTER TO HAVE VICTORY...
DID HE MEAN THE WAR ELEPHANTS ...?
...
WELL FOUGHT, EVERYONE!

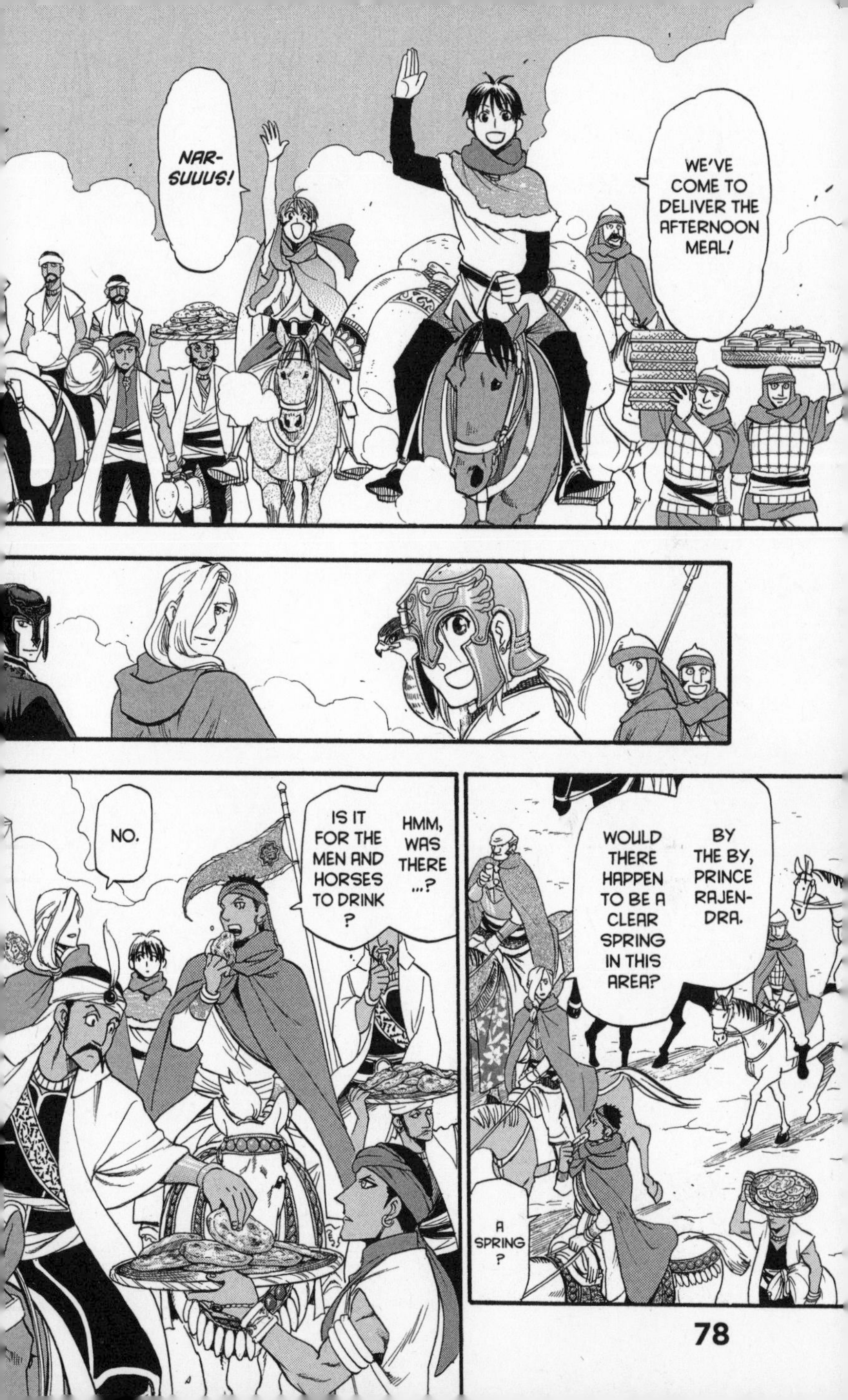
WE'VE COME TO DELIVER THE AFTERNOON MEAL!
NAR-SUUUS!
BY THE BY, PRINCE RAJEN-DRA.
WOULD THERE HAPPEN TO BE A CLEAR SPRING IN THIS AREA?
A SPRING?
HMM, WAS THERE ...?
IS IT FOR THE MEN AND HORSES TO DRINK?
NO.

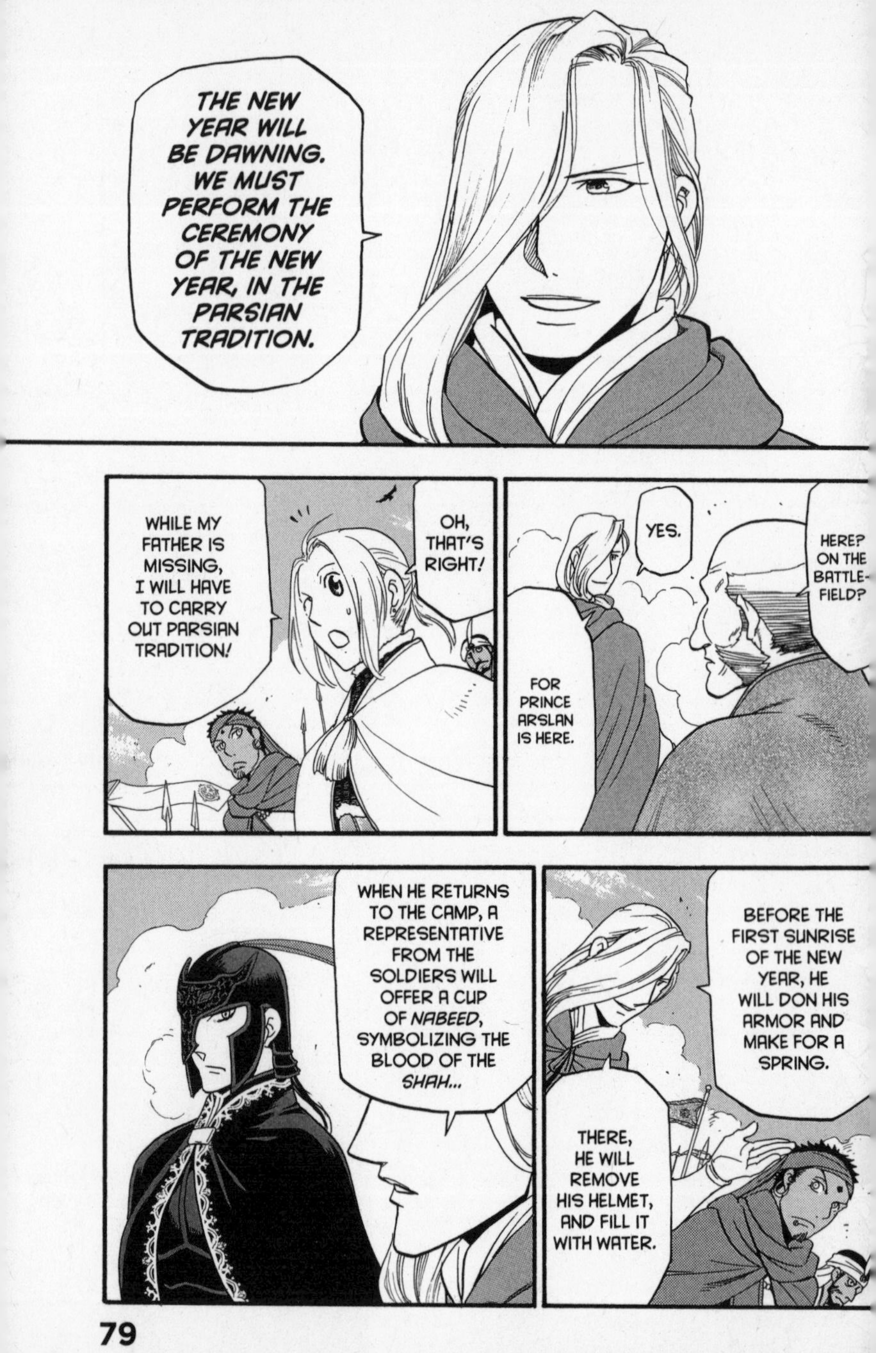
THE NEW YEAR WILL BE DAWNING. WE MUST PERFORM THE CEREMONY OF THE NEW YEAR, IN THE PARSIAN TRADITION.
HERE? ON THE BATTLE-FIELD?
YES.
FOR PRINCE ARSLAN IS HERE.
OH, THAT'S RIGHT!
WHILE MY FATHER IS MISSING, I WILL HAVE TO CARRY OUT PARSIAN TRADITION!
BEFORE THE FIRST SUNRISE OF THE NEW YEAR, HE WILL DON HIS ARMOR AND MAKE FOR A SPRING.
THERE, HE WILL REMOVE HIS HELMET, AND FILL IT WITH WATER.
WHEN HE RETURNS TO THE CAMP, A REPRESENTATIVE FROM THE SOLDIERS WILL OFFER A CUP OF *NABEED*, SYMBOLIZING THE BLOOD OF THE *SHAH*...

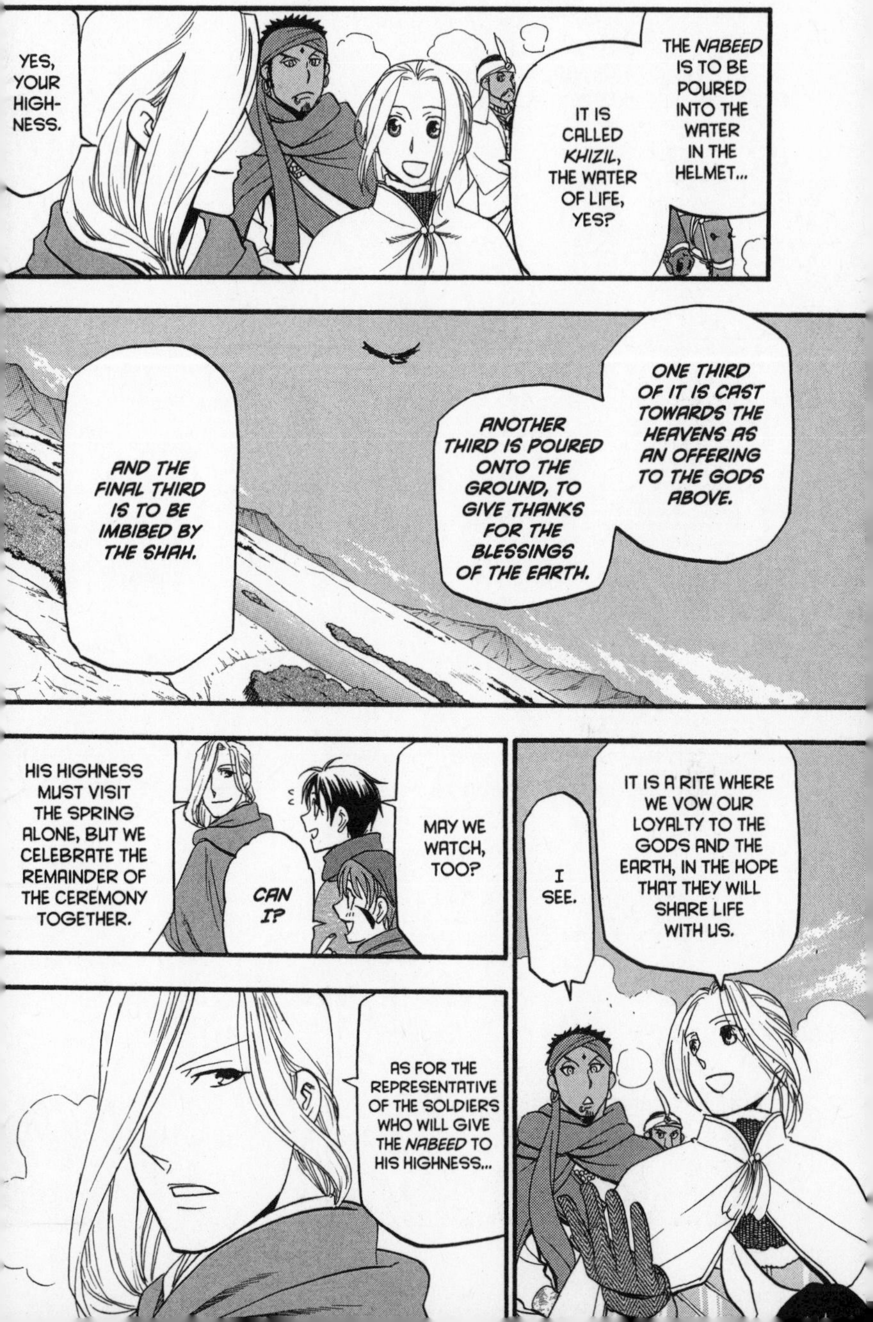
THE NABEED IS TO BE POURED INTO THE WATER IN THE HELMET...
IT IS CALLED KHIZIL, THE WATER OF LIFE, YES?
YES, YOUR HIGH-NESS.
ONE THIRD OF IT IS CAST TOWARDS THE HEAVENS AS AN OFFERING TO THE GODS ABOVE.
ANOTHER THIRD IS POURED ONTO THE GROUND, TO GIVE THANKS FOR THE BLESSINGS OF THE EARTH.
AND THE FINAL THIRD IS TO BE IMBIBED BY THE SHAH.
IT IS A RITE WHERE WE VOW OUR LOYALTY TO THE GODS AND THE EARTH, IN THE HOPE THAT THEY WILL SHARE LIFE WITH US.
I SEE.
MAY WE WATCH, TOO?
CAN I?
HIS HIGHNESS MUST VISIT THE SPRING ALONE, BUT WE CELEBRATE THE REMAINDER OF THE CEREMONY TOGETHER.
AS FOR THE REPRESENTATIVE OF THE SOLDIERS WHO WILL GIVE THE NABEED TO HIS HIGHNESS...

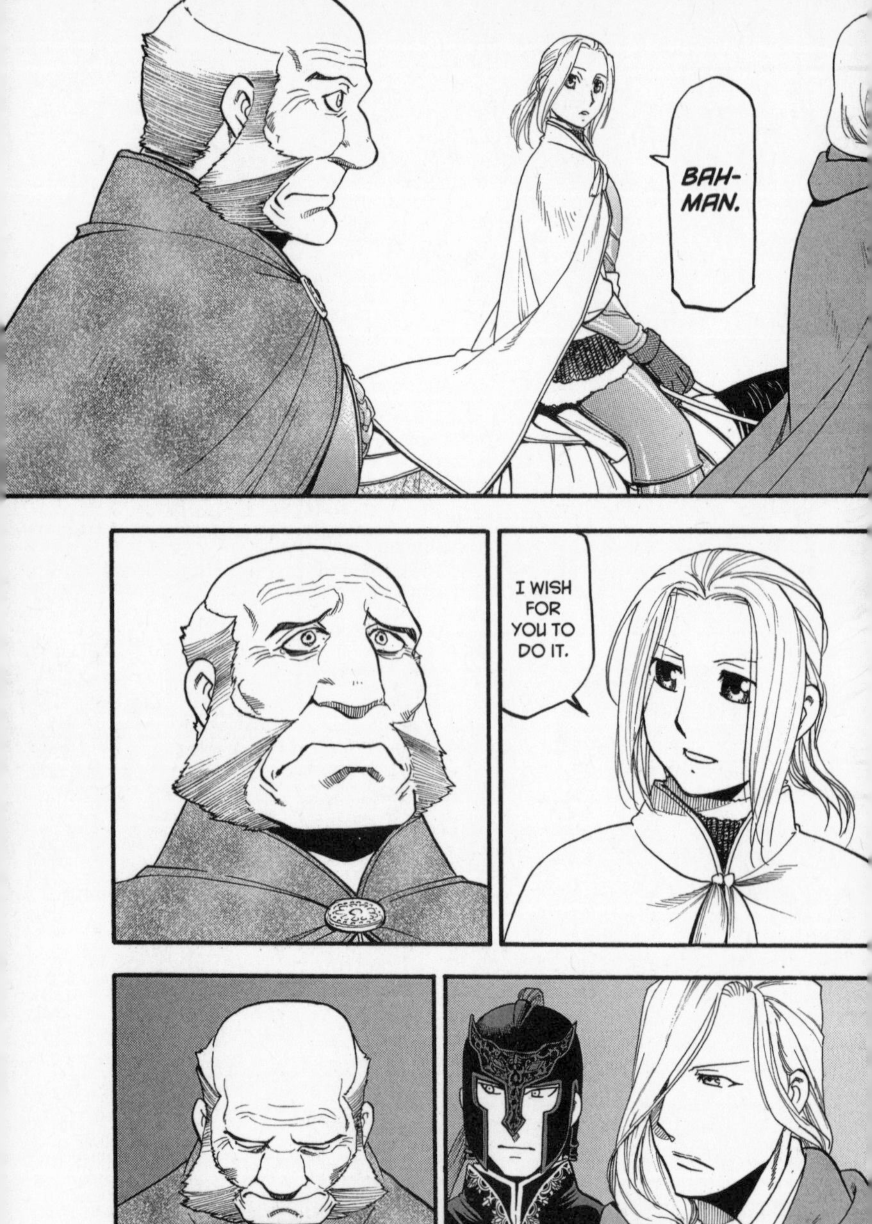
BAH-MAN.
I WISH FOR YOU TO DO IT.

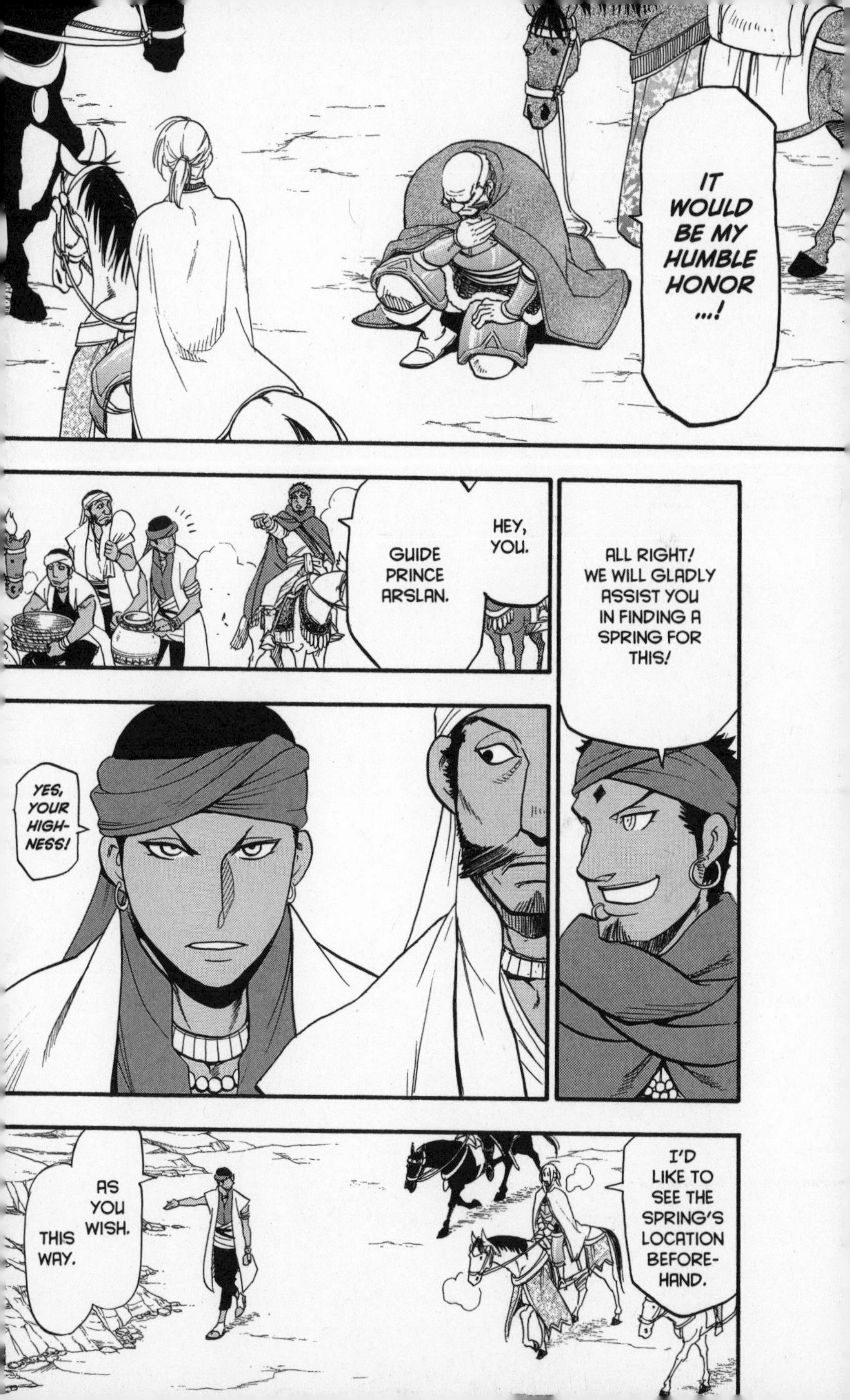
IT WOULD BE MY HUMBLE HONOR ...!
HEY, YOU.
GUIDE PRINCE ARSLAN.
ALL RIGHT! WE WILL GLADLY ASSIST YOU IN FINDING A SPRING FOR THIS!
YES, YOUR HIGH-NESS!
I'D LIKE TO SEE THE SPRING'S LOCATION BEFORE-HAND.
AS YOU WISH.
THIS WAY.

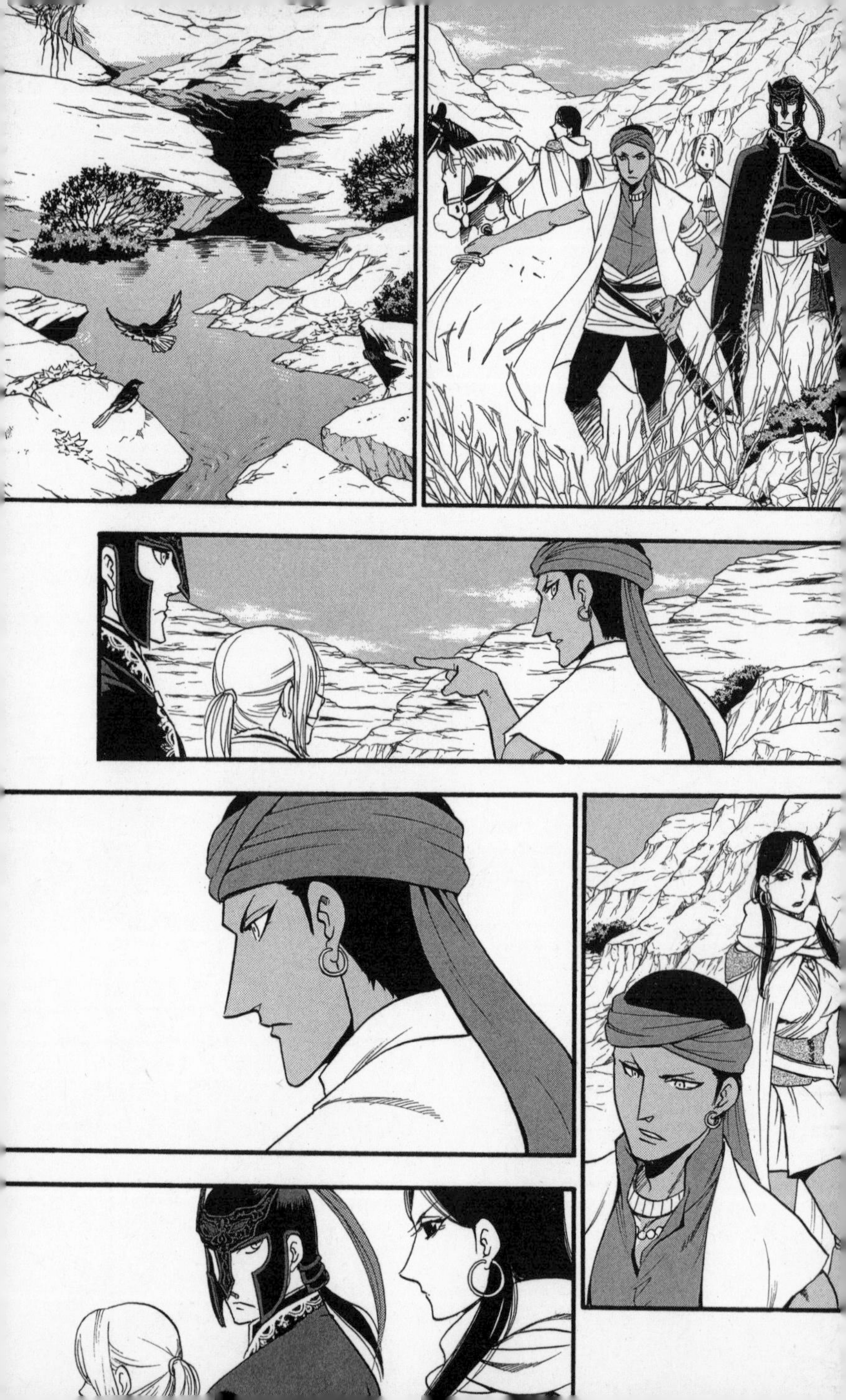

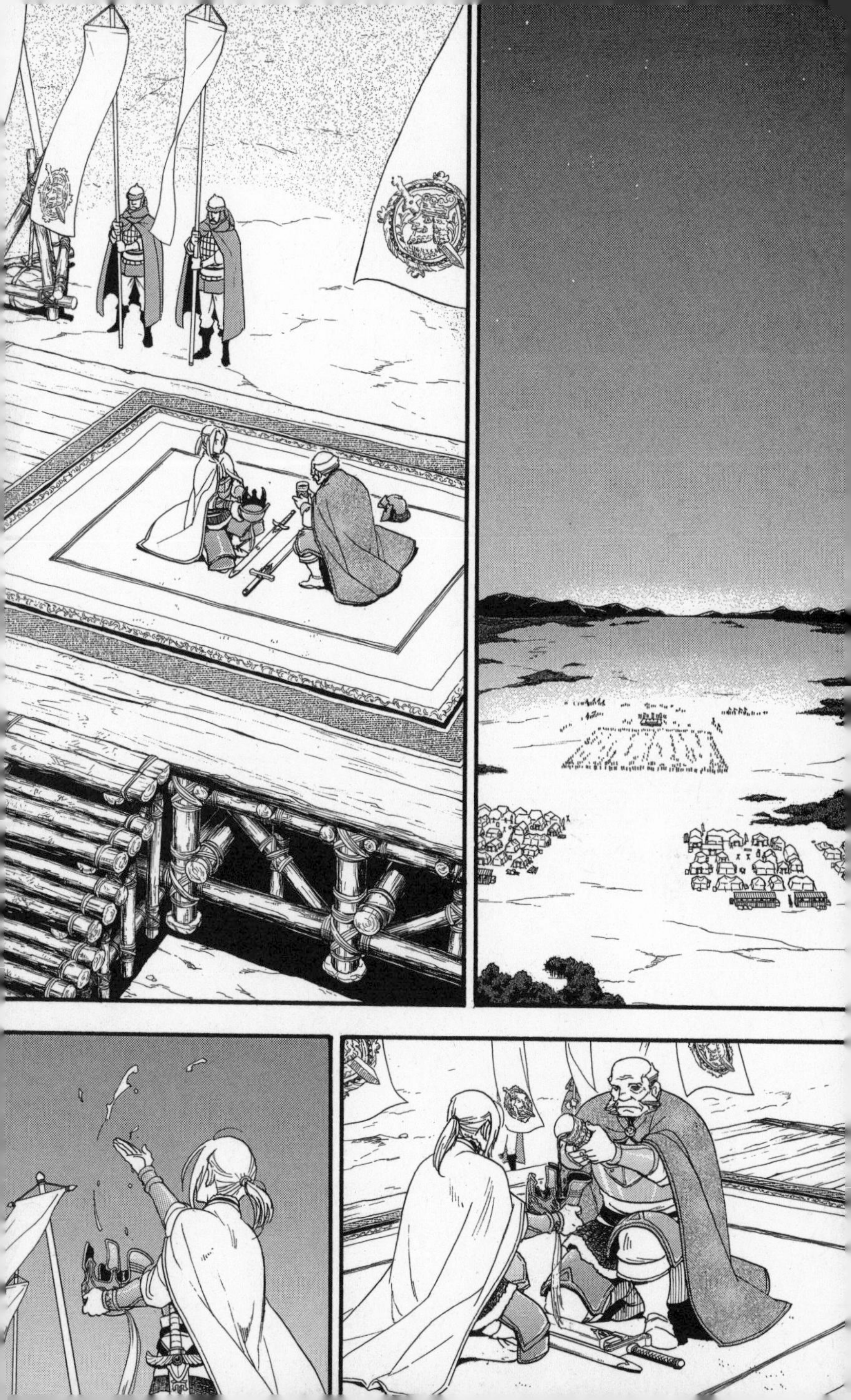

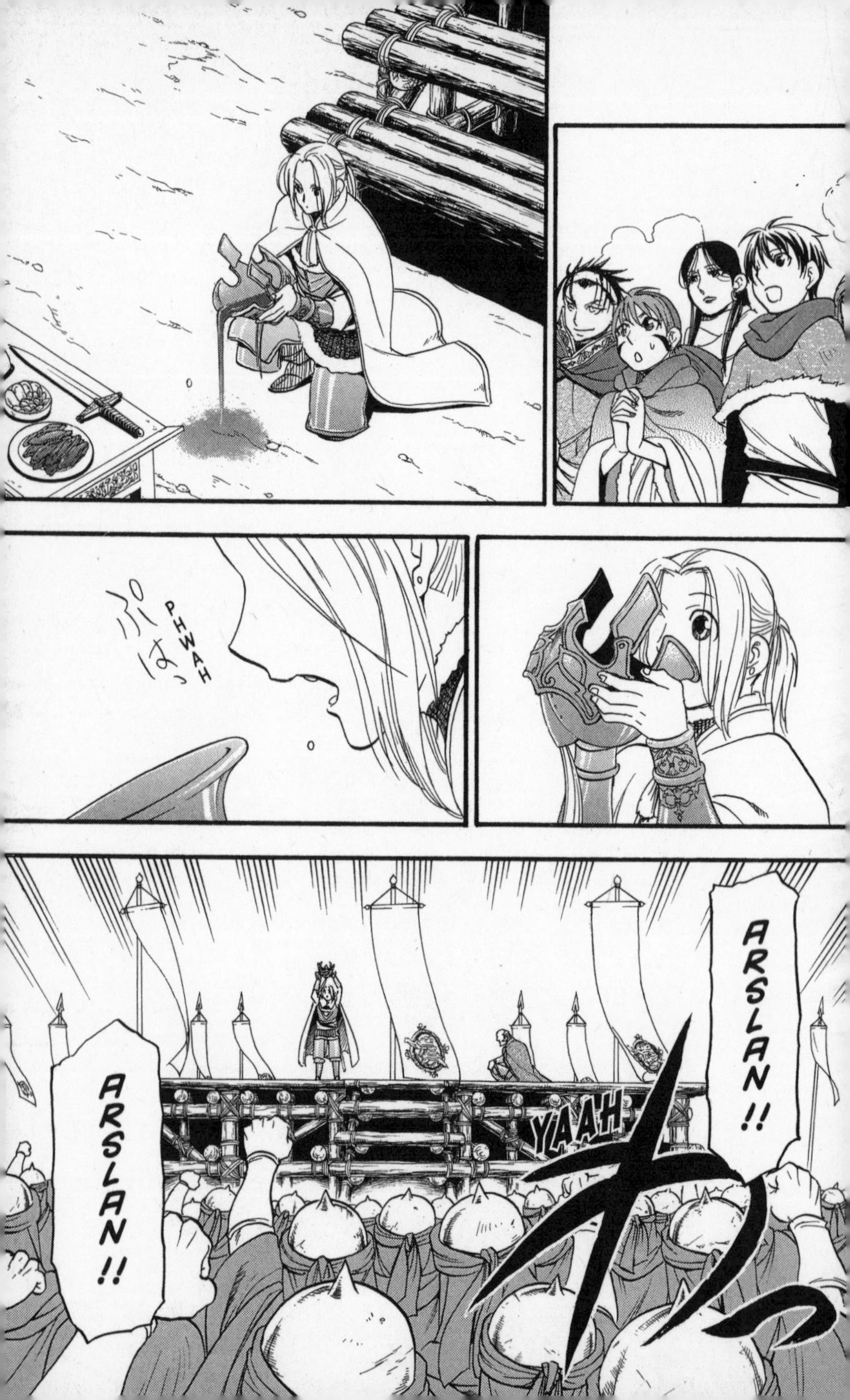
ぷはっ
PHWAH
ARSLAN!!
YAAH
ARSLAN!!

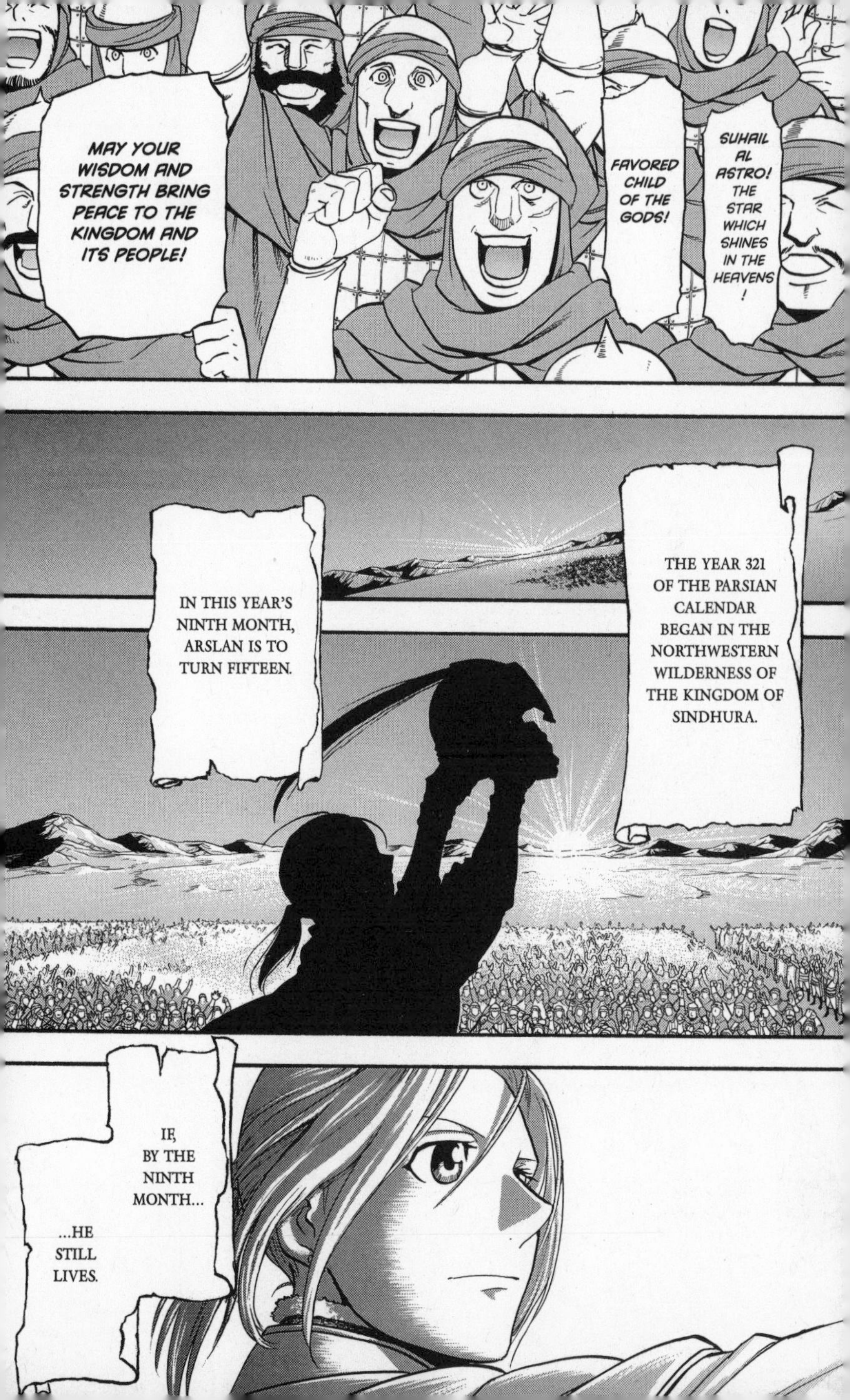
SUHAIL AL ASTRO! THE STAR WHICH SHINES IN THE HEAVENS!
FAVORED CHILD OF THE GODS!
MAY YOUR WISDOM AND STRENGTH BRING PEACE TO THE KINGDOM AND ITS PEOPLE!
THE YEAR 321 OF THE PARSIAN CALENDAR BEGAN IN THE NORTHWESTERN WILDERNESS OF THE KINGDOM OF SINDHURA.
IN THIS YEAR'S NINTH MONTH, ARSLAN IS TO TURN FIFTEEN.
IF, BY THE NINTH MONTH...
...HE STILL LIVES.

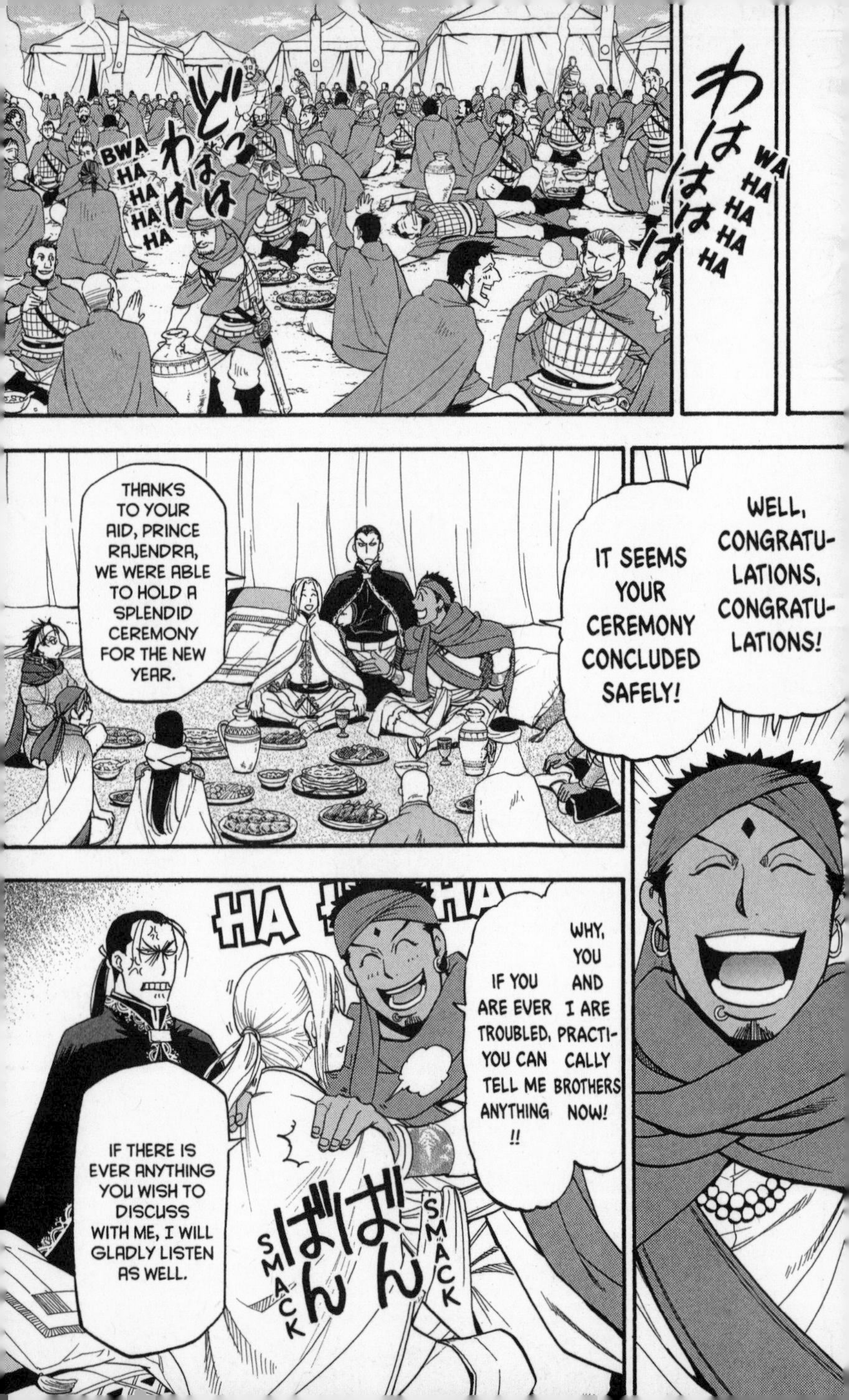
わははは
WA HA HA HA HA
どっ
わはは
BWA HA HA HA HA
WELL, CONGRATU-LATIONS, CONGRATU-LATIONS!
IT SEEMS YOUR CEREMONY CONCLUDED SAFELY!
THANKS TO YOUR AID, PRINCE RAJENDRA, WE WERE ABLE TO HOLD A SPLENDID CEREMONY FOR THE NEW YEAR.
HA HA
WHY, YOU AND I ARE PRACTI-CALLY BROTHERS NOW!
IF YOU ARE EVER TROUBLED, YOU CAN TELL ME ANYTHING!!
ばん
SMACK
ばん
SMACK
IF THERE IS EVER ANYTHING YOU WISH TO DISCUSS WITH ME, I WILL GLADLY LISTEN AS WELL.

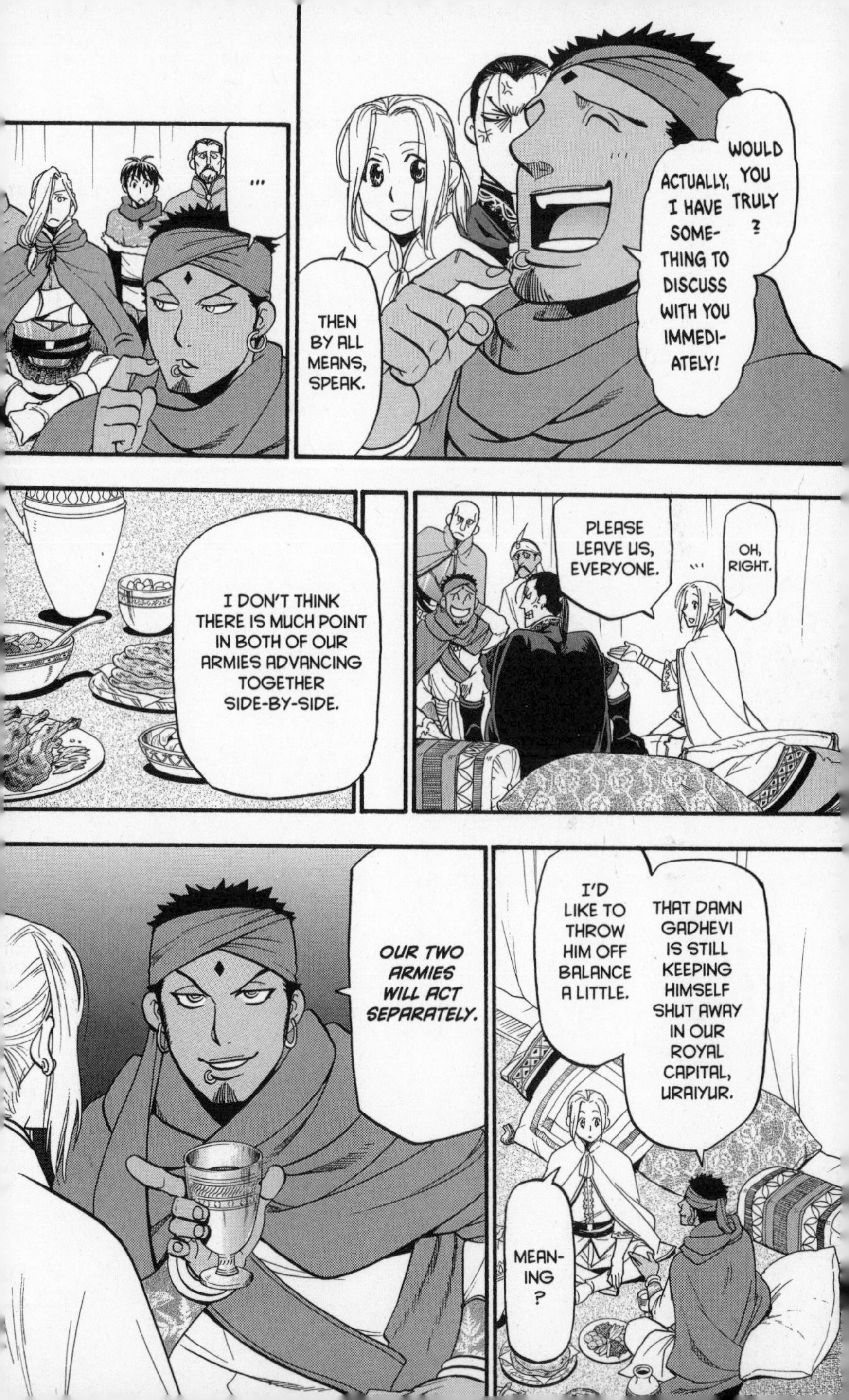

WOULD YOU TRULY?
ACTUALLY, I HAVE SOMETHING TO DISCUSS WITH YOU IMMEDIATELY!
THEN BY ALL MEANS, SPEAK.
...
PLEASE LEAVE US, EVERYONE.
...
OH, RIGHT.
I DON'T THINK THERE IS MUCH POINT IN BOTH OF OUR ARMIES ADVANCING TOGETHER SIDE-BY-SIDE.
THAT DAMN GADHEVI IS STILL KEEPING HIMSELF SHUT AWAY IN OUR ROYAL CAPITAL, URAIYUR.
I'D LIKE TO THROW HIM OFF BALANCE A LITTLE.
MEANING?
OUR TWO ARMIES WILL ACT SEPARATELY.

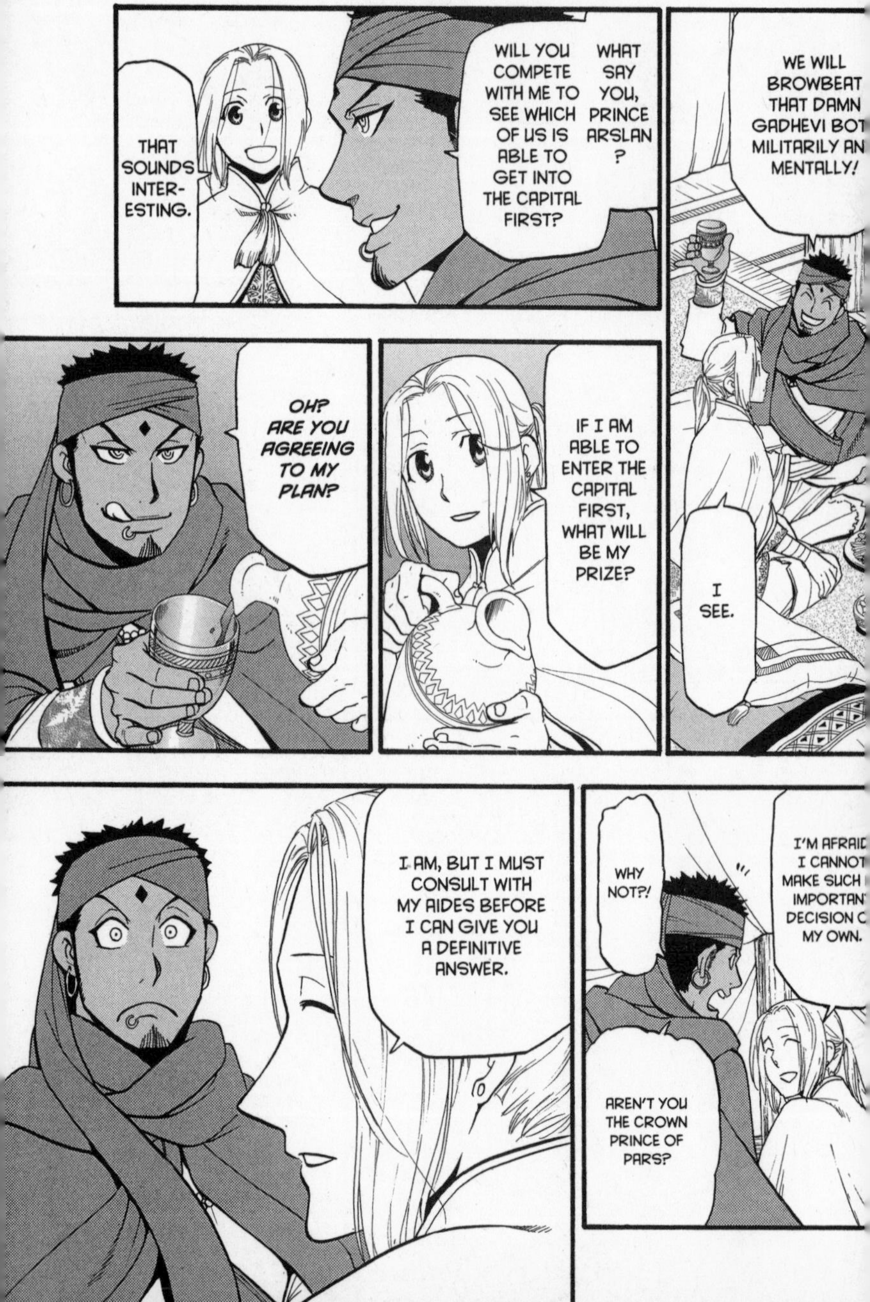
WE WILL BROWBEAT THAT DAMN GADHEVI BOT MILITARILY AN MENTALLY!
I SEE.
WHAT SAY YOU, PRINCE ARSLAN?
WILL YOU COMPETE WITH ME TO SEE WHICH OF US IS ABLE TO GET INTO THE CAPITAL FIRST?
THAT SOUNDS INTER-ESTING.
IF I AM ABLE TO ENTER THE CAPITAL FIRST, WHAT WILL BE MY PRIZE?
OH? ARE YOU AGREEING TO MY PLAN?
I'M AFRAID I CANNOT MAKE SUCH IMPORTAN DECISION C MY OWN.
WHY NOT?!
AREN'T YOU THE CROWN PRINCE OF PARS?
I AM, BUT I MUST CONSULT WITH MY AIDES BEFORE I CAN GIVE YOU A DEFINITIVE ANSWER.

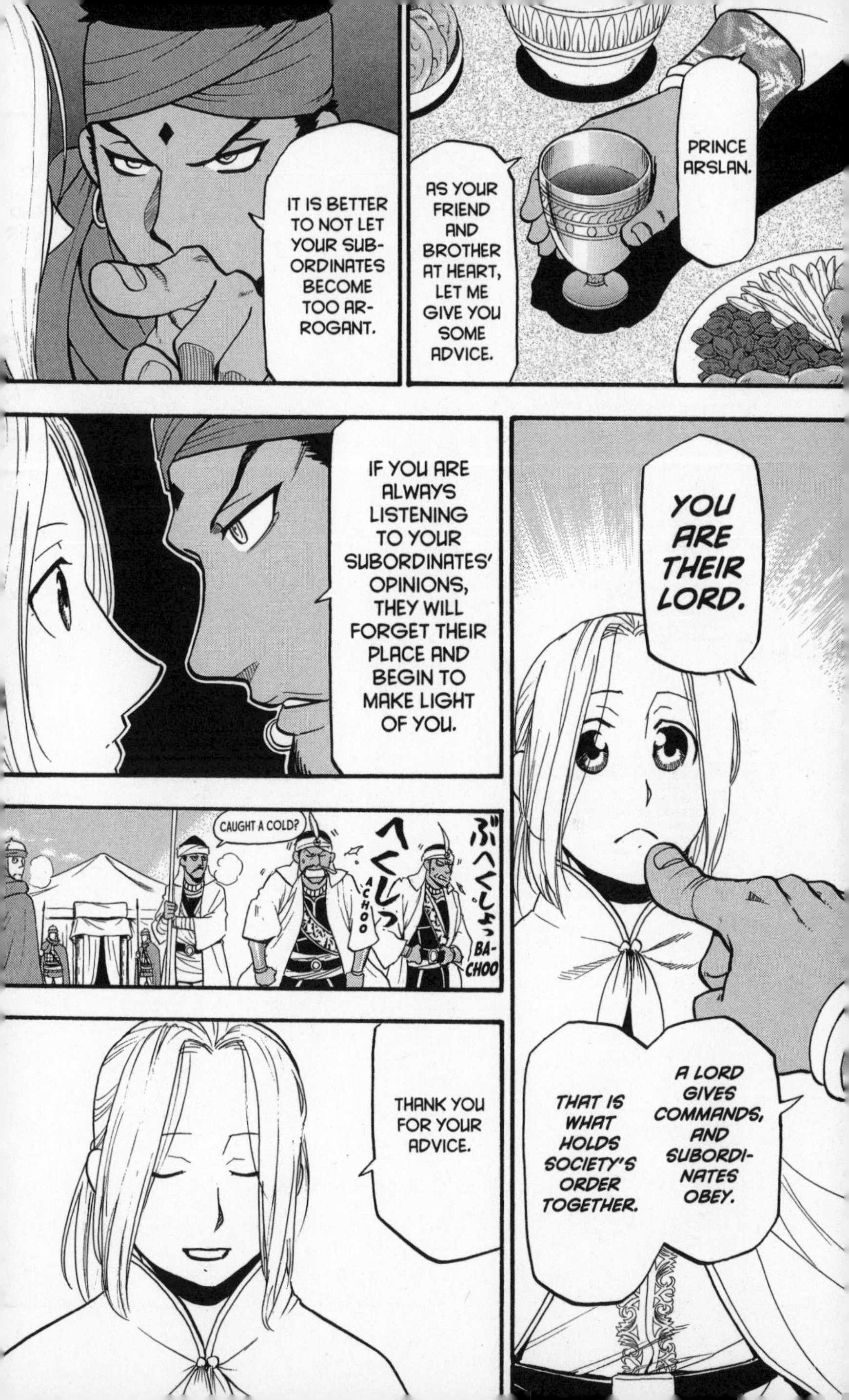
PRINCE ARSLAN.
AS YOUR FRIEND AND BROTHER AT HEART, LET ME GIVE YOU SOME ADVICE.
IT IS BETTER TO NOT LET YOUR SUBORDINATES BECOME TOO ARROGANT.
YOU ARE THEIR LORD.
A LORD GIVES COMMANDS, AND SUBORDINATES OBEY.
THAT IS WHAT HOLDS SOCIETY'S ORDER TOGETHER.
IF YOU ARE ALWAYS LISTENING TO YOUR SUBORDINATES' OPINIONS, THEY WILL FORGET THEIR PLACE AND BEGIN TO MAKE LIGHT OF YOU.
ぶへくしょっ
BA-CHOO
へくしっ
ACHOO
CAUGHT A COLD?
THANK YOU FOR YOUR ADVICE.

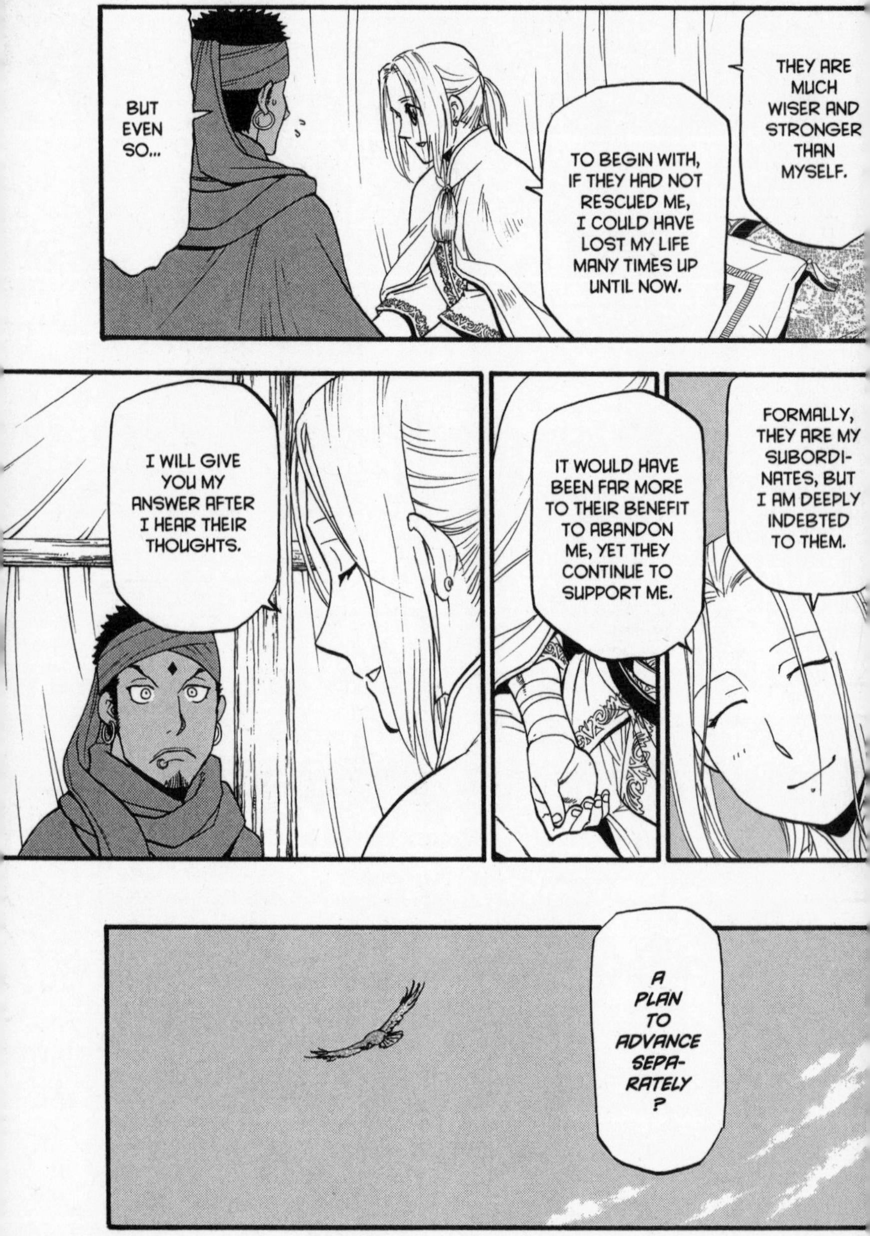
THEY ARE MUCH WISER AND STRONGER THAN MYSELF.
TO BEGIN WITH, IF THEY HAD NOT RESCUED ME, I COULD HAVE LOST MY LIFE MANY TIMES UP UNTIL NOW.
BUT EVEN SO...
FORMALLY, THEY ARE MY SUBORDI-NATES, BUT I AM DEEPLY INDEBTED TO THEM.
IT WOULD HAVE BEEN FAR MORE TO THEIR BENEFIT TO ABANDON ME, YET THEY CONTINUE TO SUPPORT ME.
I WILL GIVE YOU MY ANSWER AFTER I HEAR THEIR THOUGHTS.
A PLAN TO ADVANCE SEPA-RATELY ?

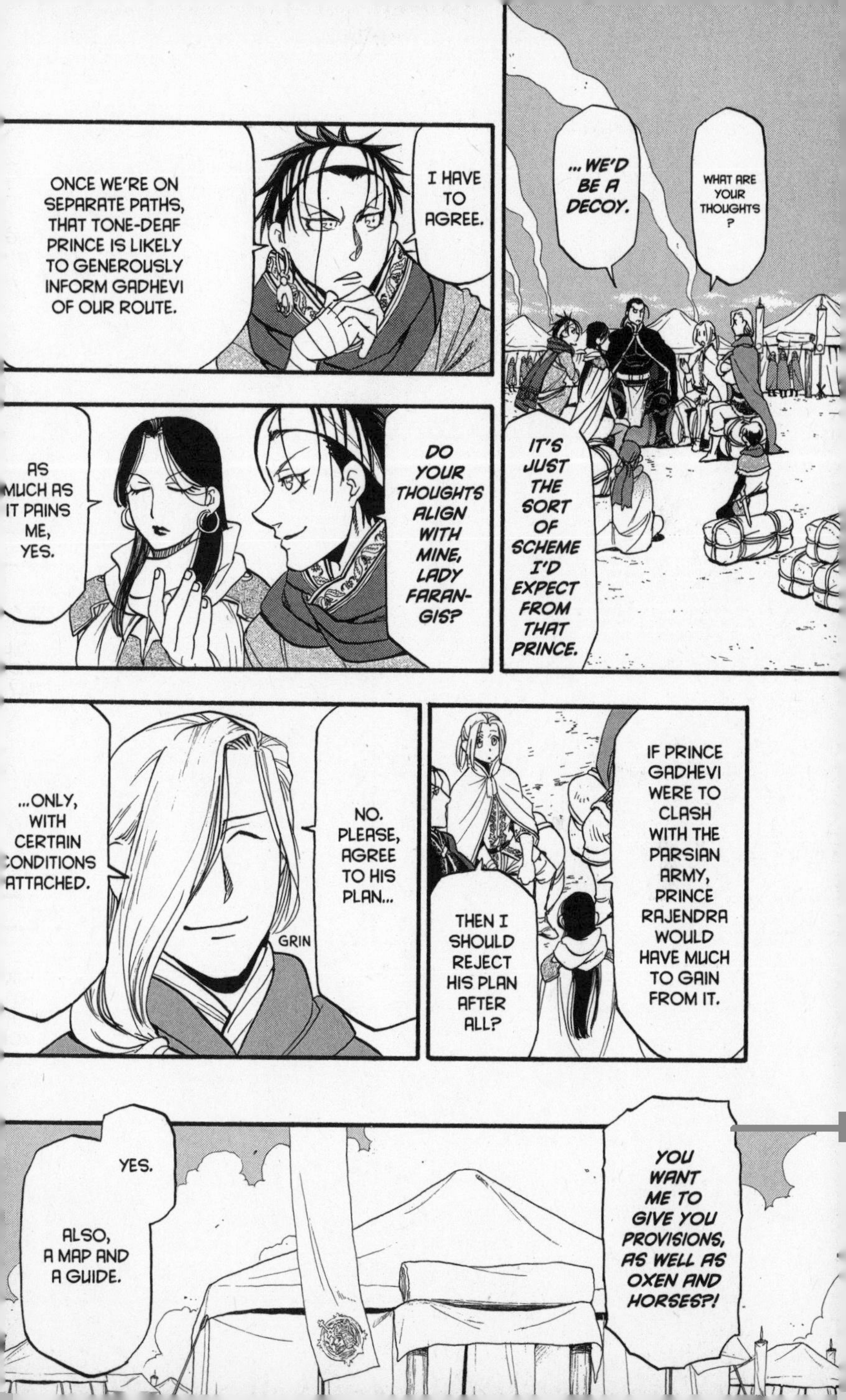
WHAT ARE YOUR THOUGHTS?
...WE'D BE A DECOY.
IT'S JUST THE SORT OF SCHEME I'D EXPECT FROM THAT PRINCE.
I HAVE TO AGREE.
ONCE WE'RE ON SEPARATE PATHS, THAT TONE-DEAF PRINCE IS LIKELY TO GENEROUSLY INFORM GADHEVI OF OUR ROUTE.
DO YOUR THOUGHTS ALIGN WITH MINE, LADY FARANGIS?
AS MUCH AS IT PAINS ME, YES.
IF PRINCE GADHEVI WERE TO CLASH WITH THE PARSIAN ARMY, PRINCE RAJENDRA WOULD HAVE MUCH TO GAIN FROM IT.
THEN I SHOULD REJECT HIS PLAN AFTER ALL?
NO. PLEASE, AGREE TO HIS PLAN...
GRIN
...ONLY, WITH CERTAIN CONDITIONS ATTACHED.
YOU WANT ME TO GIVE YOU PROVISIONS, AS WELL AS OXEN AND HORSES?!
YES.
ALSO, A MAP AND A GUIDE.

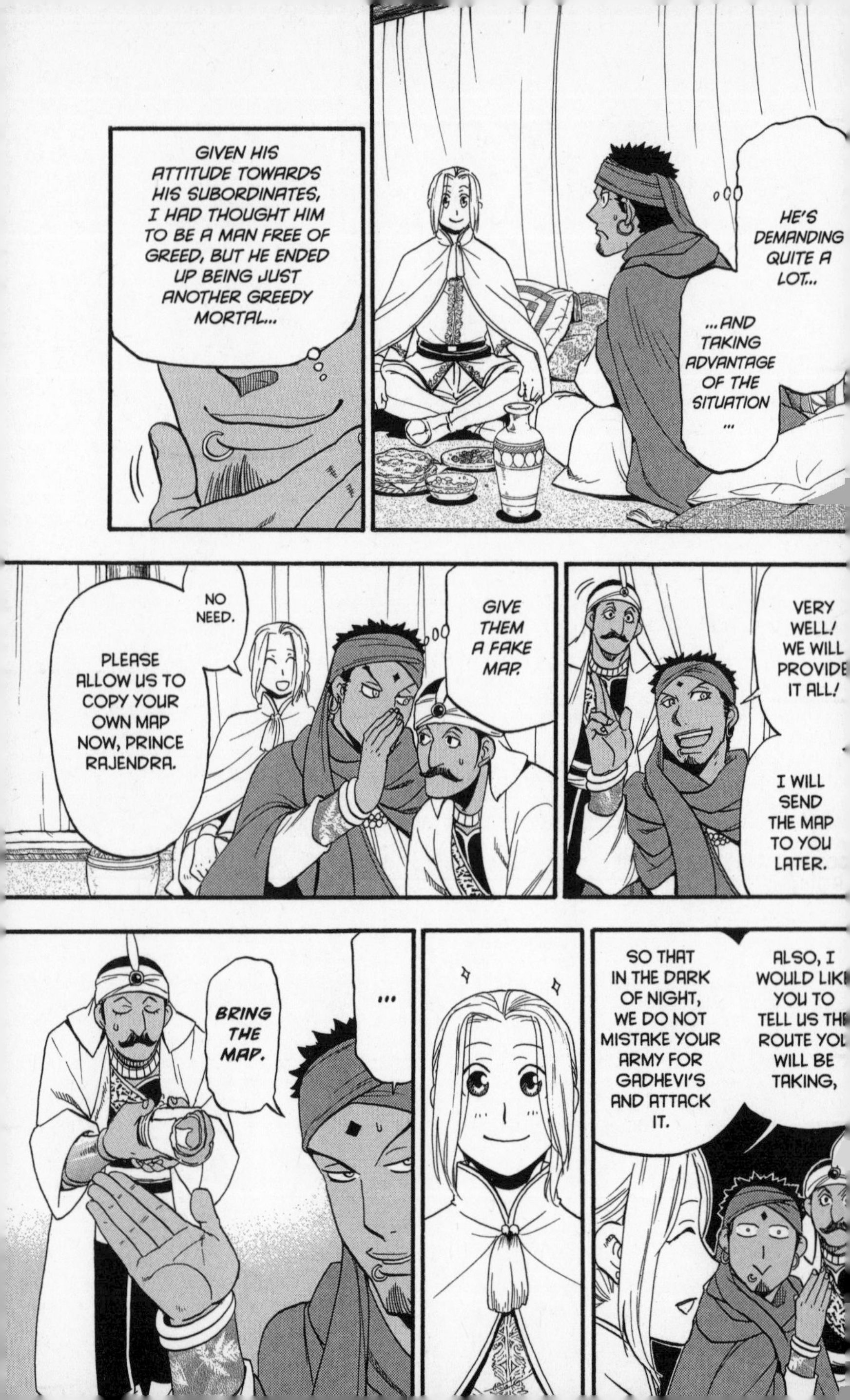
HE'S DEMANDING QUITE A LOT...
...AND TAKING ADVANTAGE OF THE SITUATION ...
GIVEN HIS ATTITUDE TOWARDS HIS SUBORDINATES, I HAD THOUGHT HIM TO BE A MAN FREE OF GREED, BUT HE ENDED UP BEING JUST ANOTHER GREEDY MORTAL...
VERY WELL! WE WILL PROVID IT ALL!
I WILL SEND THE MAP TO YOU LATER.
GIVE THEM A FAKE MAP.
NO NEED.
PLEASE ALLOW US TO COPY YOUR OWN MAP NOW, PRINCE RAJENDRA.
ALSO, I WOULD LIK YOU TO TELL US TH ROUTE YO WILL BE TAKING,
SO THAT IN THE DARK OF NIGHT, WE DO NOT MISTAKE YOUR ARMY FOR GADHEVI'S AND ATTACK IT.
...
BRING THE MAP.

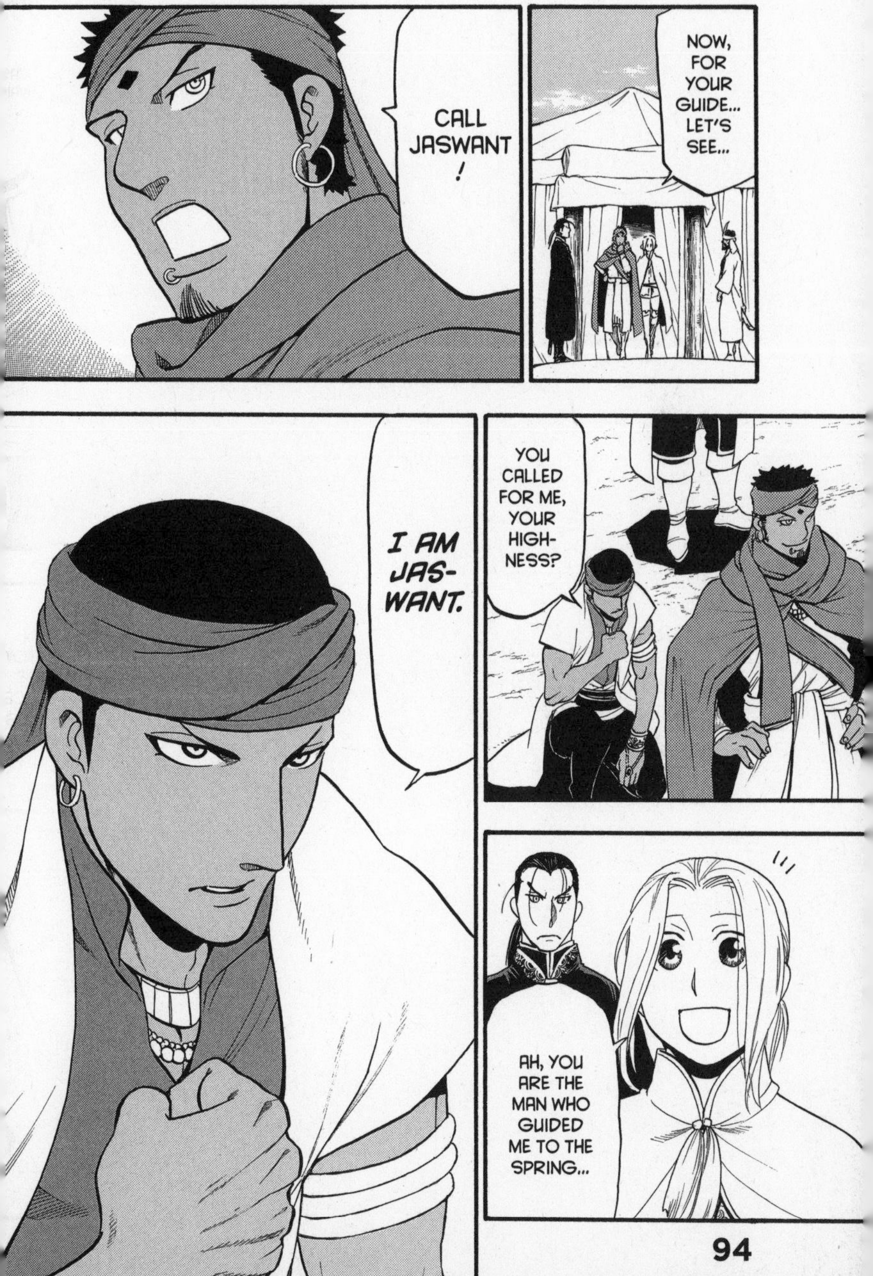
NOW, FOR YOUR GUIDE... LET'S SEE...
CALL JASWANT!
YOU CALLED FOR ME, YOUR HIGHNESS?
AH, YOU ARE THE MAN WHO GUIDED ME TO THE SPRING...
I AM JASWANT.

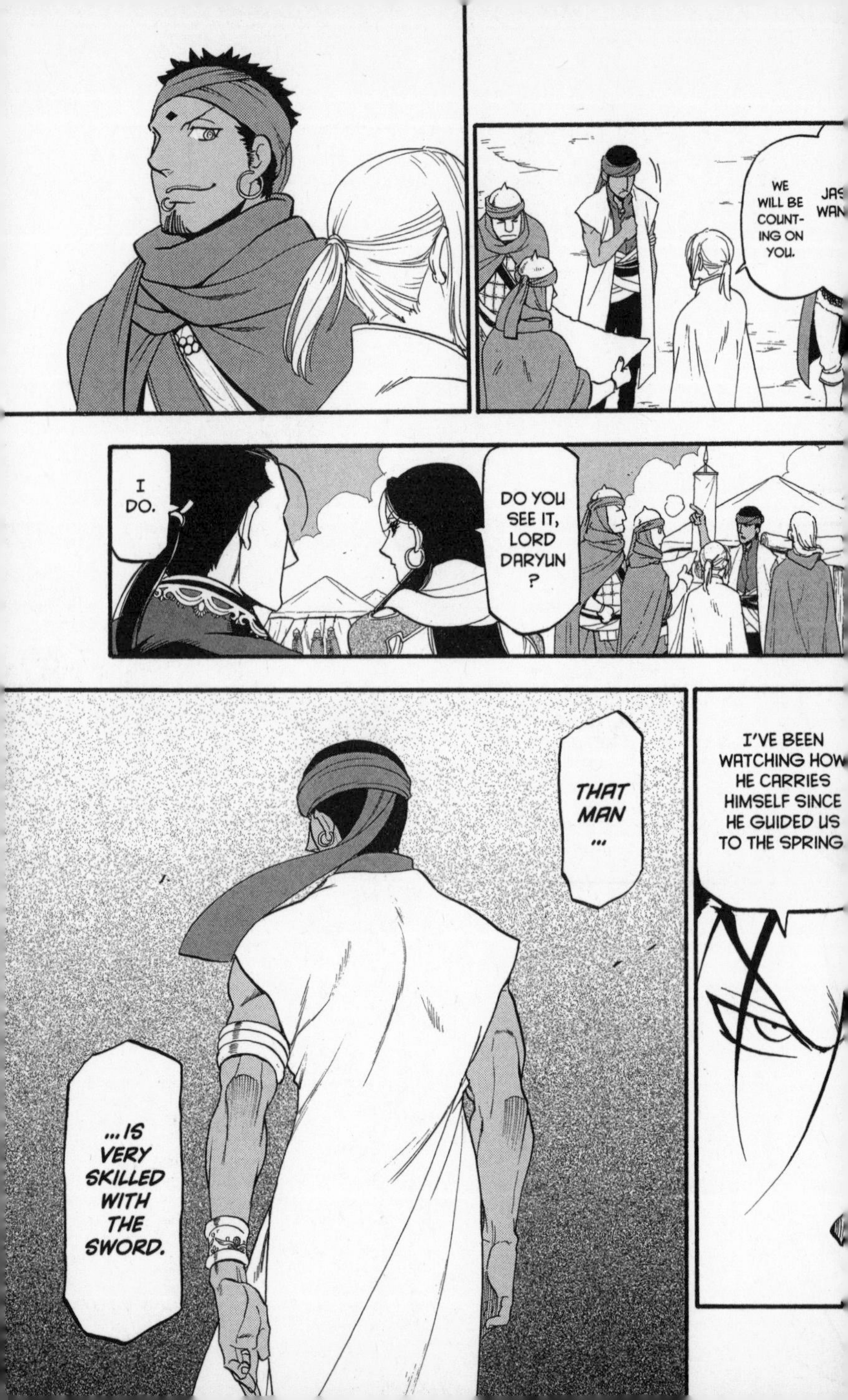
JAS
WAN
WE WILL BE COUNTING ON YOU.
DO YOU SEE IT, LORD DARYUN?
I DO.
I'VE BEEN WATCHING HOW HE CARRIES HIMSELF SINCE HE GUIDED US TO THE SPRING
THAT MAN ...
...IS VERY SKILLED WITH THE SWORD.

THE HEROIC LEGEND OF
ARSLAN

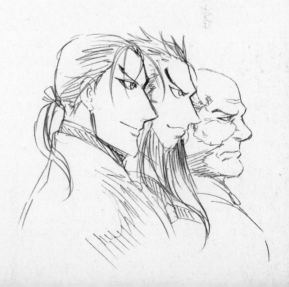

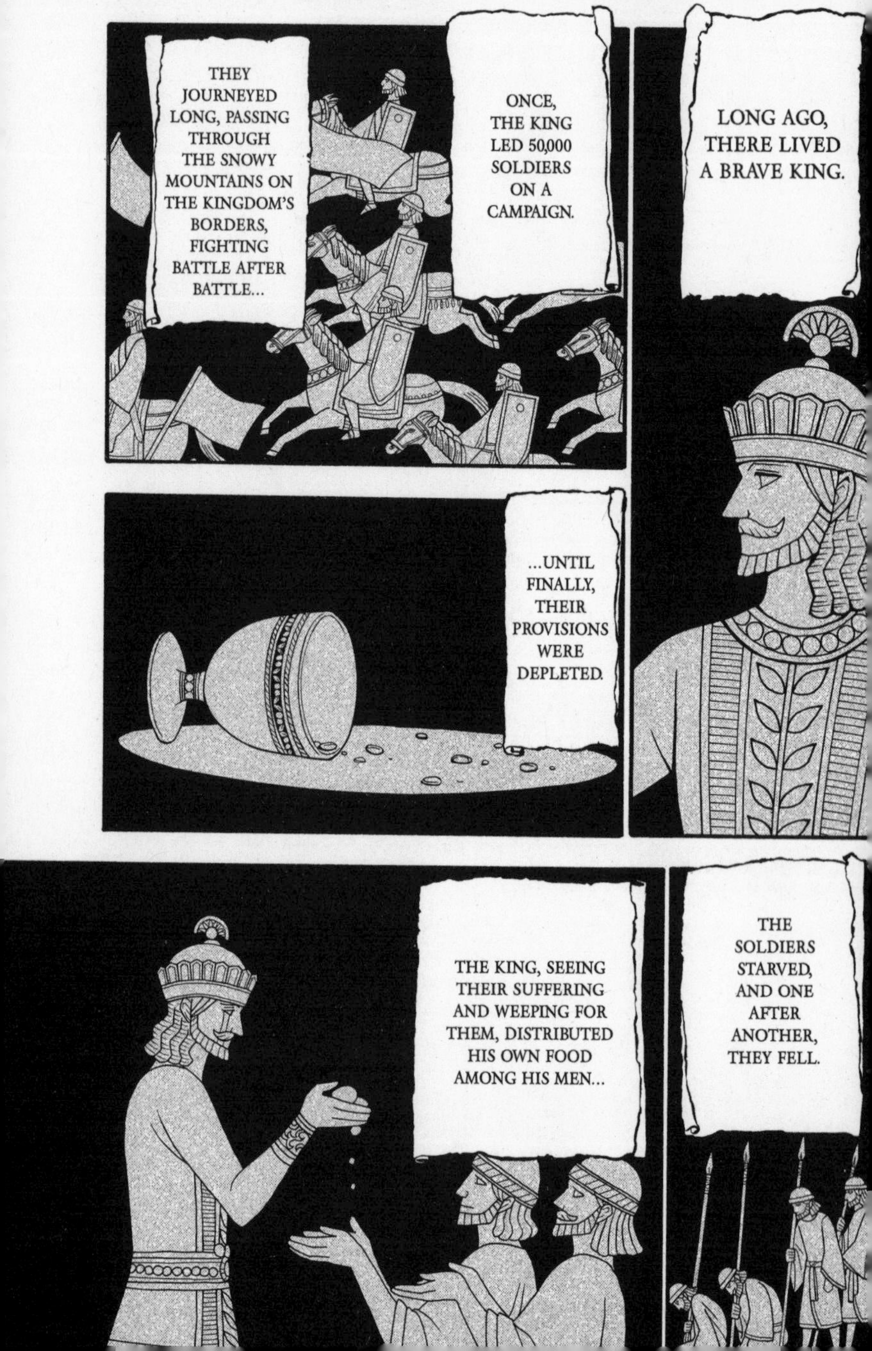
LONG AGO, THERE LIVED A BRAVE KING.
ONCE, THE KING LED 50,000 SOLDIERS ON A CAMPAIGN.
THEY JOURNEYED LONG, PASSING THROUGH THE SNOWY MOUNTAINS ON THE KINGDOM'S BORDERS, FIGHTING BATTLE AFTER BATTLE...
...UNTIL FINALLY, THEIR PROVISIONS WERE DEPLETED.
THE SOLDIERS STARVED, AND ONE AFTER ANOTHER, THEY FELL.
THE KING, SEEING THEIR SUFFERING AND WEEPING FOR THEM, DISTRIBUTED HIS OWN FOOD AMONG HIS MEN...

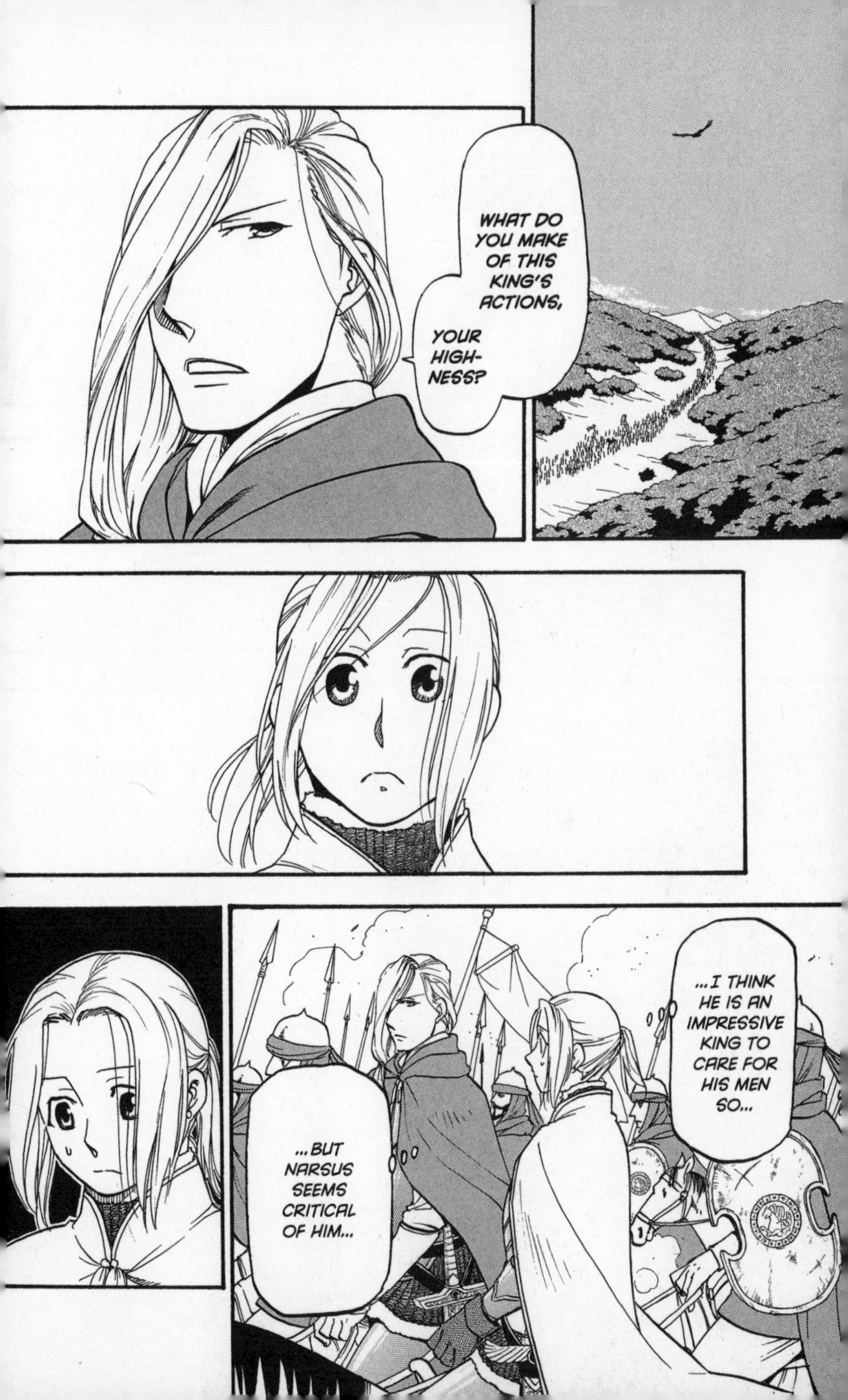
WHAT DO YOU MAKE OF THIS KING'S ACTIONS,
YOUR HIGHNESS?
...I THINK HE IS AN IMPRESSIVE KING TO CARE FOR HIS MEN SO...
...BUT NARSUS SEEMS CRITICAL OF HIM...

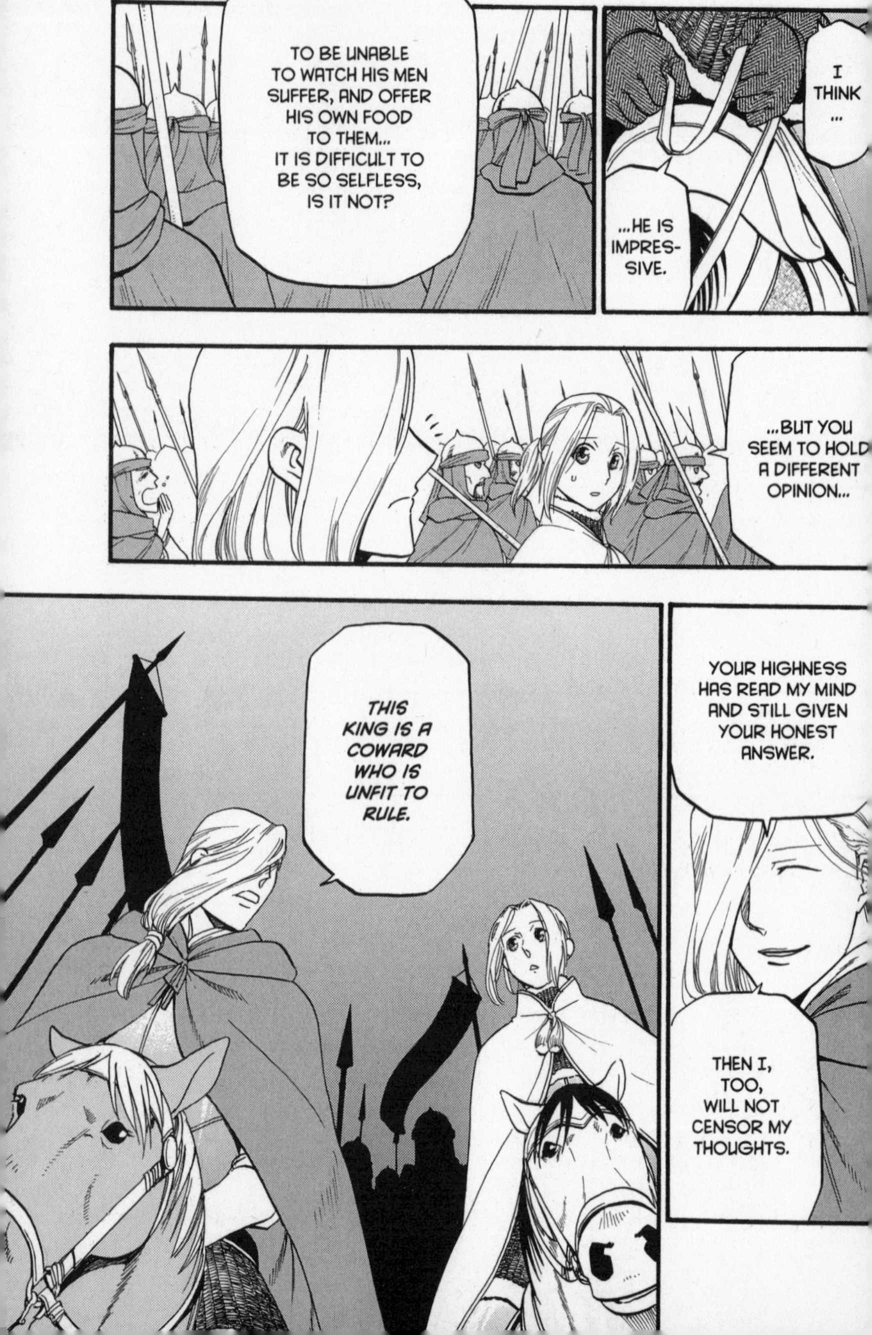
I THINK ...
...HE IS IMPRES-SIVE.
TO BE UNABLE TO WATCH HIS MEN SUFFER, AND OFFER HIS OWN FOOD TO THEM... IT IS DIFFICULT TO BE SO SELFLESS, IS IT NOT?
...BUT YOU SEEM TO HOLD A DIFFERENT OPINION...
YOUR HIGHNESS HAS READ MY MIND AND STILL GIVEN YOUR HONEST ANSWER.
THEN I, TOO, WILL NOT CENSOR MY THOUGHTS.
THIS KING IS A COWARD WHO IS UNFIT TO RULE.

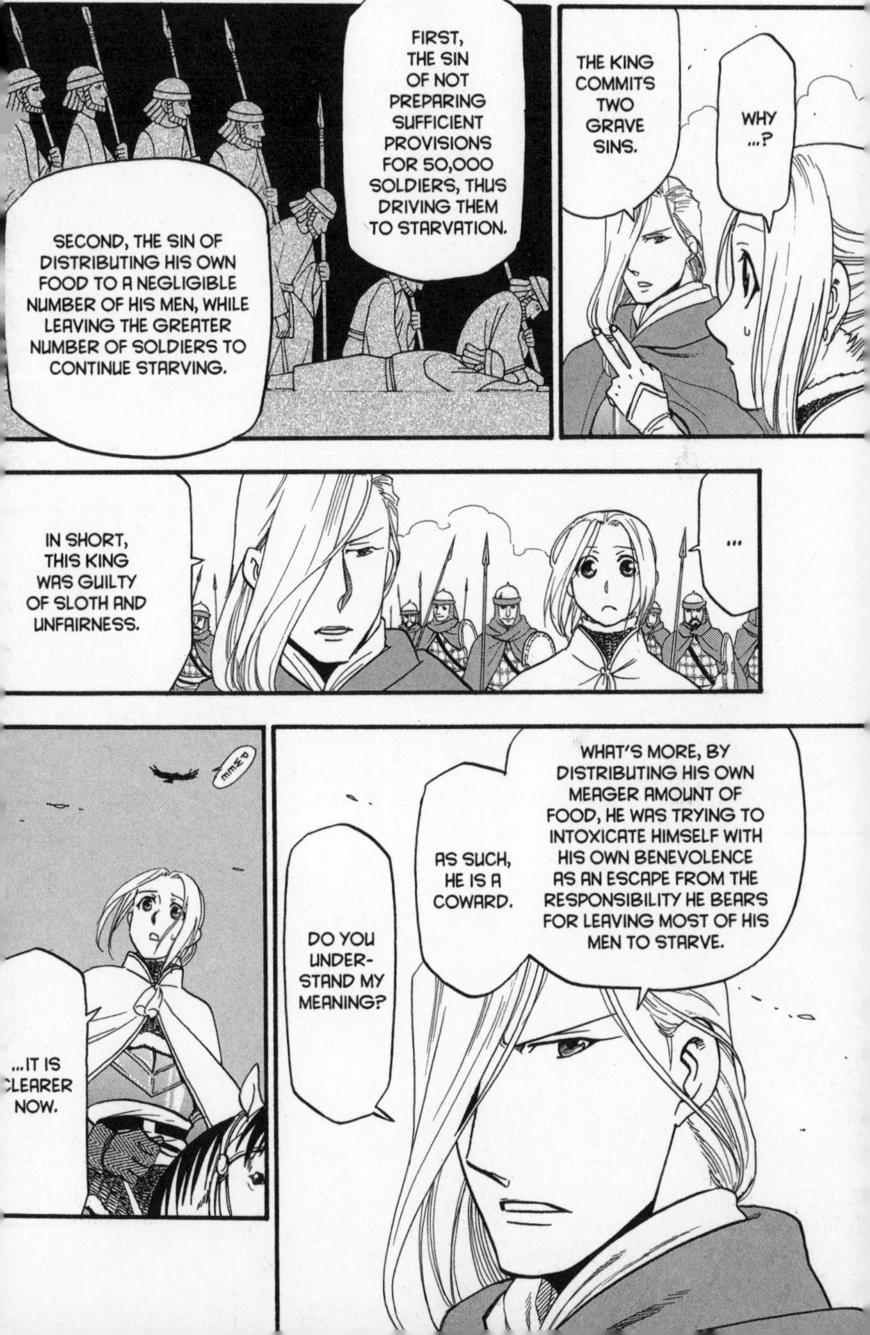
WHY ...?
THE KING COMMITS TWO GRAVE SINS.
FIRST, THE SIN OF NOT PREPARING SUFFICIENT PROVISIONS FOR 50,000 SOLDIERS, THUS DRIVING THEM TO STARVATION.
SECOND, THE SIN OF DISTRIBUTING HIS OWN FOOD TO A NEGLIGIBLE NUMBER OF HIS MEN, WHILE LEAVING THE GREATER NUMBER OF SOLDIERS TO CONTINUE STARVING.
...
IN SHORT, THIS KING WAS GUILTY OF SLOTH AND UNFAIRNESS.
WHAT'S MORE, BY DISTRIBUTING HIS OWN MEAGER AMOUNT OF FOOD, HE WAS TRYING TO INTOXICATE HIMSELF WITH HIS OWN BENEVOLENCE AS AN ESCAPE FROM THE RESPONSIBILITY HE BEARS FOR LEAVING MOST OF HIS MEN TO STARVE.
AS SUCH, HE IS A COWARD.
DO YOU UNDER-STAND MY MEANING?
...IT IS CLEARER NOW.

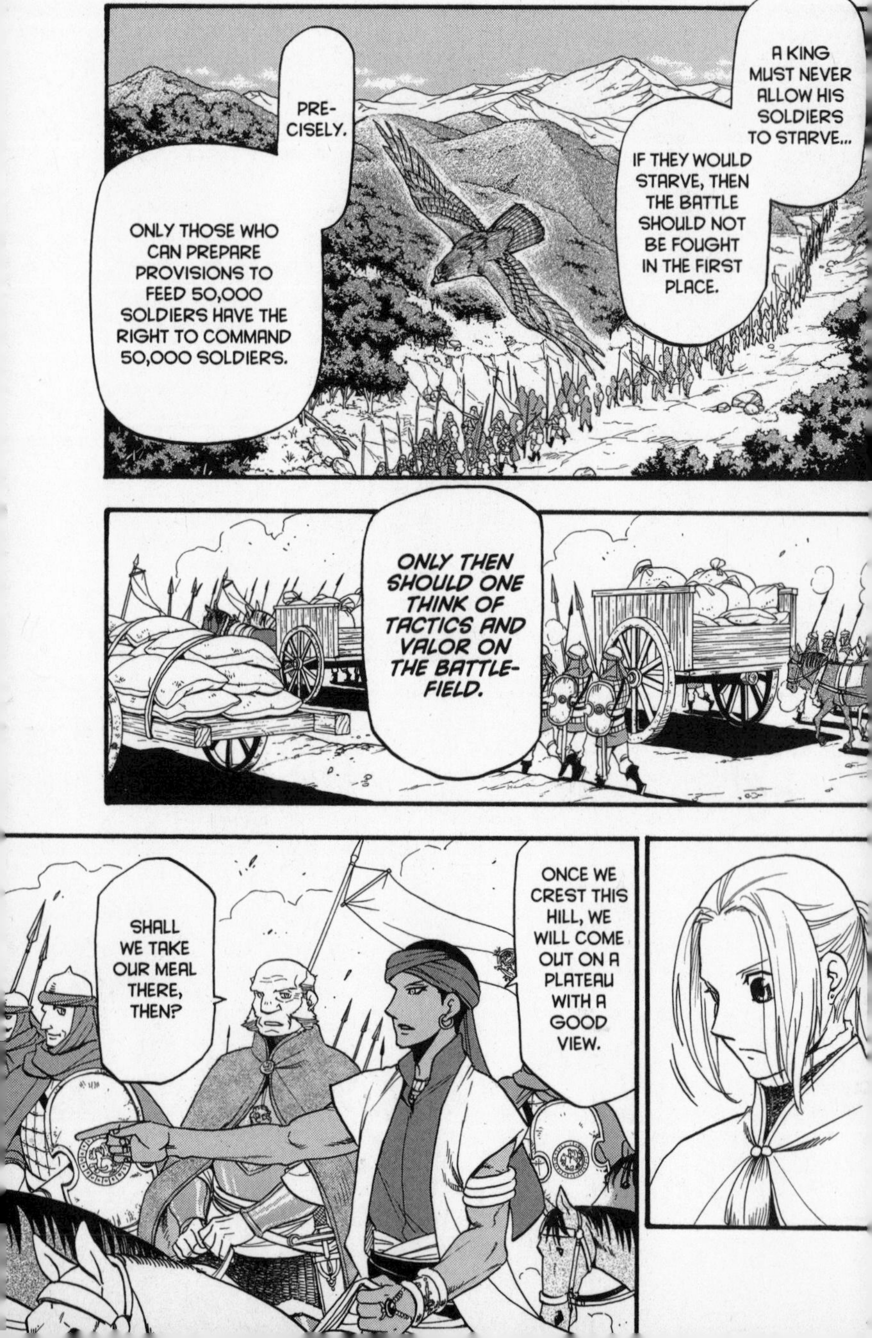
A KING MUST NEVER ALLOW HIS SOLDIERS TO STARVE...
IF THEY WOULD STARVE, THEN THE BATTLE SHOULD NOT BE FOUGHT IN THE FIRST PLACE.
PRE-CISELY.
ONLY THOSE WHO CAN PREPARE PROVISIONS TO FEED 50,000 SOLDIERS HAVE THE RIGHT TO COMMAND 50,000 SOLDIERS.
ONLY THEN SHOULD ONE THINK OF TACTICS AND VALOR ON THE BATTLE-FIELD.
ONCE WE CREST THIS HILL, WE WILL COME OUT ON A PLATEAU WITH A GOOD VIEW.
SHALL WE TAKE OUR MEAL THERE, THEN?

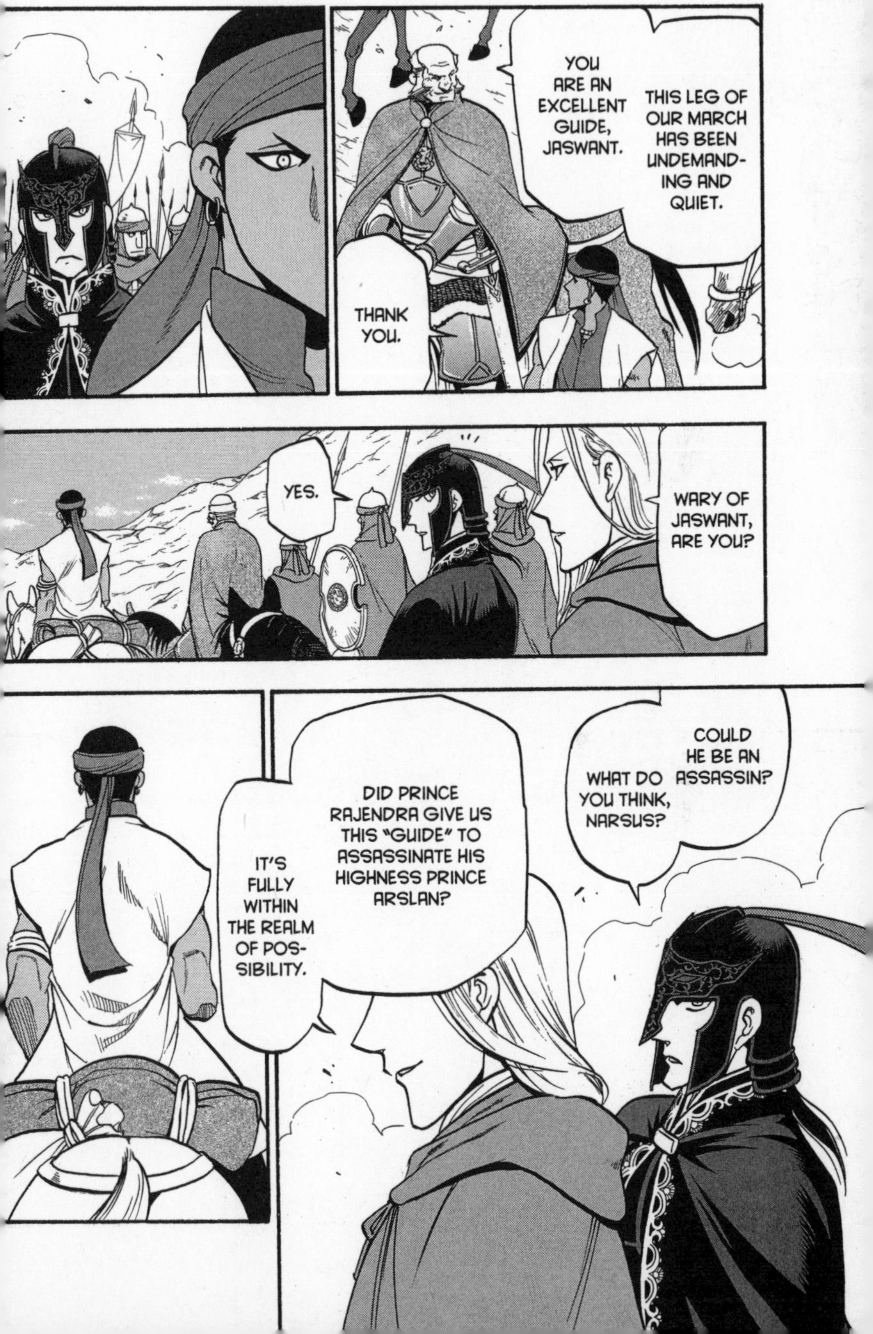
THIS LEG OF OUR MARCH HAS BEEN UNDEMAND-ING AND QUIET.
YOU ARE AN EXCELLENT GUIDE, JASWANT.
THANK YOU.
WARY OF JASWANT, ARE YOU?
YES.
COULD HE BE AN ASSASSIN?
WHAT DO YOU THINK, NARSUS?
DID PRINCE RAJENDRA GIVE US THIS "GUIDE" TO ASSASSINATE HIS HIGHNESS PRINCE ARSLAN?
IT'S FULLY WITHIN THE REALM OF POS-SIBILITY.

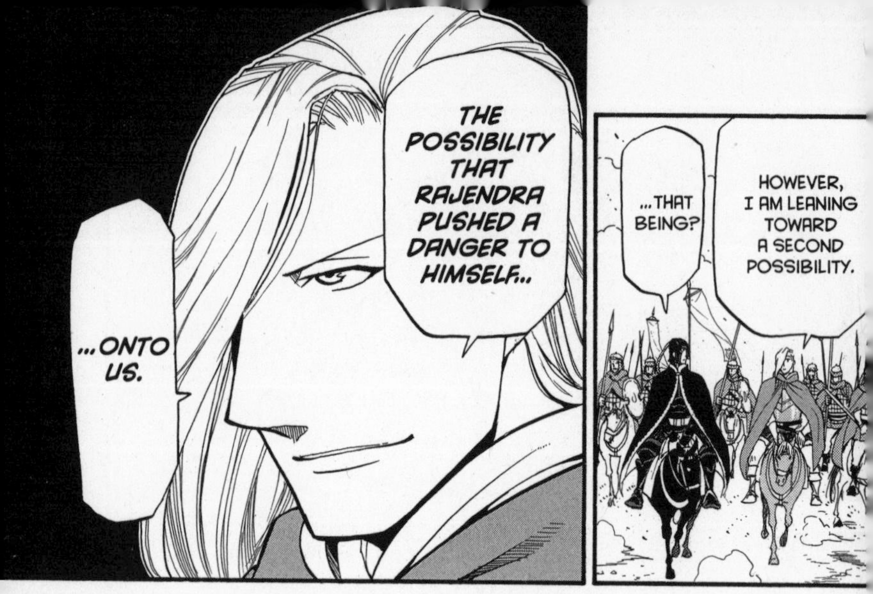
HOWEVER, I AM LEANING TOWARD A SECOND POSSIBILITY.
...THAT BEING?
THE POSSIBILITY THAT RAJENDRA PUSHED A DANGER TO HIMSELF...
...ONTO US.

Chapter 44: The Guide in the Dark of Night

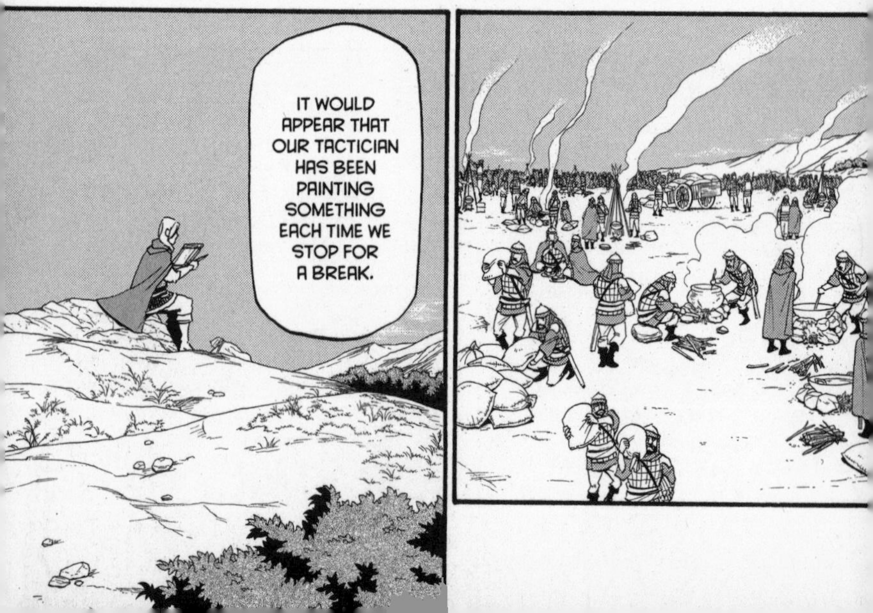
IT WOULD APPEAR THAT OUR TACTICIAN HAS BEEN PAINTING SOMETHING EACH TIME WE STOP FOR A BREAK.

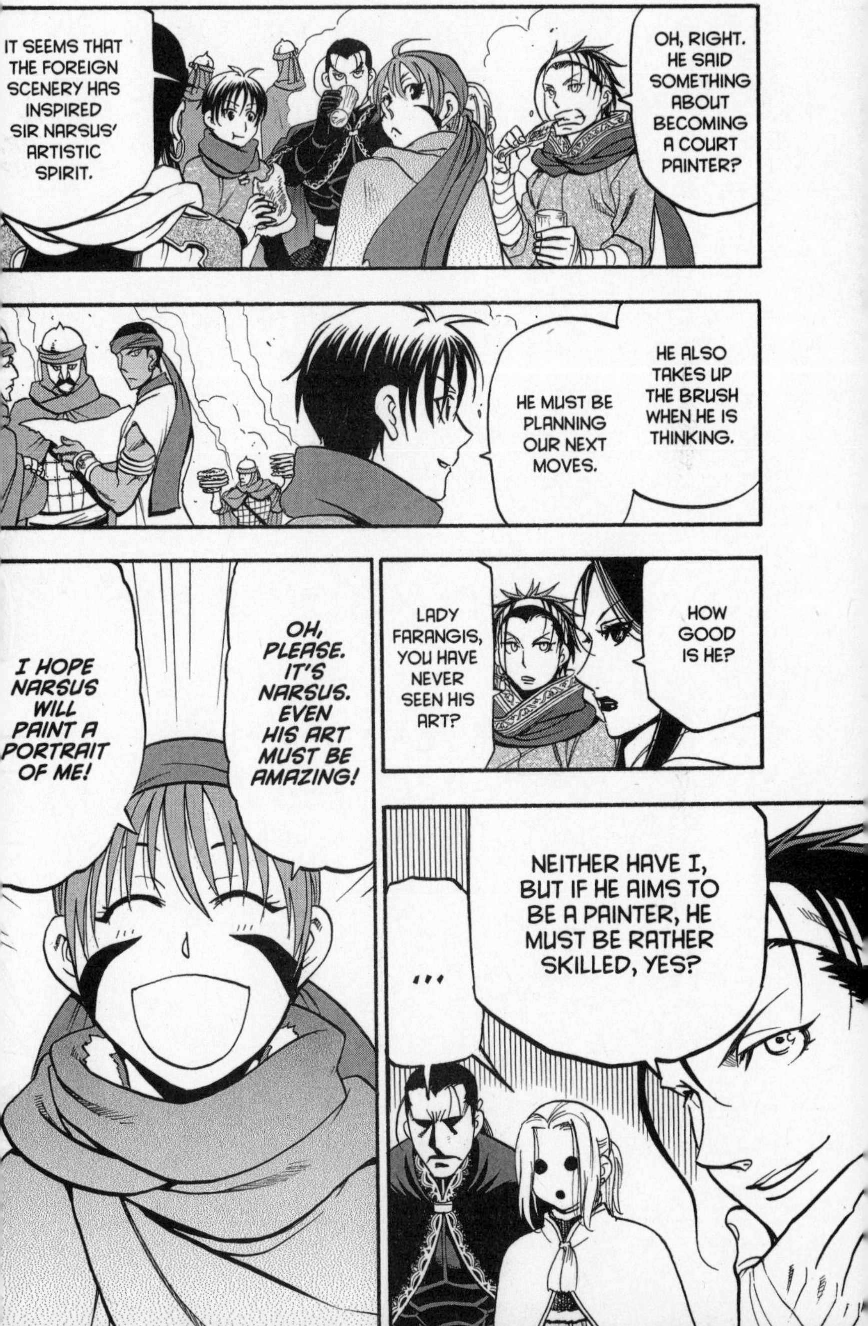
OH, RIGHT. HE SAID SOMETHING ABOUT BECOMING A COURT PAINTER?
IT SEEMS THAT THE FOREIGN SCENERY HAS INSPIRED SIR NARSUS' ARTISTIC SPIRIT.
HE ALSO TAKES UP THE BRUSH WHEN HE IS THINKING.
HE MUST BE PLANNING OUR NEXT MOVES.
HOW GOOD IS HE?
LADY FARANGIS, YOU HAVE NEVER SEEN HIS ART?
NEITHER HAVE I, BUT IF HE AIMS TO BE A PAINTER, HE MUST BE RATHER SKILLED, YES?
...
OH, PLEASE. IT'S NARSUS. EVEN HIS ART MUST BE AMAZING!
I HOPE NARSUS WILL PAINT A PORTRAIT OF ME!

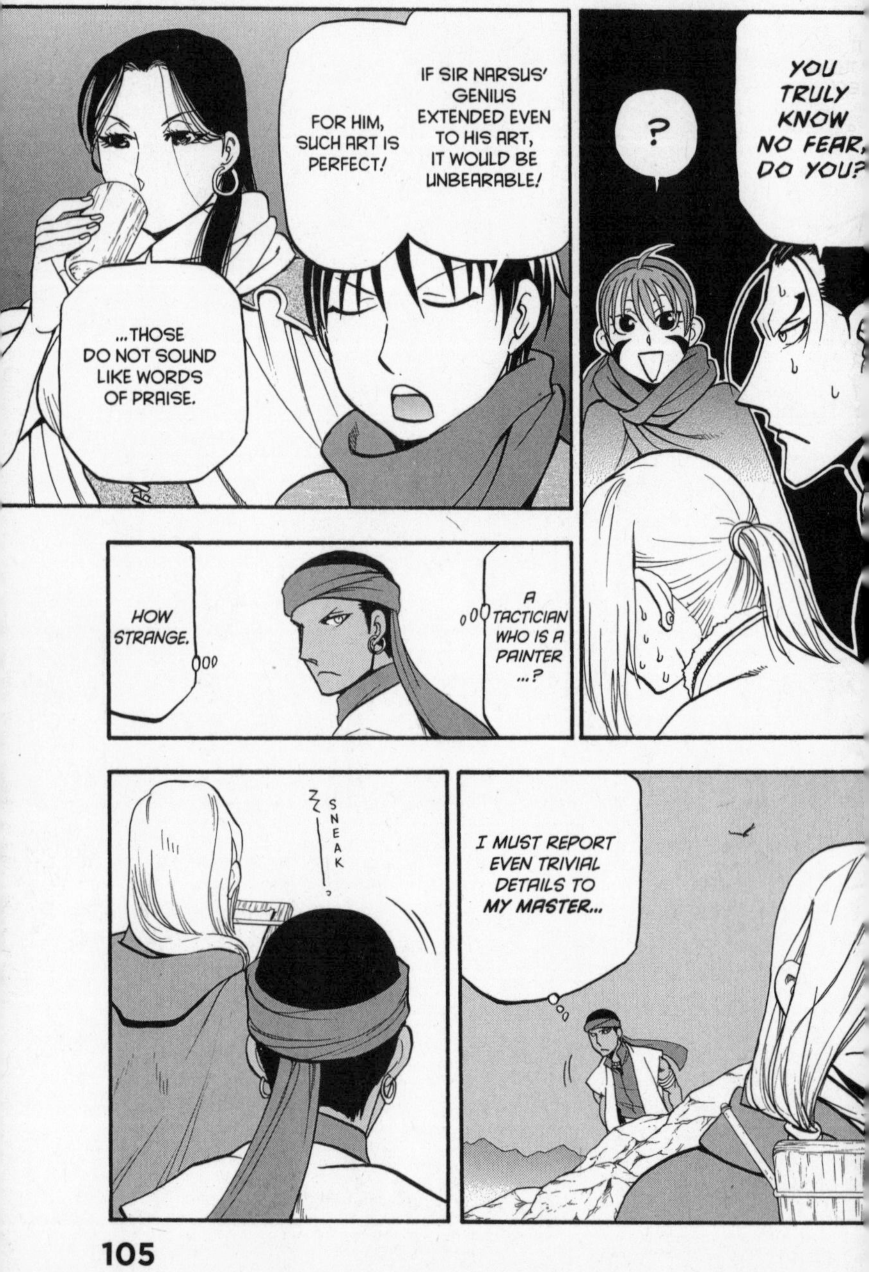
YOU TRULY KNOW NO FEAR, DO YOU?
?
IF SIR NARSUS' GENIUS EXTENDED EVEN TO HIS ART, IT WOULD BE UNBEARABLE!
FOR HIM, SUCH ART IS PERFECT!
...THOSE DO NOT SOUND LIKE WORDS OF PRAISE.
A TACTICIAN WHO IS A PAINTER ...?
HOW STRANGE.
I MUST REPORT EVEN TRIVIAL DETAILS TO MY MASTER...
SNEAK

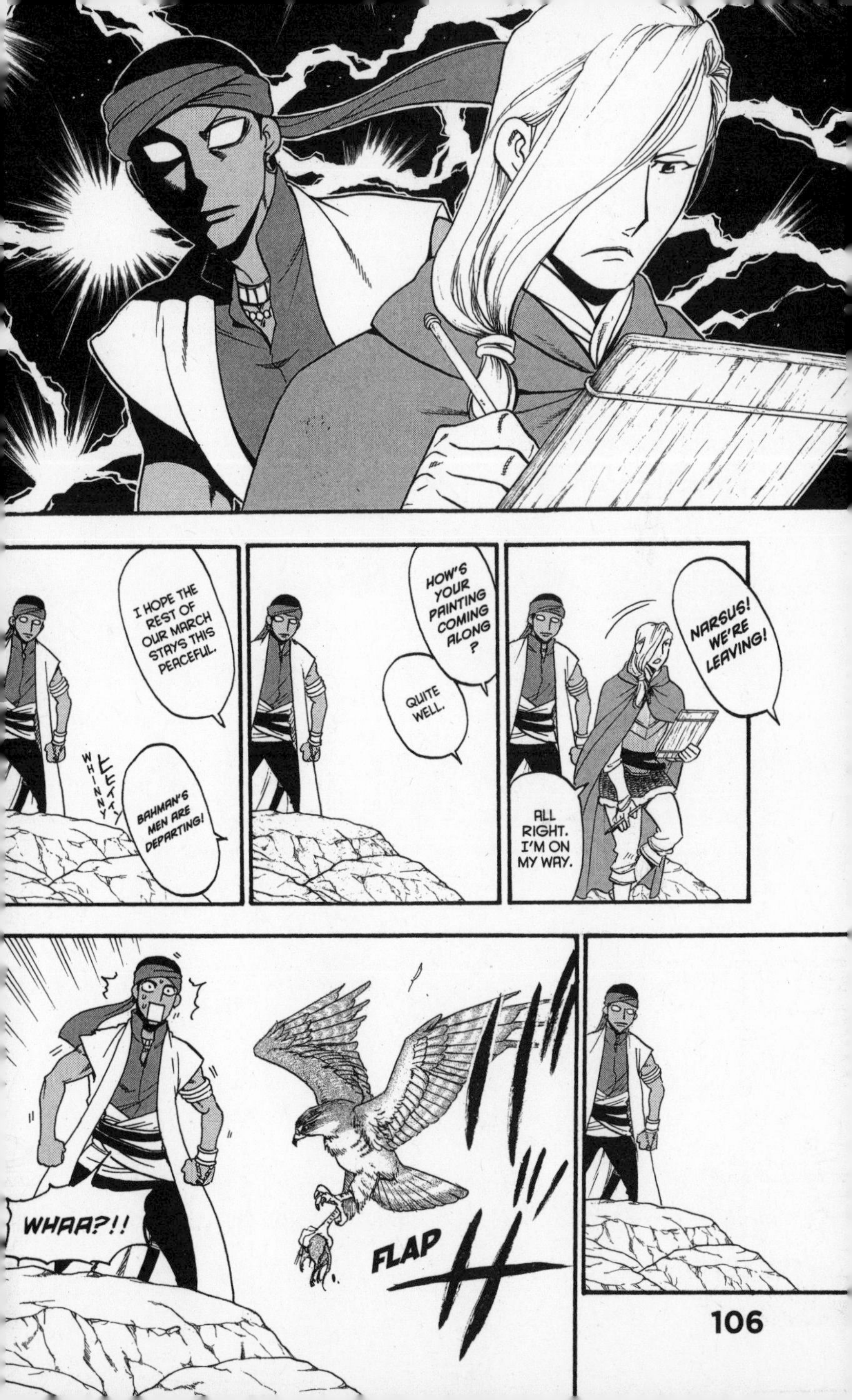
NARSUS! WE'RE LEAVING!
ALL RIGHT. I'M ON MY WAY.
HOW'S YOUR PAINTING COMING ALONG?
QUITE WELL.
I HOPE THE REST OF OUR MARCH STAYS THIS PEACEFUL.
WHINNY
BAHMAN'S MEN ARE DEPARTING!
FLAP
WHAA?!!

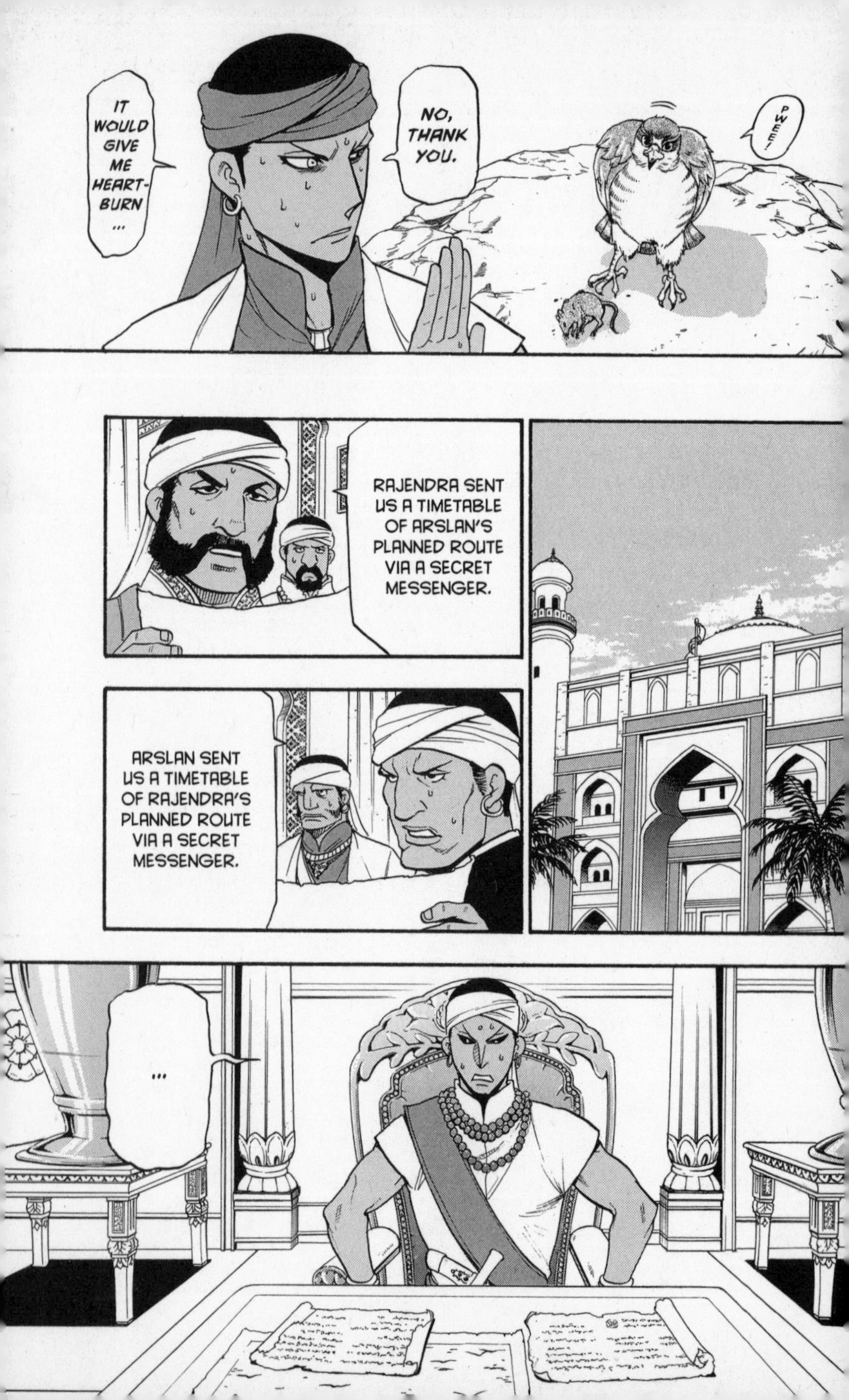
PWEE!
NO, THANK YOU.
IT WOULD GIVE ME HEART-BURN ...
RAJENDRA SENT US A TIMETABLE OF ARSLAN'S PLANNED ROUTE VIA A SECRET MESSENGER.
ARSLAN SENT US A TIMETABLE OF RAJENDRA'S PLANNED ROUTE VIA A SECRET MESSENGER.
...

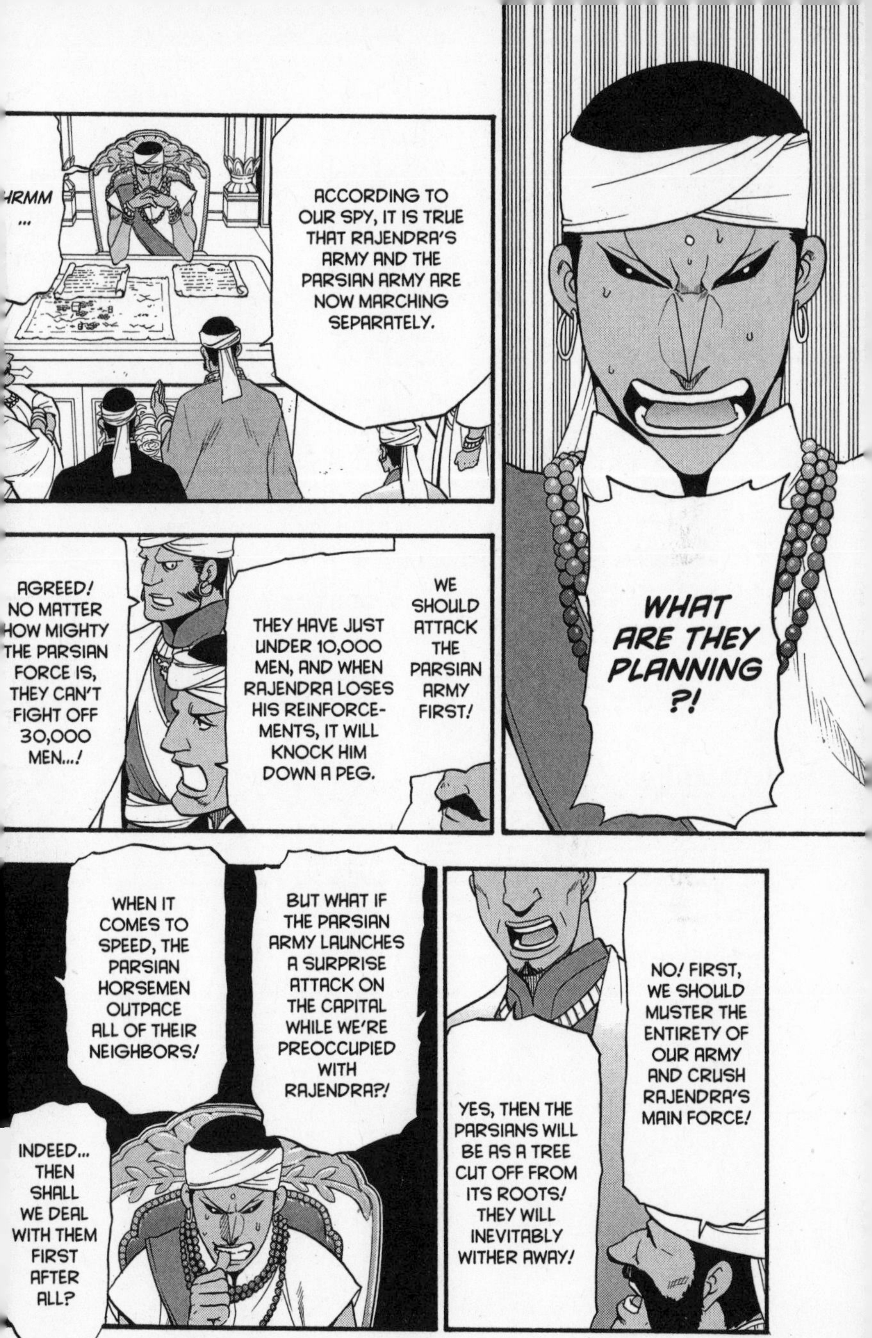
WHAT ARE THEY PLANNING ?!
ACCORDING TO OUR SPY, IT IS TRUE THAT RAJENDRA'S ARMY AND THE PARSIAN ARMY ARE NOW MARCHING SEPARATELY.
HRMM ...
WE SHOULD ATTACK THE PARSIAN ARMY FIRST!
THEY HAVE JUST UNDER 10,000 MEN, AND WHEN RAJENDRA LOSES HIS REINFORCE-MENTS, IT WILL KNOCK HIM DOWN A PEG.
AGREED! NO MATTER HOW MIGHTY THE PARSIAN FORCE IS, THEY CAN'T FIGHT OFF 30,000 MEN...!
NO! FIRST, WE SHOULD MUSTER THE ENTIRETY OF OUR ARMY AND CRUSH RAJENDRA'S MAIN FORCE!
YES, THEN THE PARSIANS WILL BE AS A TREE CUT OFF FROM ITS ROOTS! THEY WILL INEVITABLY WITHER AWAY!
BUT WHAT IF THE PARSIAN ARMY LAUNCHES A SURPRISE ATTACK ON THE CAPITAL WHILE WE'RE PREOCCUPIED WITH RAJENDRA?!
WHEN IT COMES TO SPEED, THE PARSIAN HORSEMEN OUTPACE ALL OF THEIR NEIGHBORS!
INDEED... THEN SHALL WE DEAL WITH THEM FIRST AFTER ALL?

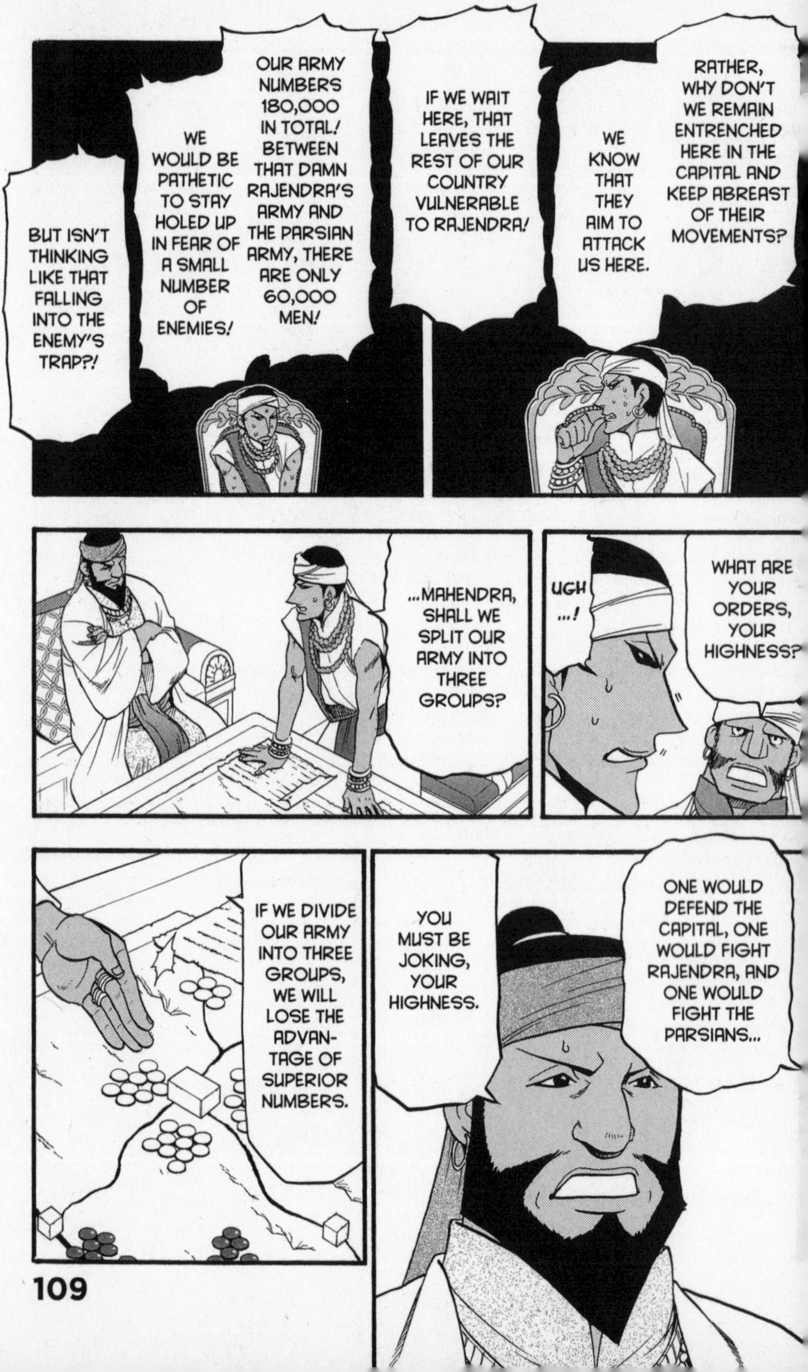
RATHER, WHY DON'T WE REMAIN ENTRENCHED HERE IN THE CAPITAL AND KEEP ABREAST OF THEIR MOVEMENTS?
WE KNOW THAT THEY AIM TO ATTACK US HERE.
IF WE WAIT HERE, THAT LEAVES THE REST OF OUR COUNTRY VULNERABLE TO RAJENDRA!
OUR ARMY NUMBERS 180,000 IN TOTAL! BETWEEN THAT DAMN RAJENDRA'S ARMY AND THE PARSIAN ARMY, THERE ARE ONLY 60,000 MEN!
WE WOULD BE PATHETIC TO STAY HOLED UP IN FEAR OF A SMALL NUMBER OF ENEMIES!
BUT ISN'T THINKING LIKE THAT FALLING INTO THE ENEMY'S TRAP?!
WHAT ARE YOUR ORDERS, YOUR HIGHNESS?
UGH ...!
...MAHENDRA, SHALL WE SPLIT OUR ARMY INTO THREE GROUPS?
ONE WOULD DEFEND THE CAPITAL, ONE WOULD FIGHT RAJENDRA, AND ONE WOULD FIGHT THE PARSIANS...
YOU MUST BE JOKING, YOUR HIGHNESS.
IF WE DIVIDE OUR ARMY INTO THREE GROUPS, WE WILL LOSE THE ADVAN-TAGE OF SUPERIOR NUMBERS.

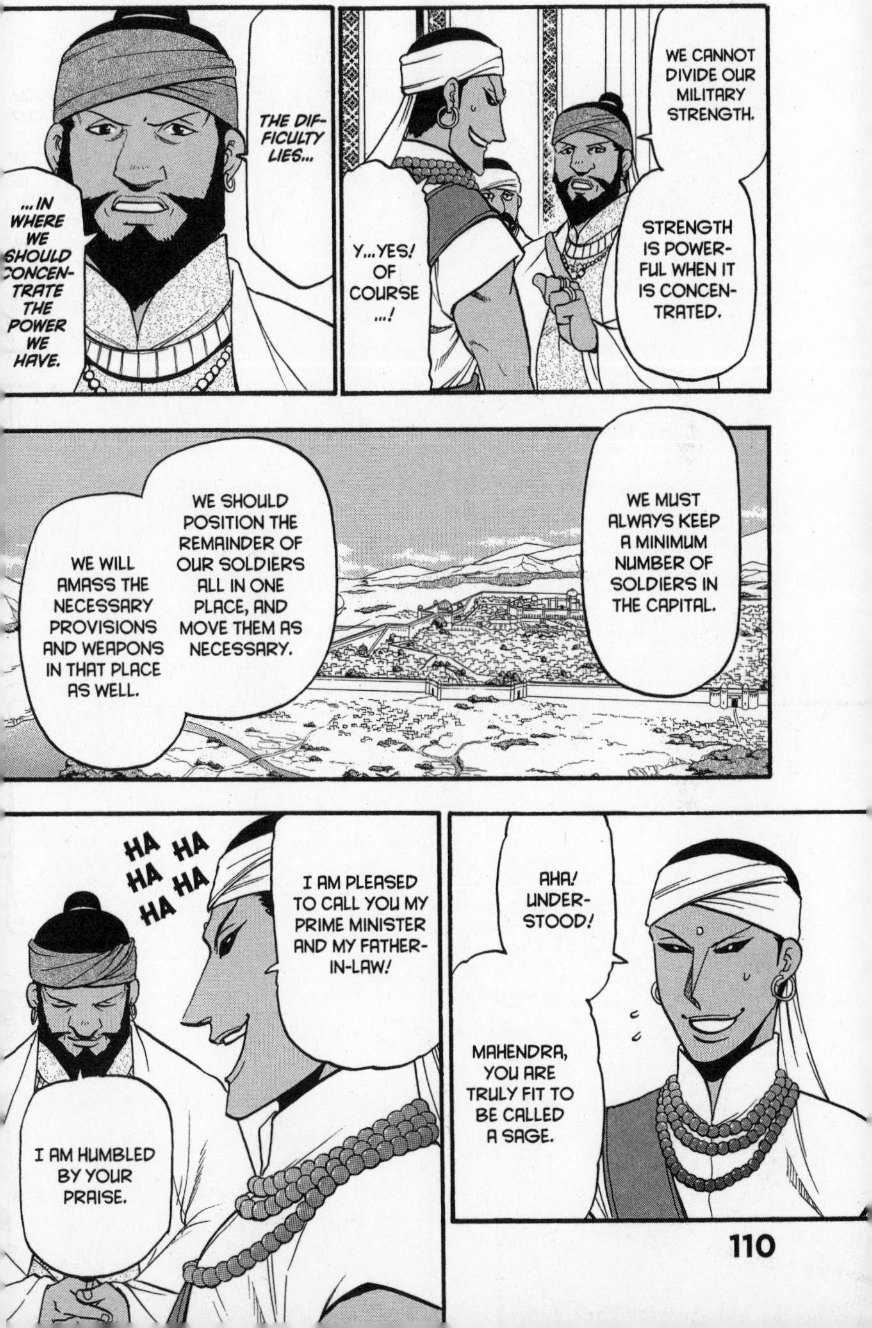
WE CANNOT DIVIDE OUR MILITARY STRENGTH.
STRENGTH IS POWERFUL WHEN IT IS CONCENTRATED.
Y...YES! OF COURSE ...!
THE DIFFICULTY LIES...
...IN WHERE WE SHOULD CONCENTRATE THE POWER WE HAVE.
WE MUST ALWAYS KEEP A MINIMUM NUMBER OF SOLDIERS IN THE CAPITAL.
WE SHOULD POSITION THE REMAINDER OF OUR SOLDIERS ALL IN ONE PLACE, AND MOVE THEM AS NECESSARY.
WE WILL AMASS THE NECESSARY PROVISIONS AND WEAPONS IN THAT PLACE AS WELL.
AHA! UNDERSTOOD!
MAHENDRA, YOU ARE TRULY FIT TO BE CALLED A SAGE.
HA HA HA HA HA HA
I AM PLEASED TO CALL YOU MY PRIME MINISTER AND MY FATHER-IN-LAW!
I AM HUMBLED BY YOUR PRAISE.

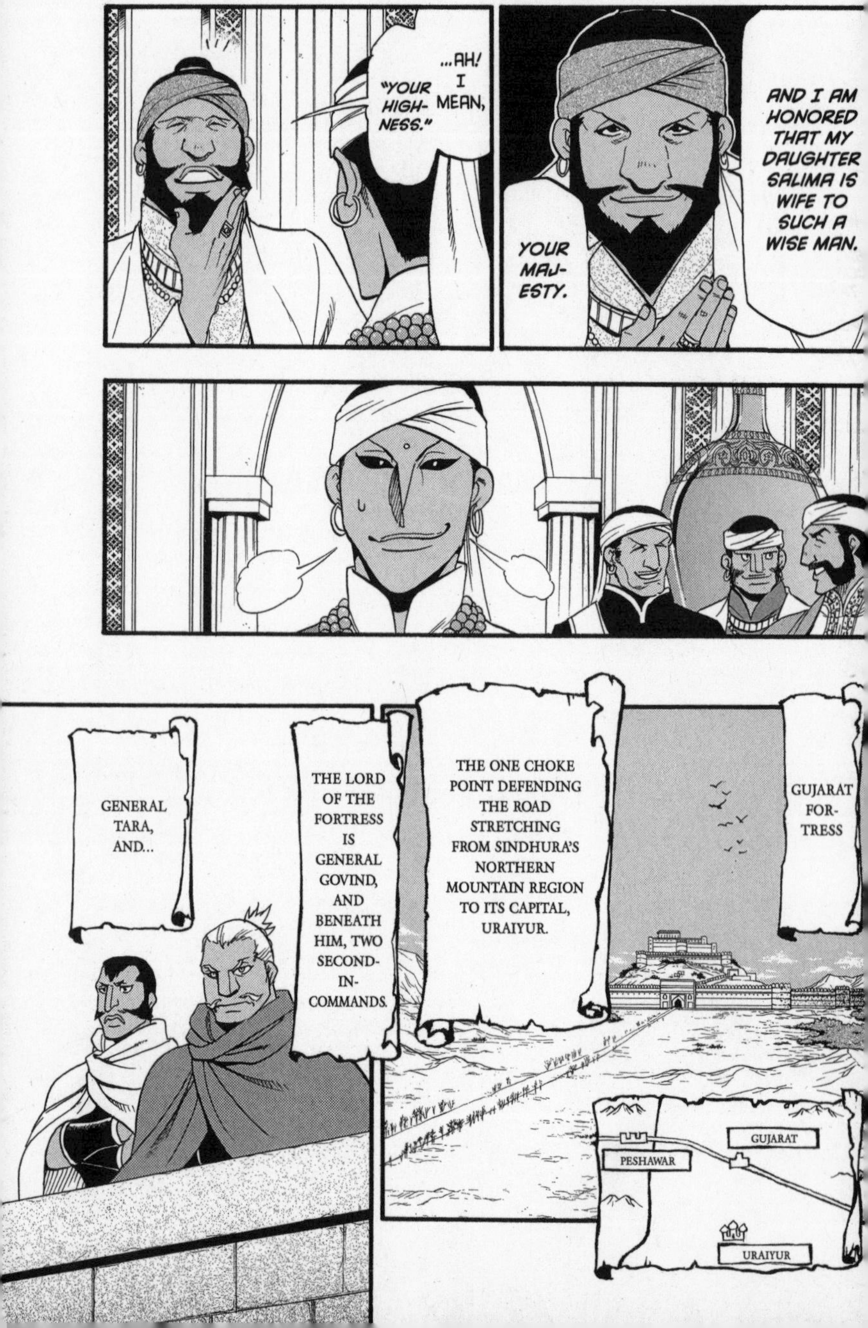
AND I AM HONORED THAT MY DAUGHTER SALIMA IS WIFE TO SUCH A WISE MAN.
YOUR MAJESTY.
...AH! I MEAN,
"YOUR HIGHNESS."
GUJARAT FORTRESS
THE ONE CHOKE POINT DEFENDING THE ROAD STRETCHING FROM SINDHURA'S NORTHERN MOUNTAIN REGION TO ITS CAPITAL, URAIYUR.
GUJARAT
PESHAWAR
URAIYUR
THE LORD OF THE FORTRESS IS GENERAL GOVIND, AND BENEATH HIM, TWO SECOND-IN-COMMANDS.
GENERAL TARA, AND...

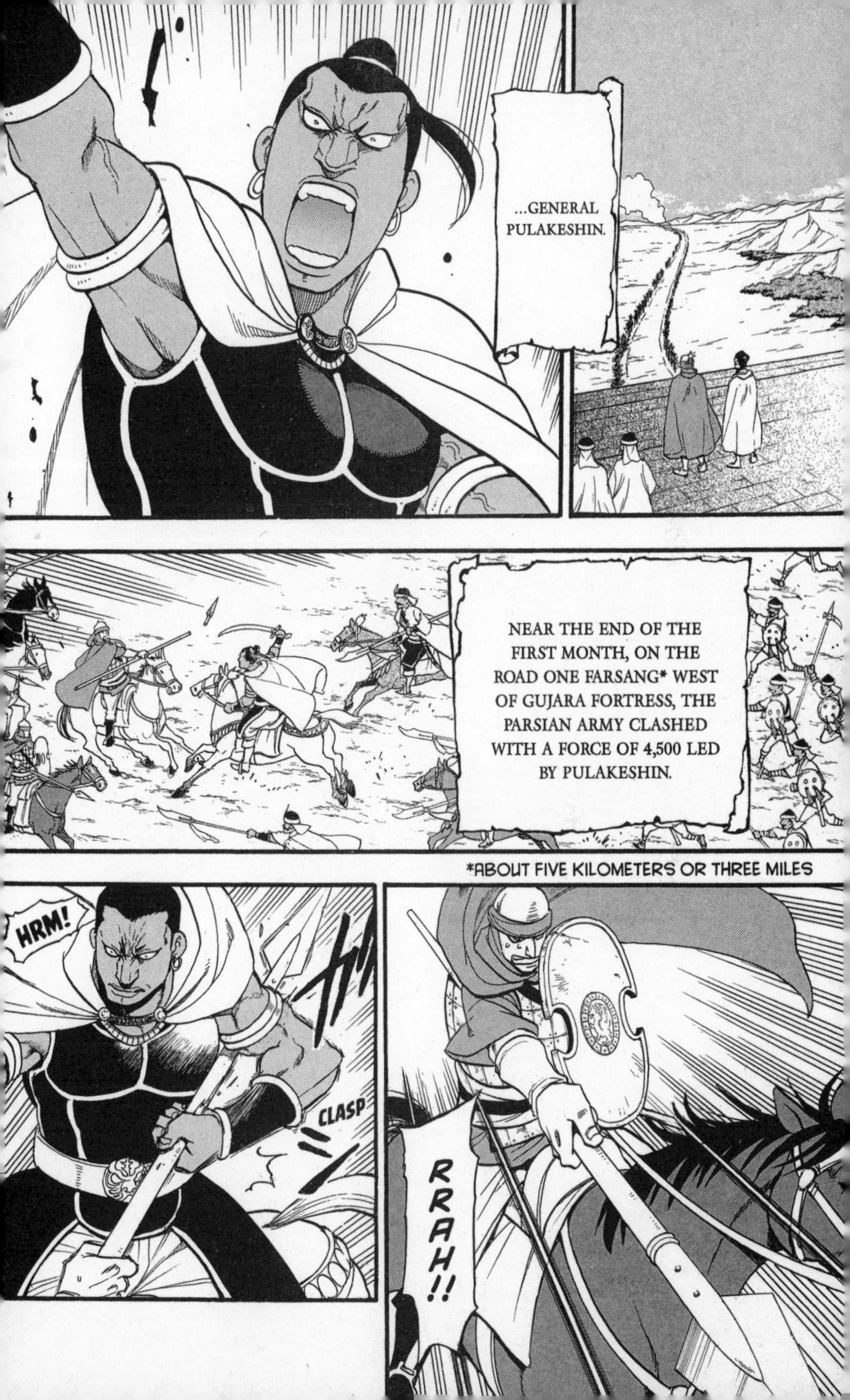
...GENERAL PULAKESHIN.
NEAR THE END OF THE FIRST MONTH, ON THE ROAD ONE FARSANG* WEST OF GUJARA FORTRESS, THE PARSIAN ARMY CLASHED WITH A FORCE OF 4,500 LED BY PULAKESHIN.
*ABOUT FIVE KILOMETERS OR THREE MILES
RRAH!!
HRM!
CLASP

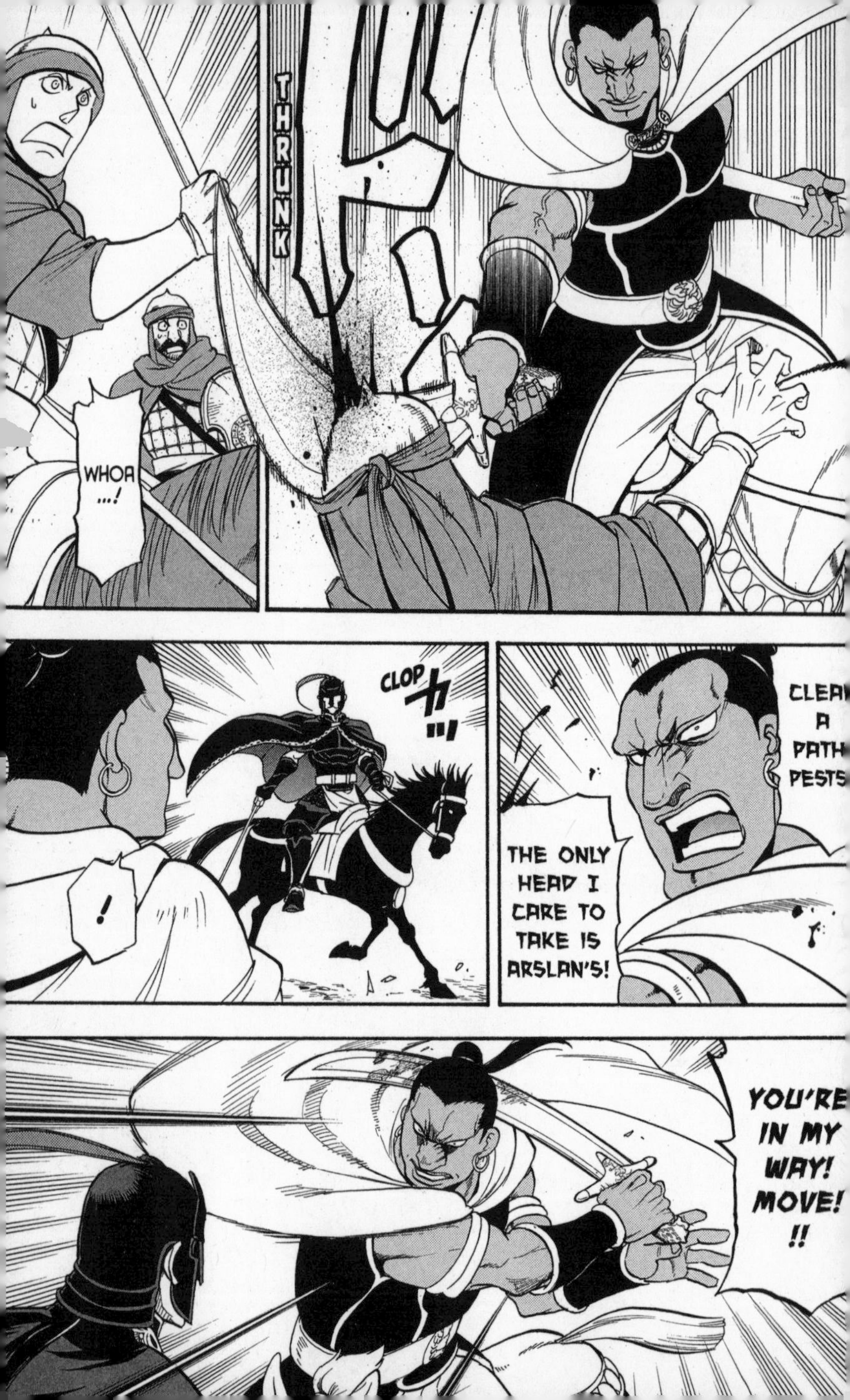
THRUNK
WHOA ...!
CLEA A PATH PESTS
THE ONLY HEAD I CARE TO TAKE IS ARSLAN'S!
CLOP
!
YOU'RE IN MY WAY! MOVE! !!

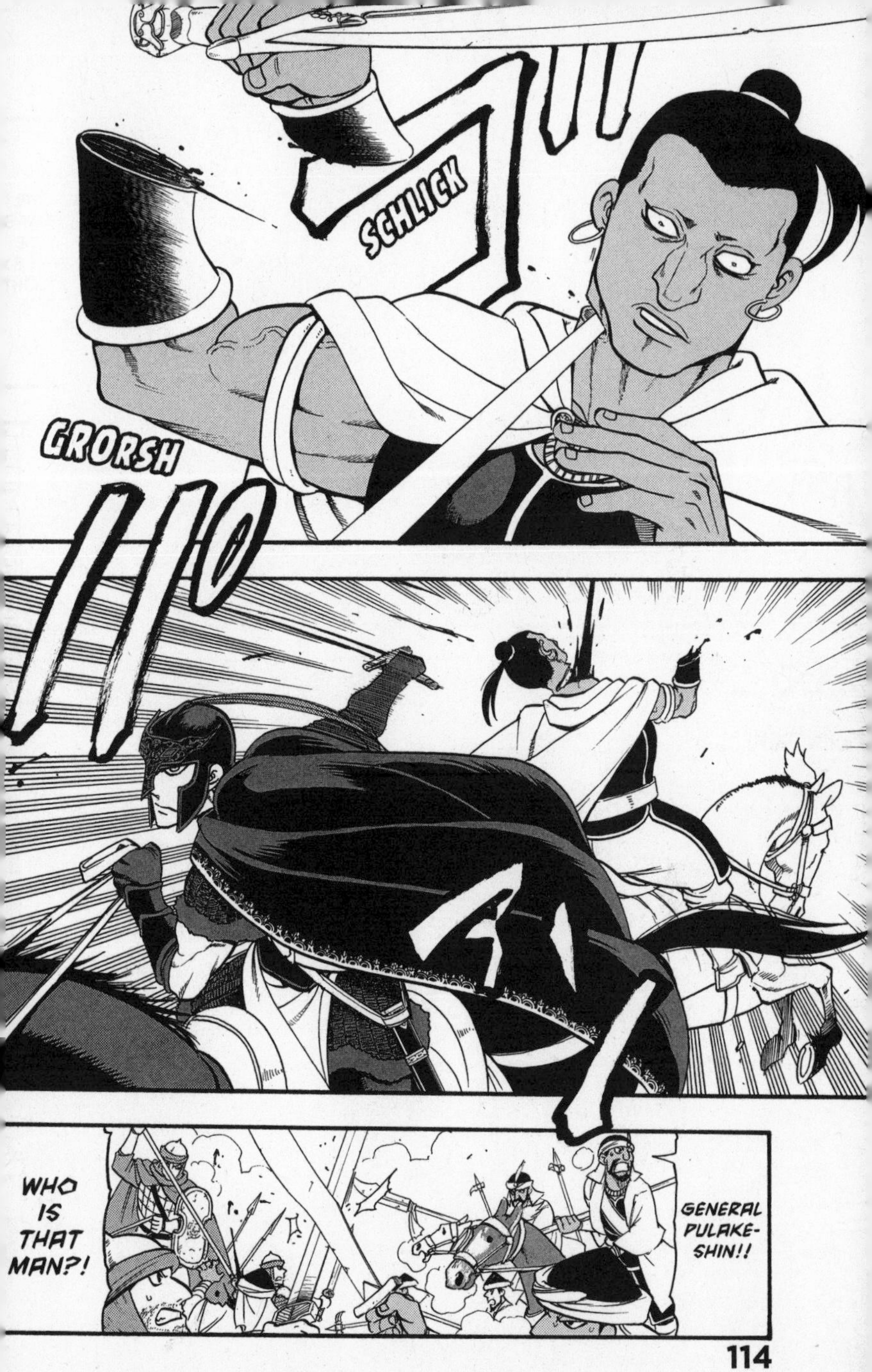
SCHLICK
GRORSH
GENERAL PULAKE-SHIN!!
WHO IS THAT MAN?!

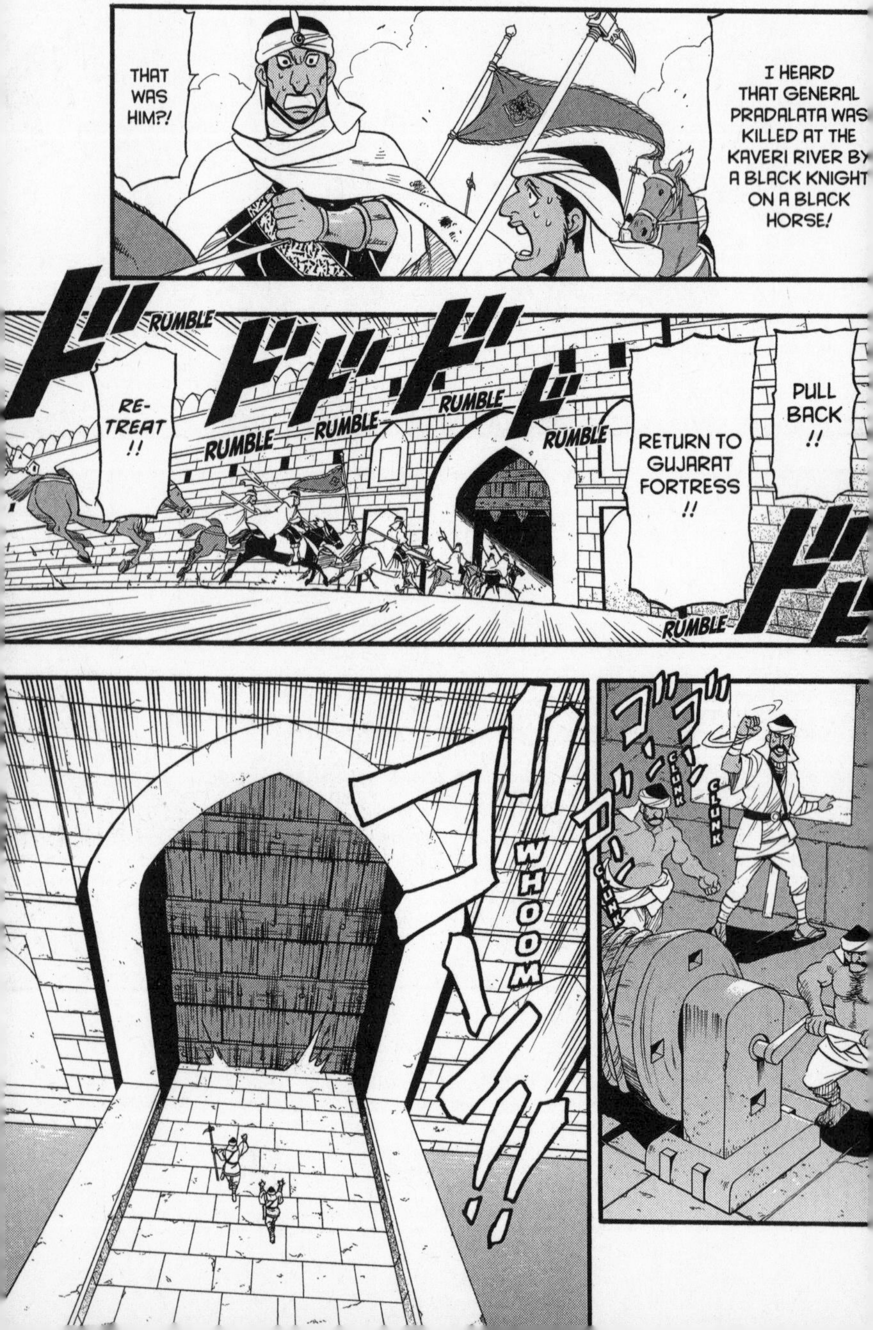
I HEARD THAT GENERAL PRADALATA WAS KILLED AT THE KAVERI RIVER BY A BLACK KNIGHT ON A BLACK HORSE!
THAT WAS HIM?!
PULL BACK!!
RETURN TO GUJARAT FORTRESS!!
RUMBLE
RUMBLE
RUMBLE
RUMBLE
RUMBLE
RE-TREAT!!
RUMBLE
CLUNK
CLUNK
CLUNK
WHOOM

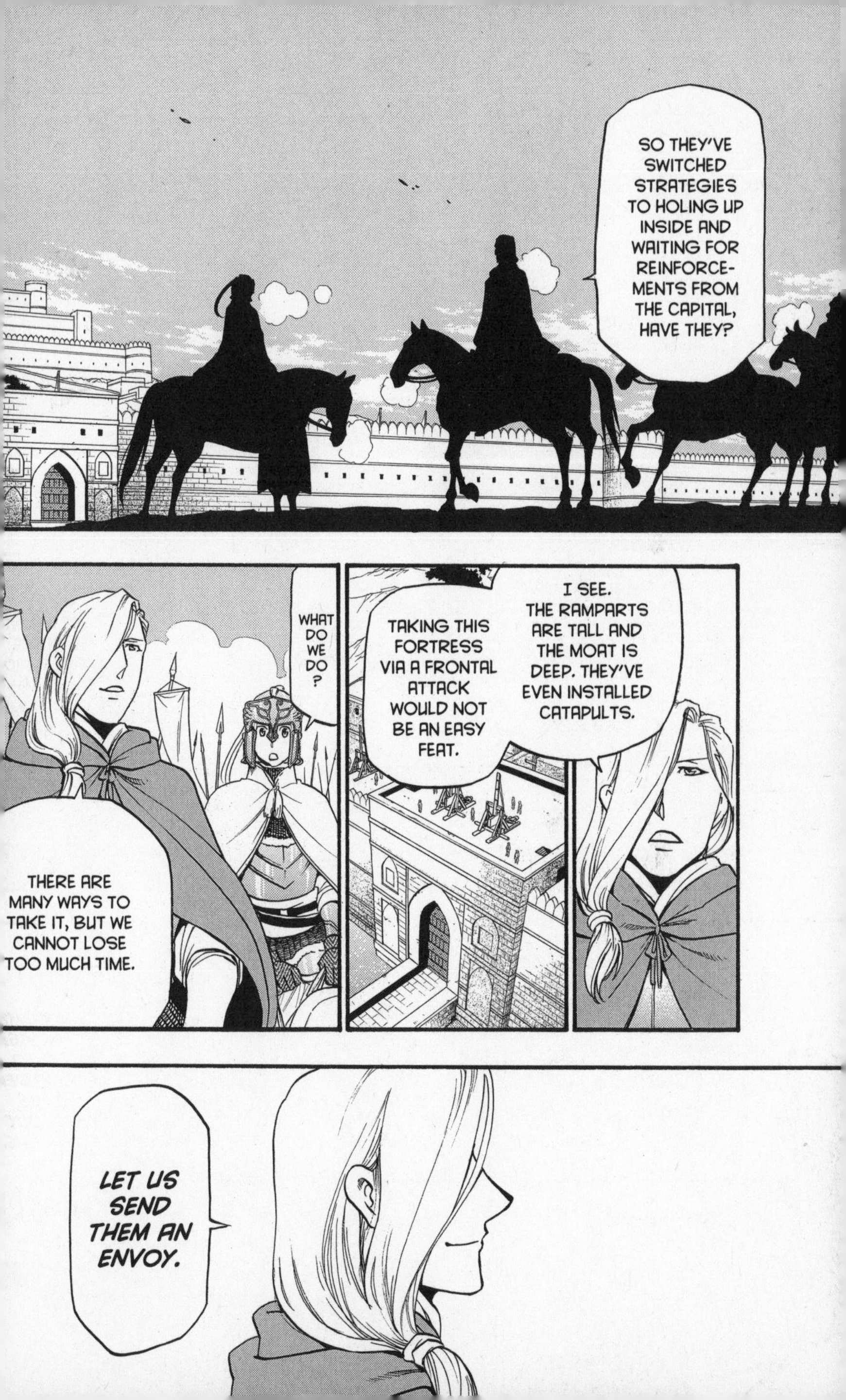
SO THEY'VE SWITCHED STRATEGIES TO HOLING UP INSIDE AND WAITING FOR REINFORCE-MENTS FROM THE CAPITAL, HAVE THEY?
I SEE. THE RAMPARTS ARE TALL AND THE MOAT IS DEEP. THEY'VE EVEN INSTALLED CATAPULTS.
TAKING THIS FORTRESS VIA A FRONTAL ATTACK WOULD NOT BE AN EASY FEAT.
WHAT DO WE DO?
THERE ARE MANY WAYS TO TAKE IT, BUT WE CANNOT LOSE TOO MUCH TIME.
LET US SEND THEM AN ENVOY.

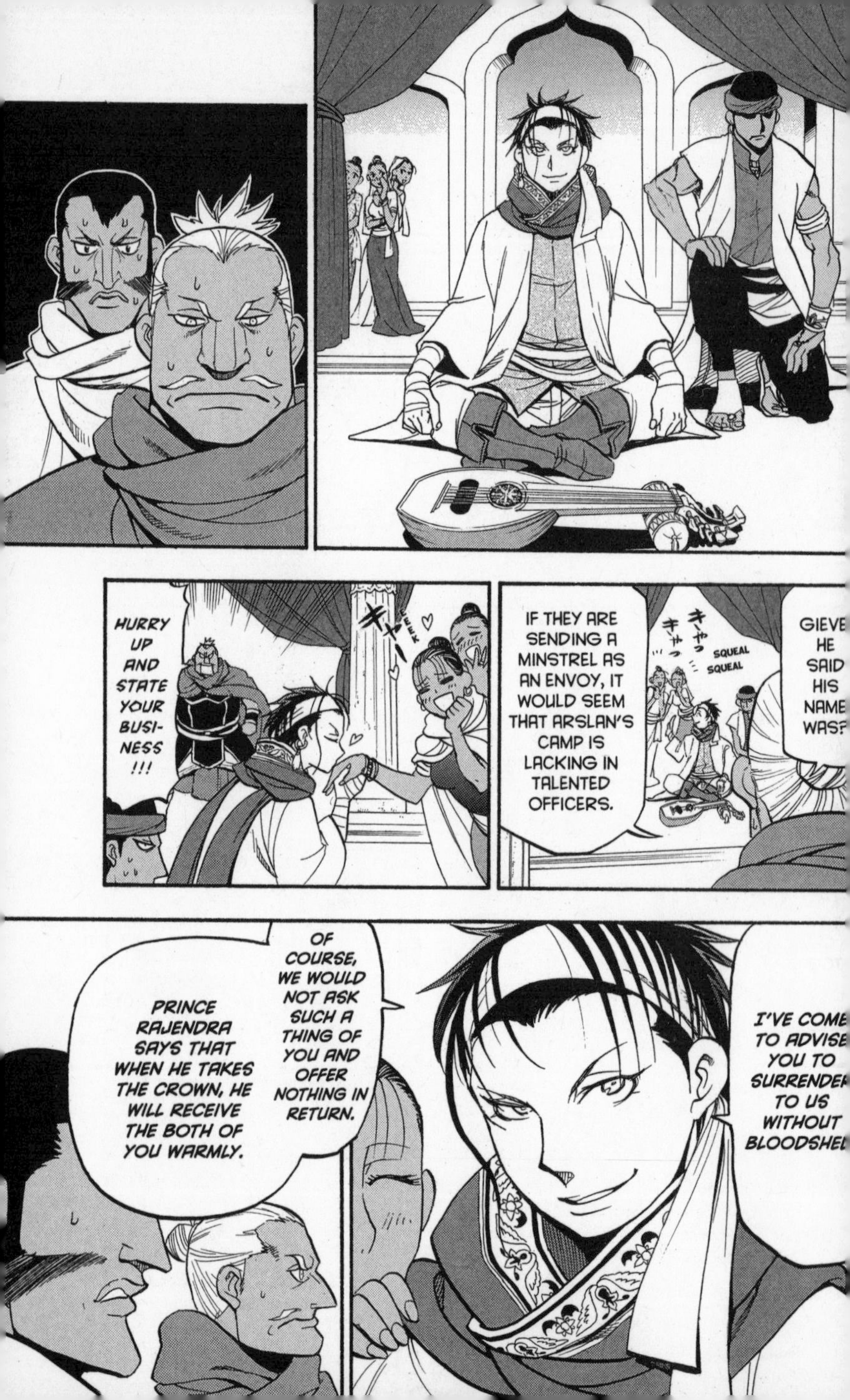
GIEVE HE SAID HIS NAME WAS?
IF THEY ARE SENDING A MINSTREL AS AN ENVOY, IT WOULD SEEM THAT ARSLAN'S CAMP IS LACKING IN TALENTED OFFICERS.
キャッ キャッ
SQUEAL SQUEAL
キャー
EEK
HURRY UP AND STATE YOUR BUSINESS!!!
I'VE COME TO ADVISE YOU TO SURRENDER TO US WITHOUT BLOODSHED
OF COURSE, WE WOULD NOT ASK SUCH A THING OF YOU AND OFFER NOTHING IN RETURN.
PRINCE RAJENDRA SAYS THAT WHEN HE TAKES THE CROWN, HE WILL RECEIVE THE BOTH OF YOU WARMLY.

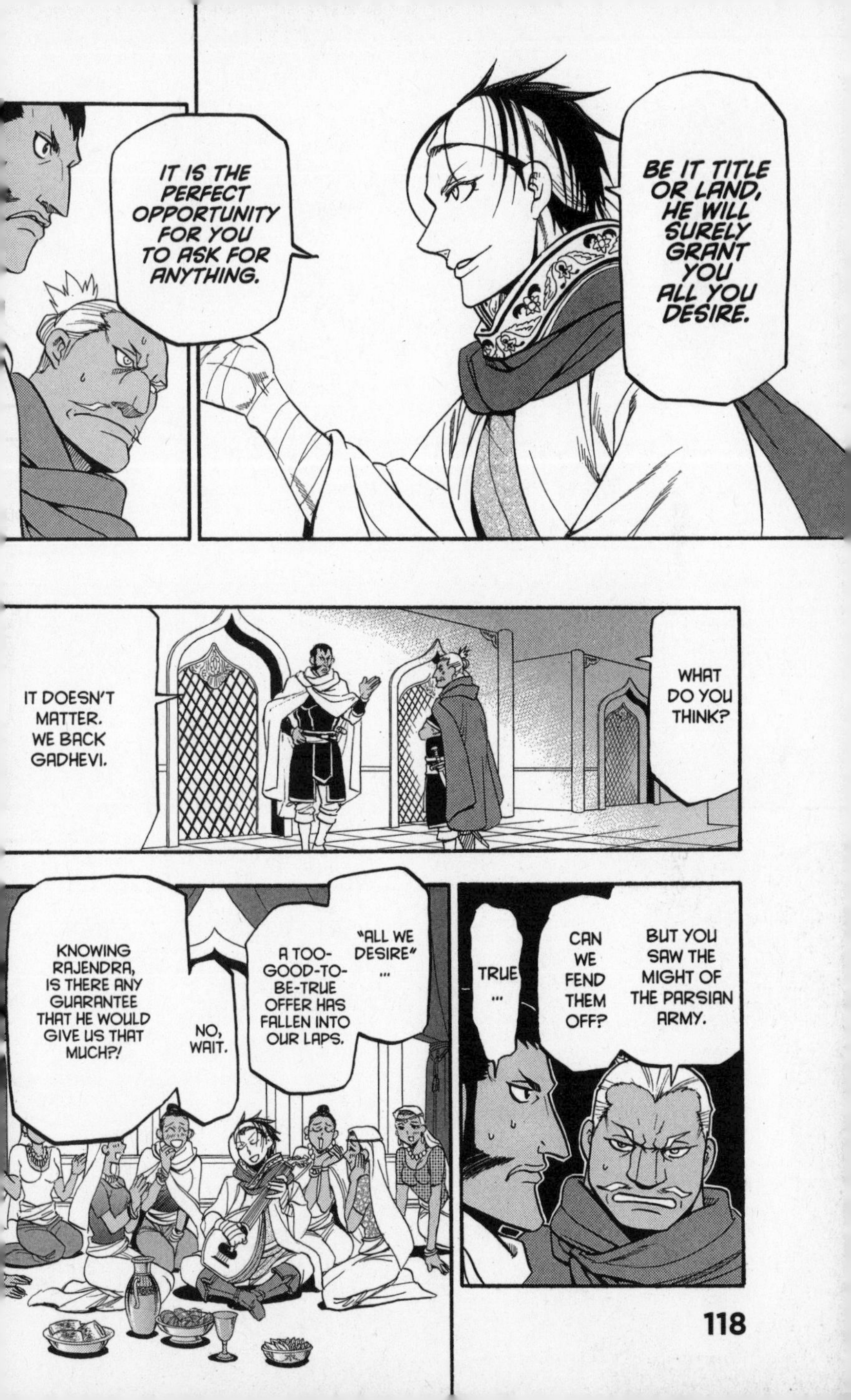
BE IT TITLE OR LAND, HE WILL SURELY GRANT YOU ALL YOU DESIRE.
IT IS THE PERFECT OPPORTUNITY FOR YOU TO ASK FOR ANYTHING.
WHAT DO YOU THINK?
IT DOESN'T MATTER. WE BACK GADHEVI.
BUT YOU SAW THE MIGHT OF THE PARSIAN ARMY.
CAN WE FEND THEM OFF?
TRUE ...
"ALL WE DESIRE" ...
A TOO-GOOD-TO-BE-TRUE OFFER HAS FALLEN INTO OUR LAPS.
NO, WAIT.
KNOWING RAJENDRA, IS THERE ANY GUARANTEE THAT HE WOULD GIVE US THAT MUCH?!

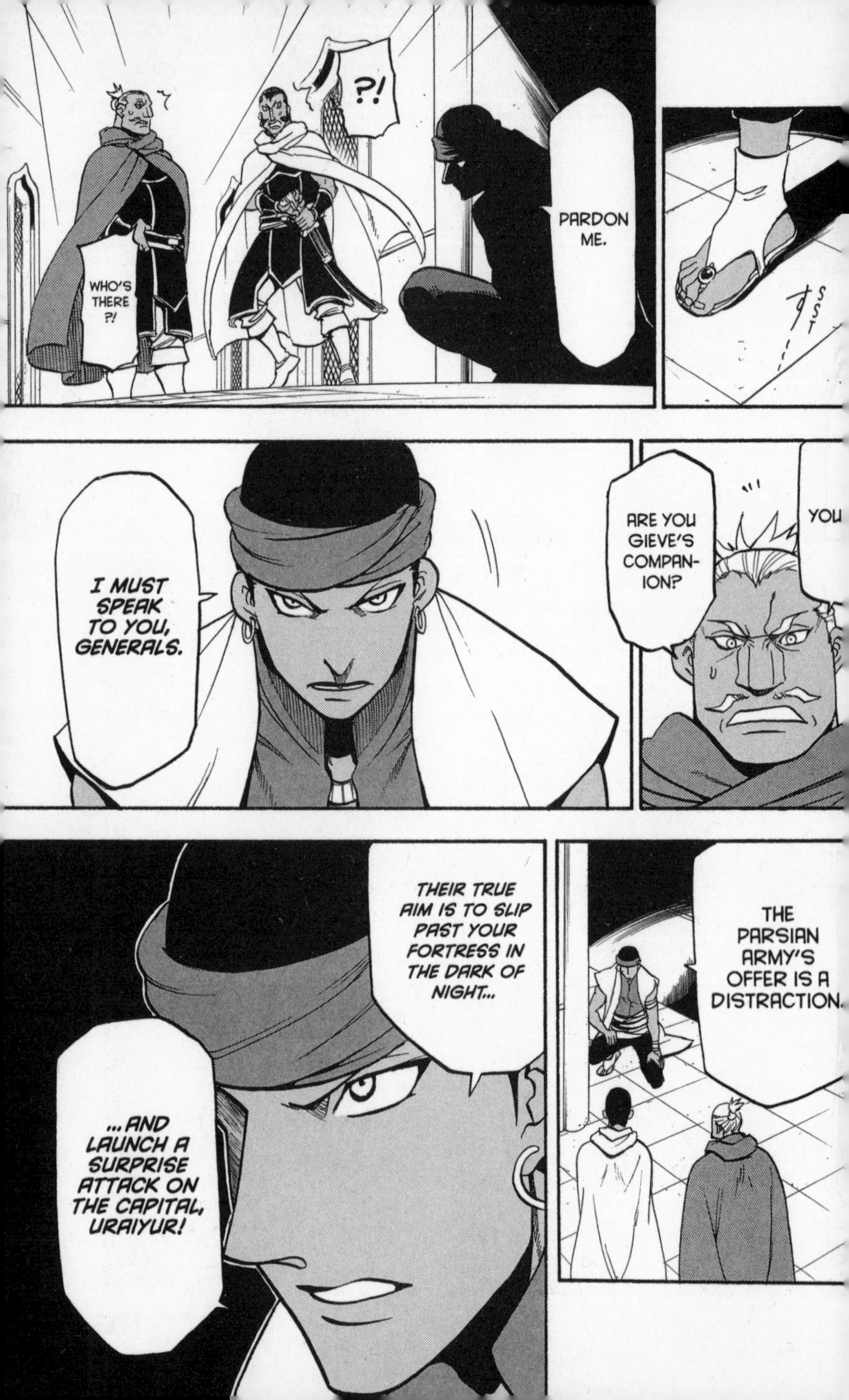
す
SST
PARDON ME.
?!
WHO'S THERE ?!
YOU
ARE YOU GIEVE'S COMPANION?
I MUST SPEAK TO YOU, GENERALS.
THE PARSIAN ARMY'S OFFER IS A DISTRACTION.
THEIR TRUE AIM IS TO SLIP PAST YOUR FORTRESS IN THE DARK OF NIGHT...
...AND LAUNCH A SURPRISE ATTACK ON THE CAPITAL, URAIYUR!

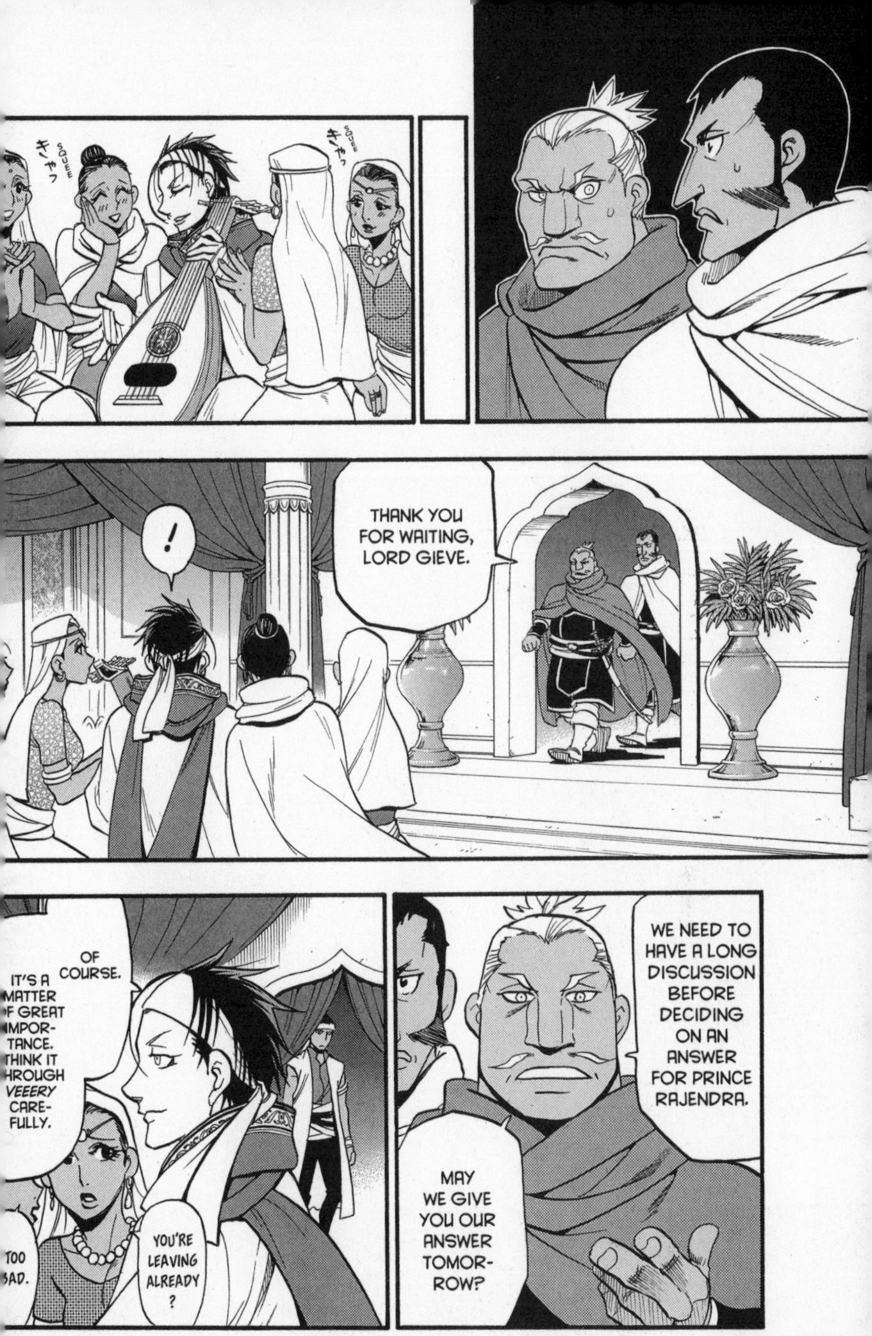
SQUEE
きゃっ
SQUEE
きゃフ
THANK YOU FOR WAITING, LORD GIEVE.
!
WE NEED TO HAVE A LONG DISCUSSION BEFORE DECIDING ON AN ANSWER FOR PRINCE RAJENDRA.
MAY WE GIVE YOU OUR ANSWER TOMORROW?
OF COURSE.
IT'S A MATTER F GREAT MPORTANCE. THINK IT HROUGH VEEERY CAREFULLY.
YOU'RE LEAVING ALREADY?
TOO AD.

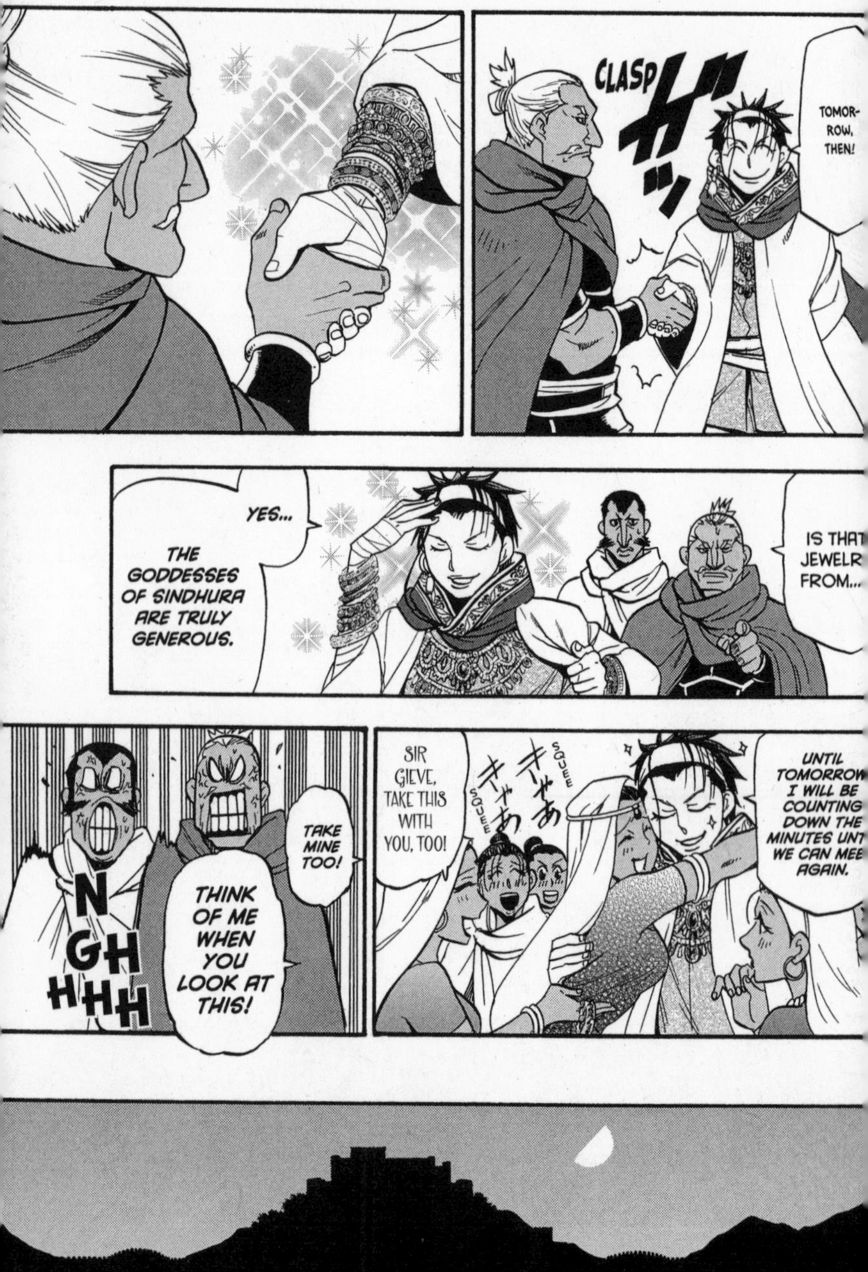
CLASP
TOMOR-ROW, THEN!
IS THAT JEWELR FROM...
YES...
THE GODDESSES OF SINDHURA ARE TRULY GENEROUS.
UNTIL TOMORROW I WILL BE COUNTING DOWN THE MINUTES UNT WE CAN MEE AGAIN.
SQUEE
SQUEE
SIR GIEVE, TAKE THIS WITH YOU, TOO!
TAKE MINE TOO!
THINK OF ME WHEN YOU LOOK AT THIS!
NGHHHH

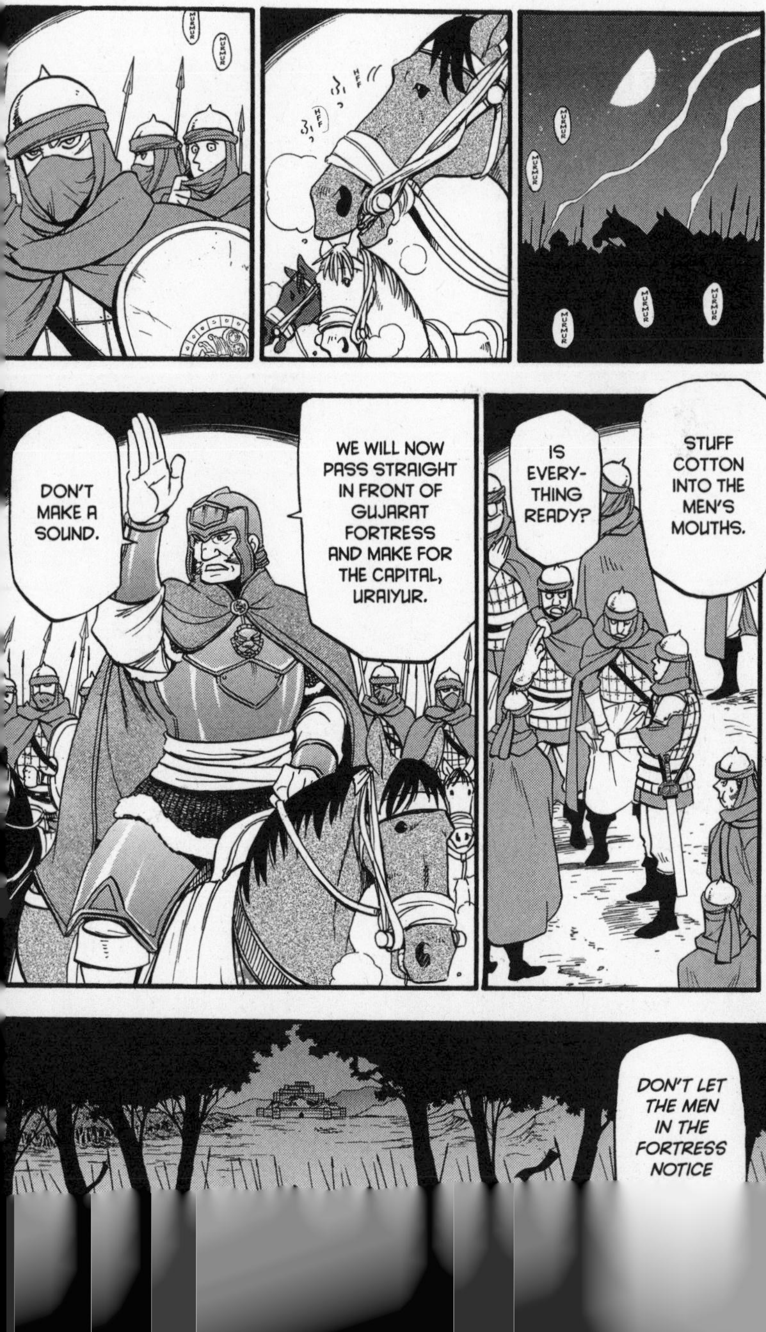
MURMUR
MURMUR
MURMUR
MURMUR
MURMUR
HFF
HFF
MURMUR
MURMUR
STUFF COTTON INTO THE MEN'S MOUTHS.
IS EVERY-THING READY?
WE WILL NOW PASS STRAIGHT IN FRONT OF GUJARAT FORTRESS AND MAKE FOR THE CAPITAL, URAIYUR.
DON'T MAKE A SOUND.
DON'T LET THE MEN IN THE FORTRESS NOTICE

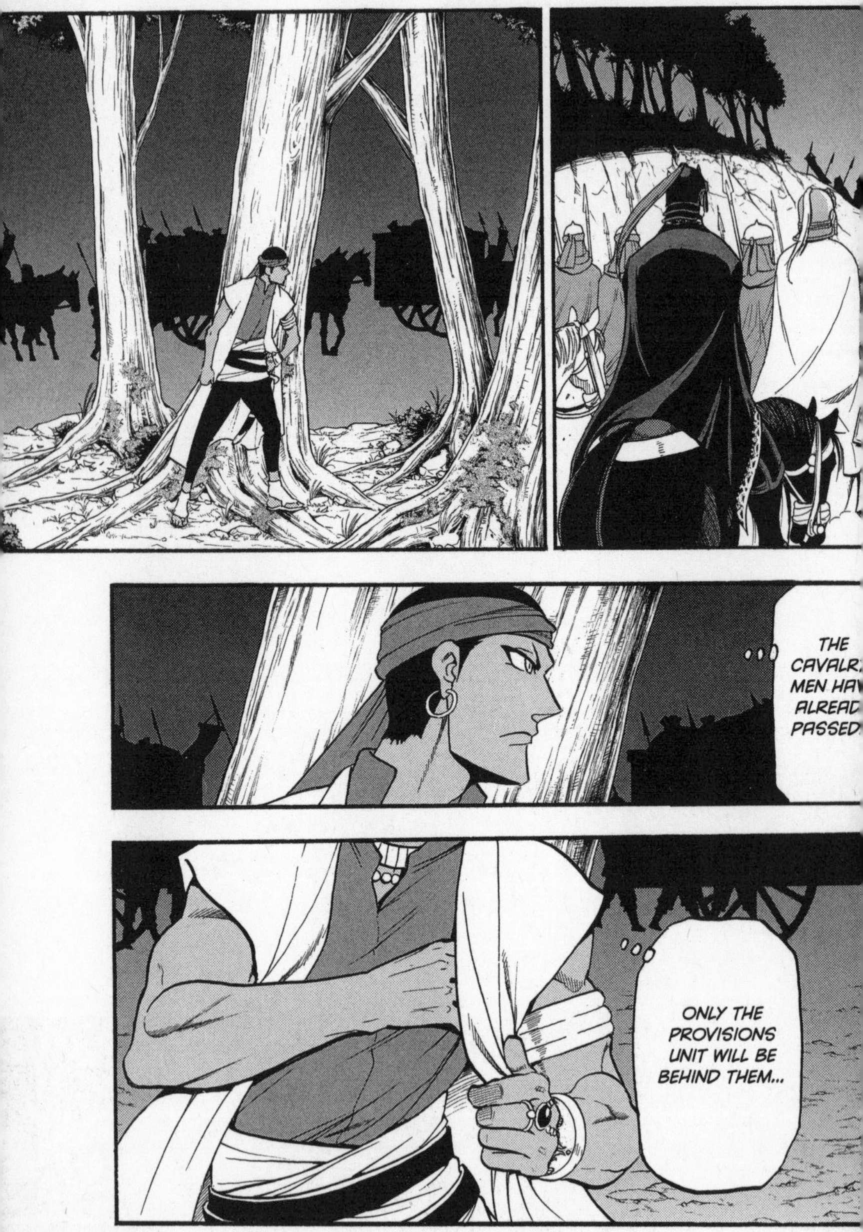
THE CAVALR[Y] MEN HA[VE] ALREA[DY] PASSED...
ONLY THE PROVISIONS UNIT WILL BE BEHIND THEM...

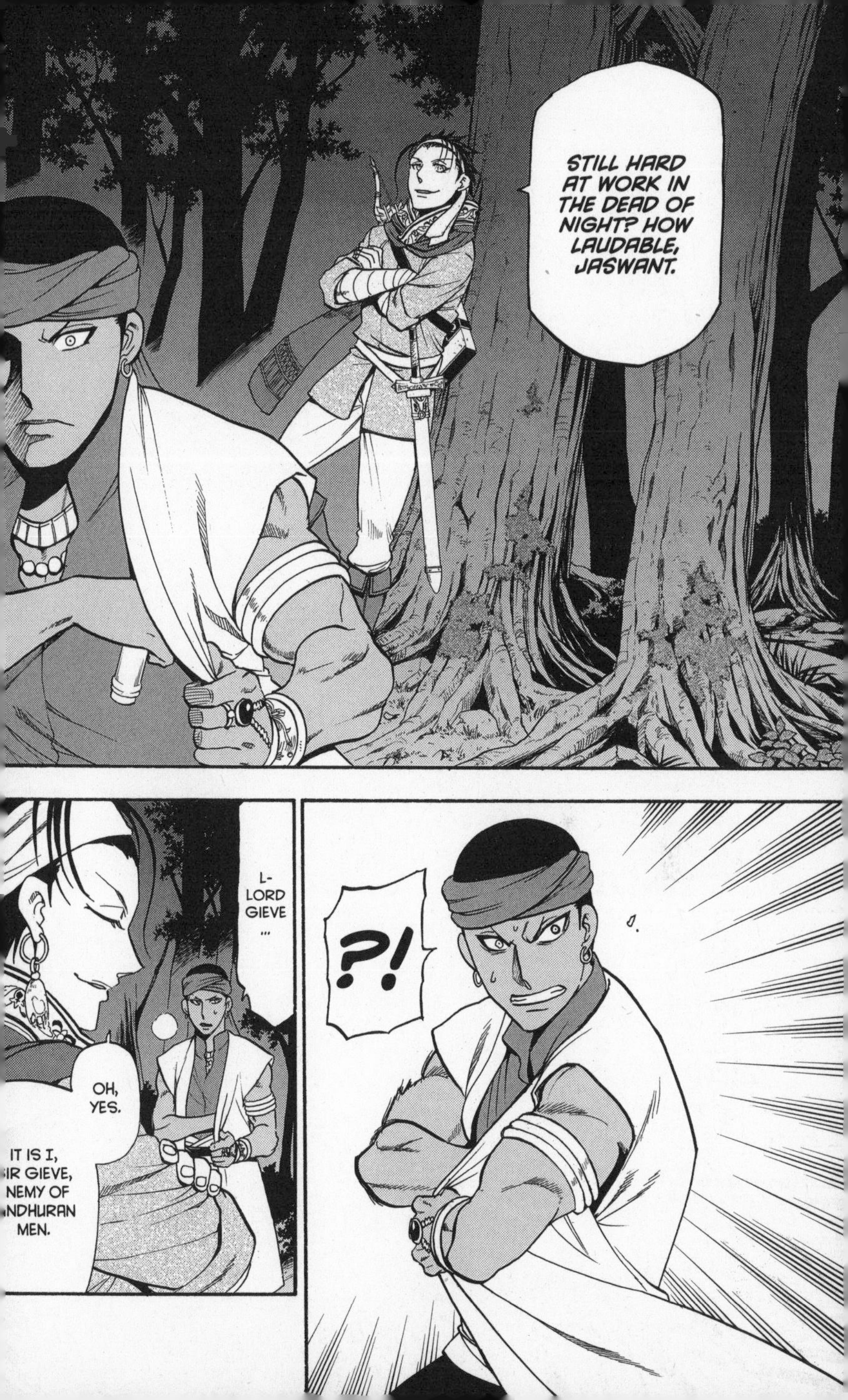
STILL HARD AT WORK IN THE DEAD OF NIGHT? HOW LAUDABLE, JASWANT.
?!
L-LORD GIEVE ...
OH, YES.
IT IS I, IR GIEVE, NEMY OF NDHURAN MEN.

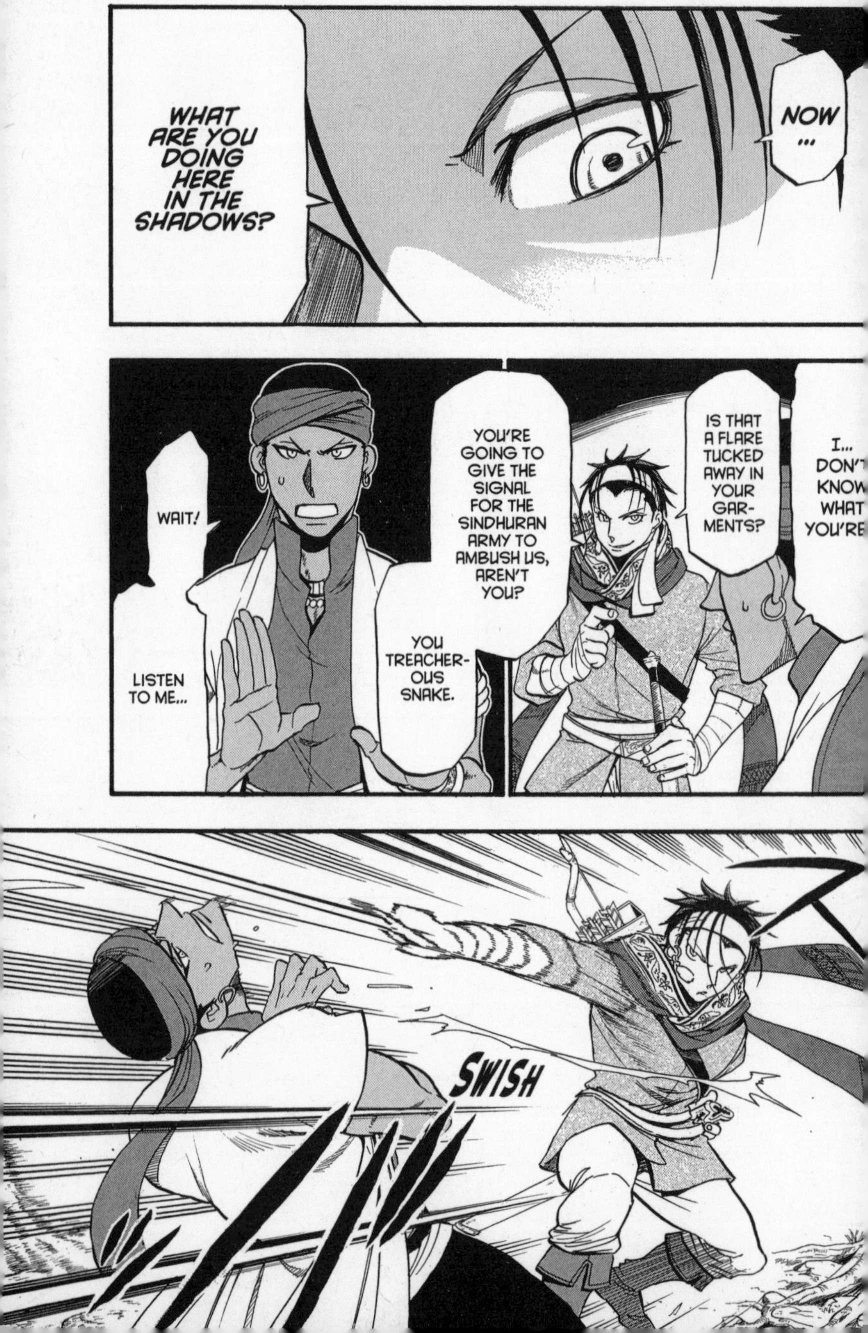
NOW ...
WHAT ARE YOU DOING HERE IN THE SHADOWS?
I... DON'T KNOW WHAT YOU'RE
IS THAT A FLARE TUCKED AWAY IN YOUR GAR-MENTS?
YOU'RE GOING TO GIVE THE SIGNAL FOR THE SINDHURAN ARMY TO AMBUSH US, AREN'T YOU?
YOU TREACHER-OUS SNAKE.
WAIT!
LISTEN TO ME...
SWISH

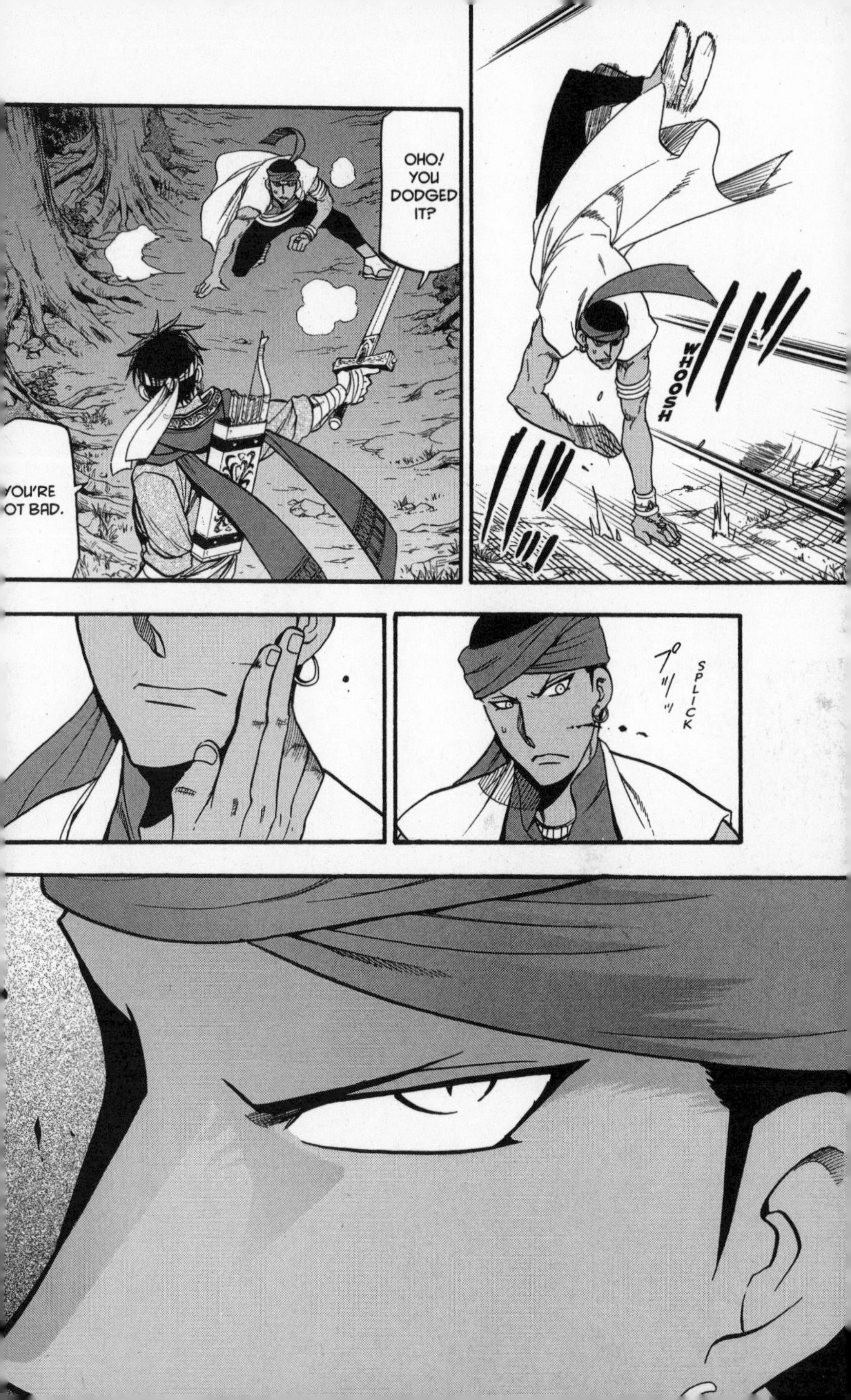
WHOOSH
OHO! YOU DODGED IT?
YOU'RE OT BAD.
プツッ
SPLICK

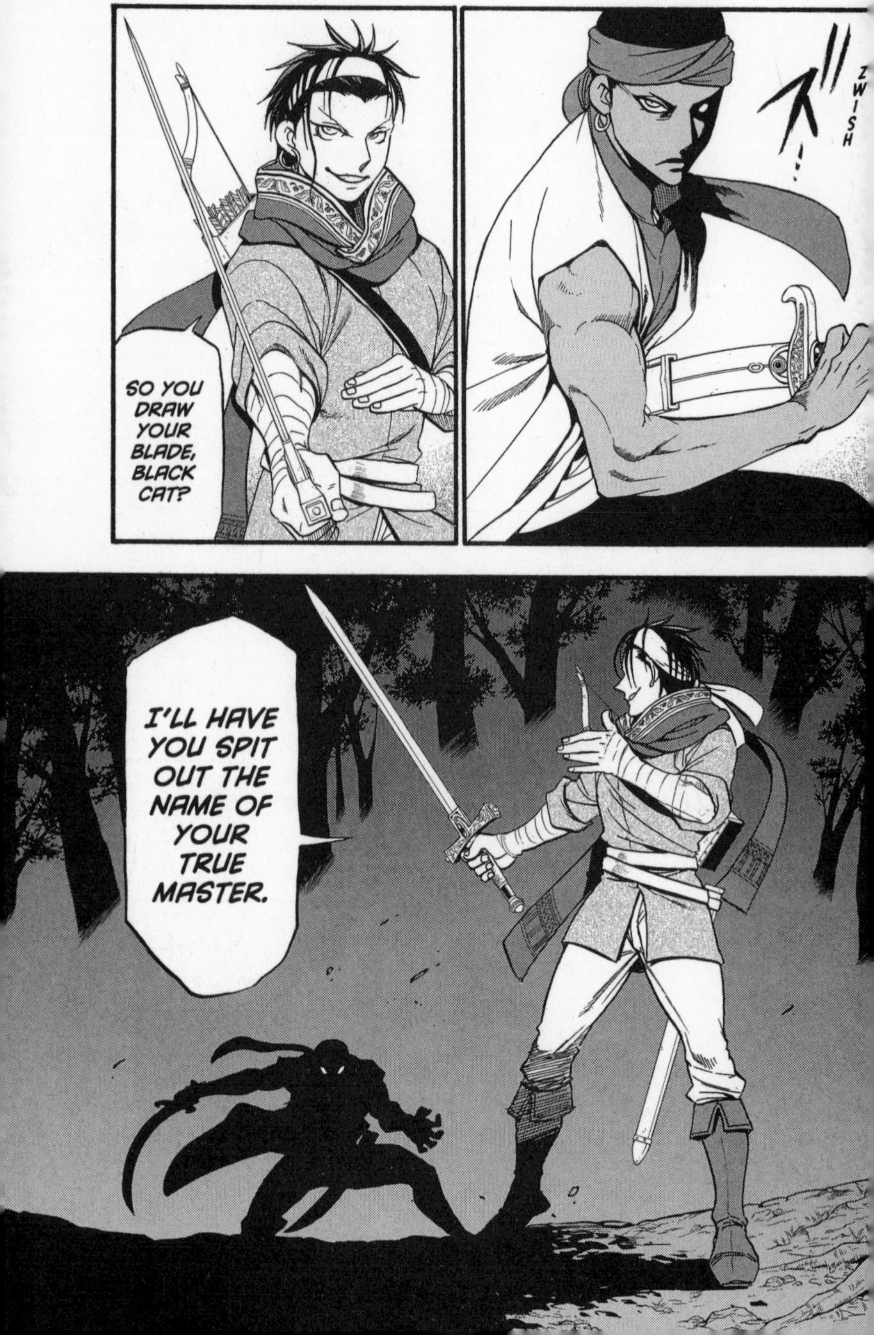
ZWISH
SO YOU DRAW YOUR BLADE, BLACK CAT?
I'LL HAVE YOU SPIT OUT THE NAME OF YOUR TRUE MASTER.

THE HEROIC LEGEND OF
ARSLAN

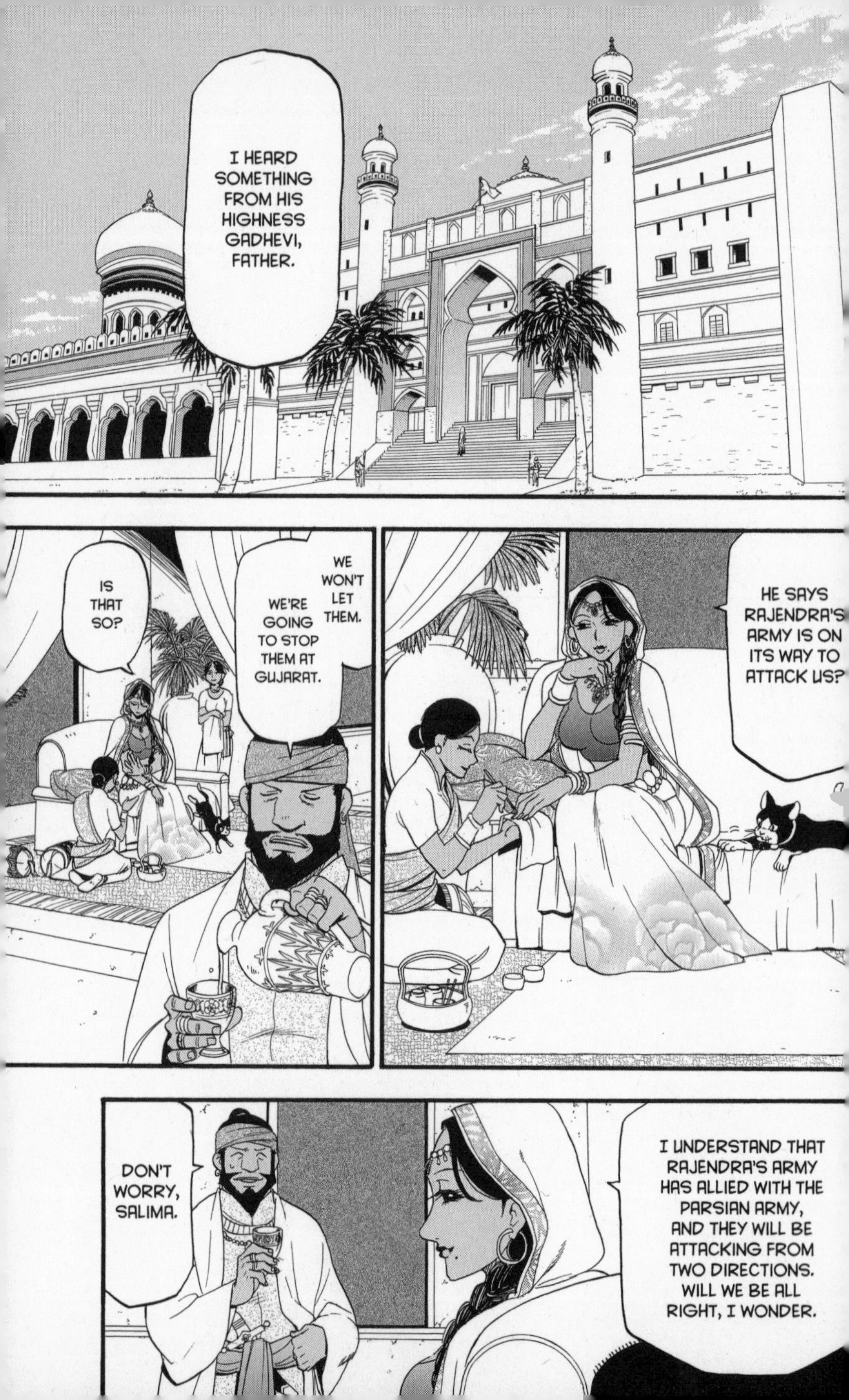
I HEARD SOMETHING FROM HIS HIGHNESS GADHEVI, FATHER.
HE SAYS RAJENDRA'S ARMY IS ON ITS WAY TO ATTACK US?
WE WON'T LET THEM.
WE'RE GOING TO STOP THEM AT GUJARAT.
IS THAT SO?
I UNDERSTAND THAT RAJENDRA'S ARMY HAS ALLIED WITH THE PARSIAN ARMY, AND THEY WILL BE ATTACKING FROM TWO DIRECTIONS. WILL WE BE ALL RIGHT, I WONDER.
DON'T WORRY, SALIMA.

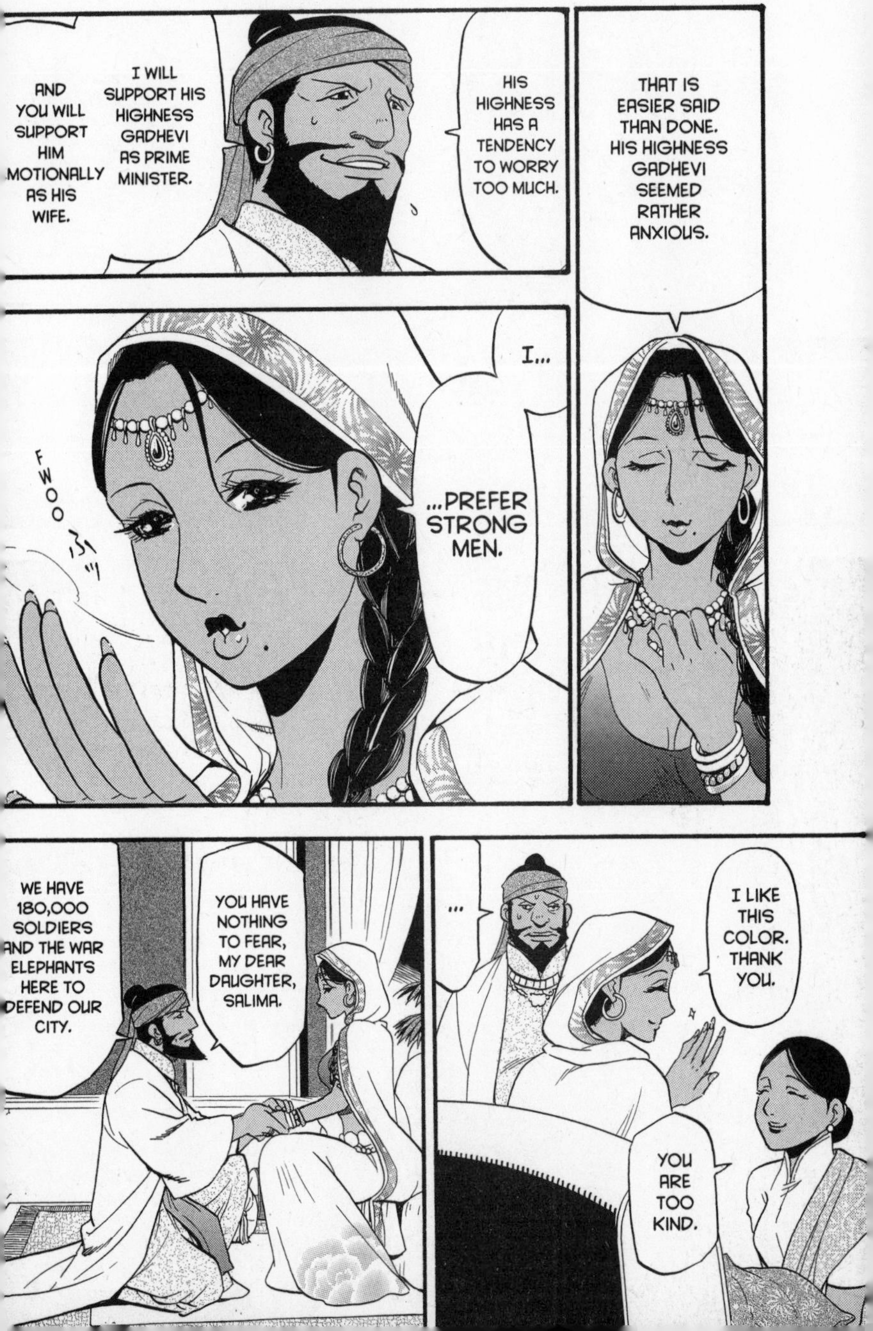
THAT IS EASIER SAID THAN DONE. HIS HIGHNESS GADHEVI SEEMED RATHER ANXIOUS.
HIS HIGHNESS HAS A TENDENCY TO WORRY TOO MUCH.
I WILL SUPPORT HIS HIGHNESS GADHEVI AS PRIME MINISTER.
AND YOU WILL SUPPORT HIM MOTIONALLY AS HIS WIFE.
I...
...PREFER STRONG MEN.
FWOO
I LIKE THIS COLOR. THANK YOU.
...
YOU ARE TOO KIND.
YOU HAVE NOTHING TO FEAR, MY DEAR DAUGHTER, SALIMA.
WE HAVE 180,000 SOLDIERS ND THE WAR ELEPHANTS HERE TO EFEND OUR CITY.

Chapter 45: The Battle of Gujarat

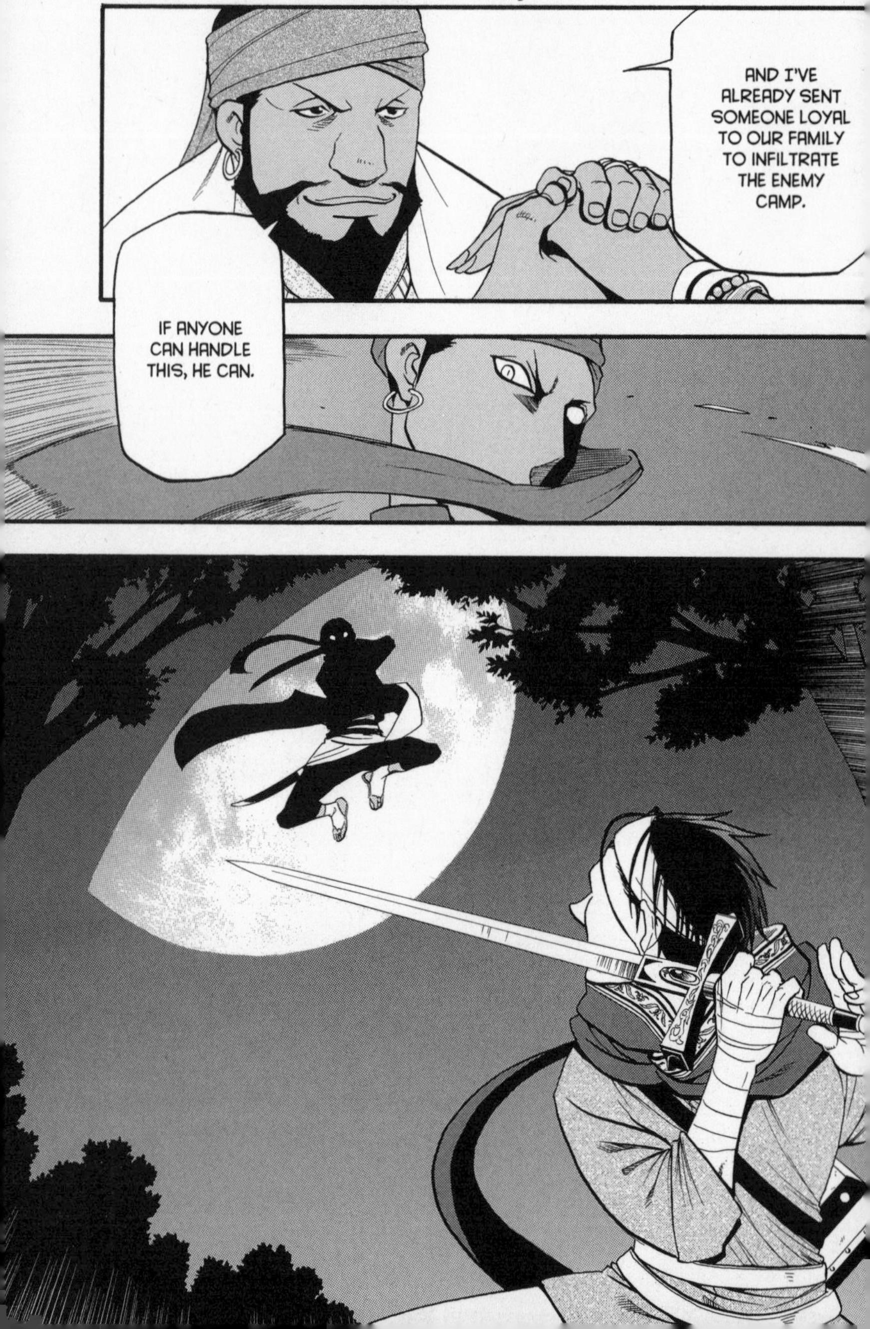
AND I'VE ALREADY SENT SOMEONE LOYAL TO OUR FAMILY TO INFILTRATE THE ENEMY CAMP.
IF ANYONE CAN HANDLE THIS, HE CAN.

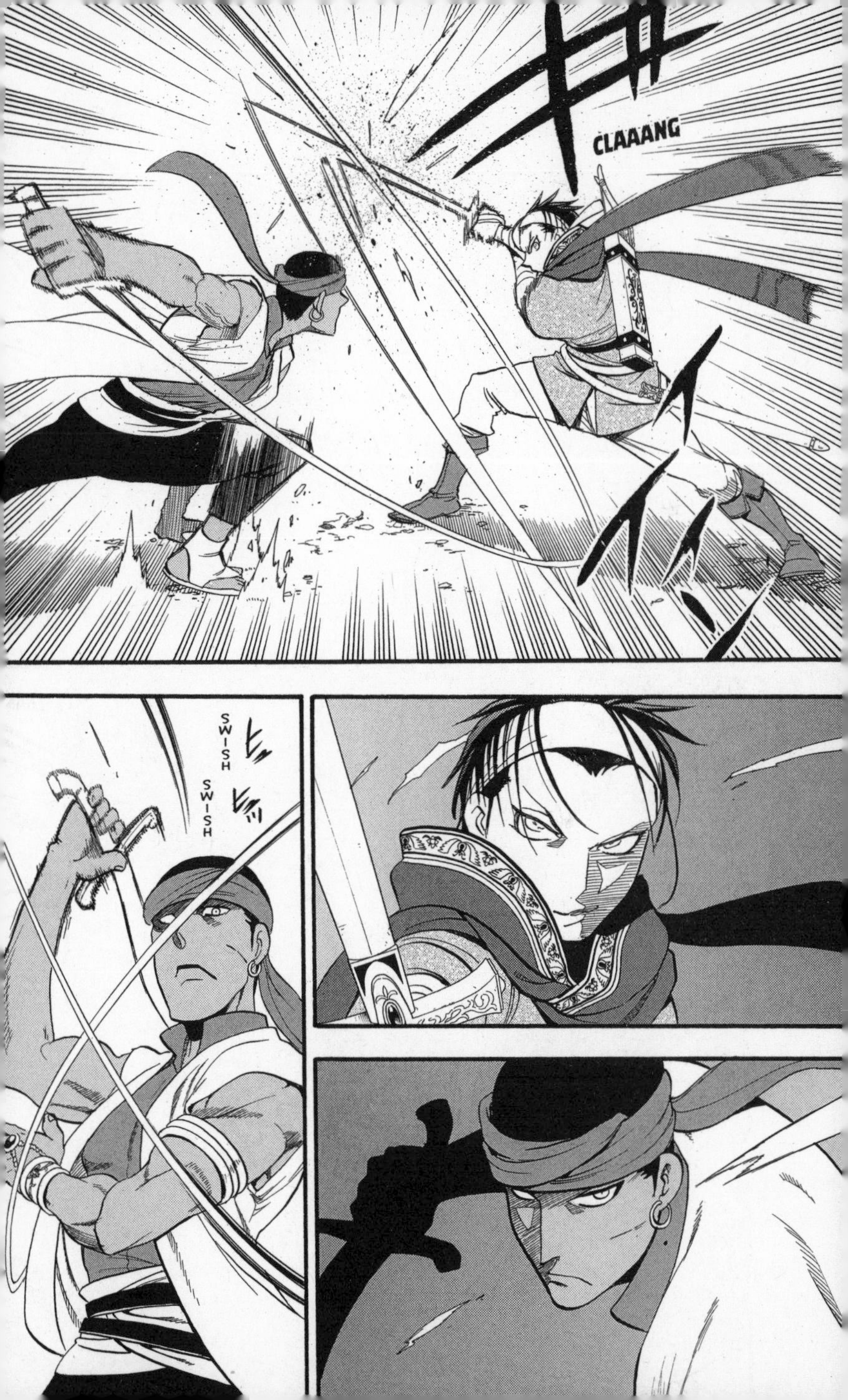
CLAAANG
SWISH
SWISH

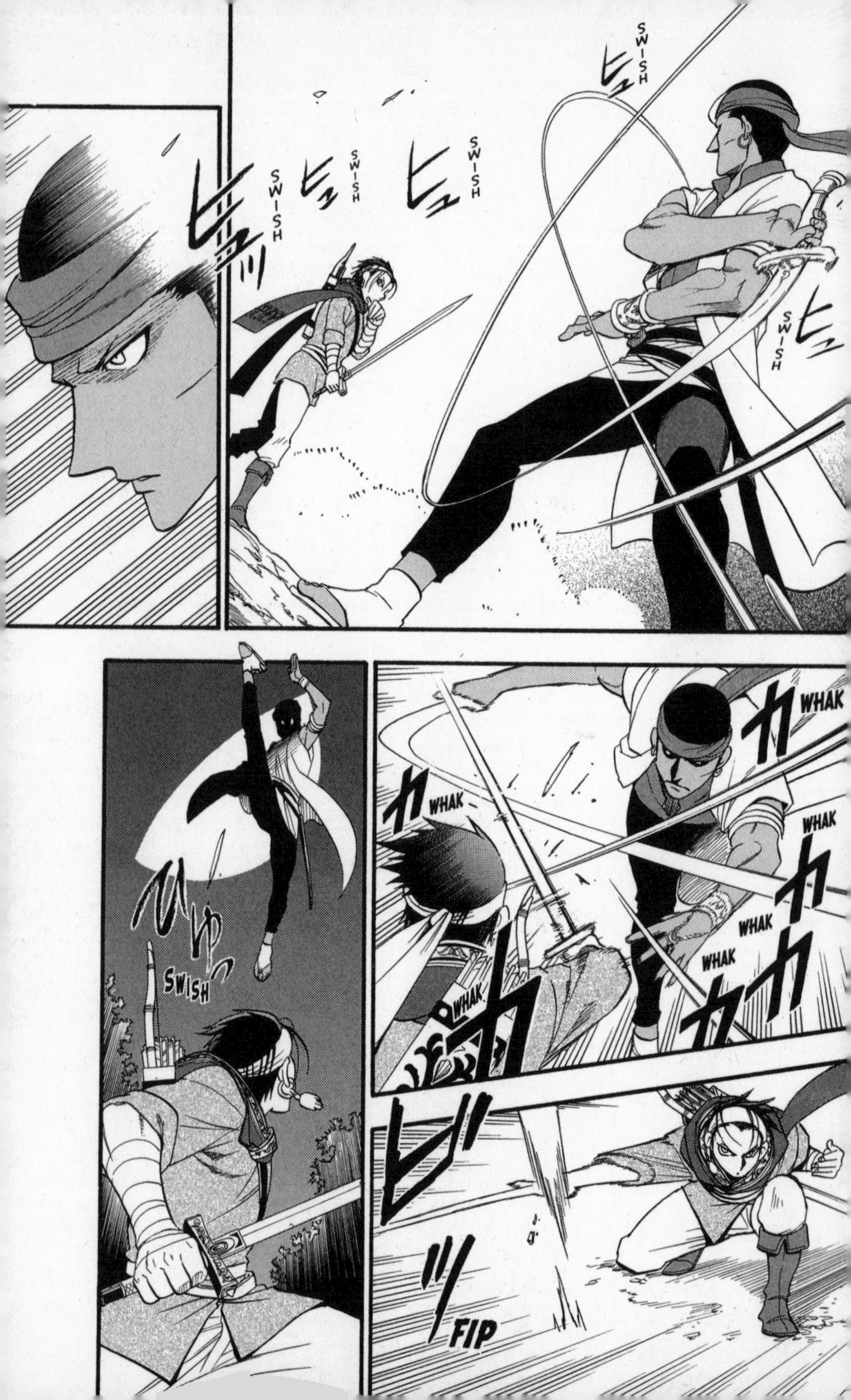
SWISH
SWISH
SWISH
SWISH
SWISH
WHAK
WHAK
WHAK
WHAK
WHAK
WHAK
FIP
SWISH

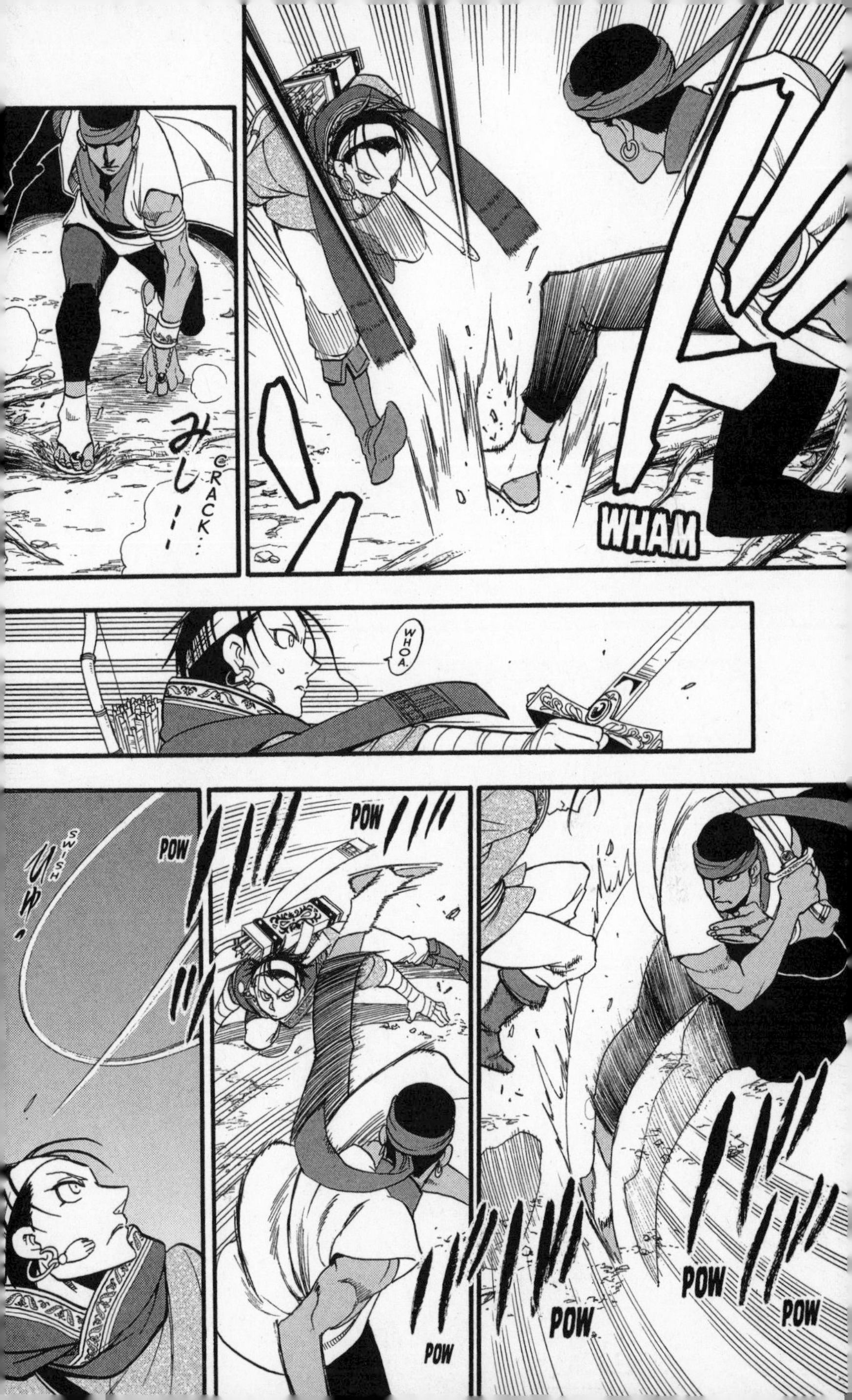
WHAM
みし...
CRACK...
WHOA.
POW
POW
POW
POW
POW
POW
SWISH
ひゅ

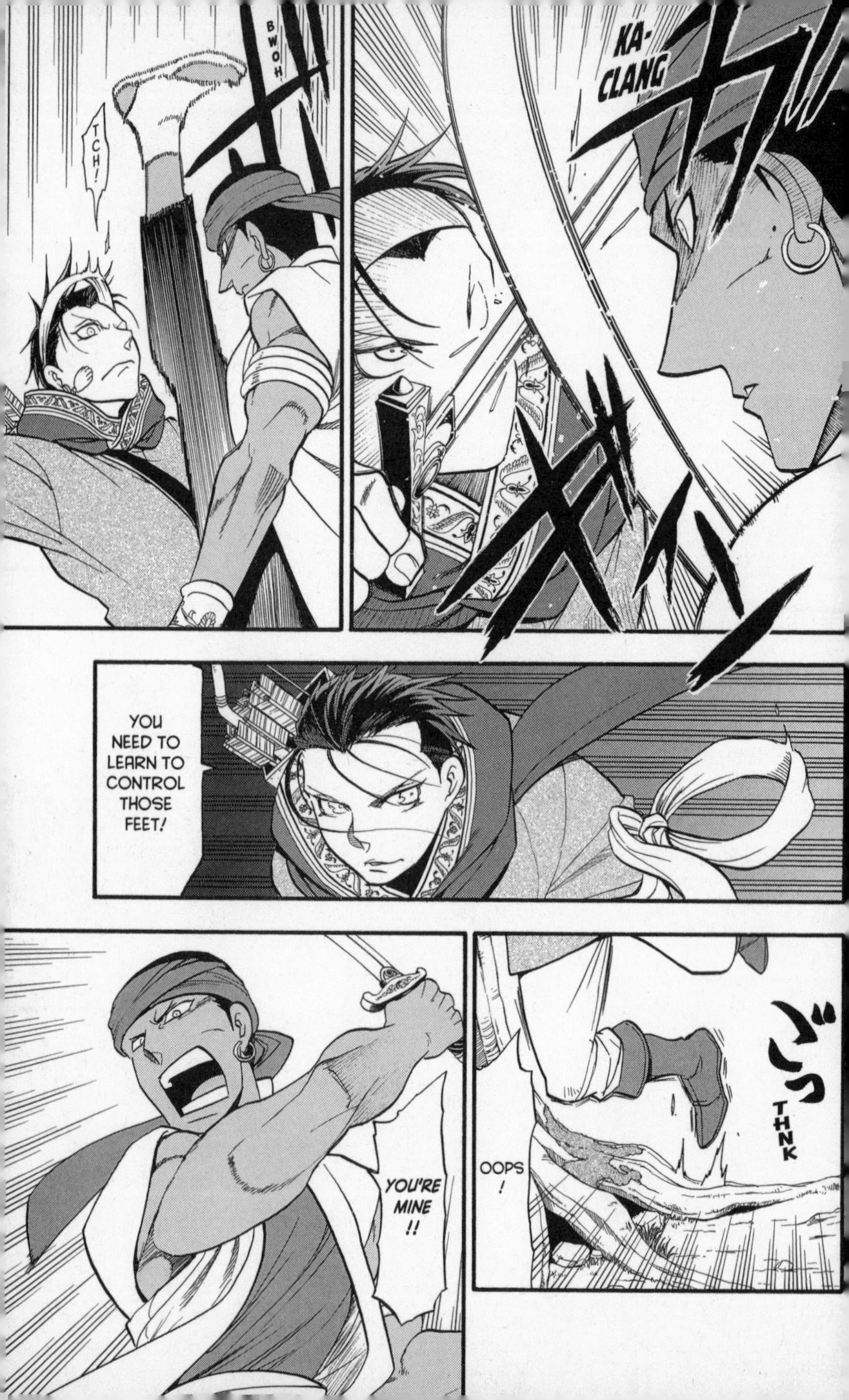
KA-
CLANG
BWOH
TCH!
YOU NEED TO LEARN TO CONTROL THOSE FEET!
ごっ
THNK
OOPS!
YOU'RE MINE!!

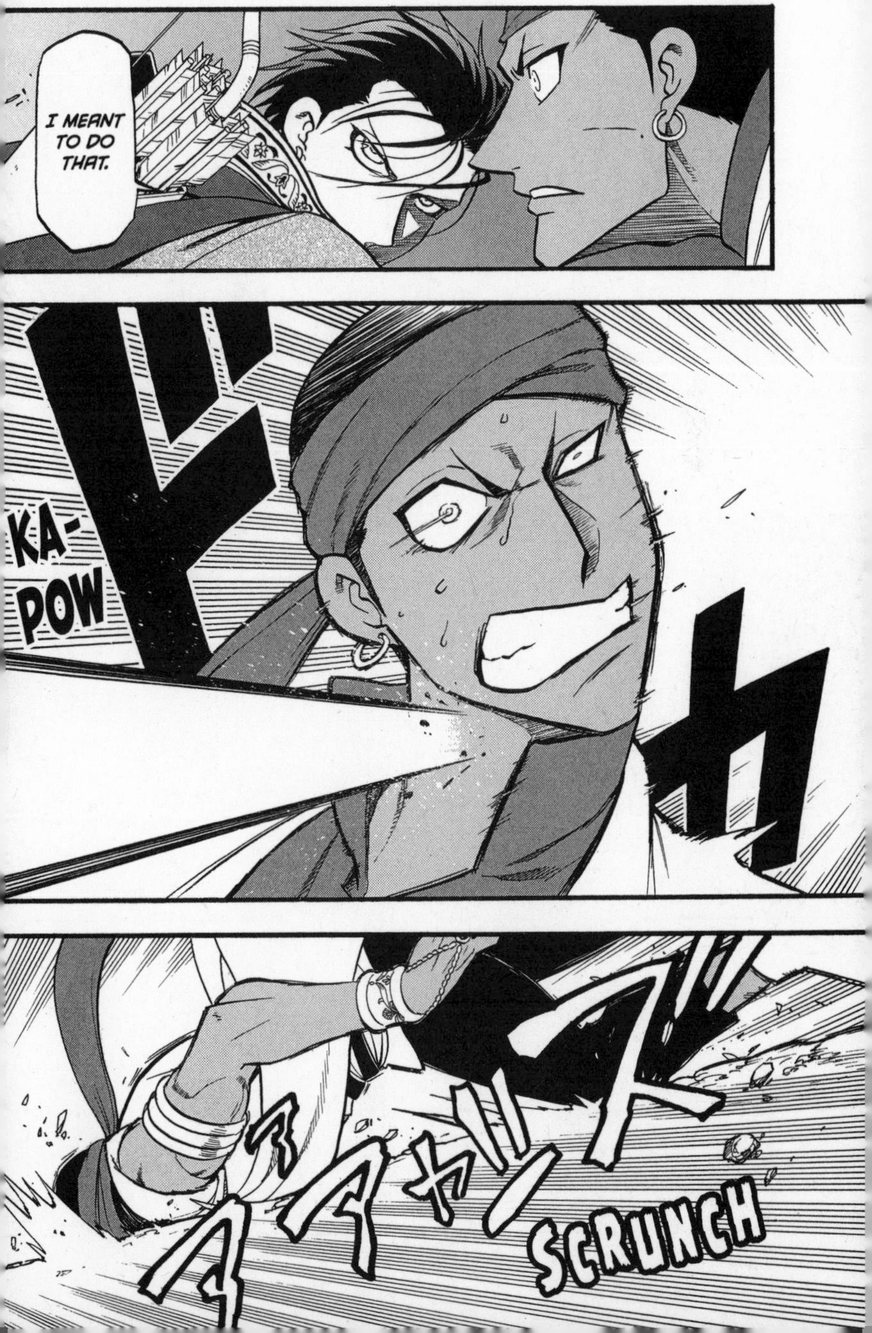
I MEANT TO DO THAT.
KA-POW
SCRUNCH

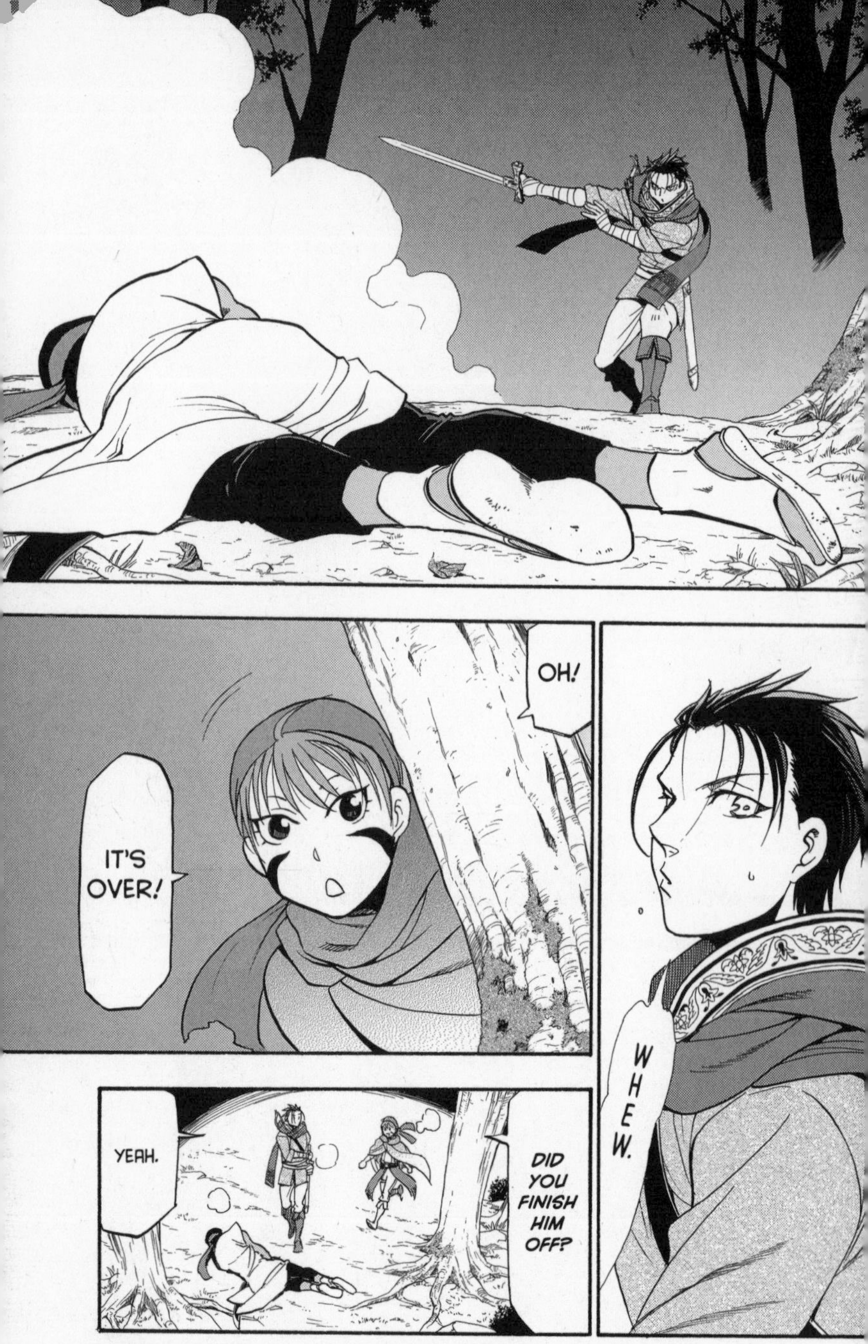
WHEW.
OH!
IT'S OVER!
DID YOU FINISH HIM OFF?
YEAH.

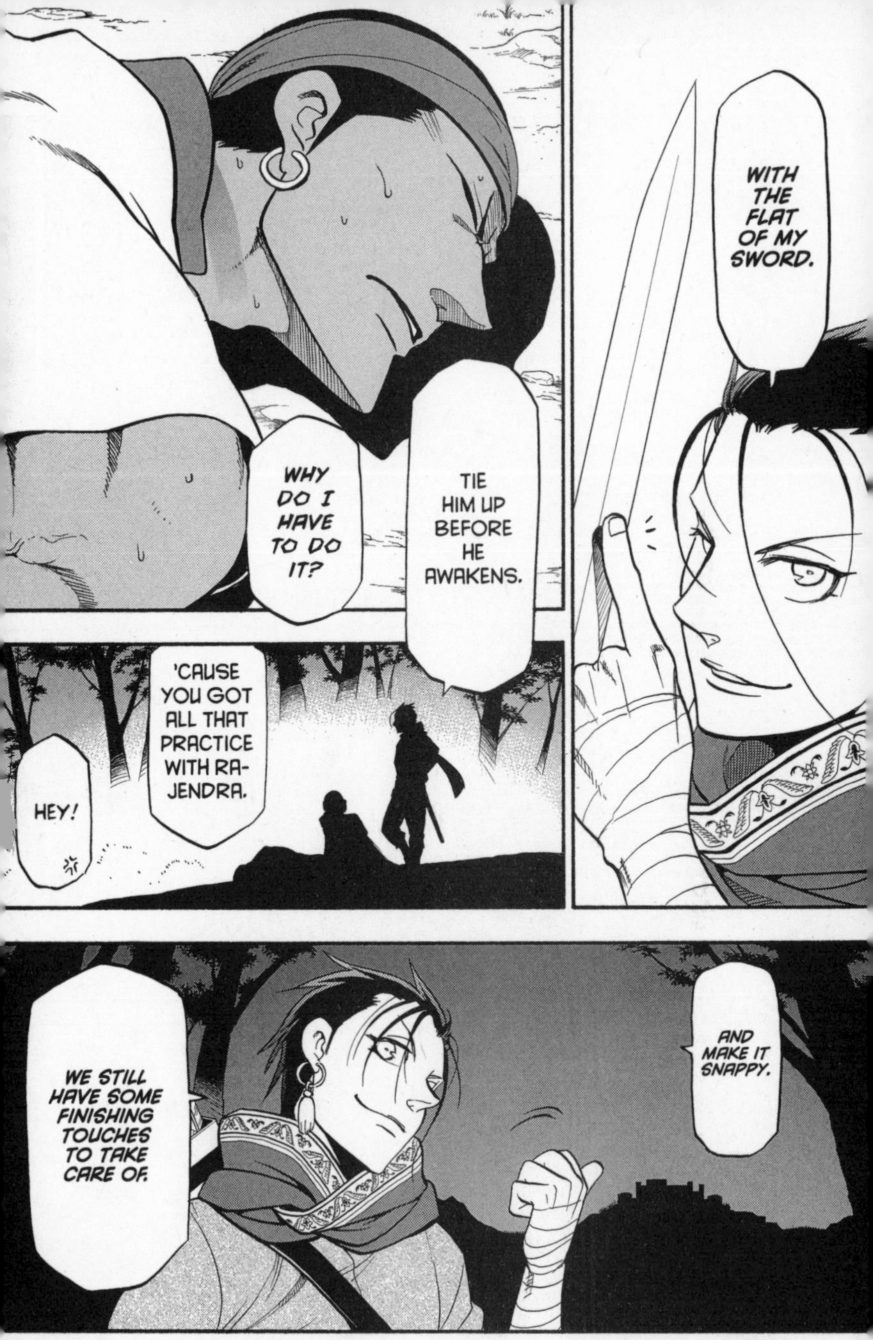
WITH THE FLAT OF MY SWORD.
TIE HIM UP BEFORE HE AWAKENS.
WHY DO I HAVE TO DO IT?
'CAUSE YOU GOT ALL THAT PRACTICE WITH RA-JENDRA.
HEY!
AND MAKE IT SNAPPY.
WE STILL HAVE SOME FINISHING TOUCHES TO TAKE CARE OF.

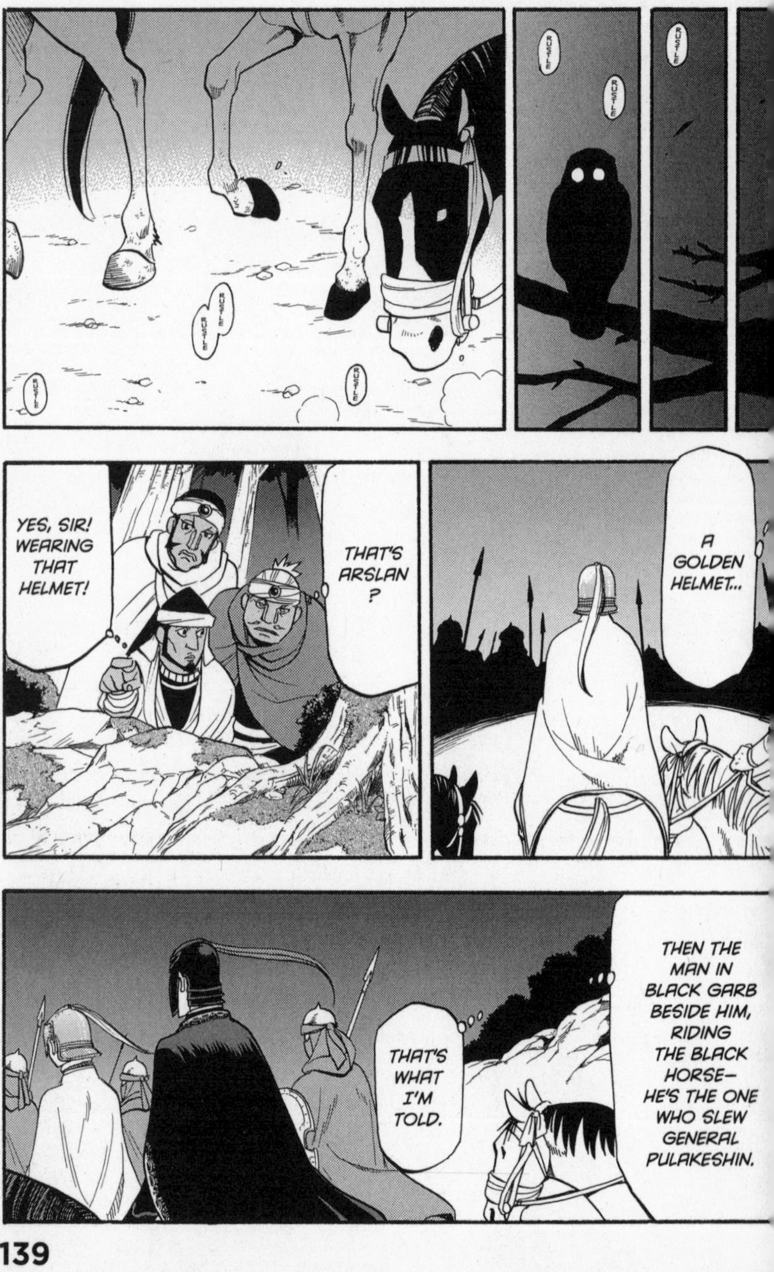
RUSTLE
RUSTLE
RUSTLE
RUSTLE
RUSTLE
RUSTLE
RUSTLE
A GOLDEN HELMET...
THAT'S ARSLAN ?
YES, SIR! WEARING THAT HELMET!
THEN THE MAN IN BLACK GARB BESIDE HIM, RIDING THE BLACK HORSE— HE'S THE ONE WHO SLEW GENERAL PULAKESHIN.
THAT'S WHAT I'M TOLD.

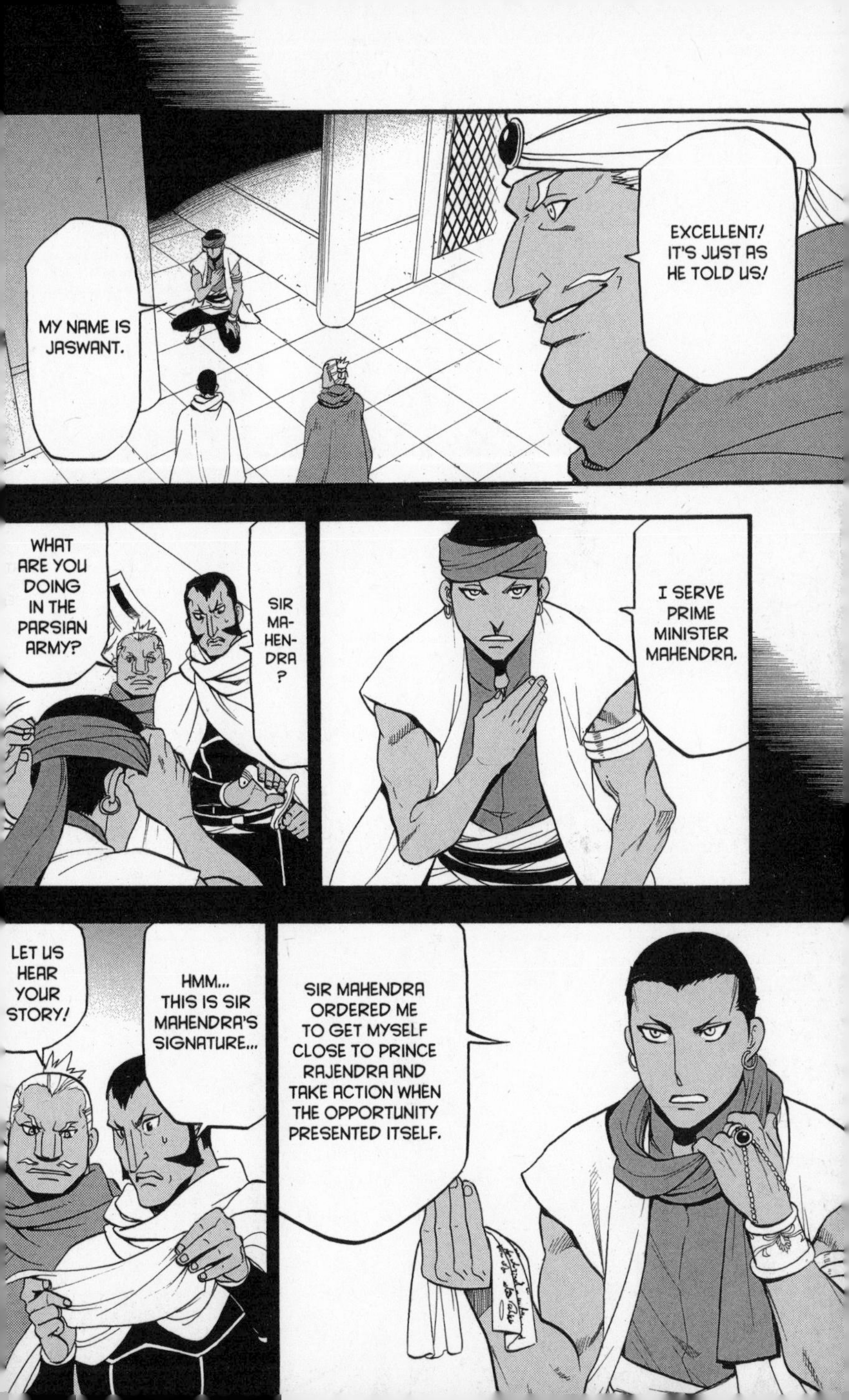
EXCELLENT! IT'S JUST AS HE TOLD US!
MY NAME IS JASWANT.
I SERVE PRIME MINISTER MAHENDRA.
SIR MA-HEN-DRA?
WHAT ARE YOU DOING IN THE PARSIAN ARMY?
SIR MAHENDRA ORDERED ME TO GET MYSELF CLOSE TO PRINCE RAJENDRA AND TAKE ACTION WHEN THE OPPORTUNITY PRESENTED ITSELF.
HMM... THIS IS SIR MAHENDRA'S SIGNATURE...
LET US HEAR YOUR STORY!

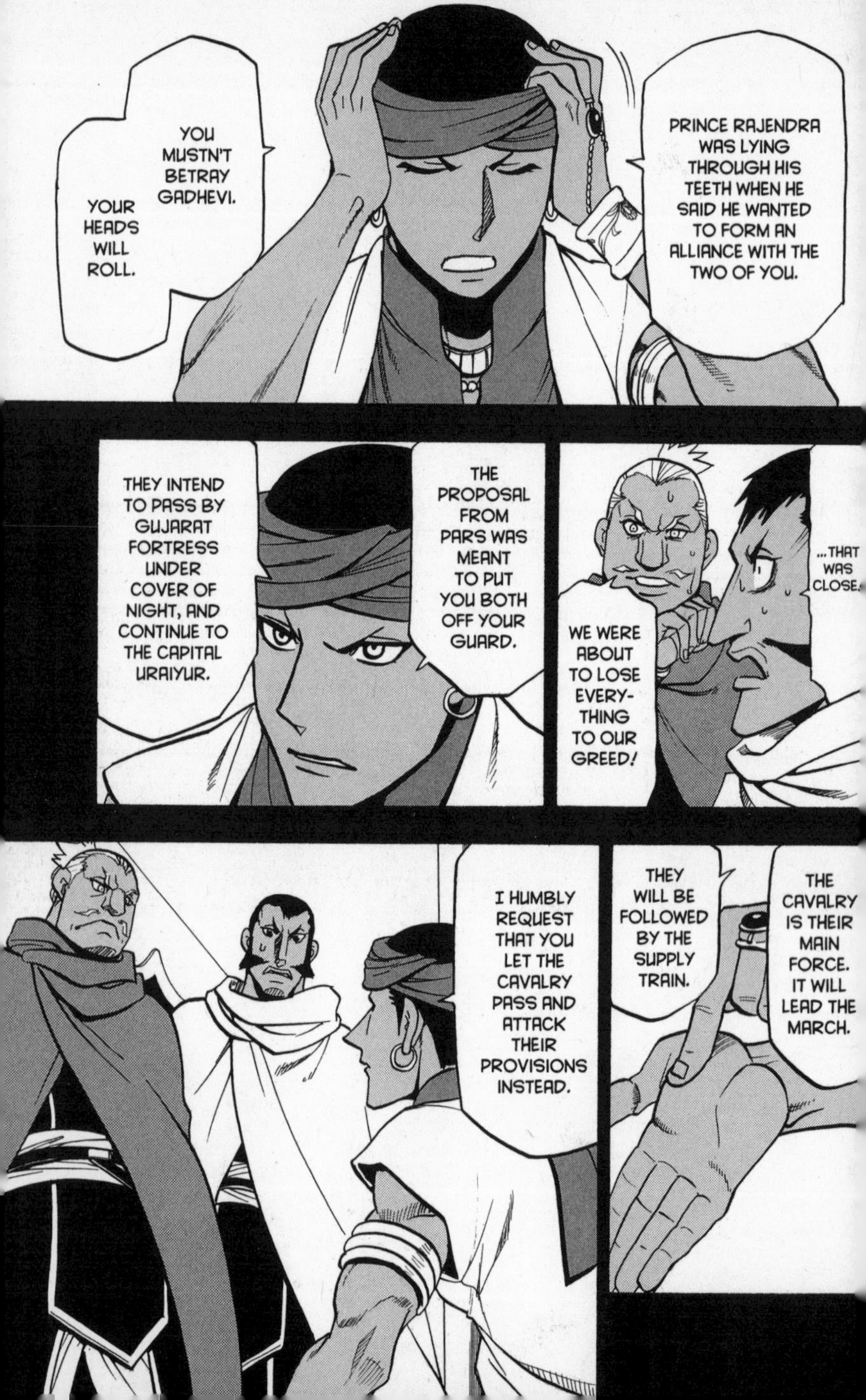
PRINCE RAJENDRA WAS LYING THROUGH HIS TEETH WHEN HE SAID HE WANTED TO FORM AN ALLIANCE WITH THE TWO OF YOU.
YOU MUSTN'T BETRAY GADHEVI.
YOUR HEADS WILL ROLL.
...THAT WAS CLOSE.
WE WERE ABOUT TO LOSE EVERY-THING TO OUR GREED!
THE PROPOSAL FROM PARS WAS MEANT TO PUT YOU BOTH OFF YOUR GUARD.
THEY INTEND TO PASS BY GUJARAT FORTRESS UNDER COVER OF NIGHT, AND CONTINUE TO THE CAPITAL URAIYUR.
THE CAVALRY IS THEIR MAIN FORCE. IT WILL LEAD THE MARCH.
THEY WILL BE FOLLOWED BY THE SUPPLY TRAIN.
I HUMBLY REQUEST THAT YOU LET THE CAVALRY PASS AND ATTACK THEIR PROVISIONS INSTEAD.

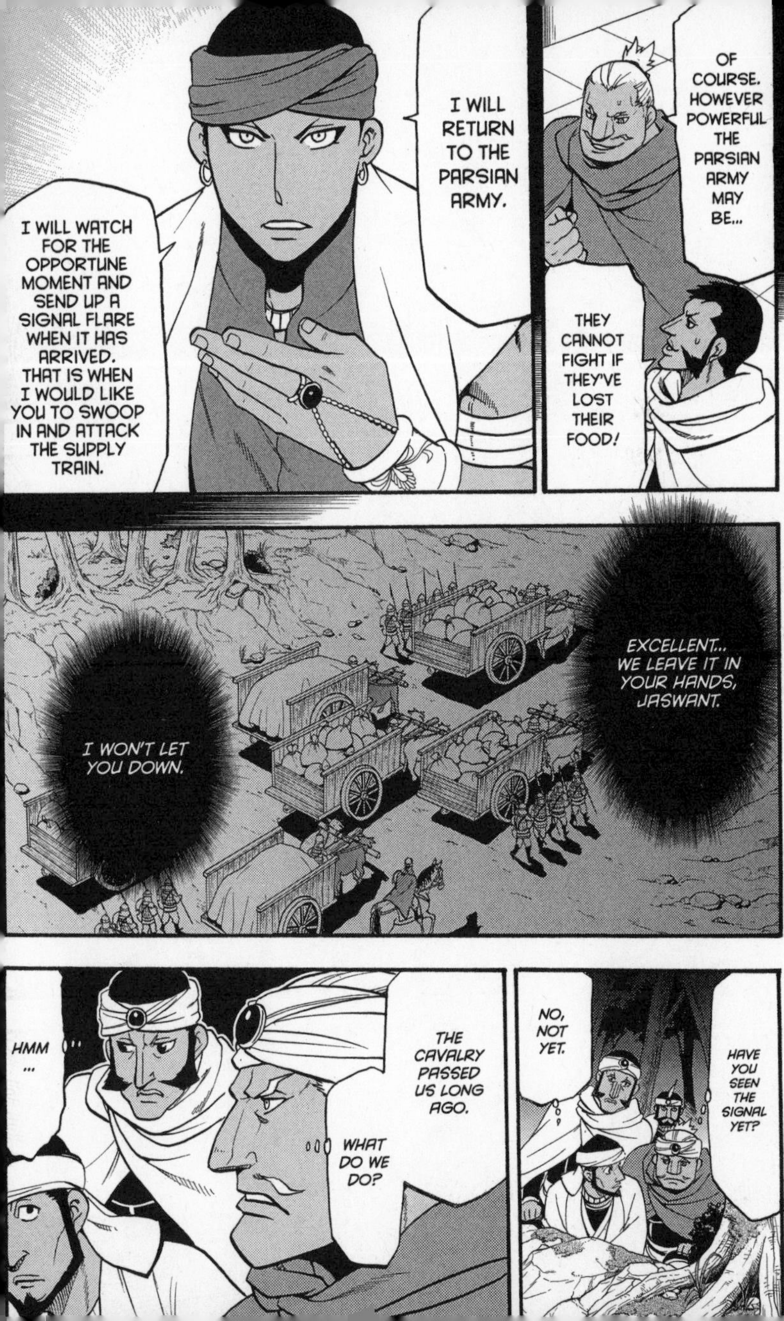
OF COURSE. HOWEVER POWERFUL THE PARSIAN ARMY MAY BE...
THEY CANNOT FIGHT IF THEY'VE LOST THEIR FOOD!
I WILL RETURN TO THE PARSIAN ARMY.
I WILL WATCH FOR THE OPPORTUNE MOMENT AND SEND UP A SIGNAL FLARE WHEN IT HAS ARRIVED. THAT IS WHEN I WOULD LIKE YOU TO SWOOP IN AND ATTACK THE SUPPLY TRAIN.
EXCELLENT... WE LEAVE IT IN YOUR HANDS, JASWANT.
I WON'T LET YOU DOWN.
HAVE YOU SEEN THE SIGNAL YET?
NO, NOT YET.
THE CAVALRY PASSED US LONG AGO.
WHAT DO WE DO?
HMM ...

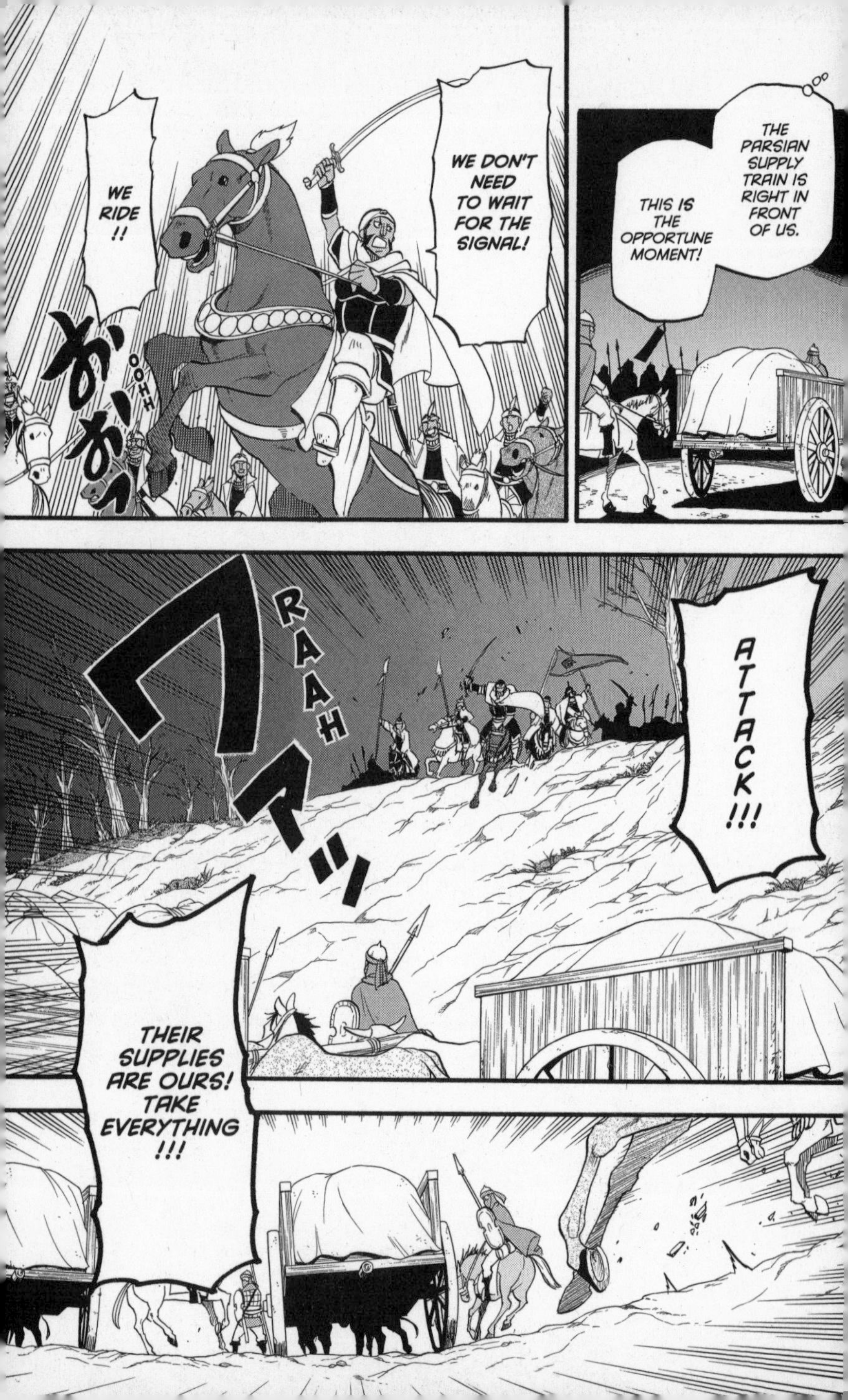
THE PARSIAN SUPPLY TRAIN IS RIGHT IN FRONT OF US.
THIS IS THE OPPORTUNE MOMENT!
WE DON'T NEED TO WAIT FOR THE SIGNAL!
WE RIDE!!
OOHH
ATTACK!!!
RAAH
THEIR SUPPLIES ARE OURS! TAKE EVERYTHING!!!

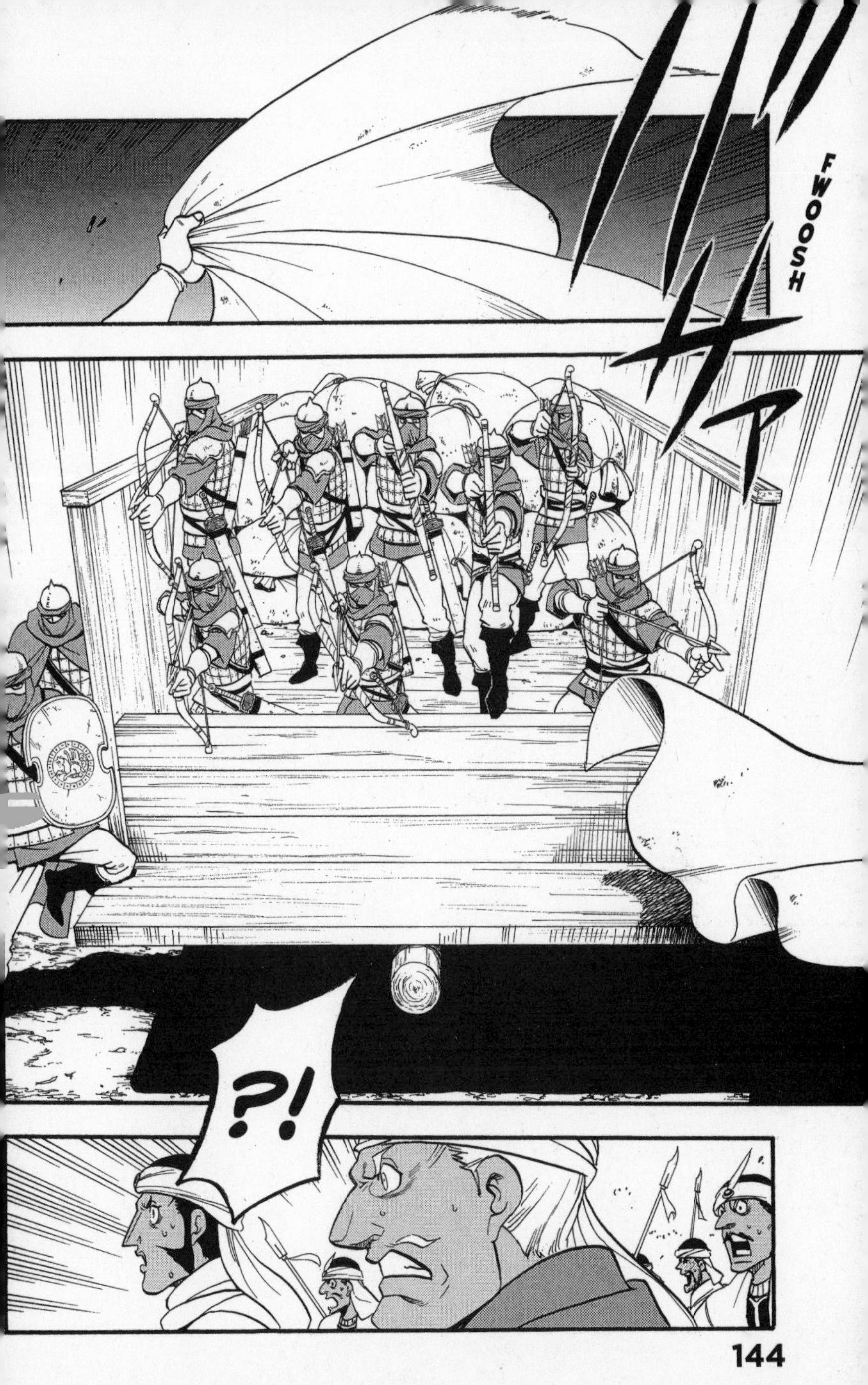
FWOOSH
?!

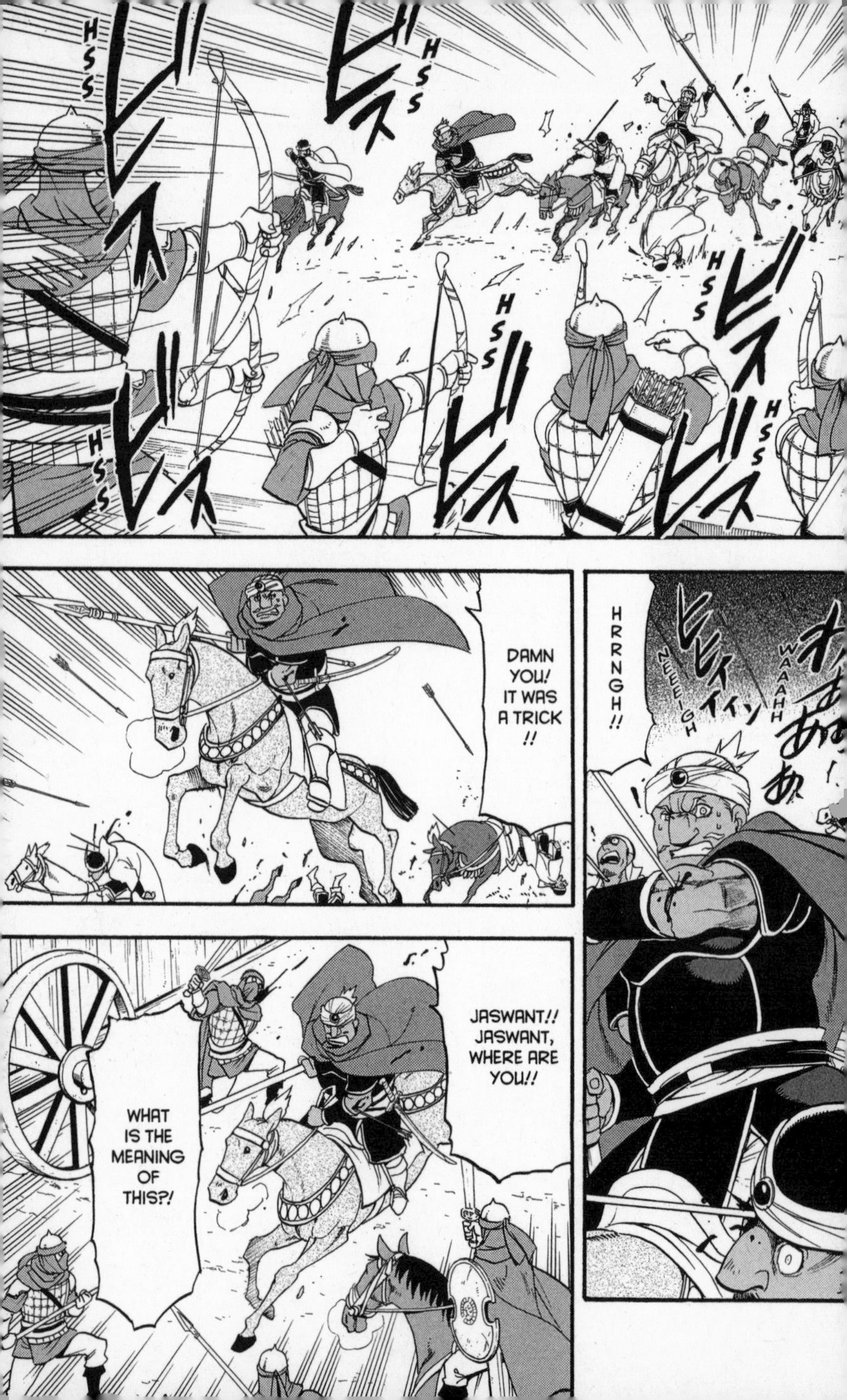

HSS
HSS
HSS
HSS
HSS
HRRNGH!!
WAAAHH
NEEEIGH
DAMN YOU! IT WAS A TRICK!!
JASWANT!! JASWANT, WHERE ARE YOU!!
WHAT IS THE MEANING OF THIS?!

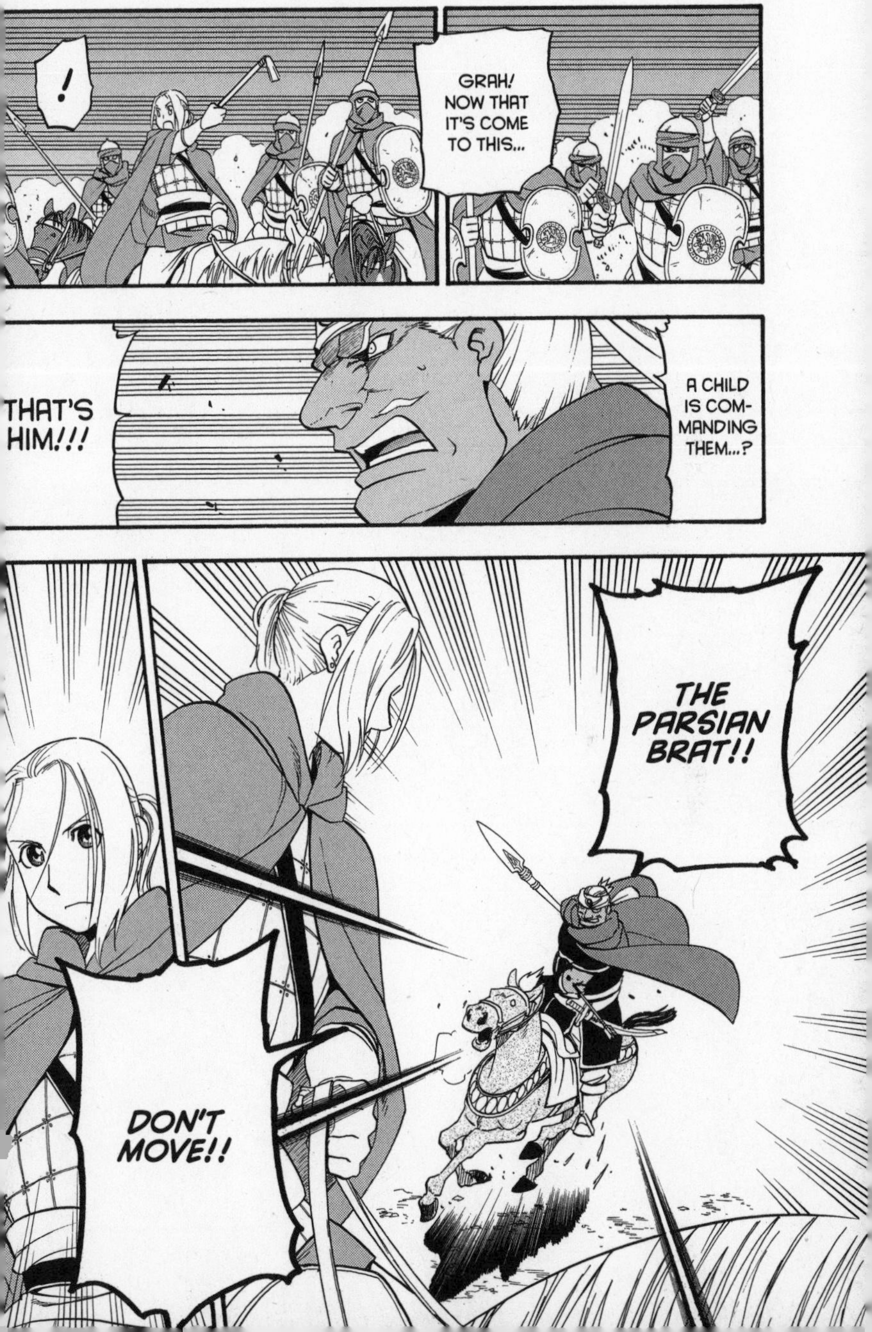
GRAH! NOW THAT IT'S COME TO THIS...
!
A CHILD IS COM-MANDING THEM...?
THAT'S HIM!!!
THE PARSIAN BRAT!!
DON'T MOVE!!

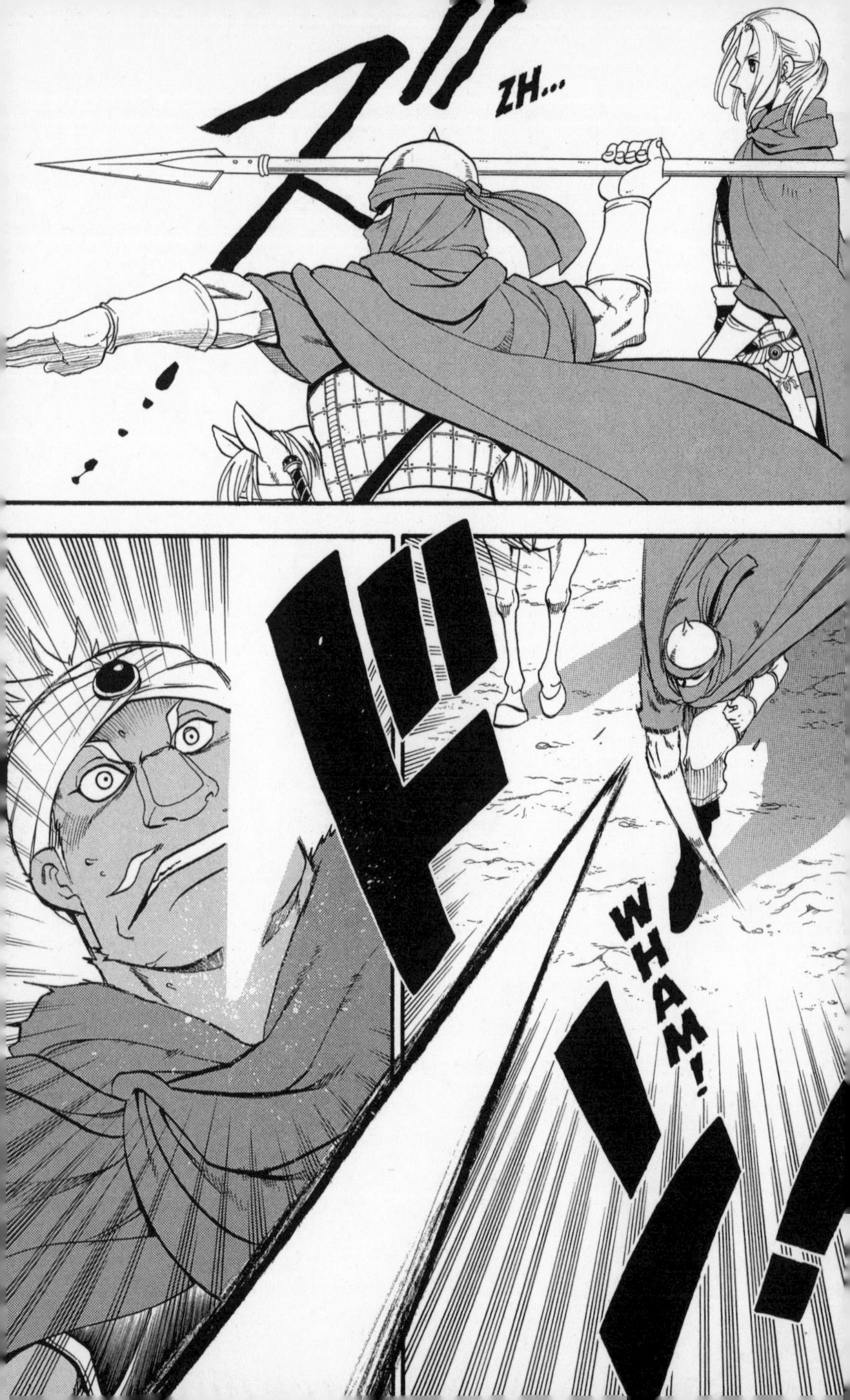
ZH...
WHAM!

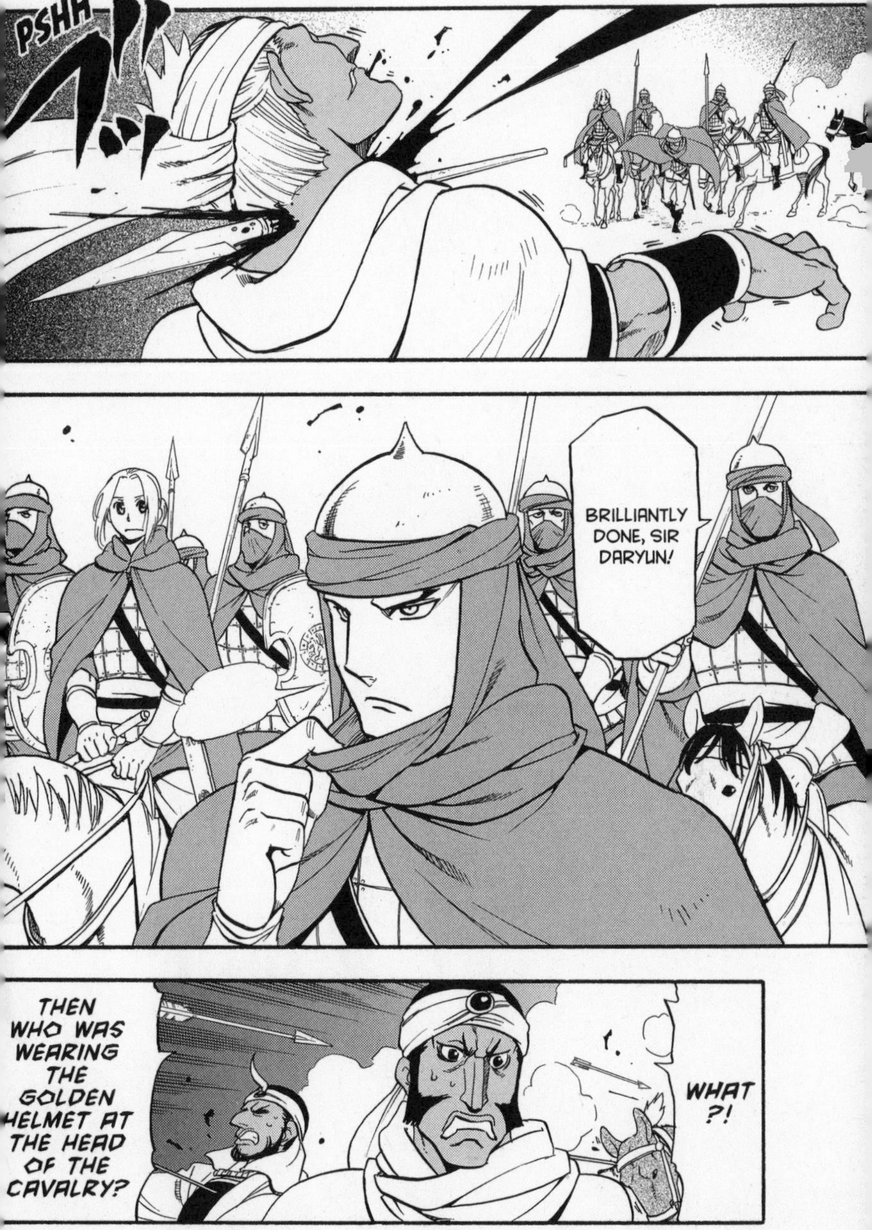
PSHH
BRILLIANTLY DONE, SIR DARYUN!
WHAT ?!
THEN WHO WAS WEARING THE GOLDEN HELMET AT THE HEAD OF THE CAVALRY?

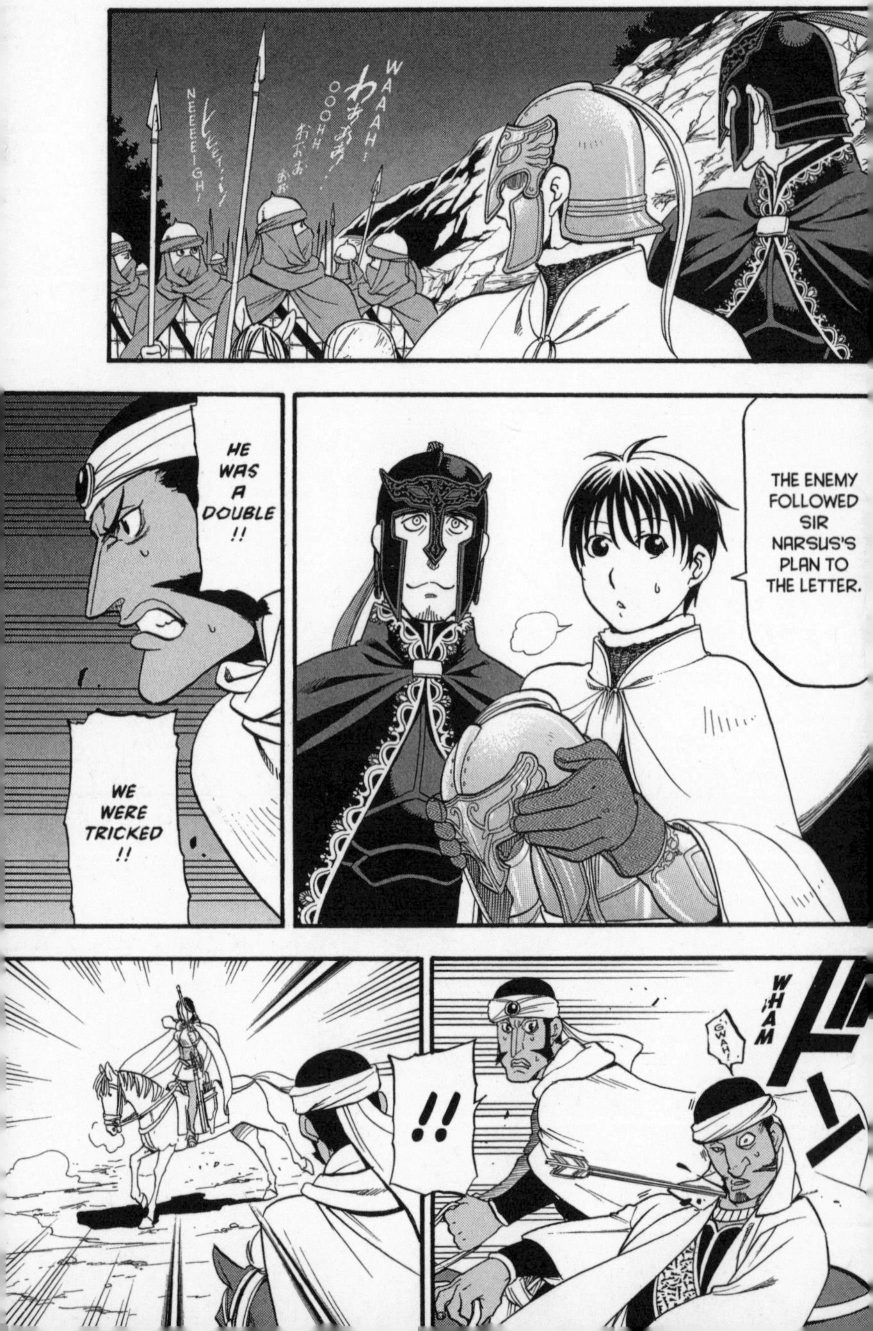
WAAAH!
OOOHH
NEEEEIGH!
THE ENEMY FOLLOWED SIR NARSUS'S PLAN TO THE LETTER.
HE WAS A DOUBLE !!
WE WERE TRICKED !!
WHAM
GWAH!
!!

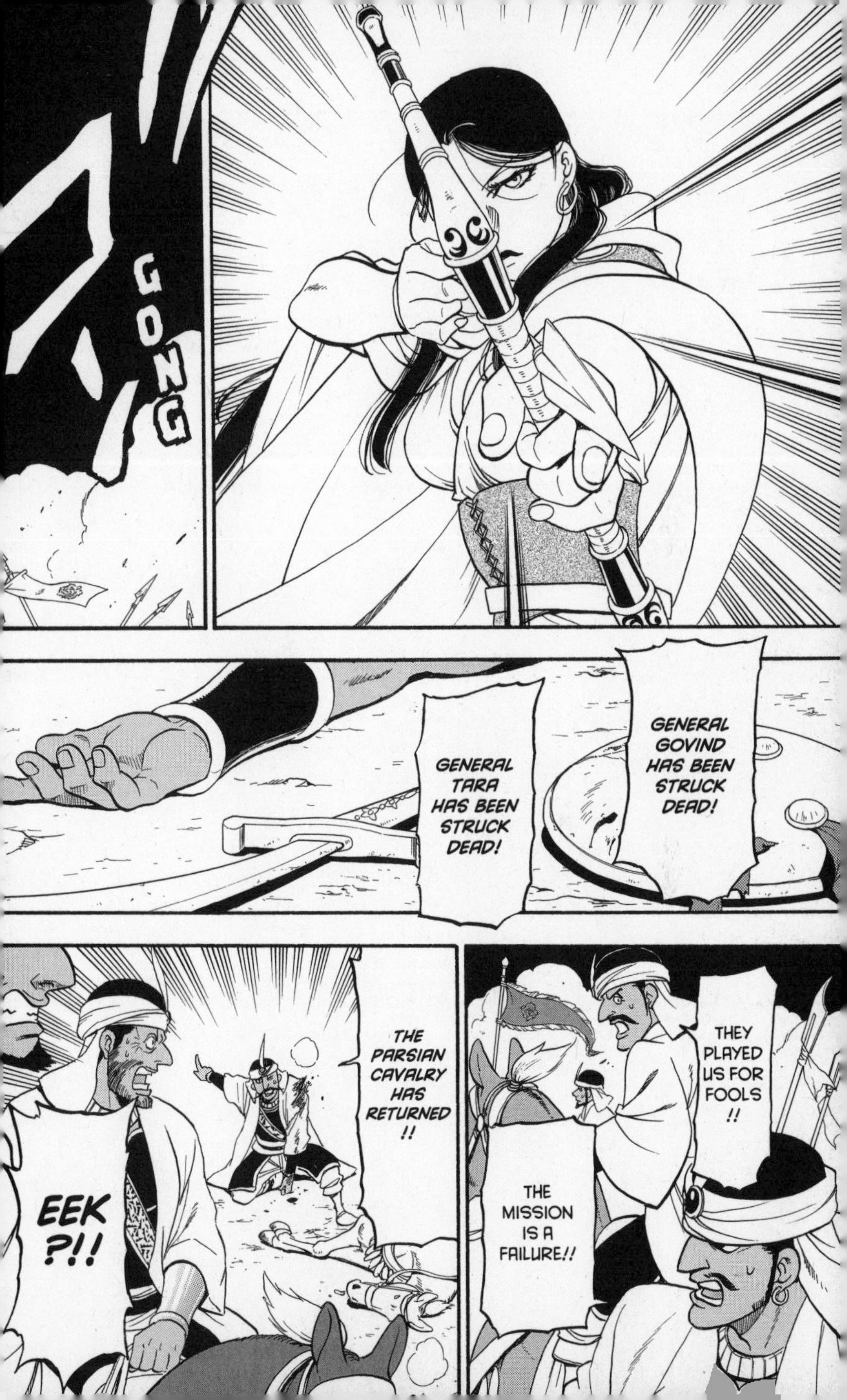
GONG
GENERAL GOVIND HAS BEEN STRUCK DEAD!
GENERAL TARA HAS BEEN STRUCK DEAD!
THEY PLAYED US FOR FOOLS!!
THE MISSION IS A FAILURE!!
THE PARSIAN CAVALRY HAS RETURNED!!
EEK?!!

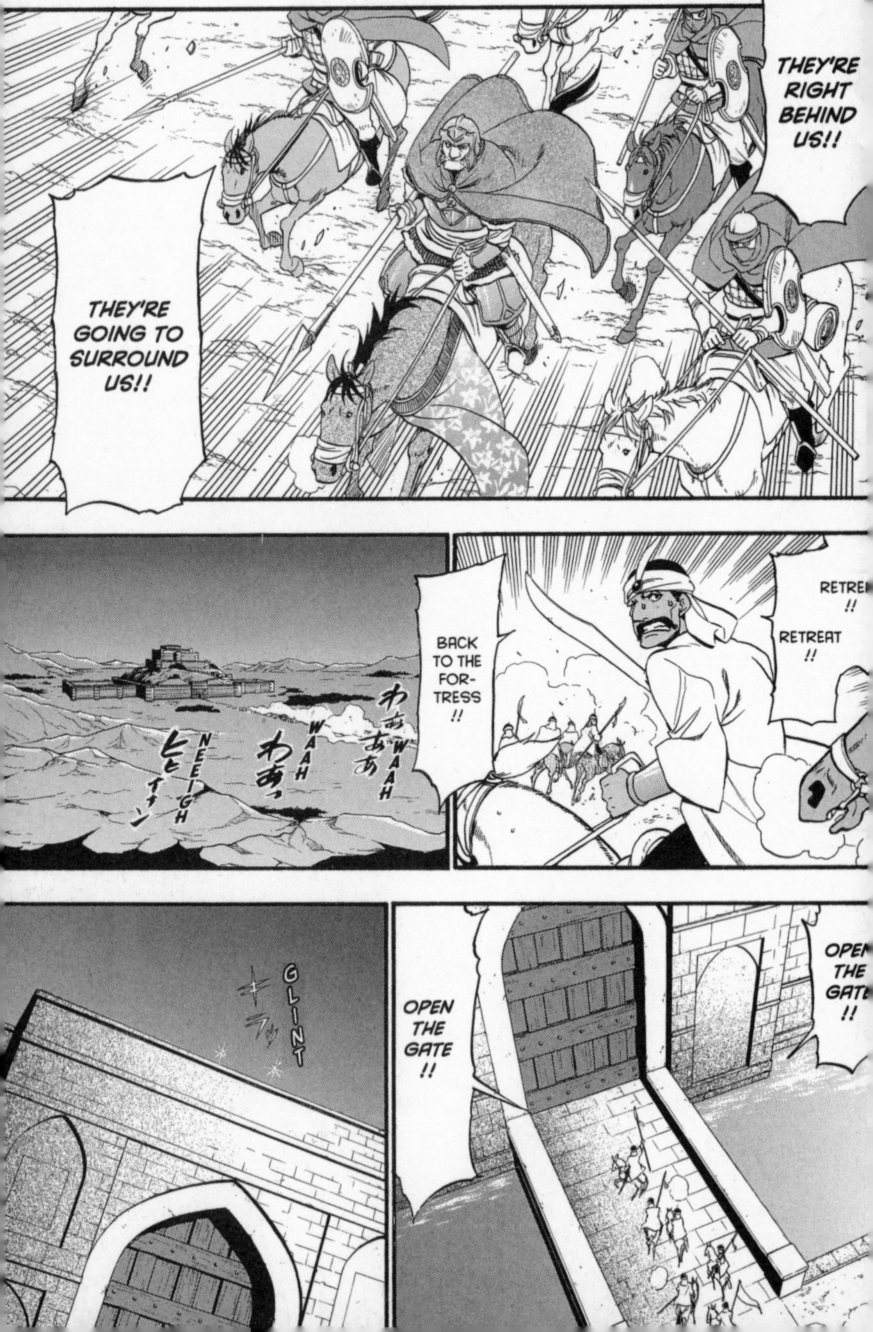
THEY'RE RIGHT BEHIND US!!
THEY'RE GOING TO SURROUND US!!
RETRE !!
RETREAT !!
BACK TO THE FOR-TRESS !!
わあああ WAAH
わあっ WAAH
ヒヒィィン NEEEIGH
OPEN THE GATE !!
OPEN THE GATE !!
GLINT

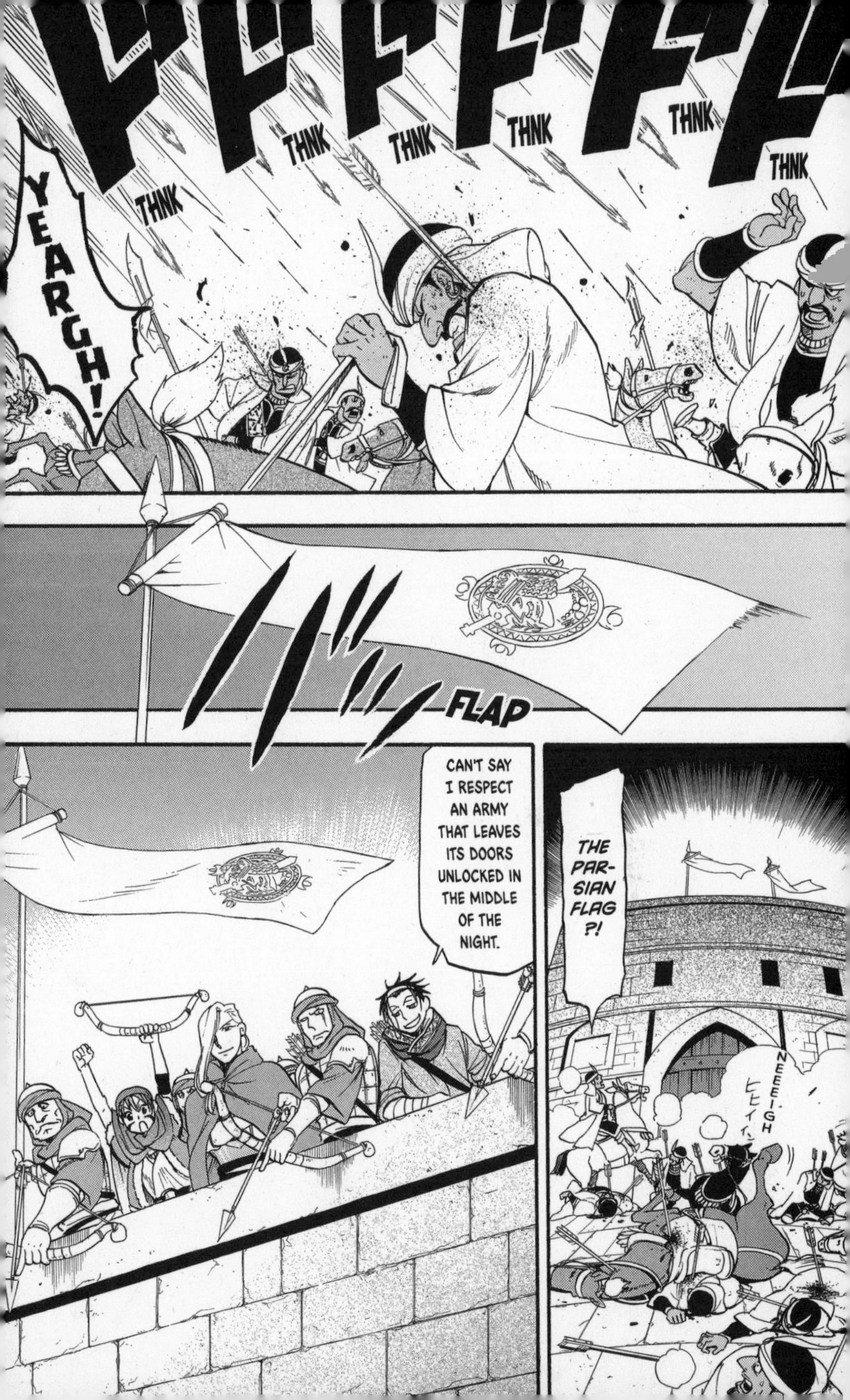
THNK
THNK
THNK
THNK
THNK
YEARGH!
THNK
FLAP
THE PAR-SIAN FLAG?!
NEEEIGH
ヒヒイーン
CAN'T SAY I RESPECT AN ARMY THAT LEAVES ITS DOORS UNLOCKED IN THE MIDDLE OF THE NIGHT.

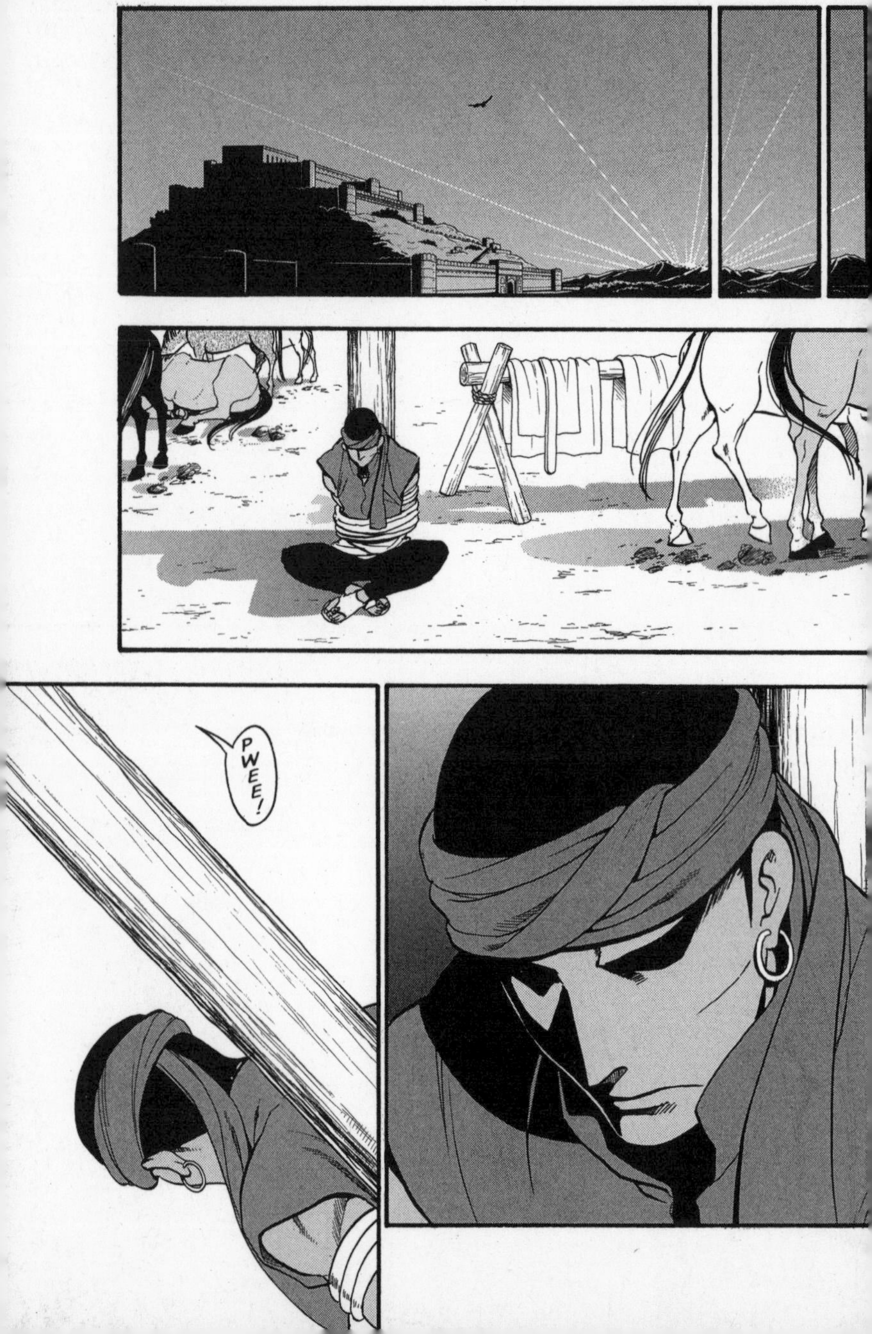
PWEE!

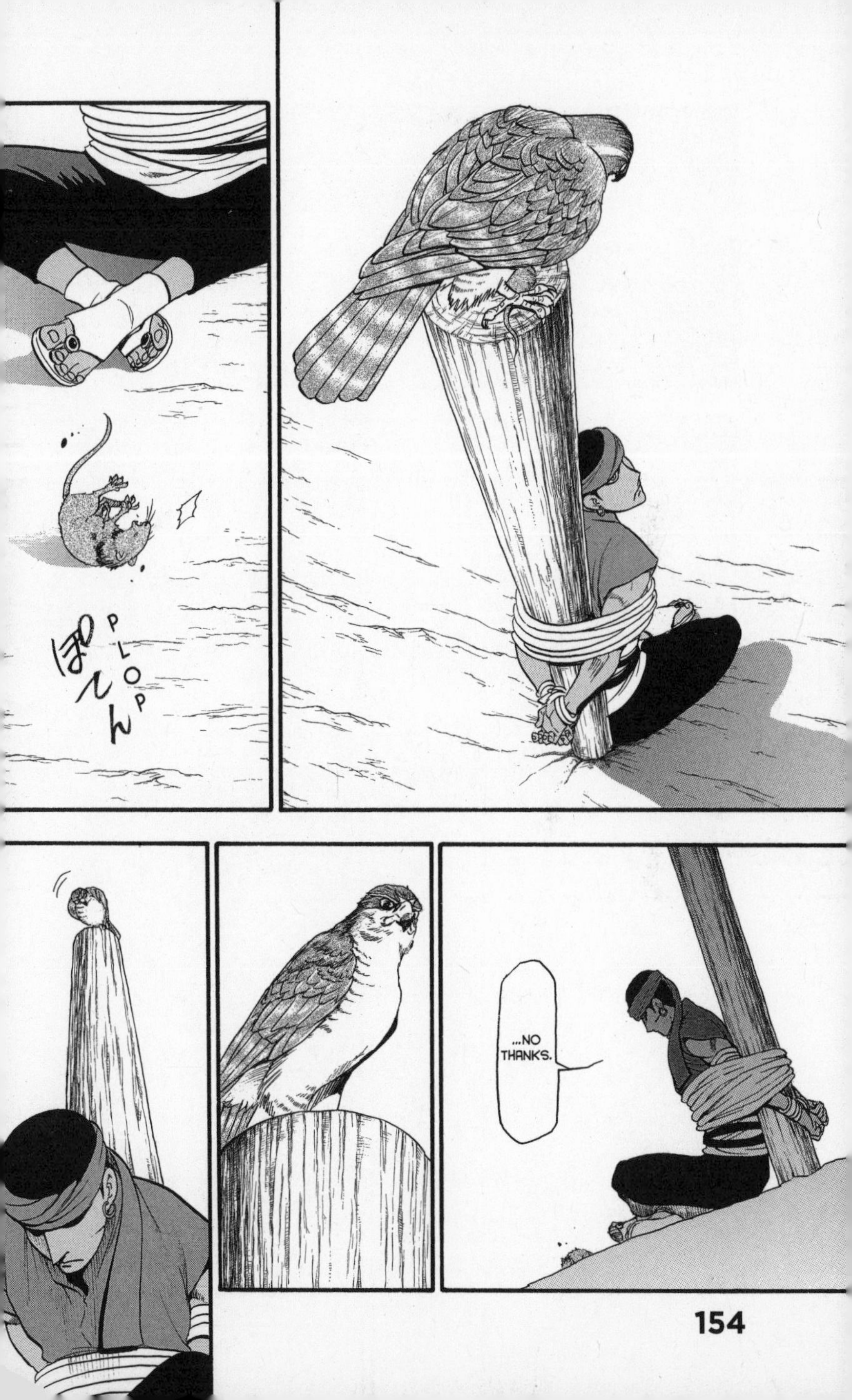

ぽてん
PLOP
...NO THANKS.

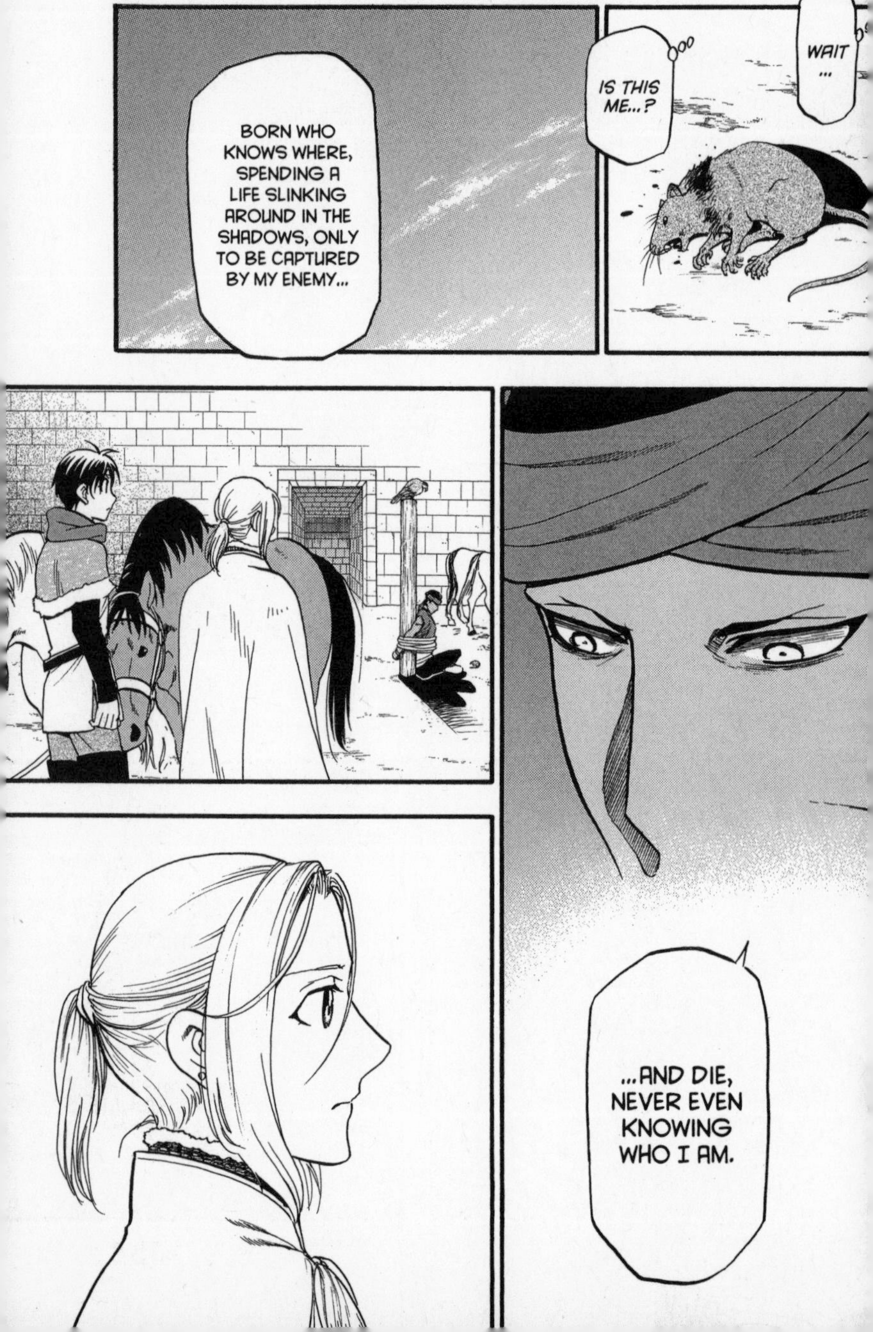
WAIT ...
IS THIS ME...?
BORN WHO KNOWS WHERE, SPENDING A LIFE SLINKING AROUND IN THE SHADOWS, ONLY TO BE CAPTURED BY MY ENEMY...
...AND DIE, NEVER EVEN KNOWING WHO I AM.

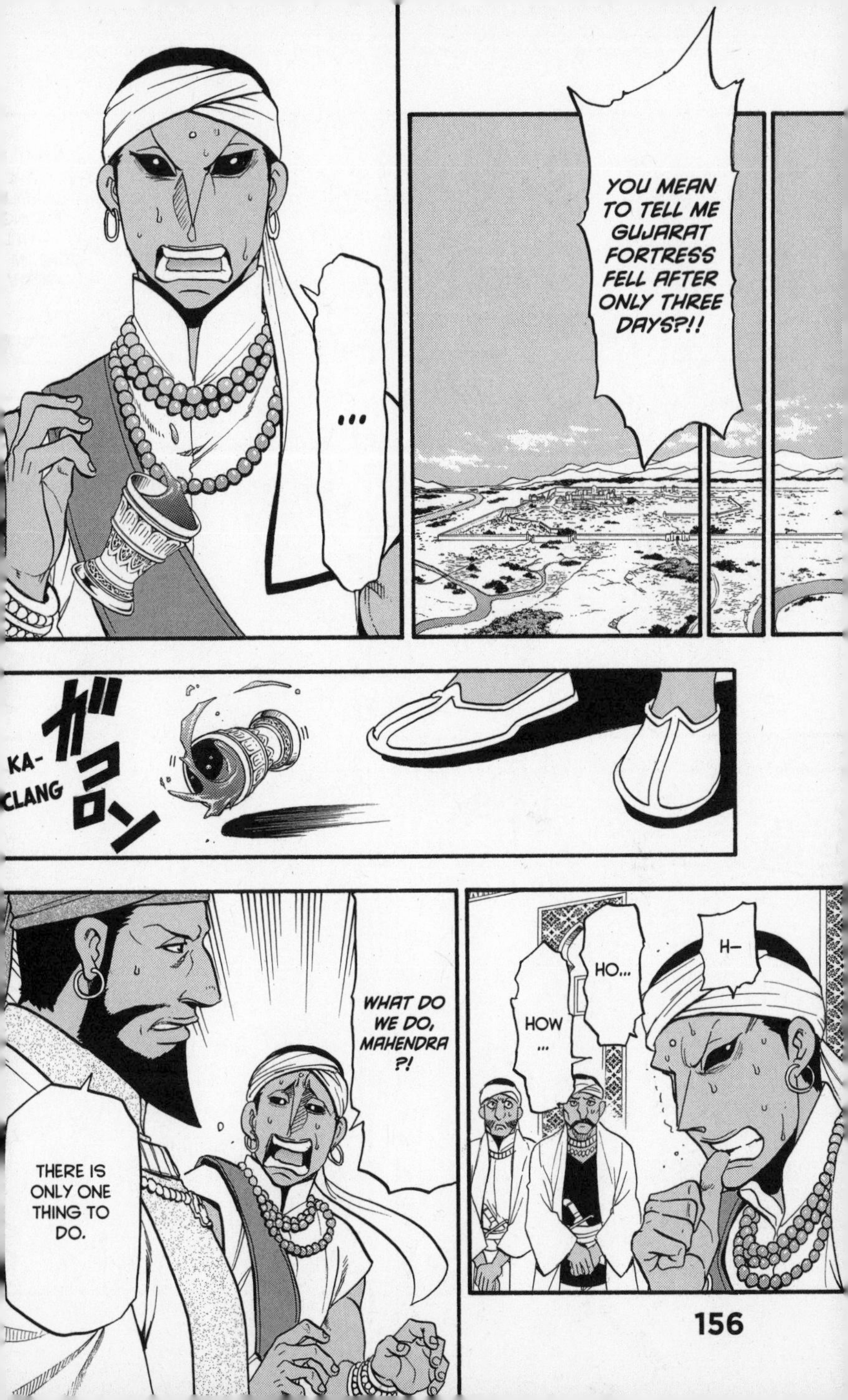
YOU MEAN TO TELL ME GUJARAT FORTRESS FELL AFTER ONLY THREE DAYS?!!
...
KA-CLANG
ガコロン
H–
HO...
HOW ...
WHAT DO WE DO, MAHENDRA ?!
THERE IS ONLY ONE THING TO DO.

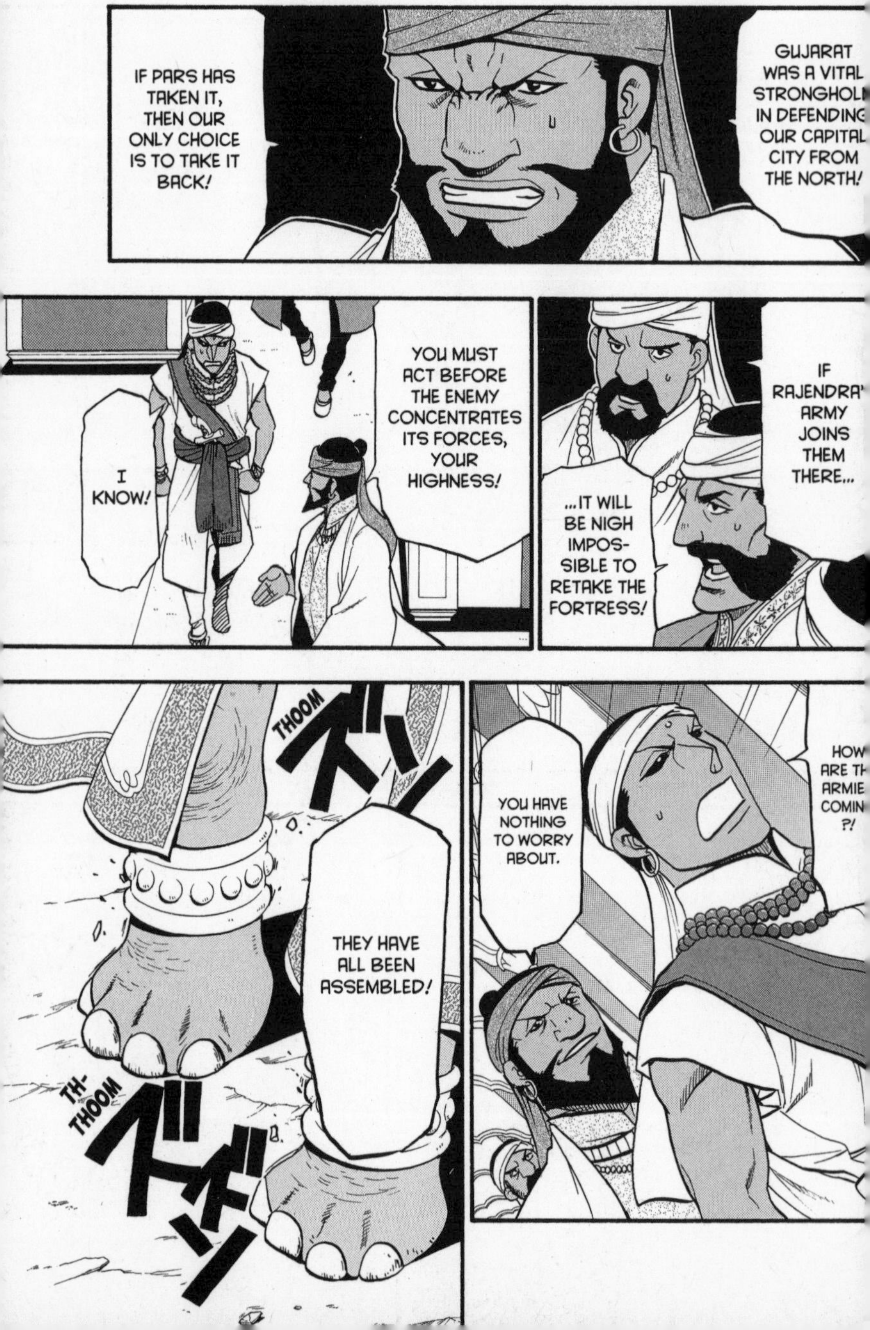
GUJARAT WAS A VITAL STRONGHOL IN DEFENDING OUR CAPITAL CITY FROM THE NORTH!
IF PARS HAS TAKEN IT, THEN OUR ONLY CHOICE IS TO TAKE IT BACK!
IF RAJENDRA' ARMY JOINS THEM THERE...
...IT WILL BE NIGH IMPOSSIBLE TO RETAKE THE FORTRESS!
YOU MUST ACT BEFORE THE ENEMY CONCENTRATES ITS FORCES, YOUR HIGHNESS!
I KNOW!
HOW ARE TH ARMIE COMIN ?!
YOU HAVE NOTHING TO WORRY ABOUT.
THEY HAVE ALL BEEN ASSEMBLED!
THOOM
TH-THOOM

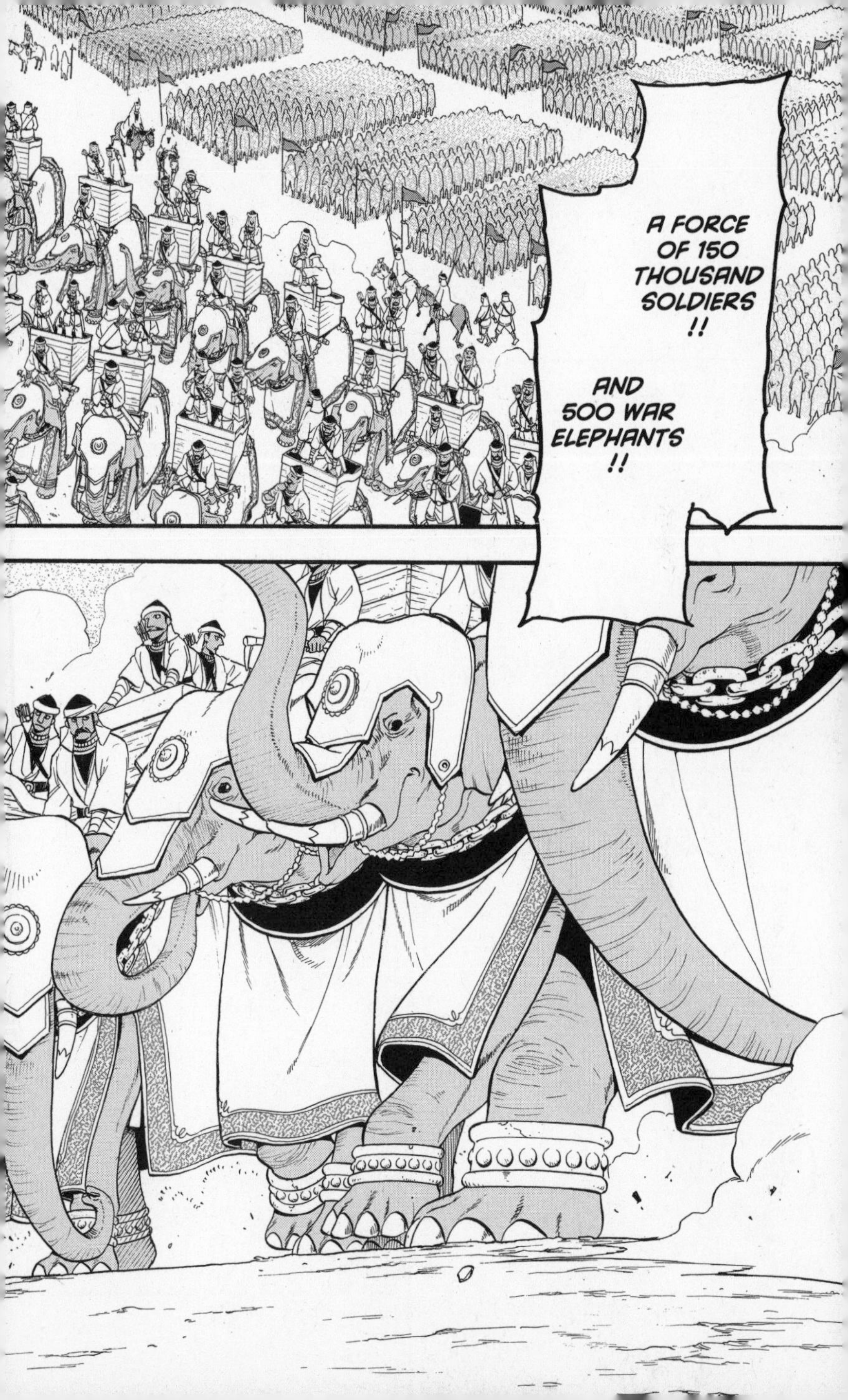
A FORCE OF 150 THOUSAND SOLDIERS !!
AND 500 WAR ELEPHANTS !!

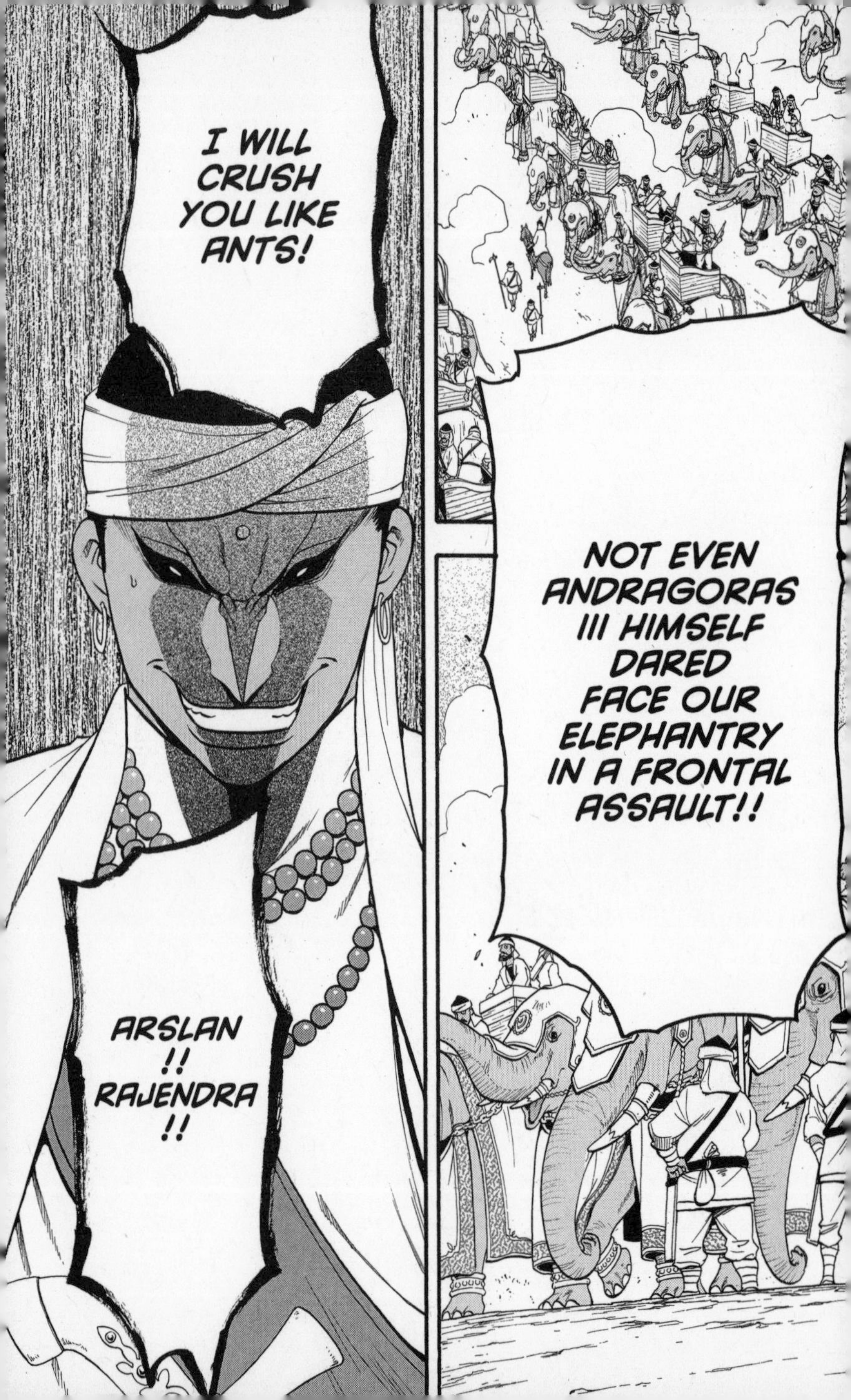
NOT EVEN ANDRAGORAS III HIMSELF DARED FACE OUR ELEPHANTRY IN A FRONTAL ASSAULT!!
I WILL CRUSH YOU LIKE ANTS!
ARSLAN!! RAJENDRA!!

THE HEROIC LEGEND OF
ARSLAN

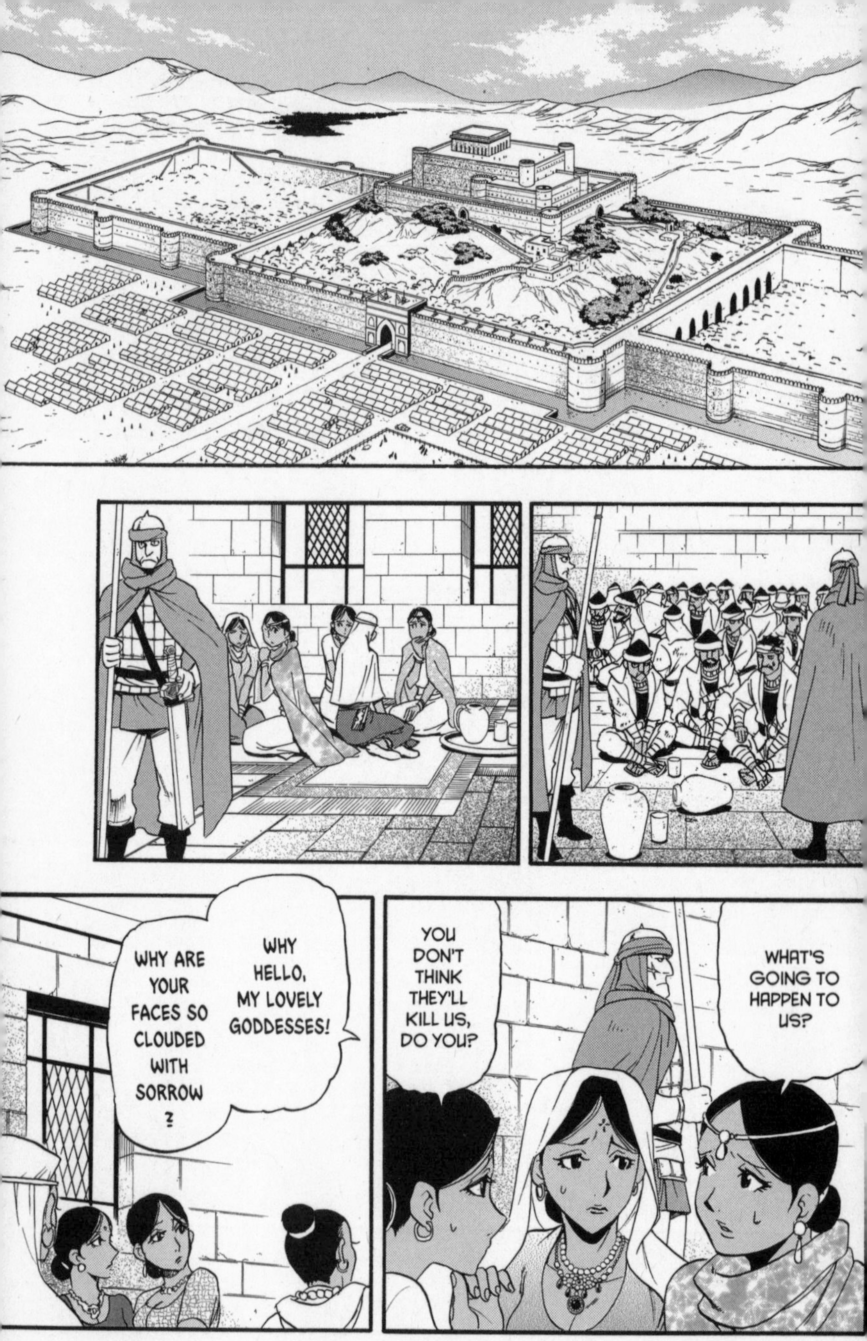
WHAT'S GOING TO HAPPEN TO US?
YOU DON'T THINK THEY'LL KILL US, DO YOU?
WHY HELLO, MY LOVELY GODDESSES!
WHY ARE YOUR FACES SO CLOUDED WITH SORROW?

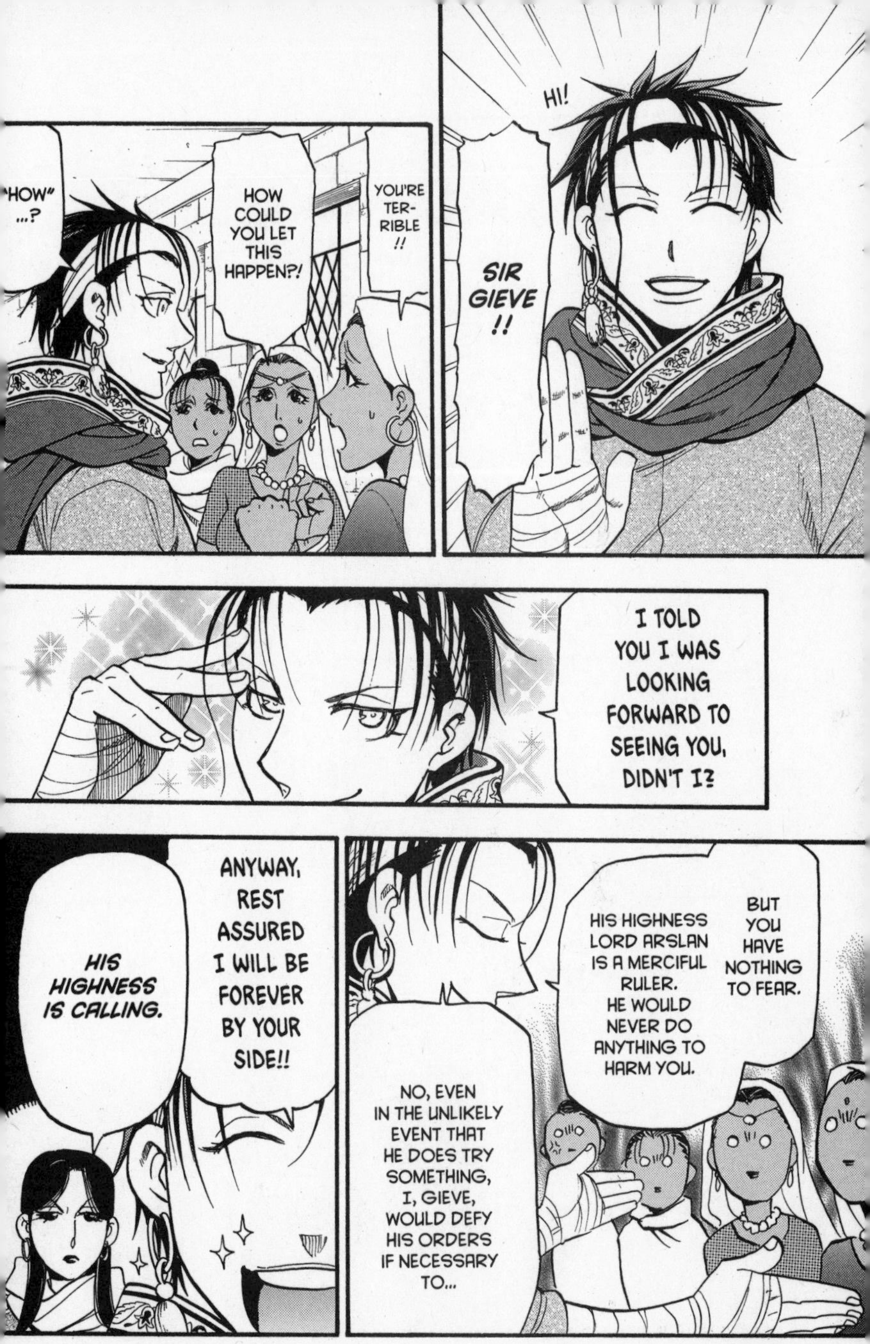
HI!
SIR GIEVE!!
YOU'RE TERRIBLE!!
HOW COULD YOU LET THIS HAPPEN?!
"HOW"...?
I TOLD YOU I WAS LOOKING FORWARD TO SEEING YOU, DIDN'T I?
BUT YOU HAVE NOTHING TO FEAR.
HIS HIGHNESS LORD ARSLAN IS A MERCIFUL RULER. HE WOULD NEVER DO ANYTHING TO HARM YOU.
NO, EVEN IN THE UNLIKELY EVENT THAT HE DOES TRY SOMETHING, I, GIEVE, WOULD DEFY HIS ORDERS IF NECESSARY TO...
ANYWAY, REST ASSURED I WILL BE FOREVER BY YOUR SIDE!!
HIS HIGHNESS IS CALLING.

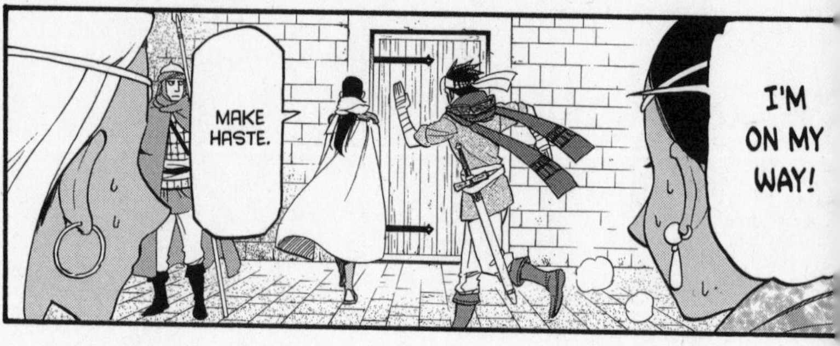
I'M ON MY WAY!
MAKE HASTE.

Chapter 46: The Bond of Servant and Master

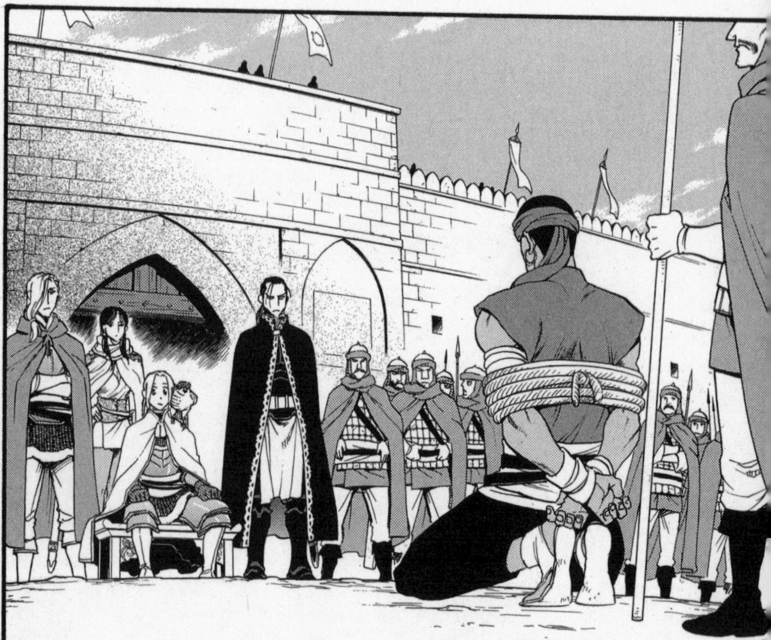

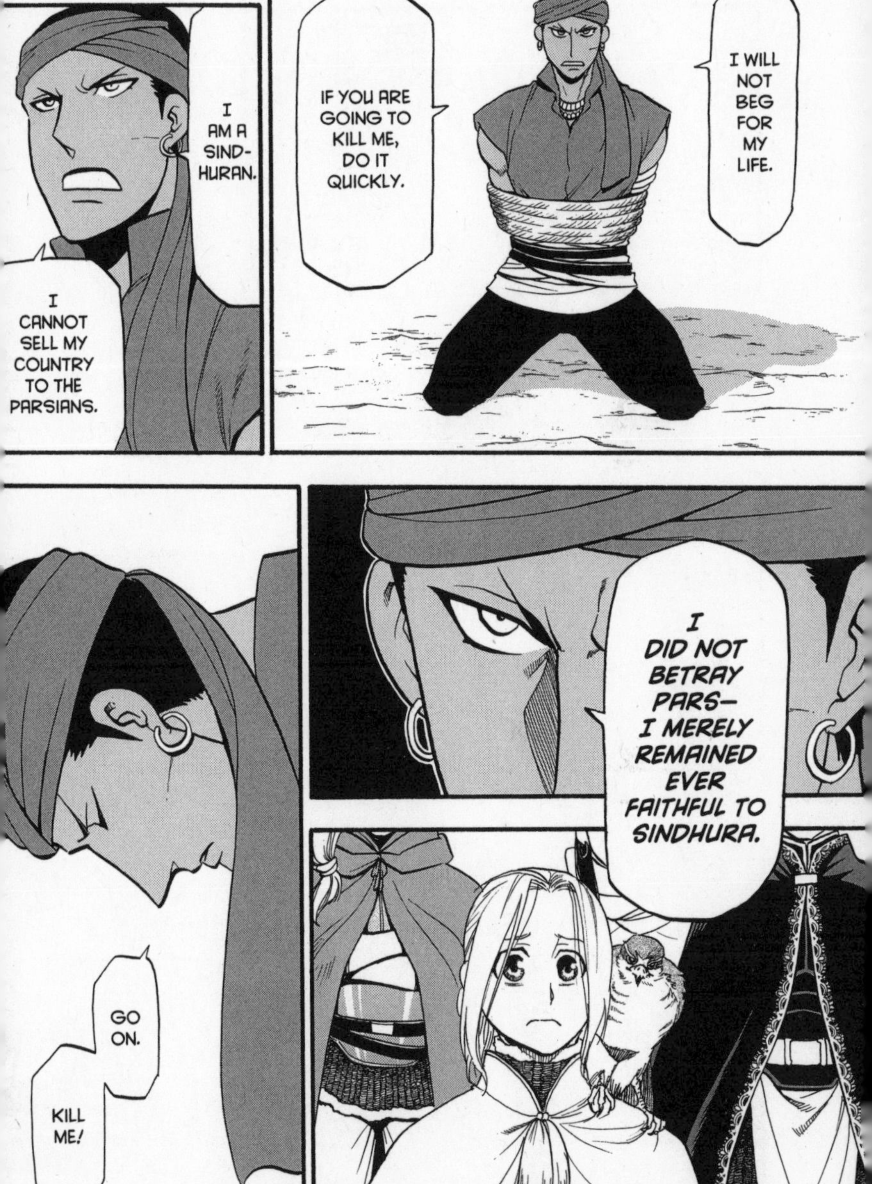
I WILL NOT BEG FOR MY LIFE.
IF YOU ARE GOING TO KILL ME, DO IT QUICKLY.
I AM A SIND-HURAN.
I CANNOT SELL MY COUNTRY TO THE PARSIANS.
I DID NOT BETRAY PARS— I MERELY REMAINED EVER FAITHFUL TO SINDHURA.
GO ON.
KILL ME!

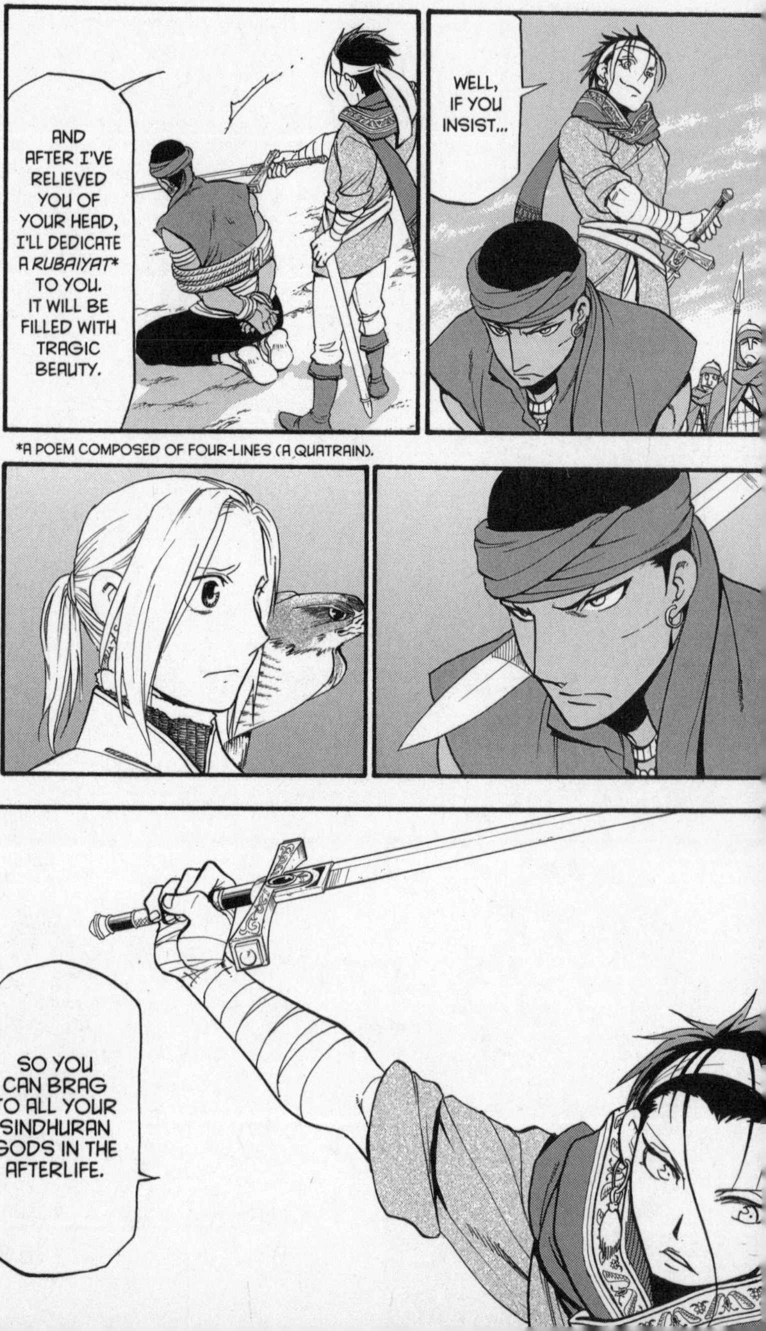
WELL, IF YOU INSIST...
AND AFTER I'VE RELIEVED YOU OF YOUR HEAD, I'LL DEDICATE A *RUBAIYAT** TO YOU. IT WILL BE FILLED WITH TRAGIC BEAUTY.
SO YOU CAN BRAG TO ALL YOUR SINDHURAN GODS IN THE AFTERLIFE.
*A POEM COMPOSED OF FOUR-LINES (A QUATRAIN).

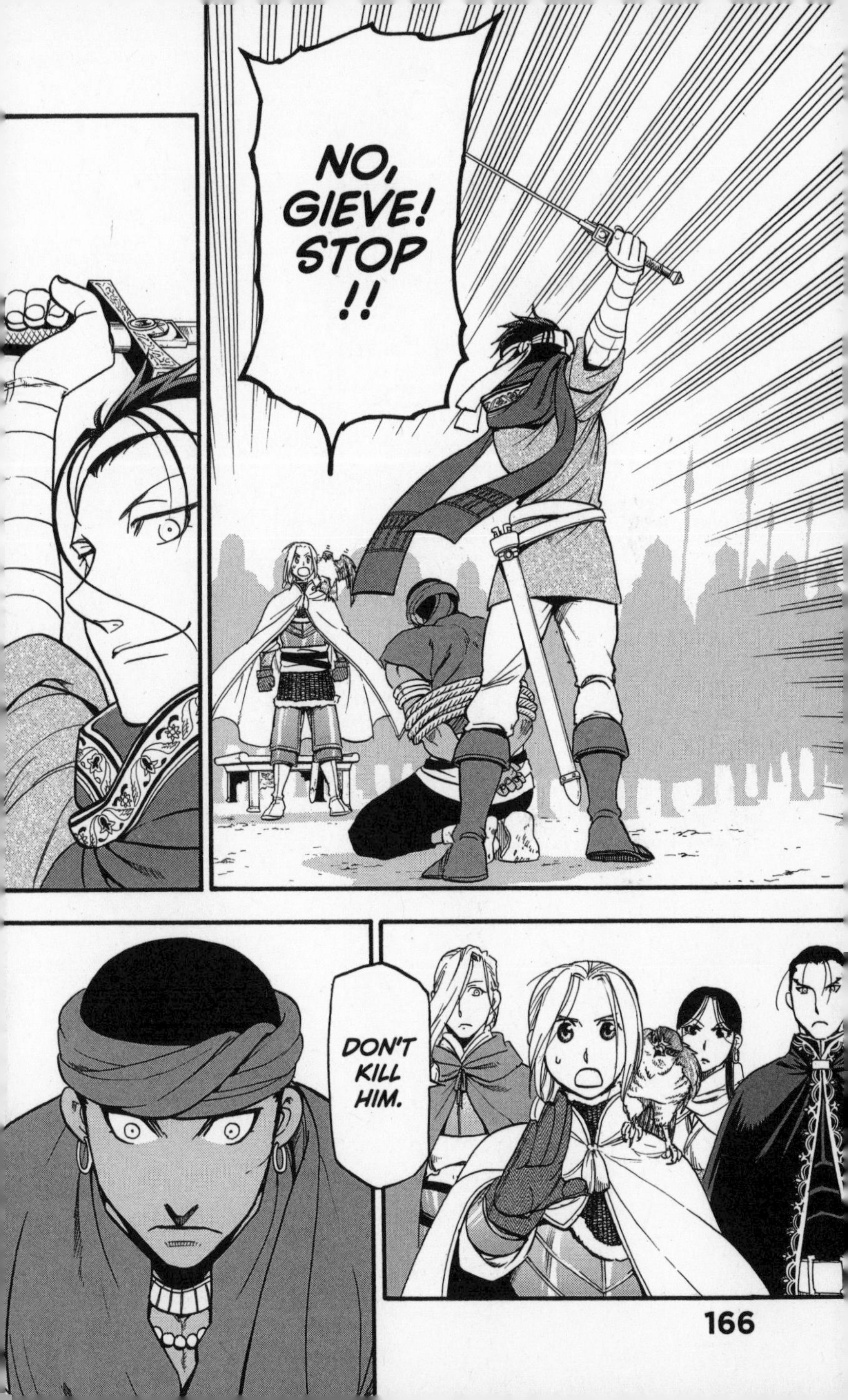
NO, GIEVE! STOP!!
DON'T KILL HIM.

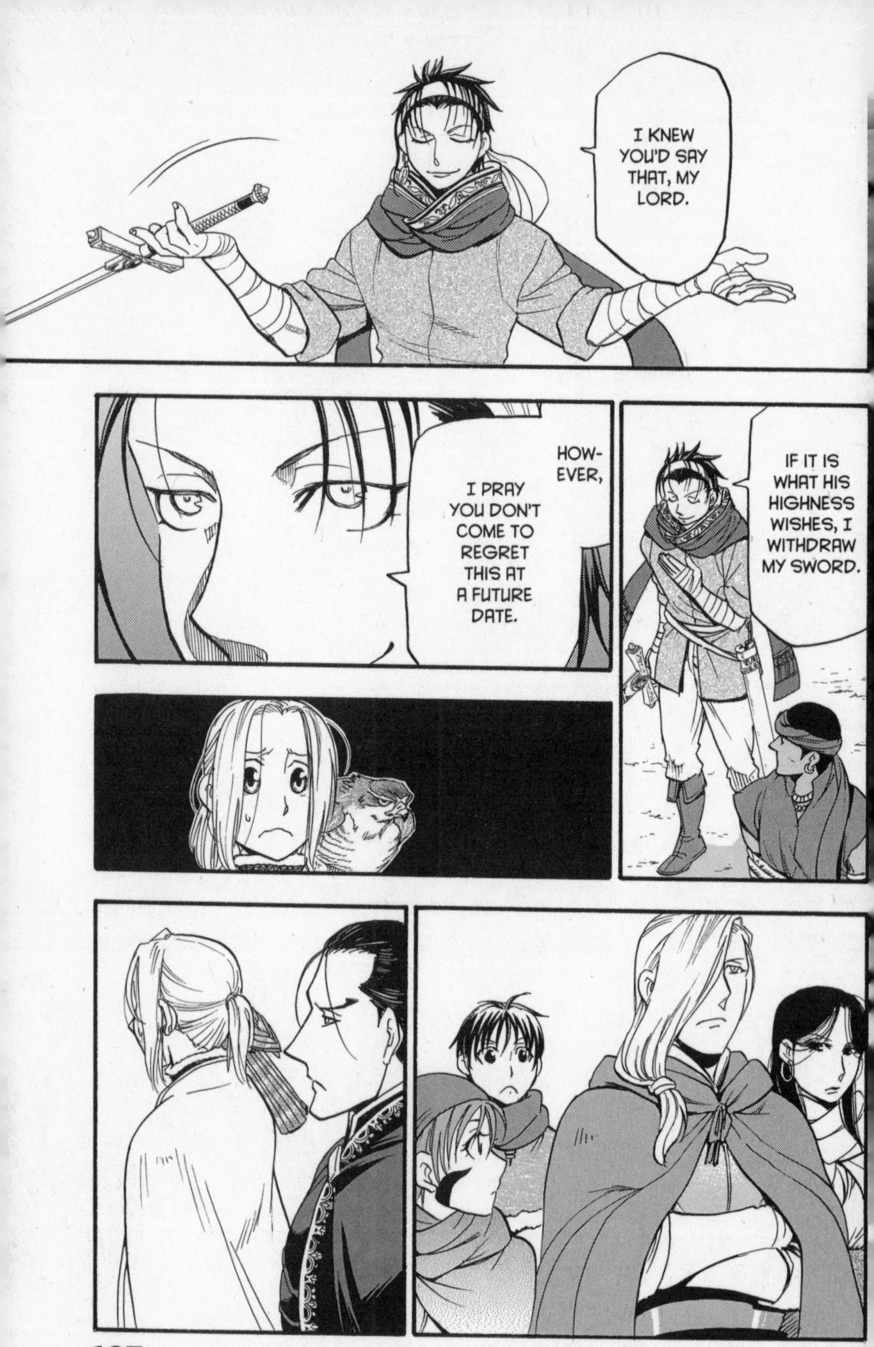
I KNEW YOU'D SAY THAT, MY LORD.
IF IT IS WHAT HIS HIGHNESS WISHES, I WITHDRAW MY SWORD.
HOW-EVER,
I PRAY YOU DON'T COME TO REGRET THIS AT A FUTURE DATE.

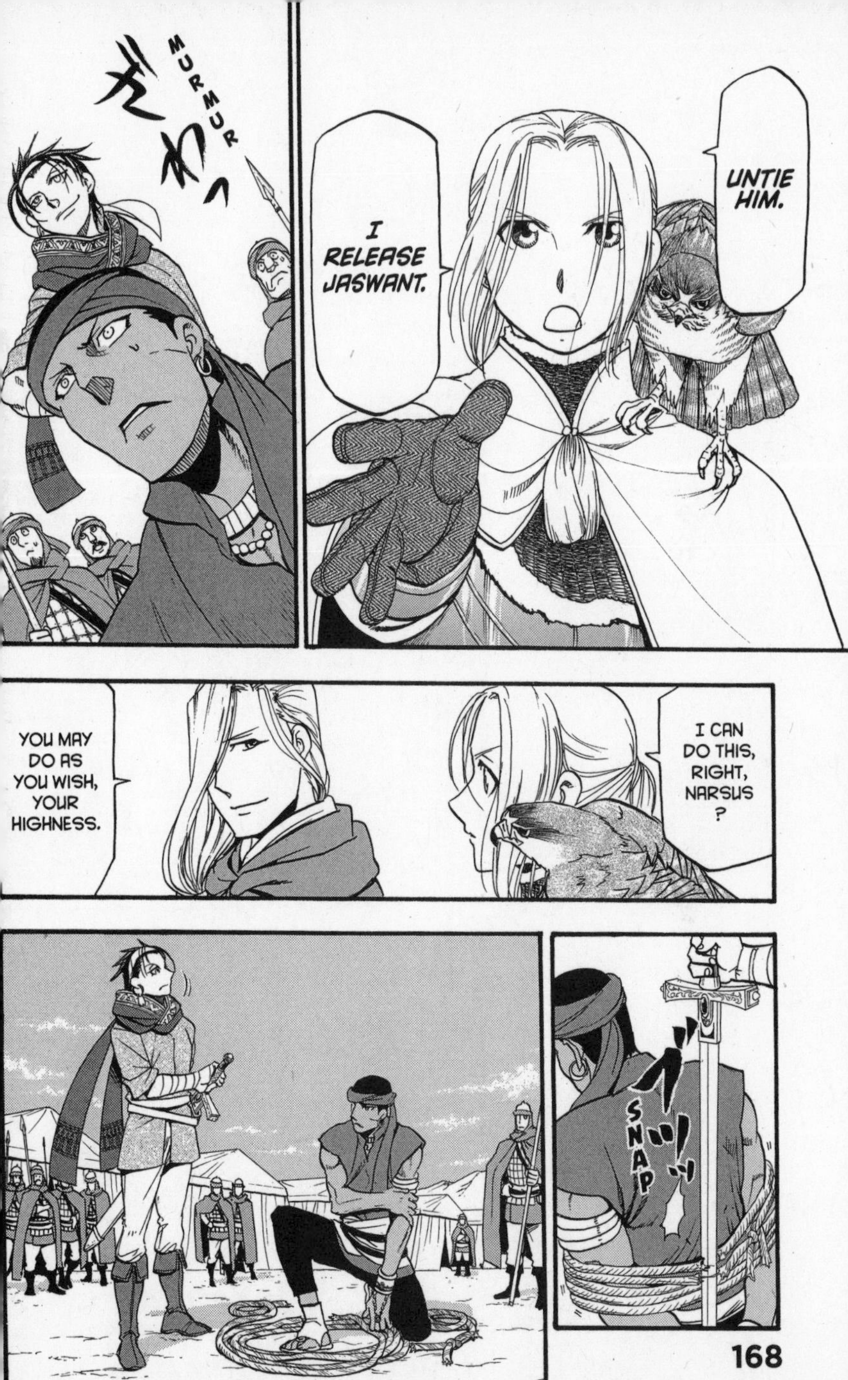
UNTIE HIM.
I RELEASE JASWANT.
MURMUR
I CAN DO THIS, RIGHT, NARSUS?
YOU MAY DO AS YOU WISH, YOUR HIGHNESS.
SNAP

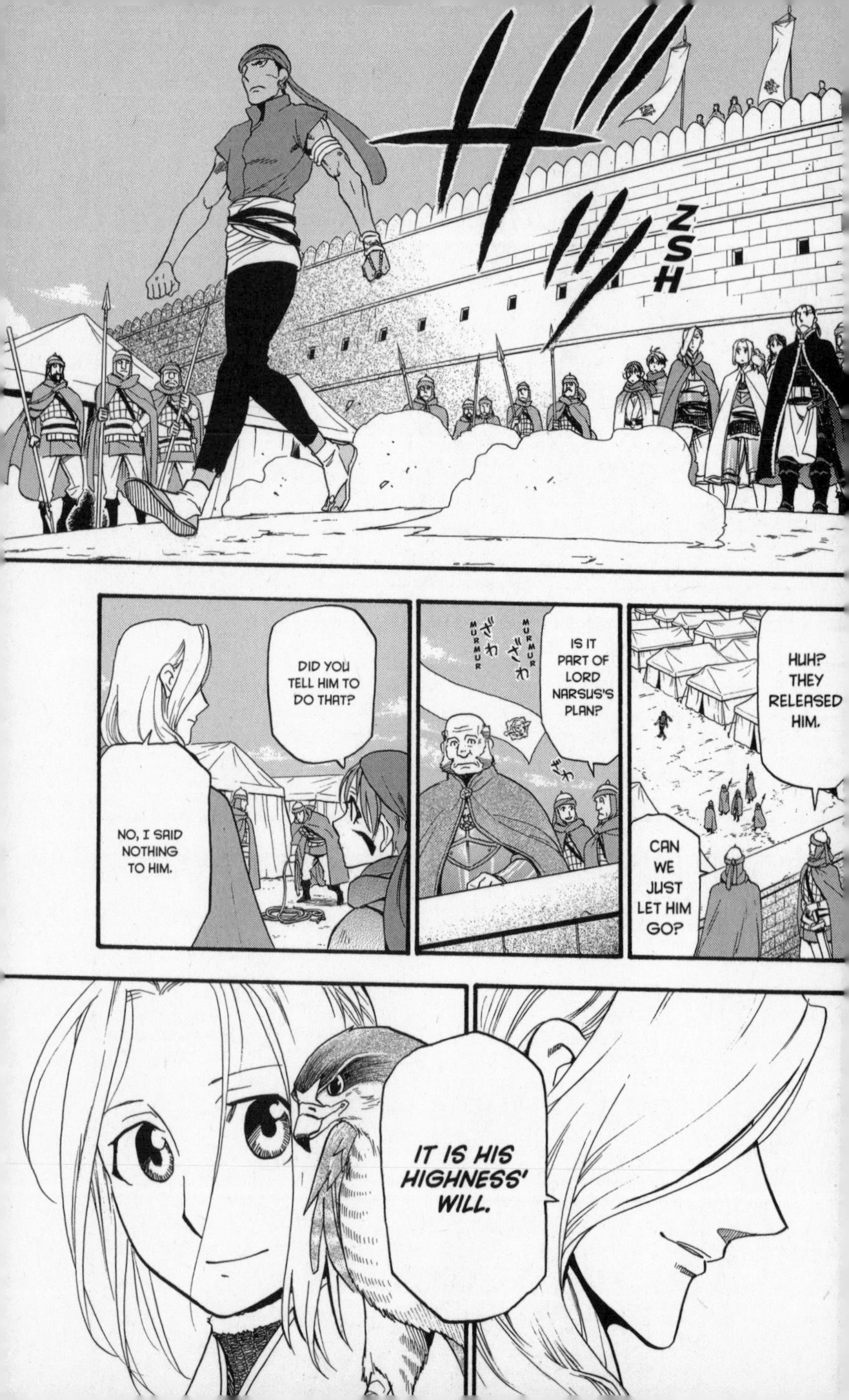
ZSH
HUH? THEY RELEASED HIM.
CAN WE JUST LET HIM GO?
MURMUR ざわ
MURMUR ざわ
IS IT PART OF LORD NARSUS'S PLAN?
ざわ
DID YOU TELL HIM TO DO THAT?
NO, I SAID NOTHING TO HIM.
IT IS HIS HIGHNESS' WILL.

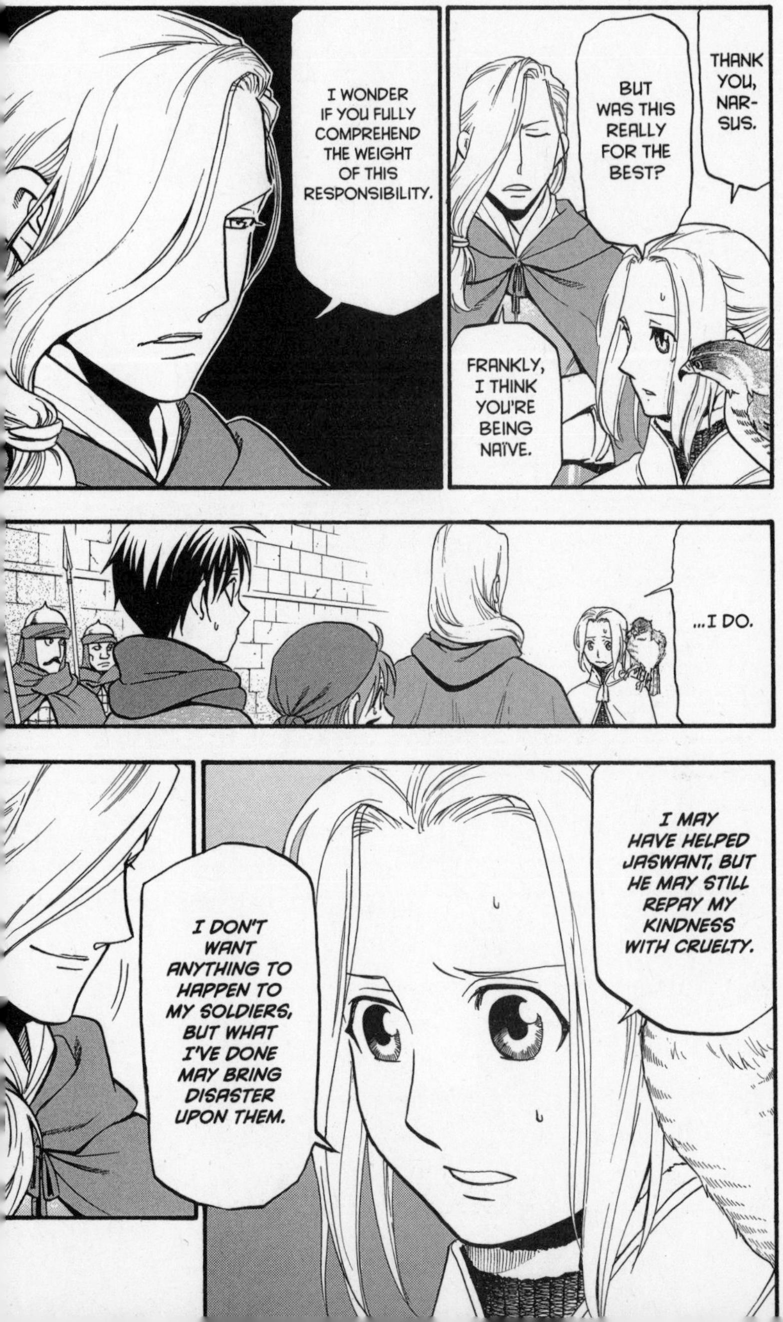
THANK YOU, NARSUS.
BUT WAS THIS REALLY FOR THE BEST?
FRANKLY, I THINK YOU'RE BEING NAÏVE.
I WONDER IF YOU FULLY COMPREHEND THE WEIGHT OF THIS RESPONSIBILITY.
...I DO.
I MAY HAVE HELPED JASWANT, BUT HE MAY STILL REPAY MY KINDNESS WITH CRUELTY.
I DON'T WANT ANYTHING TO HAPPEN TO MY SOLDIERS, BUT WHAT I'VE DONE MAY BRING DISASTER UPON THEM.

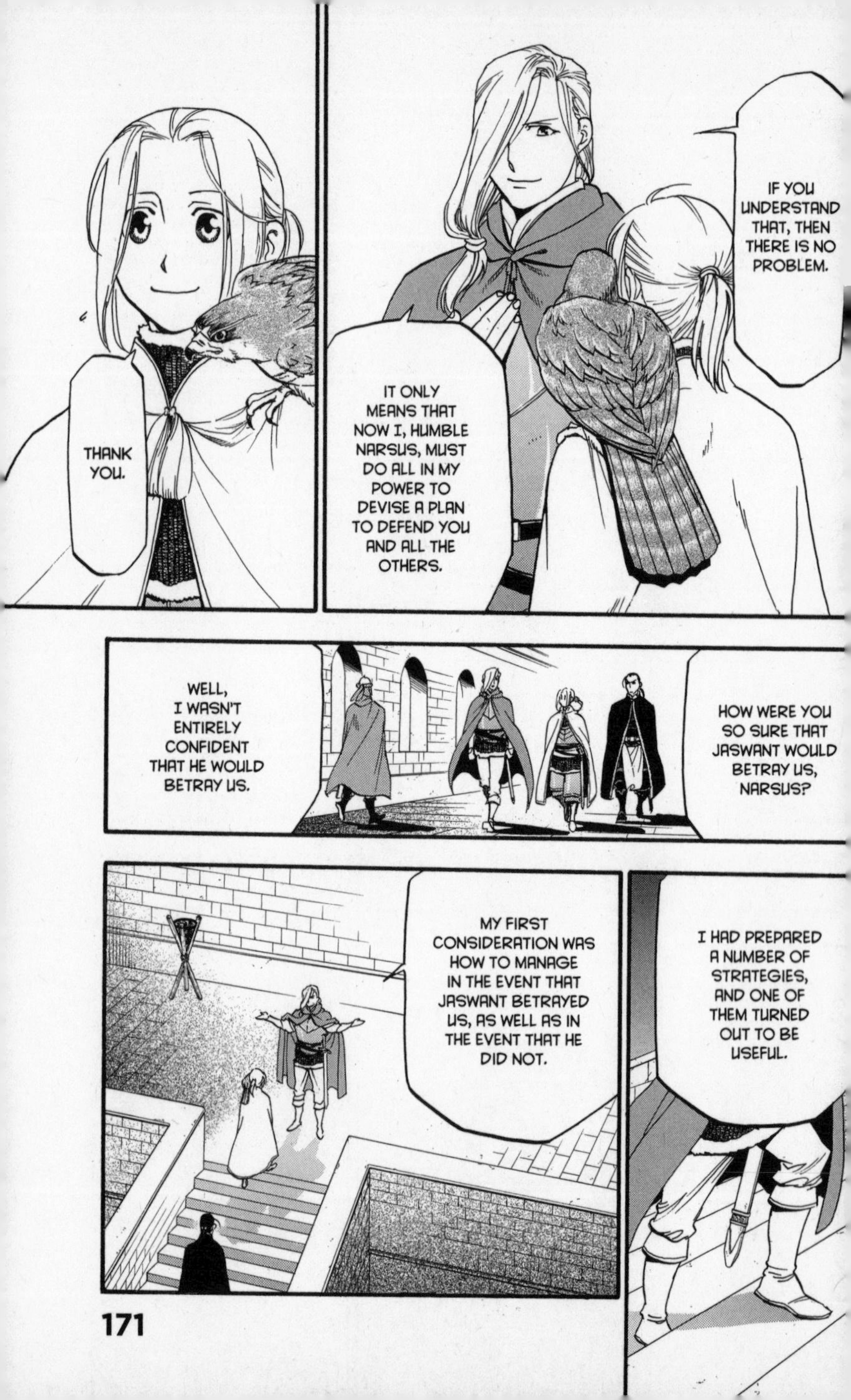
IF YOU UNDERSTAND THAT, THEN THERE IS NO PROBLEM.
IT ONLY MEANS THAT NOW I, HUMBLE NARSUS, MUST DO ALL IN MY POWER TO DEVISE A PLAN TO DEFEND YOU AND ALL THE OTHERS.
THANK YOU.
HOW WERE YOU SO SURE THAT JASWANT WOULD BETRAY US, NARSUS?
WELL, I WASN'T ENTIRELY CONFIDENT THAT HE WOULD BETRAY US.
I HAD PREPARED A NUMBER OF STRATEGIES, AND ONE OF THEM TURNED OUT TO BE USEFUL.
MY FIRST CONSIDERATION WAS HOW TO MANAGE IN THE EVENT THAT JASWANT BETRAYED US, AS WELL AS IN THE EVENT THAT HE DID NOT.

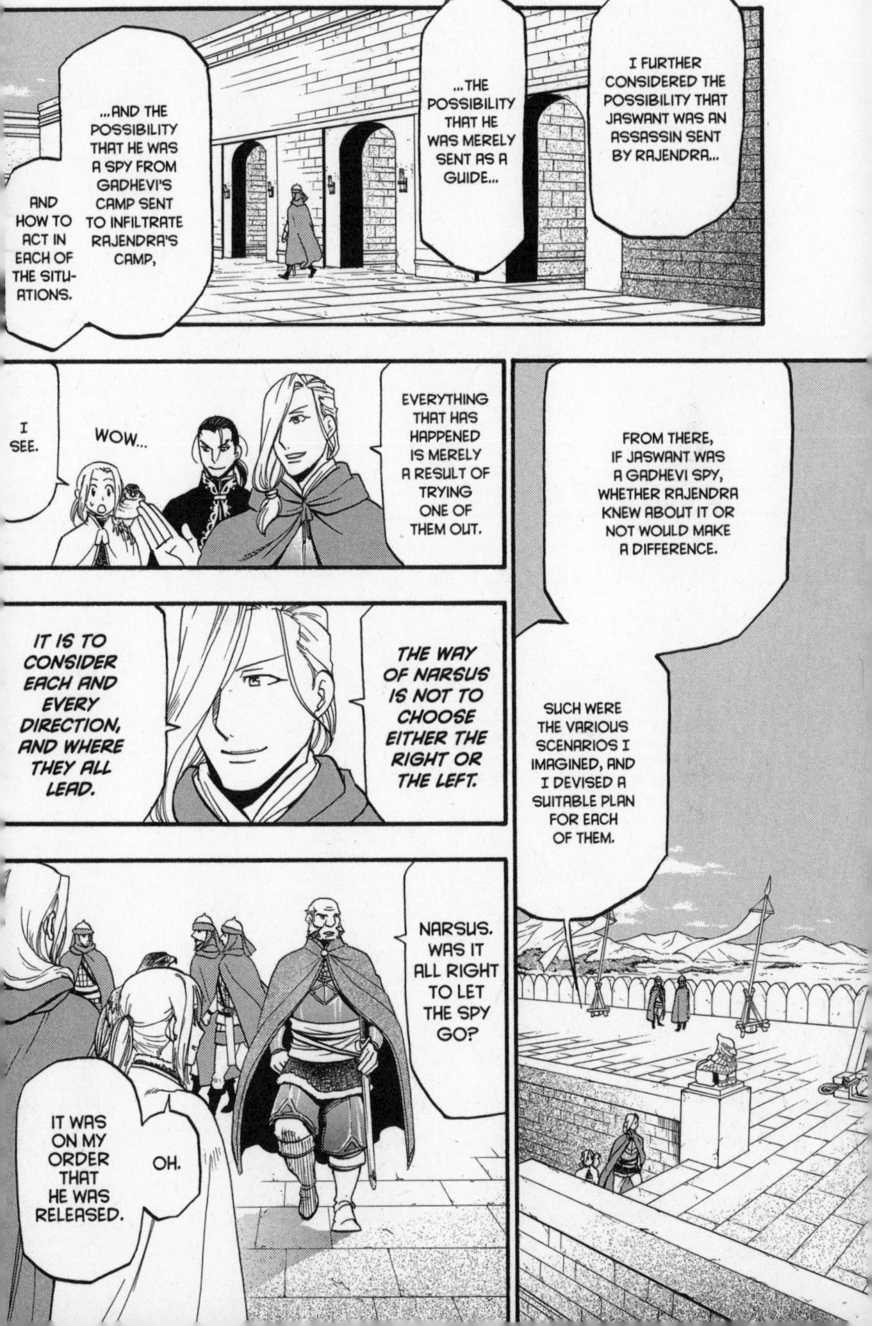
I FURTHER CONSIDERED THE POSSIBILITY THAT JASWANT WAS AN ASSASSIN SENT BY RAJENDRA...
...THE POSSIBILITY THAT HE WAS MERELY SENT AS A GUIDE...
...AND THE POSSIBILITY THAT HE WAS A SPY FROM GADHEVI'S CAMP SENT TO INFILTRATE RAJENDRA'S CAMP,
AND HOW TO ACT IN EACH OF THE SITU-ATIONS.
FROM THERE, IF JASWANT WAS A GADHEVI SPY, WHETHER RAJENDRA KNEW ABOUT IT OR NOT WOULD MAKE A DIFFERENCE.
SUCH WERE THE VARIOUS SCENARIOS I IMAGINED, AND I DEVISED A SUITABLE PLAN FOR EACH OF THEM.
EVERYTHING THAT HAS HAPPENED IS MERELY A RESULT OF TRYING ONE OF THEM OUT.
WOW...
I SEE.
THE WAY OF NARSUS IS NOT TO CHOOSE EITHER THE RIGHT OR THE LEFT.
IT IS TO CONSIDER EACH AND EVERY DIRECTION, AND WHERE THEY ALL LEAD.
NARSUS. WAS IT ALL RIGHT TO LET THE SPY GO?
OH.
IT WAS ON MY ORDER THAT HE WAS RELEASED.

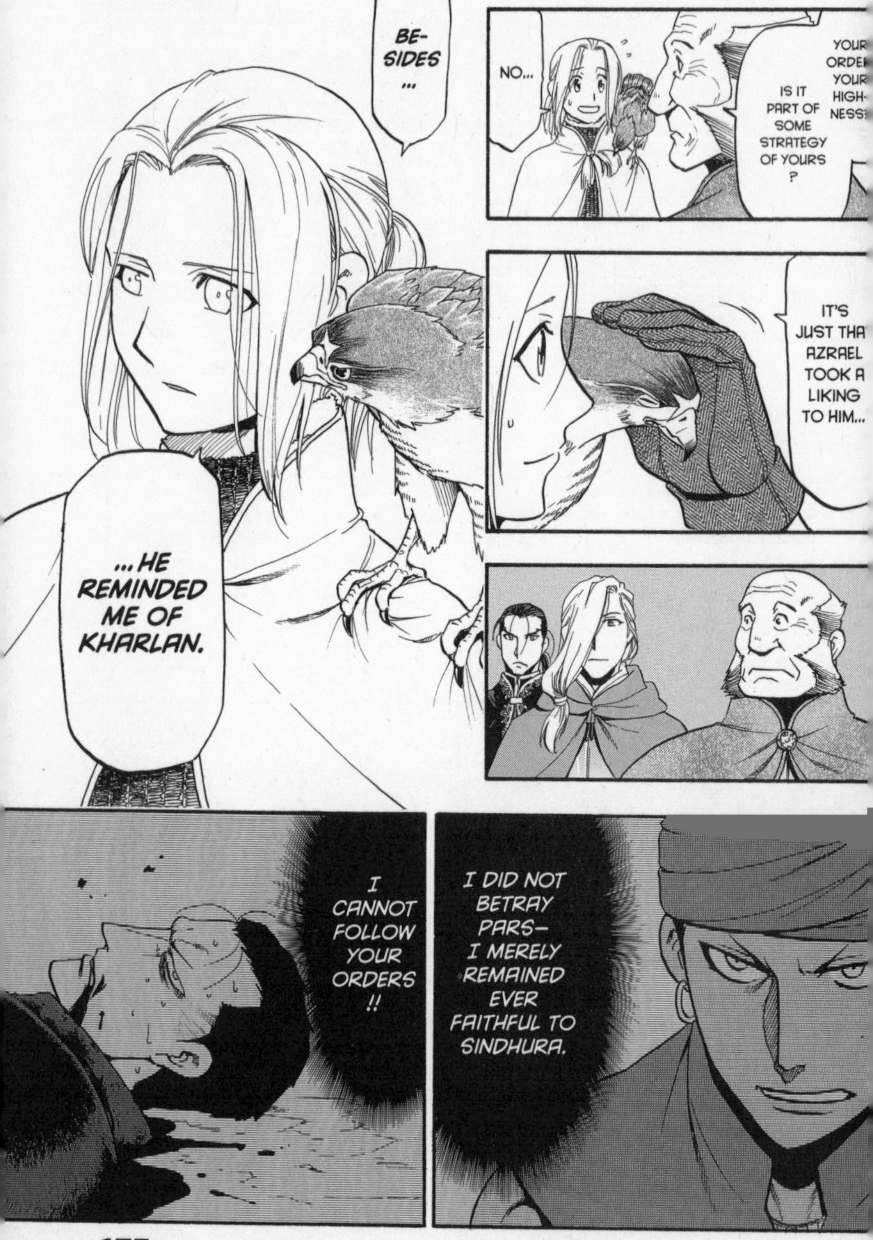
YOUR ORDE YOUR HIGH- NESS?
IS IT PART OF SOME STRATEGY OF YOURS ?
NO...
IT'S JUST THA AZRAEL TOOK A LIKING TO HIM...
BE- SIDES ...
...HE REMINDED ME OF KHARLAN.
I DID NOT BETRAY PARS— I MERELY REMAINED EVER FAITHFUL TO SINDHURA.
I CANNOT FOLLOW YOUR ORDERS !!

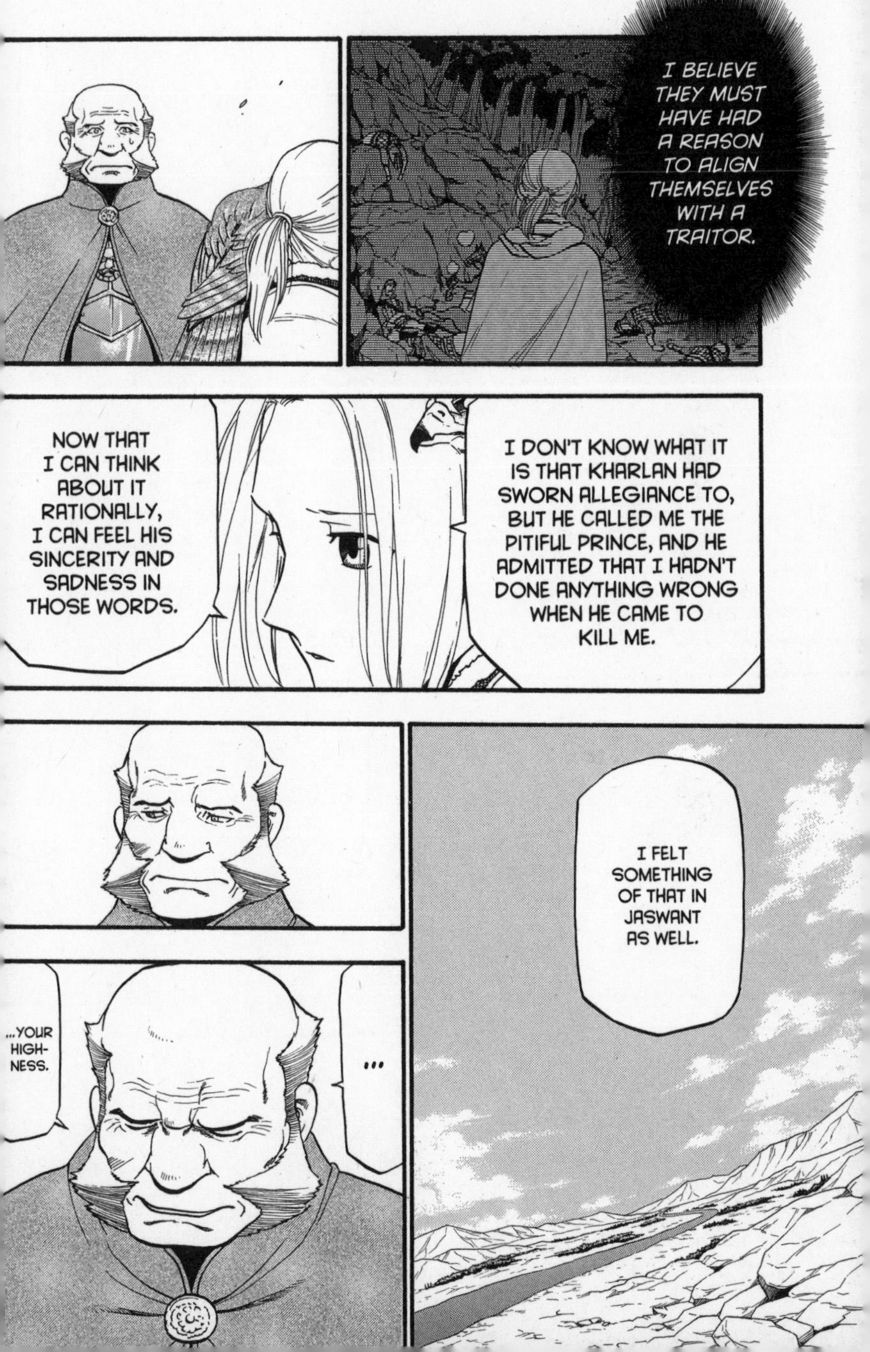
I BELIEVE THEY MUST HAVE HAD A REASON TO ALIGN THEMSELVES WITH A TRAITOR.
I DON'T KNOW WHAT IT IS THAT KHARLAN HAD SWORN ALLEGIANCE TO, BUT HE CALLED ME THE PITIFUL PRINCE, AND HE ADMITTED THAT I HADN'T DONE ANYTHING WRONG WHEN HE CAME TO KILL ME.
NOW THAT I CAN THINK ABOUT IT RATIONALLY, I CAN FEEL HIS SINCERITY AND SADNESS IN THOSE WORDS.
I FELT SOMETHING OF THAT IN JASWANT AS WELL.
...
...YOUR HIGHNESS.

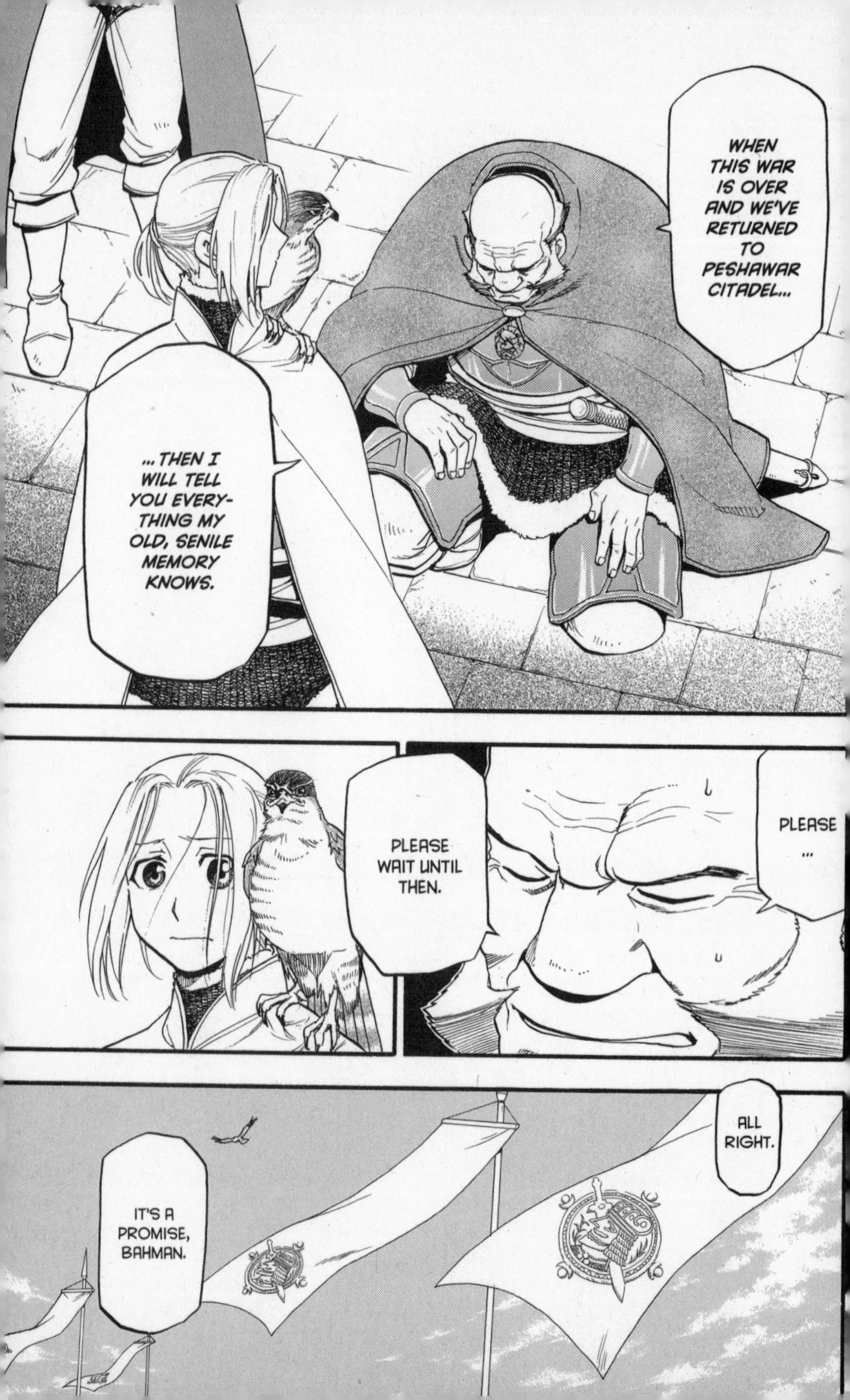
WHEN THIS WAR IS OVER AND WE'VE RETURNED TO PESHAWAR CITADEL...
...THEN I WILL TELL YOU EVERY-THING MY OLD, SENILE MEMORY KNOWS.
PLEASE ...
PLEASE WAIT UNTIL THEN.
ALL RIGHT.
IT'S A PROMISE, BAHMAN.

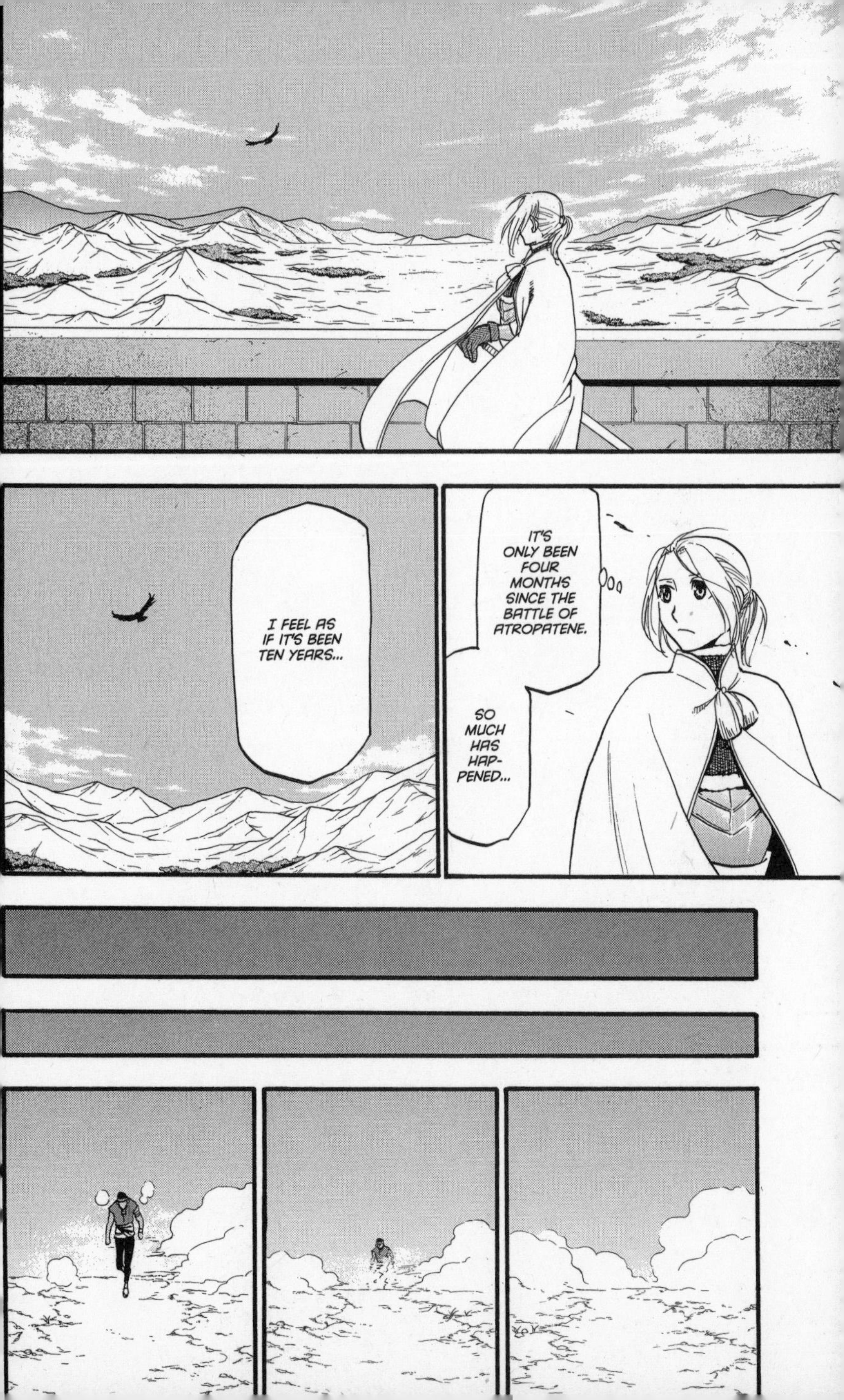
IT'S ONLY BEEN FOUR MONTHS SINCE THE BATTLE OF ATROPATENE.
SO MUCH HAS HAP-PENED...
I FEEL AS IF IT'S BEEN TEN YEARS...

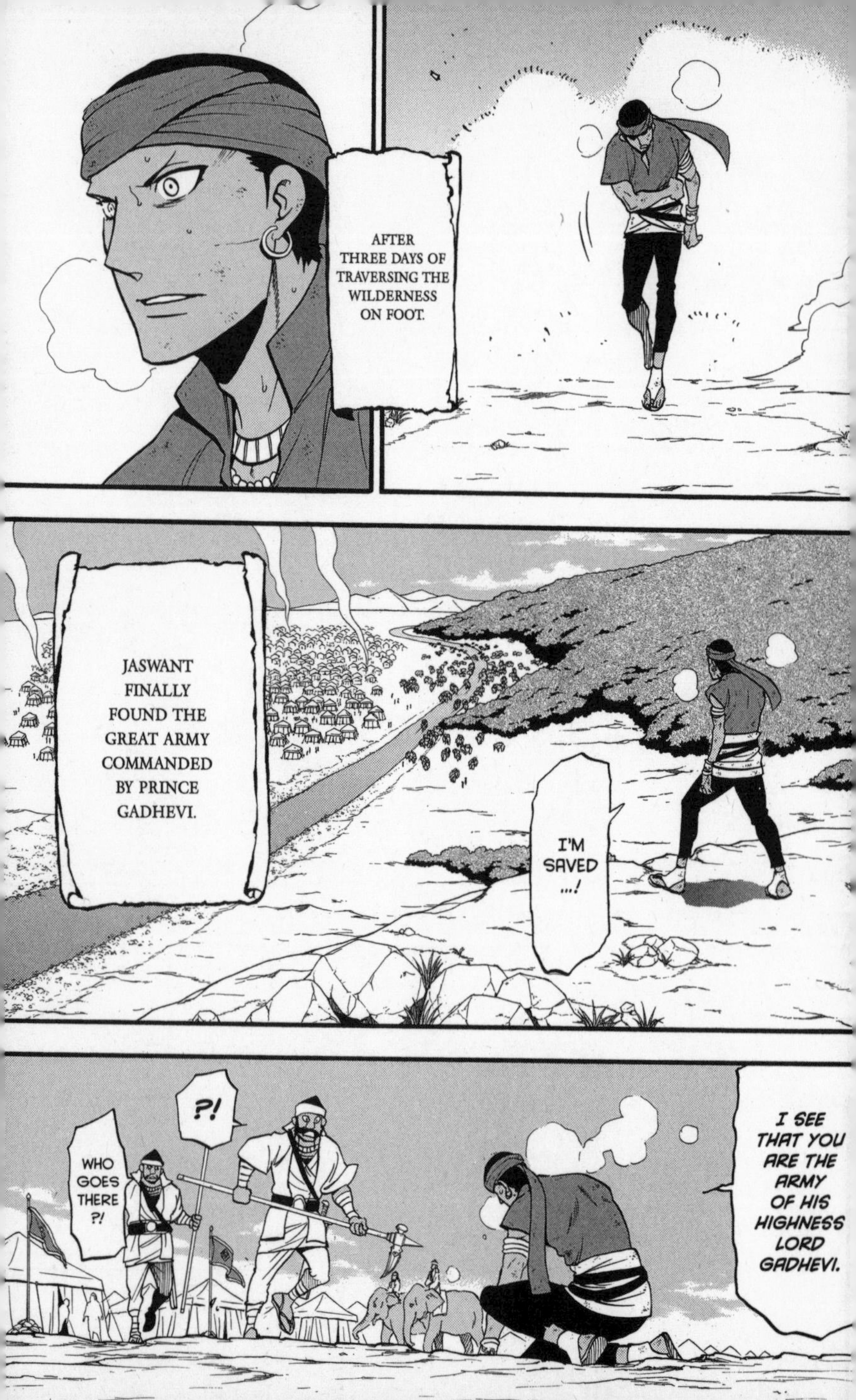
AFTER THREE DAYS OF TRAVERSING THE WILDERNESS ON FOOT.
JASWANT FINALLY FOUND THE GREAT ARMY COMMANDED BY PRINCE GADHEVI.
I'M SAVED ...!
I SEE THAT YOU ARE THE ARMY OF HIS HIGHNESS LORD GADHEVI.
?!
WHO GOES THERE ?!

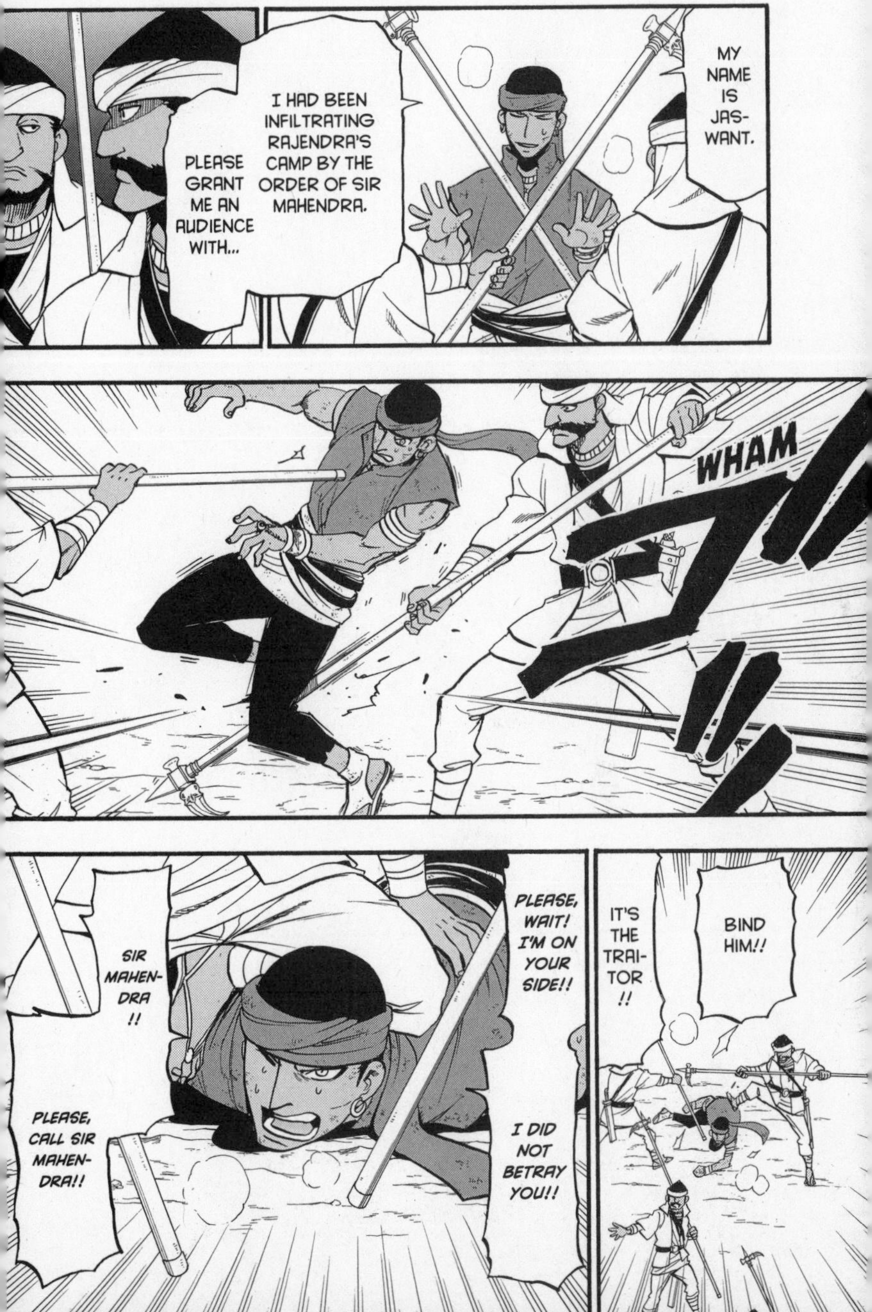
MY NAME IS JASWANT.
I HAD BEEN INFILTRATING RAJENDRA'S CAMP BY THE ORDER OF SIR MAHENDRA.
PLEASE GRANT ME AN AUDIENCE WITH...
WHAM
BIND HIM!!
IT'S THE TRAITOR!!
PLEASE, WAIT! I'M ON YOUR SIDE!!
I DID NOT BETRAY YOU!!
SIR MAHENDRA!!
PLEASE, CALL SIR MAHENDRA!!

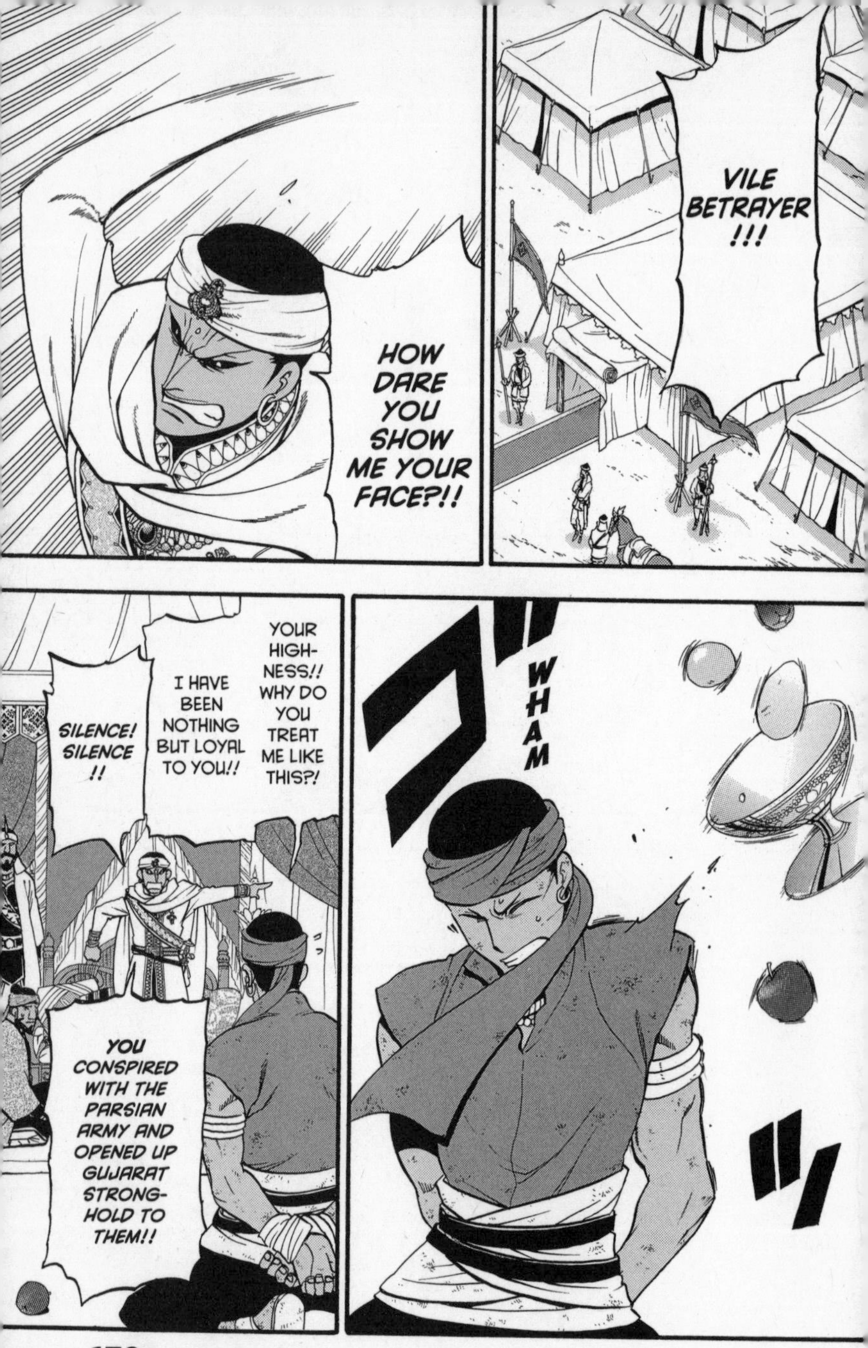
VILE BETRAYER!!!
HOW DARE YOU SHOW ME YOUR FACE?!!
WHAM
YOUR HIGHNESS!! WHY DO YOU TREAT ME LIKE THIS?!
I HAVE BEEN NOTHING BUT LOYAL TO YOU!!
SILENCE! SILENCE!!
YOU CONSPIRED WITH THE PARSIAN ARMY AND OPENED UP GUJARAT STRONGHOLD TO THEM!!

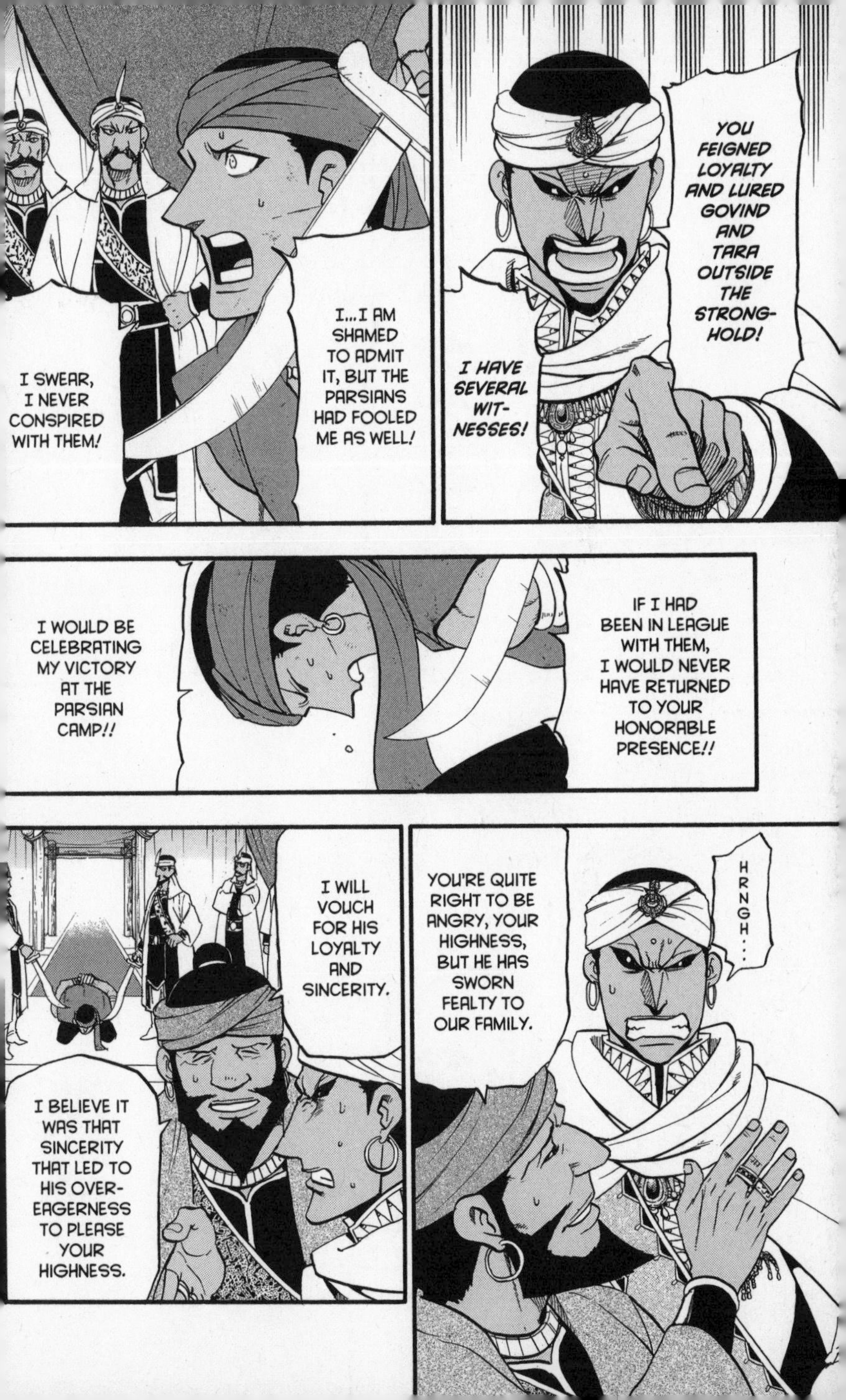
YOU FEIGNED LOYALTY AND LURED GOVIND AND TARA OUTSIDE THE STRONGHOLD!
I HAVE SEVERAL WITNESSES!
I...I AM SHAMED TO ADMIT IT, BUT THE PARSIANS HAD FOOLED ME AS WELL!
I SWEAR, I NEVER CONSPIRED WITH THEM!
IF I HAD BEEN IN LEAGUE WITH THEM, I WOULD NEVER HAVE RETURNED TO YOUR HONORABLE PRESENCE!!
I WOULD BE CELEBRATING MY VICTORY AT THE PARSIAN CAMP!!
HRNGH...
YOU'RE QUITE RIGHT TO BE ANGRY, YOUR HIGHNESS, BUT HE HAS SWORN FEALTY TO OUR FAMILY.
I WILL VOUCH FOR HIS LOYALTY AND SINCERITY.
I BELIEVE IT WAS THAT SINCERITY THAT LED TO HIS OVER-EAGERNESS TO PLEASE YOUR HIGHNESS.

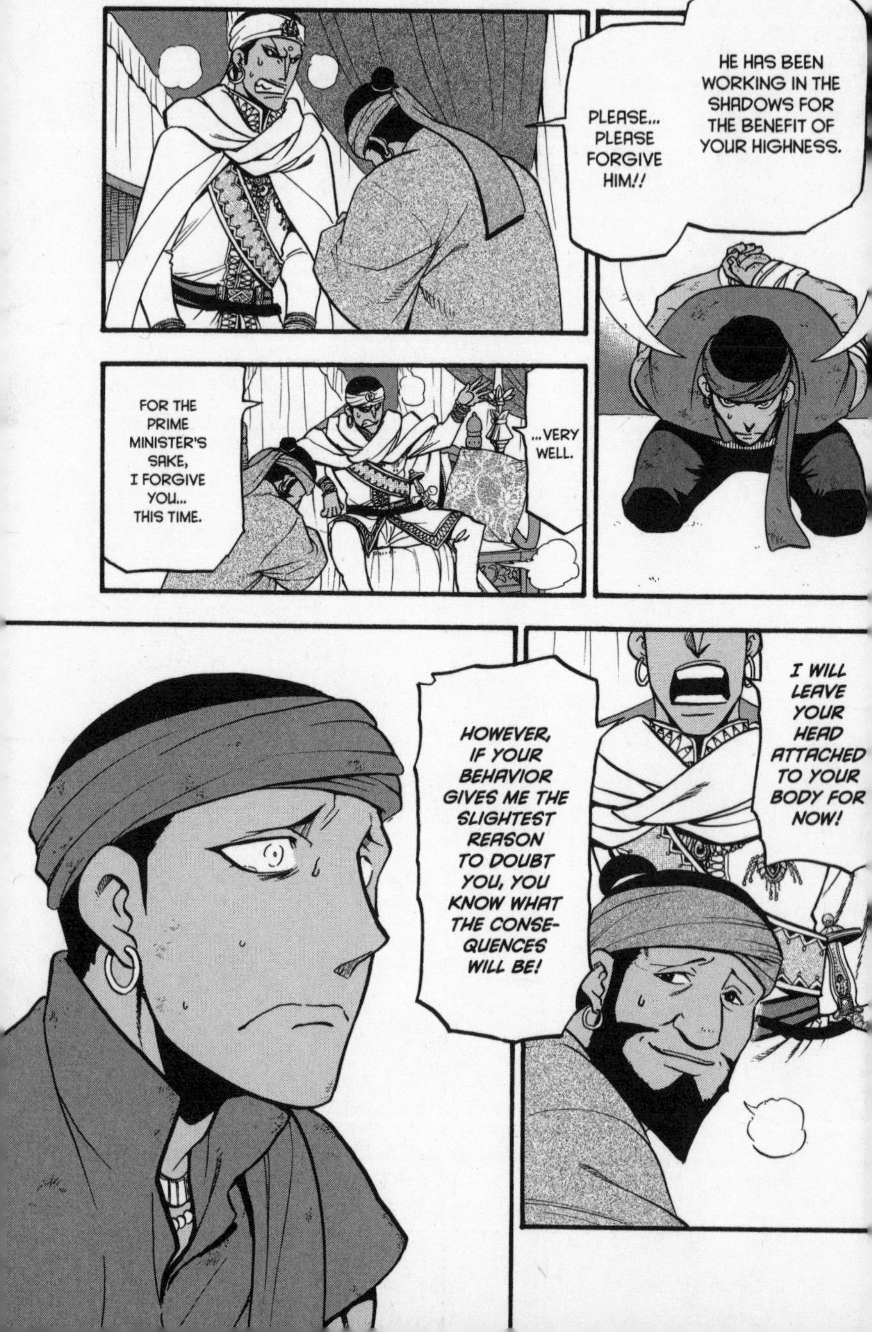
HE HAS BEEN WORKING IN THE SHADOWS FOR THE BENEFIT OF YOUR HIGHNESS.
PLEASE... PLEASE FORGIVE HIM!!
...VERY WELL.
FOR THE PRIME MINISTER'S SAKE, I FORGIVE YOU... THIS TIME.
I WILL LEAVE YOUR HEAD ATTACHED TO YOUR BODY FOR NOW!
HOWEVER, IF YOUR BEHAVIOR GIVES ME THE SLIGHTEST REASON TO DOUBT YOU, YOU KNOW WHAT THE CONSE-QUENCES WILL BE!

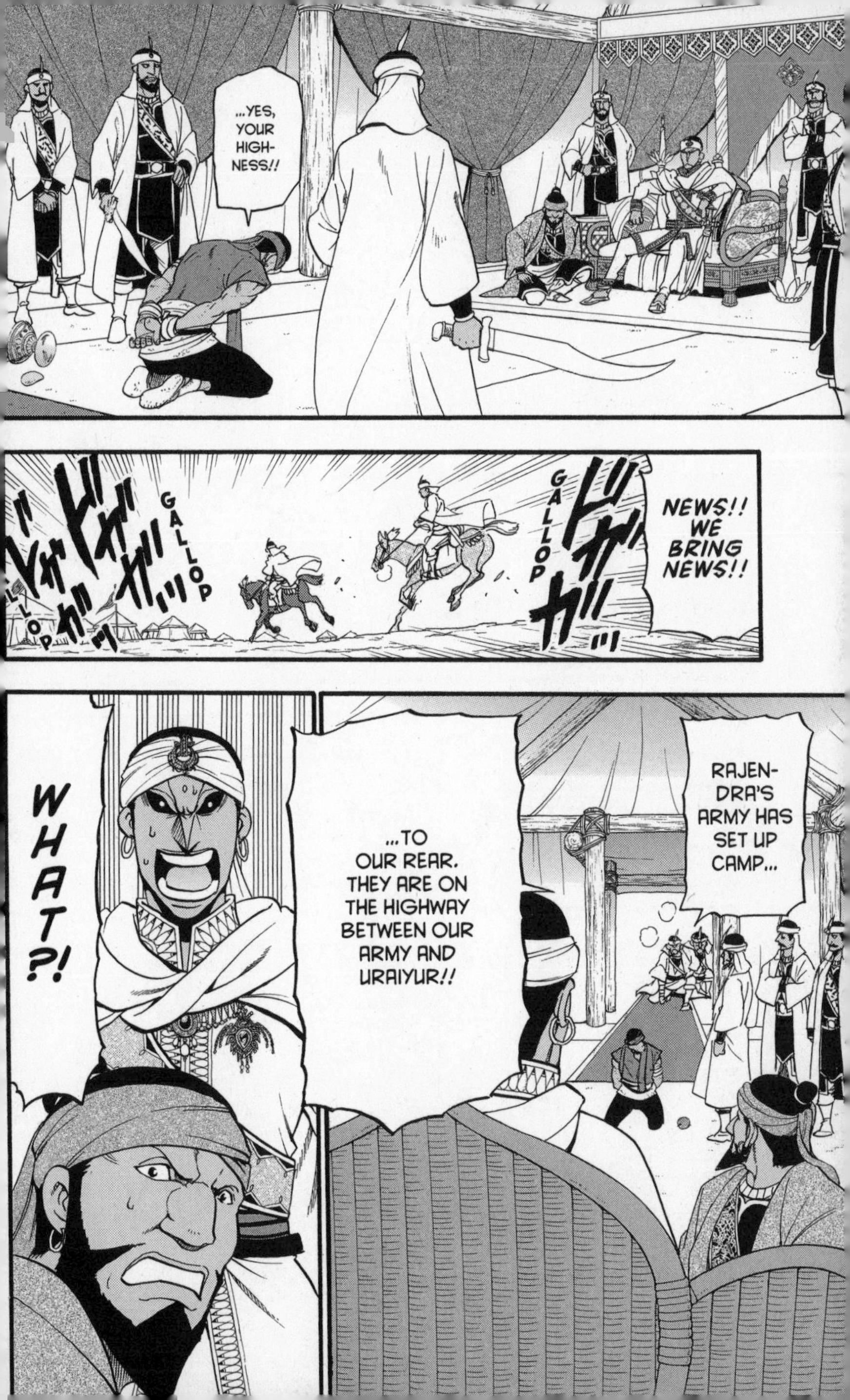
...YES, YOUR HIGH-NESS!!
NEWS!! WE BRING NEWS!!
GALLOP
GALLOP
GALLOP
RAJEN-DRA'S ARMY HAS SET UP CAMP...
...TO OUR REAR. THEY ARE ON THE HIGHWAY BETWEEN OUR ARMY AND URAIYUR!!
WHAT?!

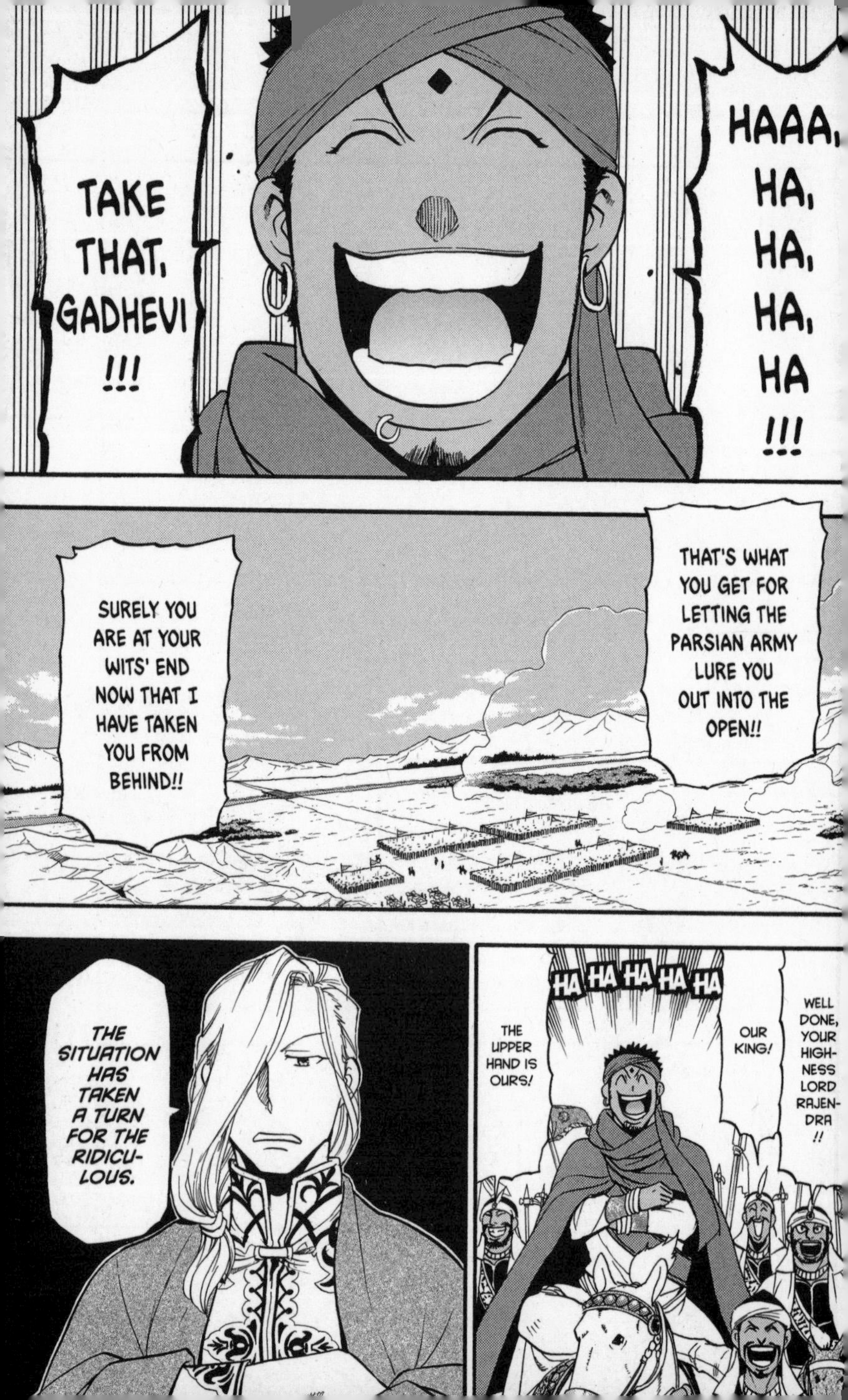
HAAA, HA, HA, HA, HA!!!
TAKE THAT, GADHEVI!!!
THAT'S WHAT YOU GET FOR LETTING THE PARSIAN ARMY LURE YOU OUT INTO THE OPEN!!
SURELY YOU ARE AT YOUR WITS' END NOW THAT I HAVE TAKEN YOU FROM BEHIND!!
WELL DONE, YOUR HIGHNESS LORD RAJENDRA!!
OUR KING!
HA HA HA HA HA
THE UPPER HAND IS OURS!
THE SITUATION HAS TAKEN A TURN FOR THE RIDICULOUS.

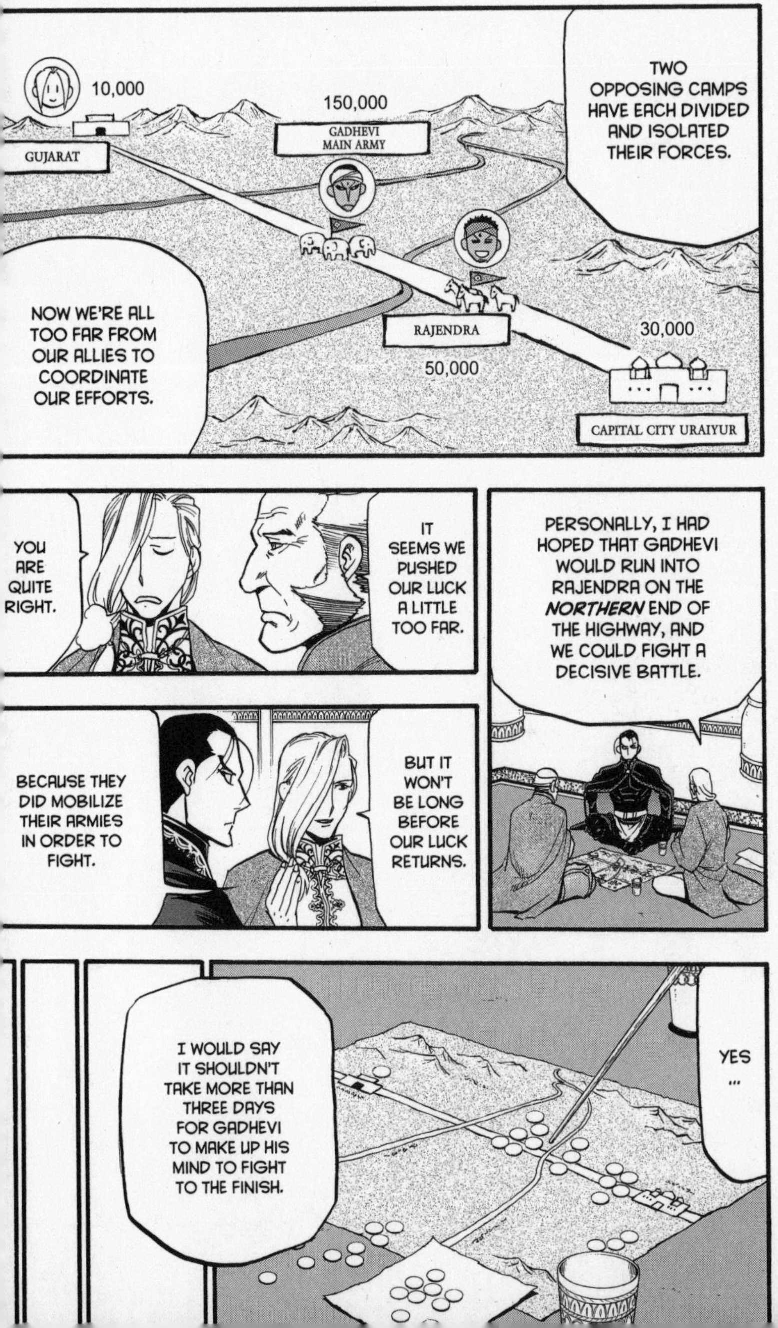
TWO OPPOSING CAMPS HAVE EACH DIVIDED AND ISOLATED THEIR FORCES.
150,000
GADHEVI MAIN ARMY
10,000
GUJARAT
30,000
RAJENDRA
50,000
CAPITAL CITY URAIYUR
NOW WE'RE ALL TOO FAR FROM OUR ALLIES TO COORDINATE OUR EFFORTS.
PERSONALLY, I HAD HOPED THAT GADHEVI WOULD RUN INTO RAJENDRA ON THE *NORTHERN* END OF THE HIGHWAY, AND WE COULD FIGHT A DECISIVE BATTLE.
IT SEEMS WE PUSHED OUR LUCK A LITTLE TOO FAR.
YOU ARE QUITE RIGHT.
BUT IT WON'T BE LONG BEFORE OUR LUCK RETURNS.
BECAUSE THEY DID MOBILIZE THEIR ARMIES IN ORDER TO FIGHT.
YES ...
I WOULD SAY IT SHOULDN'T TAKE MORE THAN THREE DAYS FOR GADHEVI TO MAKE UP HIS MIND TO FIGHT TO THE FINISH.

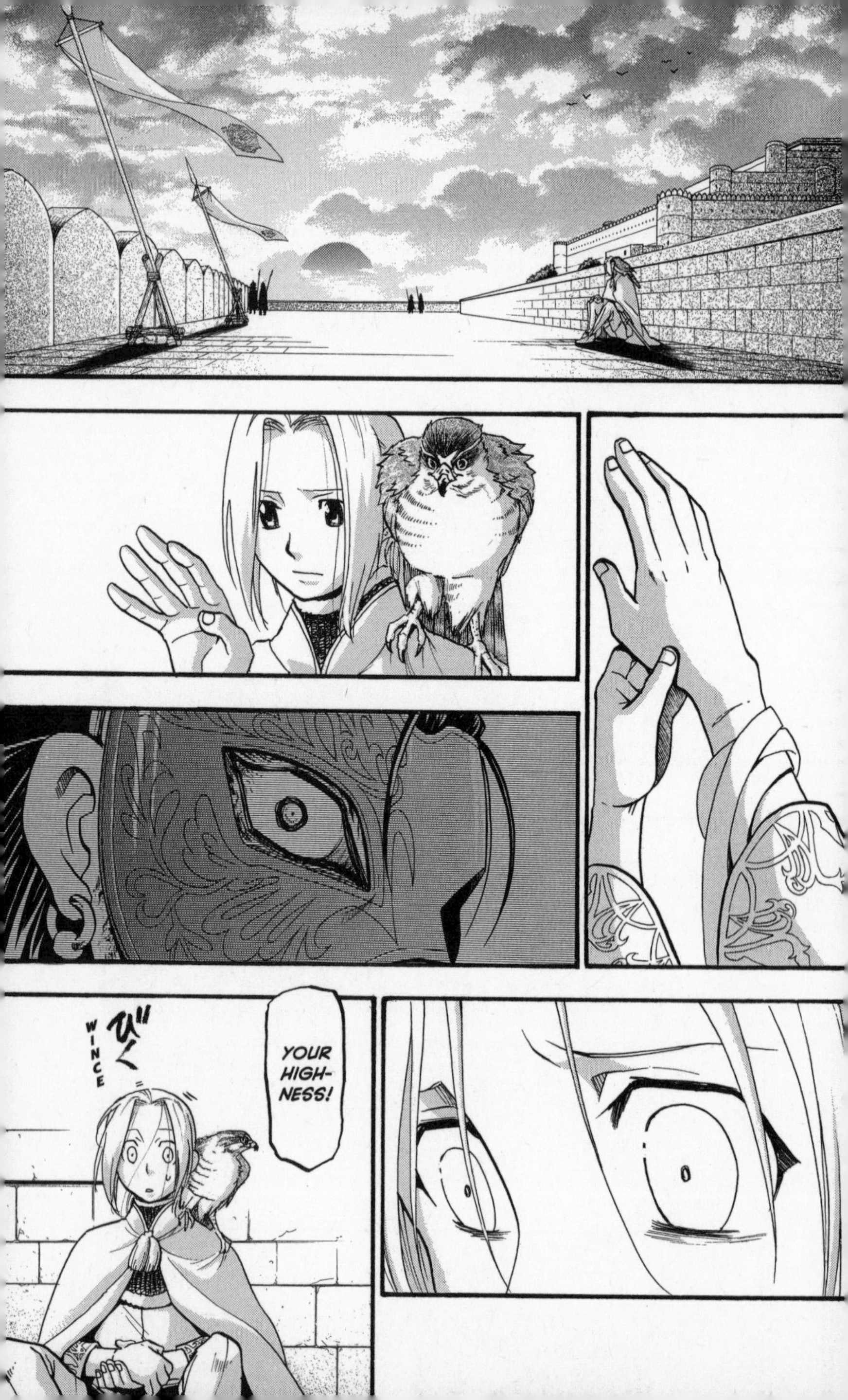
びく
WINCE
YOUR HIGH-NESS!

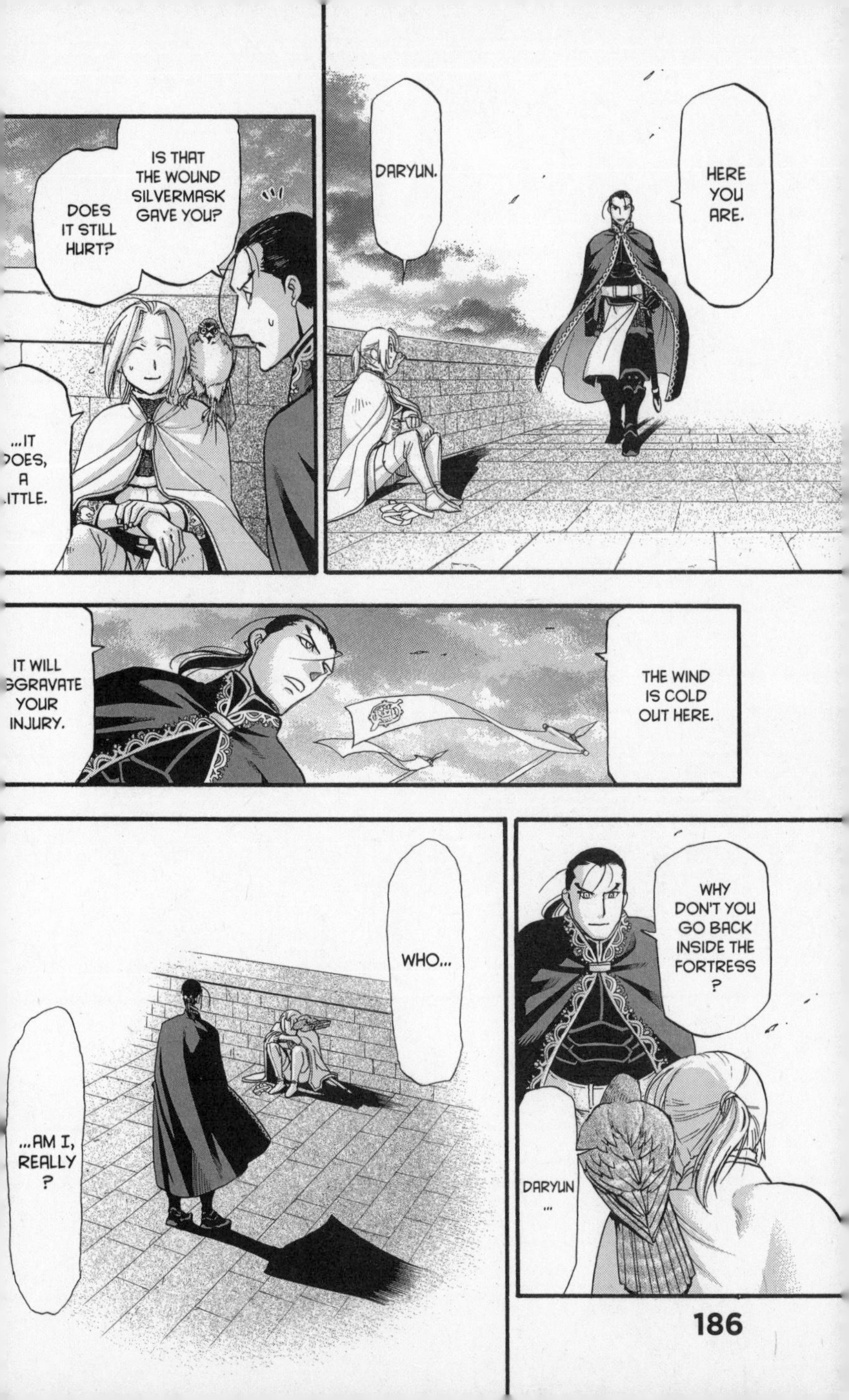

HERE YOU ARE.
DARYUN.
IS THAT THE WOUND SILVERMASK GAVE YOU?
DOES IT STILL HURT?
...IT OES, A ITTLE.
THE WIND IS COLD OUT HERE.
IT WILL GGRAVATE YOUR INJURY.
WHY DON'T YOU GO BACK INSIDE THE FORTRESS ?
DARYUN ...
WHO...
...AM I, REALLY ?

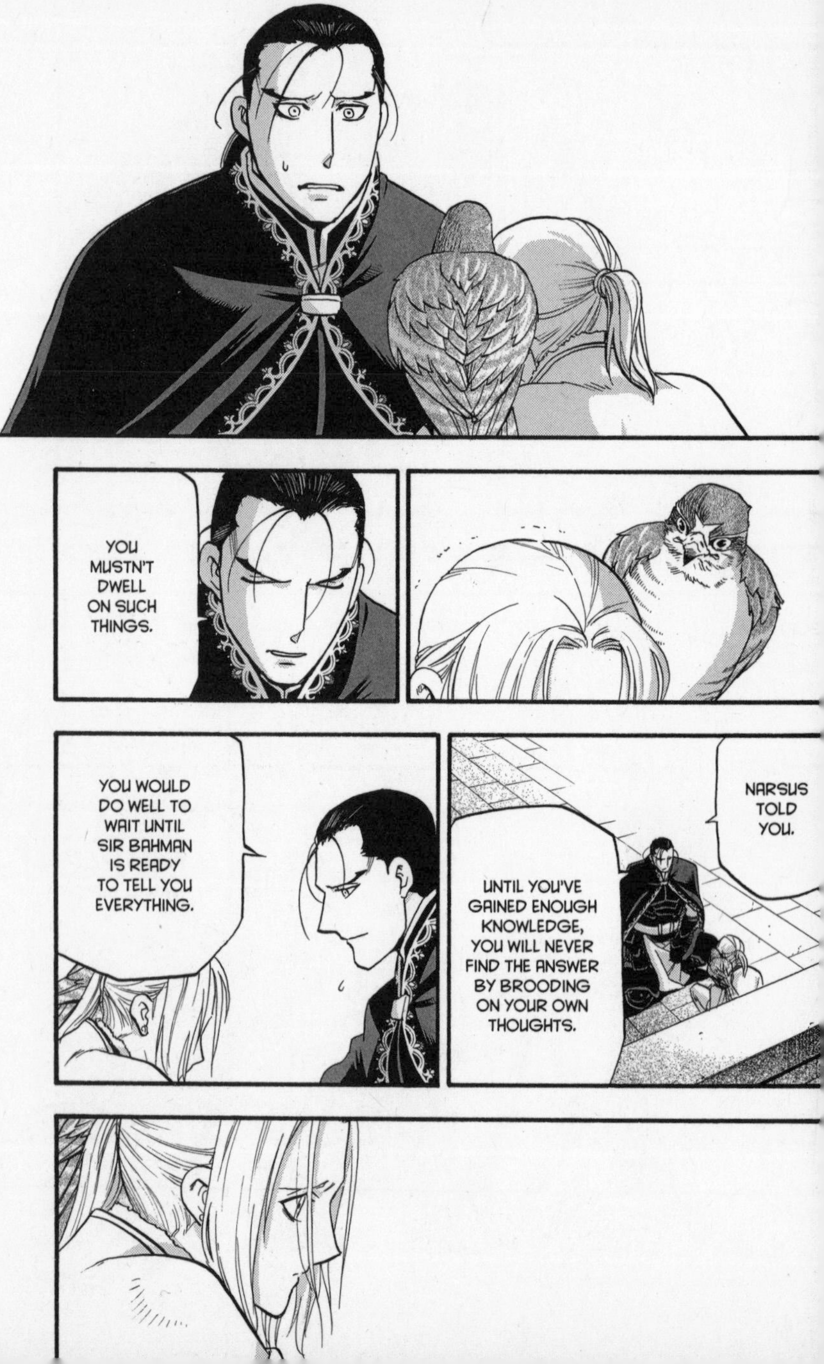
YOU MUSTN'T DWELL ON SUCH THINGS.
NARSUS TOLD YOU.
UNTIL YOU'VE GAINED ENOUGH KNOWLEDGE, YOU WILL NEVER FIND THE ANSWER BY BROODING ON YOUR OWN THOUGHTS.
YOU WOULD DO WELL TO WAIT UNTIL SIR BAHMAN IS READY TO TELL YOU EVERYTHING.

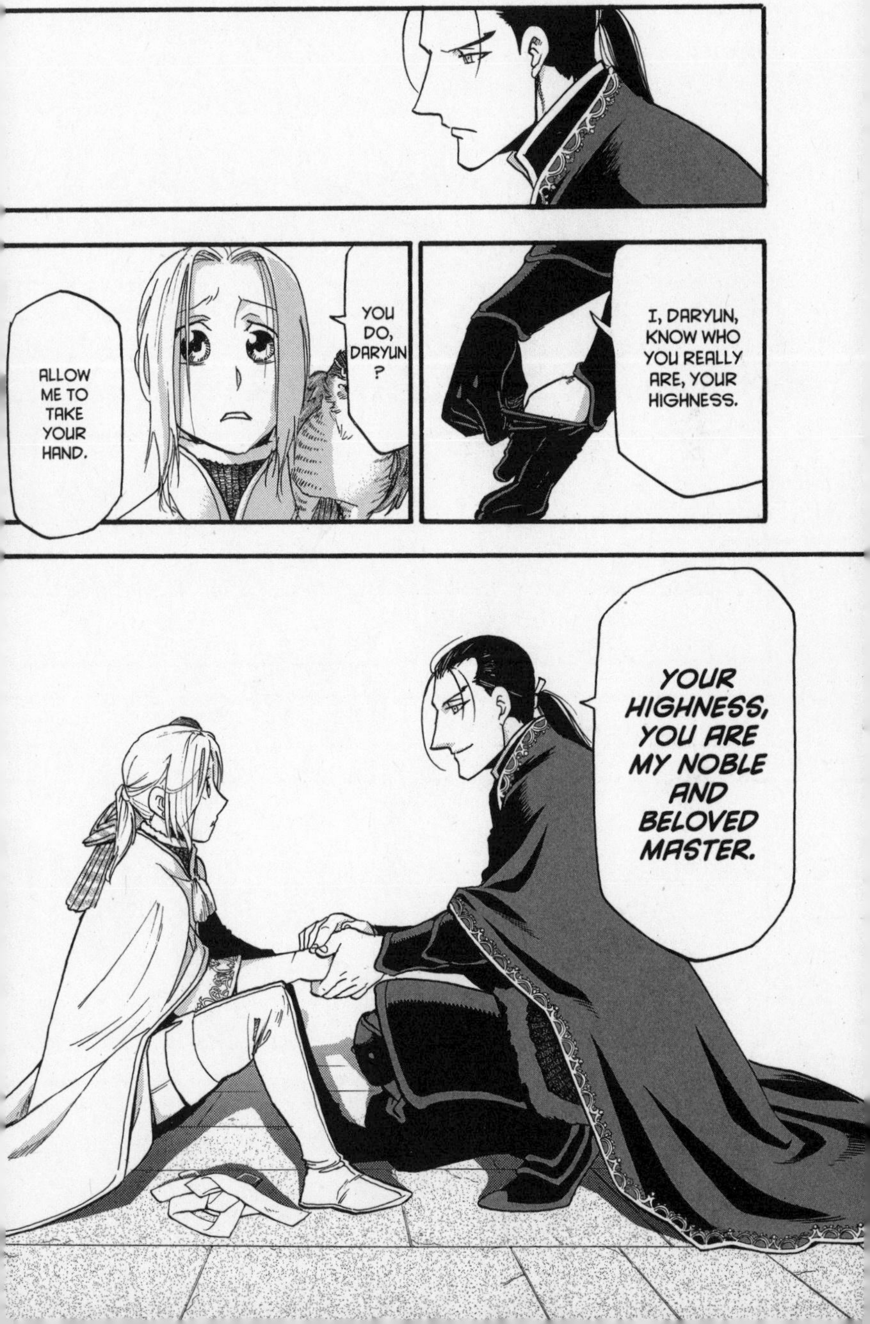
I, DARYUN, KNOW WHO YOU REALLY ARE, YOUR HIGHNESS.
YOU DO, DARYUN?
ALLOW ME TO TAKE YOUR HAND.
YOUR HIGHNESS, YOU ARE MY NOBLE AND BELOVED MASTER.

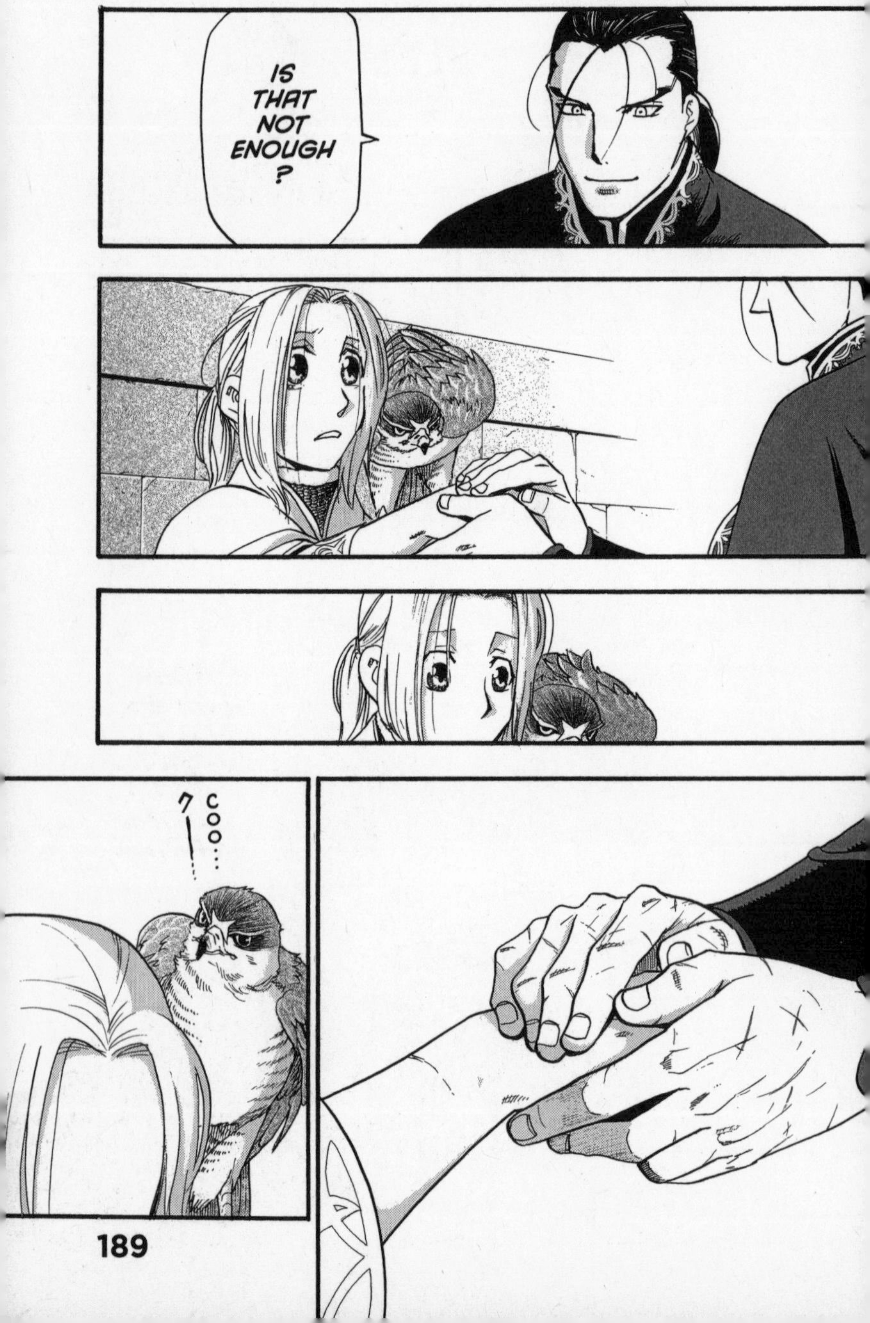
IS THAT NOT ENOUGH?
COO...

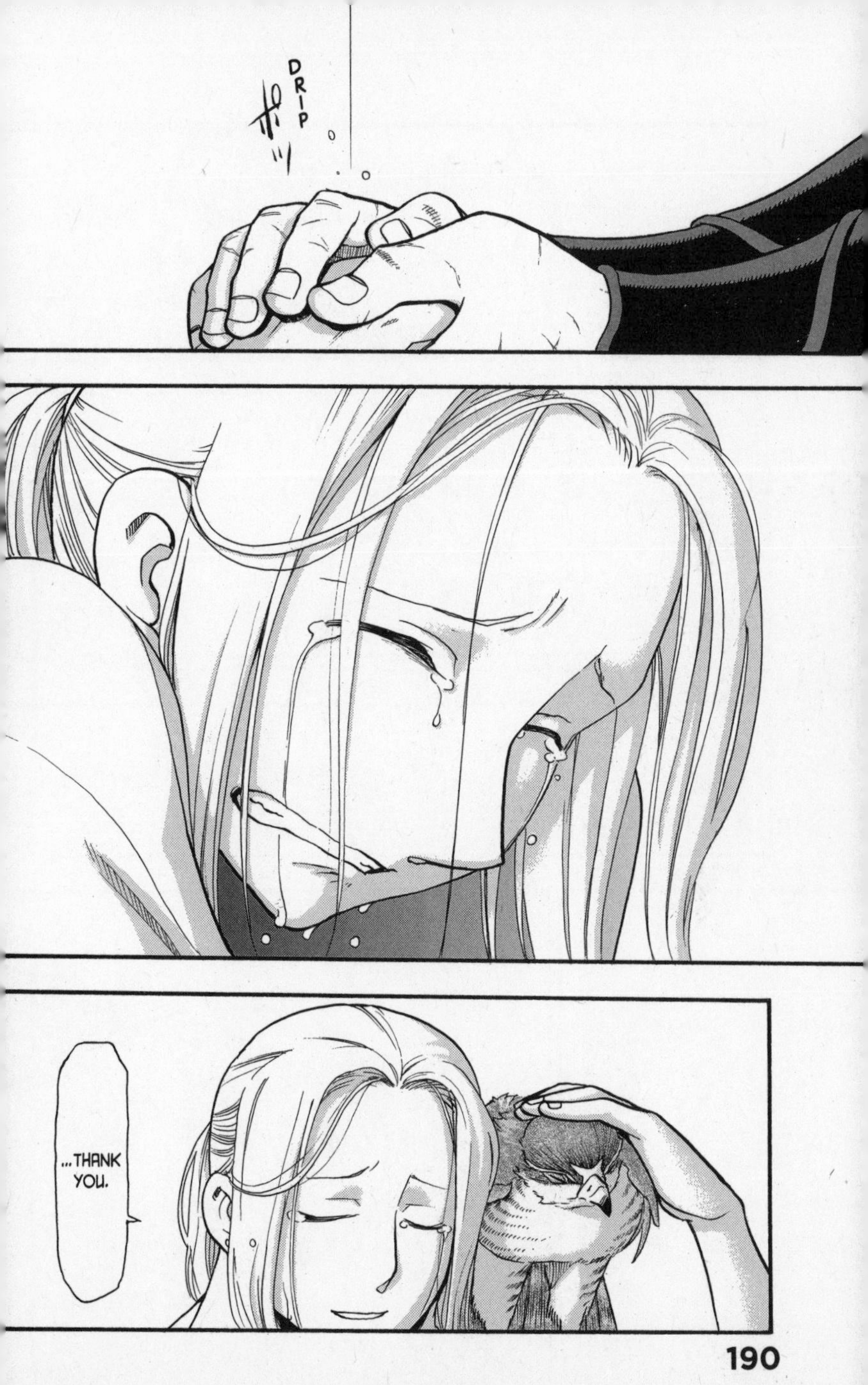
DRIP
...THANK YOU.

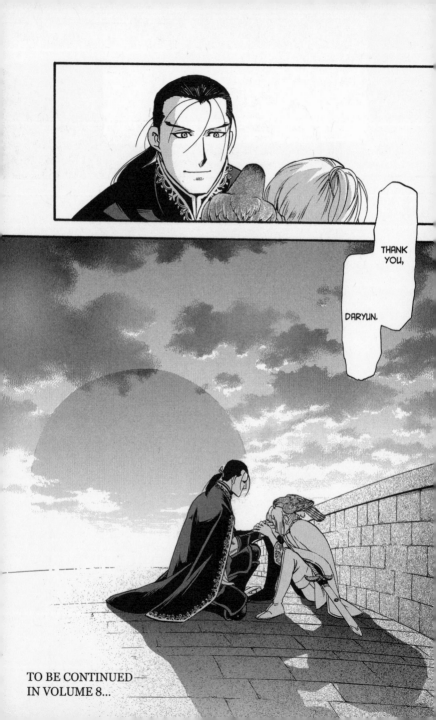

TO BE CONTINUED—
IN VOLUME 8...

The Heroic Legend of Arslan volume 7 is a work of fiction. Names, characters, places, and incidents are the products of the author's imagination or are used fictitiously. Any resemblance to actual events, locales, or persons, living or dead, is entirely coincidental.

A Kodansha Comics Trade Paperback Original.

Published in the United States by Kodansha Comics, an imprint of Kodansha USA Publishing, LLC, New York.

Publication rights for this English edition arranged through Kodansha Ltd., Tokyo.

First published in Japan in 2017 by Kodansha Ltd., Tokyo, as *Arslan Senki* volume 7.

ISBN 978-1-63236-351-0

Printed in the United States of America.

www.kodanshacomics.com

9 8 7 6 5 4 3 2 1

Translation: Amanda Haley
Lettering: James Dashiell
Editing: Ajani Oloye